September 11
Trauma and Human Bonds

RELATIONAL PERSPECTIVES BOOK SERIES

LEWIS ARON AND ADRIENNE HARRIS
Series Editors

September 11
Trauma and Human Bonds

Edited by
Susan W. Coates
Jane L. Rosenthal
Daniel S. Schechter

 THE ANALYTIC PRESS

2003   Hillsdale, NJ   London

Published by
The Analytic Press, Inc., Publishers
Editorial Offices:
101 West Street
Hillsdale, NJ 07642

www.analyticpress.com

Designed & typeset (Minister 11.5/13) by
Christopher Jaworski, Bloomfield, NJ
qualitext@earthlink.net

Library of Congress Cataloging-in-Publication Data

September 11 : trauma and human bonds / edited by Susan W. Coates,
    Jane L. Rosenthal, Daniel S. Schechter
p. cm. (Relational perspectives book series ; v. 23)
Includes bibliographical references and index.

ISBN 0-88163-381-X
1. Psychic trauma—Treatment.
2. Psychic trauma—New York Metropolitan Area.
3. Psychic trauma—Washington Metropolitan Area.
4. September 11 Terrorist Attacks, 2001—Psychological Aspects.
I. Coates, Susan W.
II. Rosenthal, Jane L.
III. Schechter, Daniel S.
IV. Series.

RC552.P67S42   2003
616.85'21—dc21
2003050206

Printed in the United States of America
10 9 8 7 6 5 4 3 2 1

Contents

(Continued)

v

Preface

Robert Alan Glick

On September 11, 2001, mental health professionals in and around New York City, no less than other residents of the area, were profoundly traumatized and burdened with uncertainty and apprehension. More than 3000 children lost parents in the terrorist attacks of that fateful day. Helping adults deal with the reactions of children (their own children and other people's) to trauma and loss while in the midst of their own traumatic grief became paramount. Tragically, as of this publication, we remain in the midst of one of the most extensive mental health crises in memory, with enormous public health policy issues created by these events.

This book is about the effects of trauma on children and adults. It brings together knowledge from attachment theory, psychoanalysis, and psychobiology to address the nature of trauma, its neuropsychological and psychosocial effects, and its transgenerational transmission. It marks an important collaboration among outstanding clinicians, researchers, scholars, and experts on social policy to explore what can and should be done to protect children and adults from the impact of massive trauma.

When Freud created psychoanalysis, he sought to heal the delayed effects of trauma in children—the persisting manifestations in adulthood of children overwhelmed by painful events beyond their understanding and control. We have learned much that he did not know about trauma—and about the parenting processes—and how it structures the brain and the mind. In considering current evidence from attachment theory, psychoanalysis, and psychobiology, certain salient facts are before us. The mind and brain of the child are plastic—robust and resilient, but highly vulnerable to the vicissitudes of the essential guardianship of the earliest relationship. Consequently, attachment, separation, and trauma are psychobiological and socially mediated processes. To protect children, we must understand how early dyadic processes mediate and moderate emotional regulation, self-organization, capacities for emotional relatedness, and identity formation. Intense and sustained negative interpersonal emotional experiences can severely compromise the formation of the psychobiological structures that allow a child to interpret the world constructively and adapt adequately in it. Parents who are psychologically lost to their children because of acute overwhelming trauma of their own, and mothers who have been the victims of violent trauma left unresolved, will in turn traumatize their children. In addition to examining the many dimensions of trauma on children and their caregivers, this volume describes how brief focused interventions can increase secure attachment, suggesting that this line of research should be further pursued in developing therapeutic strategies for breaking the tragic cycle of the transgenerational transmission of trauma.

September 11: Trauma and Human Bonds grew out of an interdisciplinary conference on the problem of the transgenerational transmission of trauma. Originally titled "When the Bough Breaks," the conference was sponsored jointly by the Parent–Infant Program of the Columbia University Center for Psychoanalytic Training and Research and the Sackler Institute for Developmental Psychology, with additional support from the Center for the Study of Science and Religion, also of Columbia University.[1] In our original planning, which took

---

[1]It is fitting that this book highlights the work of Columbia faculty, as Columbia played a pivotal role in launching modern trauma studies. Two of the founders of the Columbia University Center for Psychoanalytic Training and Research, Abram Kardiner and David Levy, were national experts on posttraumatic syndromes that were later recognized as posttraumatic stress disorder or PTSD. Kardiner described—with the keen clinical eye of a military psychiatrist and the deep curiosity about the internal world of the soldier of a psychoanalyst—the devastating effects of combat-related trauma (Kardiner and Spiegel, 1941). Levy (1945) made similarly compelling observations on

place before 9/11, we sought to review the state of trauma knowledge in relation to attachment and also from an interdisciplinary perspective. Our goal was to stimulate further research and social action. After the terrorist attacks, the conference acquired a compelling urgency none of us had anticipated, and we changed its name to "When the Bough Broke."

This important book is painful to read. In learning from it, we visit the experiences of traumatized parents and children, their searing grief, their unfolding helplessness and despair. It is painful to observe at close hand the vulnerability of children and the absoluteness of their need for our protection. It is painful to be reminded of how children and parents suffer. But this book is important to read nonetheless. It offers hope for our efforts to find ways to prevent trauma and to intervene in its aftermath to ensure our children's safety and psychological well-being.

References

Kardiner, A. & Spiegel, H. (1941), *War Stress and Neurotic Illness*. New York: Hoeber.

Levy, D. (1945), Psychic trauma of operations in children and a note on combat neurosis. *Amer. J. Dis. Child.*, 69:7–25.

---

the traumatic effects of surgery on young children. He is widely credited with being the first person systematically to study trauma in children and to develop specific techniques of intervention with traumatized children. Lenore Terr has described him as the lone voice in the wilderness who called attention to the traumatic impact of hospital policies that separated parents from their hospitalized children. More than 60 years ago, he understood that the experience of trauma was mediated by the presence of primary caretakers, and he had a huge impact on pediatric practice that led to policies that encouraged parents to stay with their children during hospitalization.

Contributors

Barbara Pape Aaron, B.A. is Director of 9/11 Projects, Department of Epidemiology, Joseph L. Mailman School of Public Health, Columbia University.

Lawrence Amsel, M.D., M.P.H. is Director of Dissemination Research for Trauma Studies and Services, New York State Psychiatric Institute; and Assistant Professor of Clinical Psychiatry, Columbia University College of Physicians and Surgeons.

Susan L. Andersen, Ph.D. is Assistant Professor of Psychiatry, Department of Psychiatry, Harvard Medical School; and Associate Chief, Laboratory of Developmental Psychopharmacology, Mailman Laboratories for Psychiatric Research, McLean Hospital, Belmont, Massachusetts.

Carl M. Anderson, Ph.D. is Instructor in Psychiatry, Harvard Medical School; and Assistant Psychobiologist, Brain Imaging Center, McLean Hospital, Belmont, Massachusetts.

Susan W. Coates, Ph.D. (Editor) is Associate Clinical Professor of Psychology in Psychiatry, Columbia University College of Physicians and Surgeons; and Director, The Parent–Infant Program, Columbia University Center for Psychoanalytic Training and Research.

Francine Cournos, M.D. is Professor of Clinical Psychiatry, Columbia University; and Director, Washington Heights Community Service, New York State Psychiatric Institute.

Cristiane S. Duarte, Ph.D. is Postdoctoral Research Fellow in Child Psychiatry/Psychiatric Epidemiology, Columbia University.

Elsa First, M.A. is Associate in Psychiatry, Columbia University College of Physicians and Surgeons; and Faculty, The Parent–Infant Program, Columbia University Center for Psychoanalytic Training and Research.

Peter Fonagy, Ph.D, F.B.A. is Freud Memorial Professor of Psycho-analysis, University College London; Director of Research at the Anna Freud Centre, London; and Director, Child and Family Center, Menninger Clinic.

Robert Alan Glick, M.D. is Professor of Clinical Psychiatry, Columbia University College of Physicians and Surgeons; Director, Columbia University Center for Psychoanalytic Training and Research; and Training and Supervising Analyst, Columbia University Center for Psychoanalytic Training and Research.

Adrienne Harris, Ph.D. is Faculty and Supervisor, New York University Postdoctoral Program in Psychoanalysis and Psychotherapy, and is in private practice in New York City.

Daniel B. Herman, D.S.W. is Assistant Professor of Clinical Epidemiology, Joseph L. Mailman School of Public Health, Columbia University; and Research Scientist, Epidemiology of Mental Disorders Research Department, New York State Psychiatric Institute.

Myron A. Hofer, M.D. is Sackler Institute Professor, Department of Psychiatry, and Director, Sackler Institute for Developmental Psychobiology, Columbia University College of Physicians and Surgeons; Research Scientist, New York State Psychiatric Institute; and Faculty, Columbia University Center for Psychoanalytic Training and Research.

Christina W. Hoven, Dr.P.H. is Child Psychiatric Epidemiologist, Department of Epidemiology, Joseph L. Mailman School of Public Health, Columbia University; and Research Scientist, Department of Child and Adolescent Psychiatry, New York State Psychiatric Institute.

Donald J. Mandell is Social Ecologist, State University of New York; and Research Scientist, Department of Child and Adolescent Psychiatry, New York State Psychiatric Institute.

Randall D. Marshall, M.D. is Director of Trauma Studies and Services and Associate Director, Anxiety Disorders Clinic, New York State

Psychiatric Institute; and Associate Professor of Clinical Psychiatry, Columbia University College of Physicians and Surgeons.

Carryl Navalta, Ph.D. is Instructor in Psychiatry, Department of Psychiatry, Harvard Medical School Developmental Biopsychiatry Research Program, McLean Hospital, Belmont, Massachusetts.

Ann Polcari, Ph.D., R.N. is Clinical Research Nurse, Developmental Biopsychiatry Research Program, McLean Hospital, Belmont, Massachusetts.

Hernán Poza III, M.S.W., C.S.W. is a bilingual Clinical Social Worker, New York City Department of Education; President, Board of Directors, Long Island Crisis Center; and a former volunteer firefighter.

Ellen Rees, M.D. is Clinical Associate Professor of Psychiatry, Weill Medical College, Cornell University; Training and Supervising Analyst, Columbia University Center for Psychoanalytic Training and Research; and Member, Editorial Board, *Journal of the American Psychoanalytic Association.*

Jane L. Rosenthal, M.D. (Editor) is Assistant Clinical Professor of Psychiatry, Columbia University College of Physicians and Surgeons; and Faculty, Columbia University Center for Psychoanalytic Training and Research.

Daniel S. Schechter, M.D. (Editor) is Assistant Professor of Clinical Psychiatry (in Pediatrics), Columbia University College of Physicians and Surgeons; Medical Director, Infant–Family Service, New York–Presbyterian Hospital; and Director of Research, Columbia University Parent–Infant Program.

Ezra S. Susser, M.D., Dr.P.H. is Professor of Public Health and Psychiatry, Columbia University College of Physicians and Surgeons; Head of Department of Epidemiology, Joseph L. Mailman School of Public Health, Columbia University; and Department Head, Epidemiology of Brain Disorders, New York State Psychiatric Institute.

Mary Target, Ph.D. is Senior Lecturer in Psychoanalysis, University College London; and Deputy Director of Research, The Anna Freud Centre, London.

Martin H. Teicher, M.D., Ph.D. is Associate Professor of Psychiatry, Department of Psychiatry, Harvard Medical School; Director, Developmental Biopsychiatry Research Program, McLean Hospital; and Chief, Laboratory of Developmental Psychopharmacology, Mailman Laboratories for Psychiatric Research, McLean Hospital, Belmont, Massachusetts.

Chapter 1

Introduction
Trauma and Human Bonds

Susan W. Coates

The original intention of the editors of this volume
was to bring into focus a new view of trauma in
relation to human bonds. That intention was transformed by the events of September 11, 2001. The
result is a multidisciplinary volume, with contributions by leading scholars, researchers, and clinicians,
that focuses on the World Trade Center attack while
trying to put the psychological consequences of that
terrible event into a context that will help clinicians
understand better the variety of human responses to
trauma as these appear in their day-to-day clinical
work.

Let us begin with our subtitle and our original intention. In the past decade, a host of new observations
have been made by psychodynamically oriented clinicians and psychoanalysts about the compelling consequences of trauma as these emerge in the course of
intensive treatment. To some extent, these observations have merely been a corrective on older, histori-
cally received views that privileged wishes over events,
internal psychic reality over the traumatic impinge-
ments of the external world, in determining what the
therapist should attend to and respond to. Most readers will already be familiar with this change in the
psychoanalytic landscape. Most clinicians now grasp
that sexual and violent physical trauma occurs with
much greater frequency in childhood than had once
been previously thought—and that when such abuse
has occurred it is likely to make its presence felt in

treatment in ways that transcend the older interpretive strategies based on the concepts of wish and defense.

But an appreciation for the reality of abuse, and the correlative though quite complex issue of traumatic memory that has lately occupied both mental-health professionals and the public at large, is but one feature of a much wider understanding of the diversity of traumatic phenomena and of the multiple meanings and manifestations that traumatic events can acquire. Indeed, so great is the diversity of phenomena that many contemporary trauma specialists are occupied at present with trying to fashion a clearer definition of what psychological trauma entails. One of the new understandings is that trauma must be understood in its relational and attachment context.

An interesting approach to the definition of trauma, on which I draw in this paper, is that of Gilkerson (1998). He has proposed that trauma be defined in relation to a continuum of arousal and emergency responses. At the lowest level of arousal, which can be defined as a "challenge," there is an increase in adrenaline and cortisol. Accompanying this limited response, there may be enhanced formation of explicit memory, or declarative memory as cognitive researchers call it, as well as enhanced emotional memory. The emotional tone may even be partially or wholly positive, entailing a feeling of exhilaration and ultimately learning and mastery. At higher levels of perceived threat, danger, or uncontrollably aversive stimuli, "challenge" shades into "stress," an equally familiar and hard-to-define psychiatric pathogen. In "stress," the hormonal activation of the hypothalamic–pituitary–adrenal axis, the sympathetic nervous system, and the limbic brain moves into higher gear. There evolves a negative impact on the formation of declarative memory, accompanied by a further heightening of emotional memory. The organism is primed for emergency action. The whole response is a marvel of evolutionary adaptation, suspending ordinary functioning and instituting an organized battle plan involving immediate deployment of all the major action systems of the brain. But as with the placement of an army in the field, the operation is incredibly costly. If it has to be sustained for any length of time, there begin to be huge secondary costs. The ordinary civilian life of the organism begins to deteriorate; the psychic economy moves to a more or less permanent wartime footing.

But this state is not yet trauma. Trauma entails yet a further escalation of the system toward a kind of dramatically hyperaroused state in which the organism's ability effectively to respond to the threat begins to break down. The threat is too massive, too immediate, too "unthinkable" in its proportions and implications to be encompassed by the organism's response systems. And yet the threatened event happens, even as behaviorally and neurophysiologically everything is being done to keep it from happening.

It is useful to pause to elaborate, from a clinical perspective, on the extreme point of Gilkerson's continuum. The events that transpire in the traumatic state will not thereafter be accessible to memory in the usual way; they will not be integrated into the individual's ordinary life narrative. In Winnicott's (1965) terms, there has been a discontinuity in "going on being." In traumatologist Lenore Terr's (1984) terms, there has been a change in the attitude toward life, a sense that things can never be quite the same again, which may bring with it a foreshortened sense of future possibility. In the understanding of the relational psychoanalyst Philip Bromberg (1998), there has been a fractioning of the self that goes beyond the ordinary day-to-day use of dissociation as a defense, such that major portions of the self can no longer be accessed except by reexperiencing the threat of traumatic dissolution.

But there is another way of thinking of Gilkerson's continuum, and it takes us to the central topic of this volume. Ordinarily, when we think of trauma we think in terms of the individual and how he or she is overwhelmed. The tendency to supplement our knowledge of the psychological experience of trauma with neurophysiological data, which have been so clarifying in terms of understanding some of the effects of trauma, particularly on memory, only strengthens this tendency to think of the traumatized person in isolation: that is, we think about the hormonal and other changes occurring within the *individual* organism. But what defines trauma in the first place, what changes a challenge into stress and stress into a genuine trauma, may in part be derived from the fact that it is undergone alone. Facing a dangerous situation with others is quite different from facing a dangerous situation alone. And the memory of terrible events can be made more tolerable when shared with others.

In short, one can begin to think of trauma and human relatedness as inversely related terms. The greater the strength of the human bonds that connect an individual to others, and the more those bonds are accessible in times of danger, the less likely it is that an individual will be severely traumatized and the more likely it is that he or she may recover afterward. There is a limit, to be sure, when even the most securely related individual will be overwhelmed by a threat that is too massive to be borne, whether it occurs in war or on the 96th floor of a burning building. But one must also remember that the basic human instinct, even on the 96th floor, is to make contact with someone else—even if it has to be by cell phone and even when it is clear that it will be futile in terms of rescue.

In retrospect, the importance of human connection as a protection against later trauma and as a means of healing afterward seems so obvious and straightforward an observation of human nature that one might suppose that clinicians have always known this. In a sense they have, but not with clarity. For the longest time, the understanding of trauma has remained connected to the events of wartime, where physical injury and death merit first consideration. Nonetheless, soldiers fight for and with their fellow soldiers. And this aspect was not lost on those who worked with them: Consider that the death of a comrade, rather than personal injury, was often identified as the cause of the traumatic reaction. And Fairbairn (1994) understood well that what might trigger a soldier's breakdown in the absence of an injury was a sudden disconnection from the officer in charge. Consider, too, the famous observation of Anna Freud and Dorothy Burlingham in their study of children in wartime London during the German blitz (Freud and Burlingham, 1943):

> The war acquires comparatively little significance for children so long as it only threatens their lives, disturbs their material comfort, or cuts their food rations. It becomes enormously significant the moment it breaks up family life and uproots the first emotional attachments of the child within the family group. London children, therefore, were on the whole much less upset by bombing than by evacuation to the country as a protection from it.

It is hard to recall now how startling the foregoing observation was at the time. Indeed, it was so novel that its full import could not be integrated into the field. What Freud and Burlingham had discovered went beyond the awful facts of the London blitz: it was the child's separation from the mother that was traumatic.

The full realization that a prolonged separation from the mother was innately traumatic for a child had to wait for the work of John Bowlby, whose legacy is hard to overestimate. Bowlby's interest in separation and loss in early childhood had multiple sources. Even though much of his career lay in front of him, as the author of the coming World Health Organization (WHO) report on homeless children in postwar Europe he already knew enough to expect trouble ahead when he was approached in 1950 by James Robertson—a young conscientious objector who had been previously employed at Anna Freud's Hampstead Clinic—to make a film about a child going to the hospital. This film was made at a time when public health policy still dictated that the child be dropped off by the parents, who had no further role to play in the treatment, until they came to retrieve the child days or weeks later. Attachment researcher Inge Bretherton (1995) tells the story:

> After two years of collecting data on hospitalized children for Bowlby's research projects, Robertson protested that he could not continue as an uninvolved research worker but felt compelled to do something for the children he had been observing. On a shoestring budget, with minimal training, a handheld cinecamera, and no artificial lighting, he made the deeply moving film *A Two-Year-Old Goes to Hospital*. . . . Foreseeing the potential impact of this film, Bowlby insisted that it be carefully planned to ensure that no one would later be able to accuse Robertson of biased recording. The target child was randomly selected, and the hospital clock on the wall served as proof that time sampling took place at regular periods of the day. Together with Spitz's film, *Grief: A Peril in Infancy*, Robertson's first film helped improve the fate of hospitalized children all over the Western world, even though it was initially highly controversial among the medical establishment [p. 50].

Again, it is difficult to recall now just how shocking Robertson's film was. Spitz's earlier film had been devastating, but it was about orphans, and the level of neglect was total. Little "Laura" in Robertson's film was an ordinary child, and she came from an ordinary family; her stay in the hospital lasted all of a week. Yet what viewers of the film witnessed as it unfolded was a manifestly terrible traumatization of the child, which culminated in a visibly profound psychological detachment toward her parents when they came to pick her up. What the viewer saw was so striking that it changed hospital policies around the world. And all that had happened was a weeklong separation.

Could the simple loss of human connectedness constitute for a child a trauma equal to the trauma of war? It was a thought almost too daunting to think. And matters shortly became yet more complicated, thanks to the work of Mary Ainsworth, who turned up in London as a skilled Rorschach expert looking for work just when Robertson began working on his film and Bowlby was finishing the WHO report. Ainsworth initially doubted that the model of a secure bond with an attachment figure, which Bowlby argued was key to the child's development, would survive cross-cultural comparison. Her studies of children in Uganda, conducted in the years immediately following, changed her mind. But when she then moved on to Baltimore, and discovered in her famous study of 26 mother–infant dyads that there actually were qualitatively different forms of the basic attachment, it was Bowlby's turn to be astonished. For a time, he did not believe what she had found. The children whom Ainsworth classified as "avoidant" seemed to be reacting in a detached way to a reunion with their mothers in the famous "strange-situation" experiment, much as little Laura had reacted in Robertson's film. Could a level of posttraumatic detachment really occur between a child and a mother who had never been separated for more than a few hours? Bowlby didn't believe it.

It turned out that the avoidant child's disregard of his or her mother in the reunion phase of the strange-situation experiment is not the same as what little Laura showed in Robertson's film. But Ainsworth's findings, including her description of the avoidant attachment style, have been replicated in study after study. It is now incontestable that there is no single kind of basic human bond between mother and child. Attachment relationships come in different styles; some are more benign, or rather secure, than others.

How might the differences in attachment style bear on what I have said about trauma and human relatedness being inversely related? This issue is extremely complicated, and it would take years to even begin to sort it out. Indeed, its proper explication required Mary Main's (George, Kaplan, and Main, 1985) development of an instrument for measuring attachment style in the adult, the Adult Attachment

Interview (AAI), which included specific questions about loss and trauma. Main was one of Ainsworth's early and most distinguished students. Further understanding of the puzzle awaited the arrival of a new generation of developmental and clinical researchers attuned to research with clinical populations, including not only Main and her principal collaborator Erik Hesse at Berkeley but also Dante Cicchetti, Sherry Toth, and their collaborators at the University of Rochester, Karlen Lyons-Ruth and her collaborators at Cambridge Hospital in Massachusetts, and Peter Fonagy and Mary Target and their collaborators in London, to name just a few of the outstanding figures in the new field of developmental psychopathology.

The basic issue that led to Bowlby's initial disbelief in Ainsworth's discovery can be stated simply: Could something be going on in an intact mother–child relationship that is somehow traumatizing to the child? That, as a generation of research has shown (and has been animating more research ever since), is a difficult question when posed to a nonclinical mother and her child. But it is akin to a much more easily approached question that was being asked by another pioneer, Selma Fraiberg, who had undertaken to set up a clinic to work with maltreating mothers and their children.

Fraiberg's famous paper, "Ghosts in the Nursery," coauthored with Edna Adelson and Vivian Shapiro, remains an enduring contribution to the understanding of trauma as it occurs within a relationship. The following scenario was caught on tape: the characters include Ms. Adelson, one of the authors; Mrs. Atreya, a tester; Mrs. March, the first woman ever seen in the clinic; and Mary, Mrs. March's five-and-a-half-month-old daughter (Fraiberg, Adelson, and Shapiro, 1975):

> Mary begins to cry. It is a hoarse, eerie cry in a baby. Mrs. Atreya discontinues the testing. On tape, we see the baby in her mother's arms screaming hopelessly; she does not turn to her mother for comfort. The mother looks distant, self-absorbed. She makes an absent gesture to comfort the baby, then gives up. She looks away. The screaming continues for five dreadful minutes on tape. In the background, we hear Mrs. Adelson's voice, gently encouraging the mother. "What do you do to comfort Mary when she cries like this?" Mrs. March murmurs something inaudible. Mrs. Adelson and Mrs. Atreya are struggling with their own feelings. They are restraining their own wishes to pick up the baby and hold her, to

murmur comforting things to her. If they should yield to their own wish, they would do the one thing they feel must not be done. For Mrs. March would then see that another woman could comfort the baby, and she would be confirmed in her own conviction that she was a bad mother. It is a dreadful five minutes for the baby, the mother, and the two psychologists. Mrs. Adelson maintains composure, speaks sympathetically to Mrs. March. Finally, the visit comes to an end when Mrs. Adelson suggests that the baby is fatigued and probably would welcome her own home and her crib, and mother and baby are helped to close the visit with plans for a third visit very soon.

As we watched this tape later in a staff session, we said to each other incredulously, "It's as if this mother doesn't *hear* her baby's cries!" This led us to the key diagnostic question: "*Why doesn't this mother hear her baby's cries?*" [pp. 389–390].

The answer to this question, many readers will recall, turned out to be that Mrs. March, herself "the outcast child of an outcast family," could not hear her *own* cries. With assistance, she could recount her own gruesome history of repeated traumatization, but she did so without feeling and without making a connection to her own suffering. As Fraiberg et al. describe it:

There were, we thought, two crying children in the living room. The mother's distant voice, her remoteness and remove we saw as defenses against grief and intolerable pain. Her terrible story had been first given factually, without visible suffering, without tears. All that was visible was the sad, empty, hopeless look upon her face. She had closed the door on the weeping child within herself as surely as she had closed the door upon her crying baby [pp. 395–396].

Though it was slow to be disseminated among the analytic community, the report of Fraiberg and her colleagues virtually single-handedly created a new field of study: the cross-generational transfer of trauma. This field became all the more important because it was launched at a time when a new generation of children had recently reached maturity and had begun to seek help for complaints that initially seemed to have no name; these were the children of survivors of the Holocaust. Thus, it gradually became clear to clinicians practicing in a wide variety of modalities that trauma could have terrible effects that reached past the individual and affected the next generation.

Thus we come full circle. Human relationships, when they are benign, provide an anodyne for trauma. But they also can become the vehicle for the transmission of trauma, whether through the repetition of maltreatment or through other mechanisms. And traumatization, when it is early and severe, can lead to profound relational difficulties that far transcend the confines of posttraumatic stress disorder.

How then to conceptualize the fundamental relationship of human bonds and trauma? In fashioning this volume, we set out to provide an understanding of the complexity of this topic. We bring together a number of domains: clinical research on trauma, developmental psychopathology, interpersonal psychobiology, epidemiology, and social policy.

The first area of knowledge is derived from the recent experiences of clinicians engaged in intensive psychotherapy and psychoanalysis. Simply put, therapists of different theoretical persuasions have begun to identify a host of phenomena in their clinical work that are related directly or indirectly to trauma. These phenomena are sometimes of a classic kind, such as an overwhelming or catastrophic event from earlier in life that is suddenly half-recalled in a dissociated state. But at other times, these phenomena are anything but classic in their presentation. Rather, they typically emerge in the relational field between patient and therapist, and as their meaning unfolds they may entail patterns of traumatization that stretch back two or three generations.

The second domain of knowledge we wished to access in this book arises from that relatively new interdisciplinary field, developmental psychopathology. This field incorporates findings from diverse disciplines, including pediatrics, child psychiatry, neurology, behavioral neuroendocrinology, developmental psychology, and the field of attachment research. In broad outline, developmental psychopathology is altering our basic conceptualizations of both childhood disorders and of the contributions of childhood factors to the development of disorders later in life. More specifically, the findings of developmental psychopathology allow us to think about trauma in childhood in dramatically altered terms. The same findings also allow us to think in similarly radically changed terms about what is entailed in retraumatization.

The emerging field of interpersonal psychobiology is demonstrating that the most fundamental biological processes are interpersonally organized. Work from epidemiologic and social policy paints with a broader brush. We believe that it is important for clinicians to conceptualize their individual work in the context of social trends and policies and to take this into account when listening to patients.

Our contention is that developments in these fields are beginning to fit together in surprisingly complementary ways. The emergent findings of these fields are interesting in their own right but far more interesting when brought together in relation to each other. Taken together, they allow us to appreciate, with a new degree of empathy and precision, a range of phenomena having to do with trauma that we see daily in our clinical work. Our intention was to bring together contributions that would directly illustrate these developments and help advance the ongoing discussion in these fields.

The editors of this volume, and most of the contributors to it, are residents of New York City and were present for the terrible events of September 11 and their aftermath. It seemed to us that, despite the preparation provided through the new knowledge in this book, the events catapulted us into a new, massively more vivid and intense understanding of what trauma is really about. Indeed, if we can say this without appearing to dramatize our own experience, it seemed to us that it was only in the process of working through what had happened to us and to our patients that we were able to resume the endeavor of putting together this volume. Conversely, putting this volume together in its new and final form was a means for us to contain the impact of those events and give them a meaningful shape that allowed us to go on.

It is too early to say what the final lessons will be of the World Trade Center disaster or how they will further change our understanding of the multiple connections between human relationships and trauma. A few points are already so clear, however, that we cannot avoid bringing them to the reader's attention.

First and foremost, trauma as a topic has undergone a fundamental transformation in that the stigma and unnecessary mystification surrounding trauma has been dispelled once and for all. It is a sad comment on psychiatric and psychoanalytic history that knowledge of the terrible traumas of war was lost twice in the 20th century. Though shell shock was seen throughout World War I, governments consistently acted to suppress psychiatric knowledge of the terrible psychological consequences of war on soldiers. The result of this general social amnesia was that psychiatry had to rediscover the reality of war trauma all over again in World War II. Army physicians, during and after the war, were thus relearning what novelists and filmmakers had already seen and attempted to memorialize after World War I: that for some men, the war never ended. Once again, however, the full impact of this realization was avoided, in part, because it was clear, and strategically crucial for further understanding, that many soldiers who had never heard a shot fired were breaking down (Fairbairn, 1994). The question of susceptibility to trauma, once pursued, led both toward a more stringent look at the personality of the soldier before the trauma and away from the trauma's brutal reality. Thus it happened that Vietnam War veterans returned home with conditions that psychiatry had seen before but had forgotten. It was almost a decade before the veterans' complaints were appreciated. Posttraumatic stress disorder (PTSD) entered the official nomenclature only in 1980, years after the war ended.

During all previous wars, the traumatized soldier was seen by many as a coward and a malingerer. His symptoms were viewed with suspicion, and he became heir to the disbelief that had previously attended abused women and victims of railway accidents (Fairbairn, 1994).

That attitude has changed. One of the aims of terrorist warfare is to impose traumatization on an entire population. In this context, to experience traumatization as a psychic consequence of a terrorist attack no longer entails a questionably patriotic stance; it is rather part of facing up to the reality that war has begun. The long-standing stigma on traumatized individuals has come to an end. One hopes the new acceptance and understanding of trauma will radiate to other traumatized conditions. If so, they will make a general contribution to society's mental health in much the same way that general education about sexuality did in the early and middle decades of the last century.

Second, though the establishment of the diagnosis of posttraumatic stress disorder as part of the official diagnostic nomenclature was a long time coming, in the wake of the events of 9/11 it has become even clearer that PTSD constitutes only one of the possible reactions to severe traumatization. As short-term descriptive accounts give way to epidemiologic studies of greater and greater longitudinal depth, we will get a picture of the diversity of traumatic reactions, and of their relative tendencies to endure, such that we have never had before.

Third, the concepts of susceptibility and vulnerability to traumatization, concepts which have bedeviled psychiatry since the 19th century, are beginning to appear in a new light as a result of recent events. Here, the combination of more acute clinical observation and the revised conceptual understandings provided by the field of developmental psychopathology found, in the crucible of events, a most telling and fruitful application. In observing how children were reacting to the events around them, clinicians were able to see how the children's attempts at comprehension and absorption were couched in terms provided by the family milieu. This observation included, but was not restricted to, the ways in which the children were dealing with their parents' simultaneous traumatization. Similarly, the reactions of adults to the trauma took on additional meaning when understood in terms of their own relational histories, including not only their own prior history of traumatization but their parents' traumas as well. These kinds of observations were idiographic, to be sure, but both the editors and the contributors to this book have been struck by how they fit into an overall framework provided by the findings of developmental psychopathology.

Perhaps a single additional finding might clarify this goodness of fit, to use a statistical metaphor. In the field of developmental psychopathology, the work of Peter Fonagy, Mary Target, and their colleagues has come to the fore as providing an unusually penetrating window into the inner workings of the transmission of trauma from one generation to the next. It has been widely known that not all traumatized parents transmit their trauma to their children (thereby traumatizing them), just as only about one third of parents abused as children end up abusing their children. Fonagy and Target have identified in a rigorous way the psychological factor that enables traumatized parents *not* to traumatize their children. This factor has been given various names, including "reflective functioning" and, as it appears in their contribution to this volume, "interpersonal interpretive function." It consists in accepting and appreciating that the child has a mind of his or her own. One of the startling findings associated with the events of 9/11 (to our minds perhaps *the* most startling finding) came in a survey conducted by Stuber, Galea, and Fairbrother (2002). Young children, whose parents did not know how they responded after September 11 and did not appreciate the minds of their children, were 11 times more likely to have trauma-related behavior problems.

Finally, we might mention that 9/11 was a comparatively unique event in the sense that the mental-health professionals involved were parties to the traumatic events. There was thus no ambiguity in anyone's mind as to what the triggering event was all about, even if it remained to be discovered what precisely an individual had seen or heard, whom he had lost, or what it meant. How this shared context affected the reports of the victims, or the reports of the authors, cannot be specified in any definite way, but our feeling is that it has allowed greater emotional clarity in terms of appreciating the nature of the traumatization. We hope that this clarity has been communicated to the full impact of the trauma.

This book is designed to help the practicing clinician make use of tools from neighboring disciplines. It attempts to provide ways of thinking about the interconnections between psychological trauma and human relationships that are equal both to the intellectual challenges of a number of evolving fields and to the emotional challenges of a radically altered world. The topic of trauma is no longer the intellectual property of any one discipline. Nor can the accumulated knowledge of what psychological trauma entails be encompassed by a single volume. There are no simple truths in the world of trauma studies, no easy-to-remember rules of thumb for the clinician to memorize. There are no tried-and-true interventions suitable across the board, no cognitive-behavioral anodynes or pharmacologic magic bullets or depth-psychological schematizations that will hold true for a majority or even a sizable minority of cases. Even within the restricted purview of being a preliminary report on a terrible national trauma, this book has its limitations and deficiencies. Our original intent and our revised post-9/11 intent will have been realized if the contributions to this volume offer the clinical reader some insight into the complexity of trauma and its relational nature.

References

Bowlby, J., Robertson, J. & Rosenbluth, D. (1952), A two-year-old goes to the hospital. *The Psychoanalytic Study of the Child*, 7:82–94. New York: International Universities Press.

Bretherton, I. (1995), The origins of attachment theory: John Bowlby and
    Mary Ainsworth. In: *Attachment Theory*, ed. S. Goldberg, R. Muir & J. Kerr.
    Hillsdale, NJ: The Analytic Press, pp. 50–84.
Bromberg, P. M. (1998), *Standing in the Spaces: Clinical Process, Trauma, and
    Dissociation*. Hillsdale, NJ: The Analytic Press.
Fairbairn, W. R. D. (1943), The war neuroses: Their nature and significance.
    In: *Psychoanalytic Studies of the Personality*. New York: Routledge, 1994, pp.
    256–288.
Fraiberg, S., Adelson, E. & Shapiro, V. (1975), Ghosts in the nursery. *J. Amer.
    Acad. Child Psychiat.*, 14:387–421.
Freud, A. & Burlingham, D. (1943), *Children in War*. New York: Medical War
    Books.
George, C., Kaplan, H. & Main, M. (1985), The Berkeley Adult Attachment
    Interview. Unpublished protocol, Department of Psychology, University
    of California, Berkeley.
Gilkerson, L. (1998), Brain care: Supporting healthy emotional development.
    Child Care Inform. Exchange, 5:66–68.
Stuber, J., Galea, G. & Fairbrother, F. (2002), The mental health of New York
    City families. Presented at Columbia University's Child Psychiatry Grand
    Rounds, September 11.
Terr, L. (1984), Time and trauma. In: *The Psychoanalytic Study of the Child*,
    39:633–665. New Haven, CT: Yale University Press.
Winnicott, D. W. (1965), *The Maturational Processes and the Facilitating Envi-
    ronment: Studies of the Theory of Emotional Development*. New York: Interna-
    tional Universities Press.

Chapter 2

A Letter from Brooklyn
September 11, 2001

Hernán Poza III

Hernán Poza III, a former volunteer firefighter, has been a social worker in New York City for more than 20 years. He has worked as a clinician with severely emotionally disturbed children for the New York City Department of Education for the past 11 years. The following account was posted on a website entitled "New York Stories." Mr. Poza composed it on the evening of the attack on the World Trade Center as an e-mail message to his friends and relatives when he became too exhausted to make or field any more phone calls. The editors sought out his piece for this volume not merely because it is a vivid eyewitness account of the trauma as it happened, but also because it captures exquisitely how a caretaker can attempt to move effectively to shield children even as his own ability to take in events is crumbling.

Mr. Poza speaks for the authors and editors of this volume who, like all New Yorkers, were faced with trying to regain their emotional and mental equilibrium in the wake of the traumatic events of 9/11.

It's early Tuesday morning, September 11, 2001, and I'm interviewing one of my children. He has scratches on his face, and it's my responsibility as the boy's therapist/social worker to make an initial determination as to the seriousness of his injuries. He describes falling off his bike and how his mother handled the situation; the injuries seem consistent with his explanation. The interview concludes abruptly as the assistant principal rushes into my office. She looks flushed and upset. I tell her his story about falling off the bike, and she says, "Okay, send him back to class."

She then asks me to hurry immediately up to the third floor of the school, a special education program for young children located in downtown Brooklyn. Our third floor houses three classrooms—two third grades and one fourth-grade class—as well as the speech teacher's office. These rooms all have magnificent skyline views of lower Manhattan, located directly across the river.

As I enter the first classroom, I see the children and their teachers crowded, transfixed, before the windows; the Twin Towers of the World Trade Center billow fiercely with smoke. My heart leaps in my chest, I lose my breath, and I remind myself to breathe.

The kids are excited and shouting,

"A plane crashed into the building!"
"Planes crashed into the big buildings!"
"We heard them crash!"
"We saw them crash!"
"They're on fire,
they're burning,
they're burning!"

My head swims at the sight of these mighty buildings bathed in the white, black, and gray smoke surging upward, up their sides, darkening the sky. The sound of sirens, shrieking and wailing, floats across the East River.

The teachers try to regain order, asking the children to return to their seats. The adults, tear-filled eyes connecting, dazed and shocked.

I suggest that we pull the lower window shades down, that we block this sight from the children. As I begin to do so, many of the children yell, "No, no, we want to watch, we want to see!" Many are now at their desks, eyes wide, crying and asking for their mothers.

I rush to the neighboring classroom and find the same sight, children and staff hypnotized before this unreal spectacle. The sky blackens with smoke, the sirens piercing louder and louder. We shut the shades to the same cries from the children, "No, no, we want to watch!" Some sob at their desks.

The third classroom repeats the unreal scene: transfixed, excited children, shocked, tearful staff. Then the protests from the children about shutting off their view. Most are now in tears, asking for their mommies, some excited and leaping from their seats, running to the windows, pulling up the shades and trying to peek out.

I move from room to room, stand before the classes, ask the children:

what they saw,
how they're feeling,
what are their worries,
their questions,
their fears.

My fellow clinicians follow, first watching, then expanding and opening this important dialogue.

The children ask me powerful questions:

"Are we safe?"
"Are the buildings in the city going to fall down?"
"Are they going to fall down on us and smash our school?"
"Why are the sirens so loud?"
"How could this happen?"
"Are all the planes going to crash from the sky?"
"Will airplanes smash into our school?"
"Who could do this?"
"Why does the smoke smell funny?"
"Why is this happening?"
"Are the buildings going to all fall down?"
"Was this an accident?"
"Why aren't they spraying water on the buildings?"
"Are people dying?"
"Are a lot of people dead?"
"What is going to happen to us?"

"How will we get home?"
"Where is my mommy?"

I answer them as best I can:

"You are very safe here in Brooklyn, in our school, we will keep
    you safe."
"The firefighters and policemen in the city are not afraid; they are
    brave and strong and smart and know how to help."
"I used to be a firefighter, and I know this is true."
"The planes will not fall from the sky."
"You are safe now."
"The firefighters and policemen are helping the people in those
    buildings right now."
"The big buildings in our city are built strong and solid and won't
    fall down."
"The buildings will not fall down on us here across the river, at
    our school in Brooklyn."
"They are fighting the fire from the inside of the building; they
    can't spray water on the outside right now."
"We will keep you safe here at school."
"We will call your families and tell them you're okay."
"We will make sure that it's safe to send you home and that you
    will get home okay."

I don't remember exactly when or why,
but I entered the speech teacher's office, finding tearful, shocked
staff standing transfixed before the windows, radios blaring
    frightening
news,
hijacked planes,
terrorists,
terror,
sirens wailing and shrieking,
and
the Twin Towers, now obscured behind massively billowing
    smoke, then,
in slow motion,
before my eyes,

THE TOWER IS GONE,
GONE.
Beneath swirling brown, gray, black smoke, it seems to shrink in
    upon
itself,
it is GONE.
    I see it fall.
    I immediately realize,
the children should not be on the third floor, their curious eyes
    cannot see this sight,
no peeking at this horror,
this is too much,
this is not real.
    I cannot explain this to them.
We cannot explain this to them,
this is for their families,
this is for history,
this is overwhelming,
this is not real,
this is a new world.
    I tell myself,
I will not feel this,
I will not feel this now,
the enormity of what I have seen,
I want my mommy and daddy,
I desperately want to know that my friends in lower Manhattan
    are okay, I
will make those calls to find out, for myself,
    the rest I will not know,
the rest I do not want to know,
the rest I will not feel,
not until I am home,
not until I have time,
not until the children are home.

The children are moved quickly to the first floor where our heroic
staff teaches lessons, shows videos to pass the slow-motion time of this
unending day.
    The remainder of my school day is a blur of activity.

First, finding out my loved ones are safe and well.
Phone calls to the parents of all the children on the third floor,
    who have directly witnessed the tragedy—advising them of how
    to talk to their children about this,
consoling stunned staff who have family members working in the
    Twin Towers,
consulting with my colleagues,
sharing stories, tears, shock, outrage, worries.
    Smelling smoke,
hearing sirens,
sneaking a look out the window on the now deserted third floor,
    the
billowing smoke and empty space where the Twin Towers once
    stood.
    At two-thirty the yellow school buses come,
the children are taken home,
the staff slowly disperses.
    the acrid smell of smoke in the air,
and sirens louder out on the street.
    In my car,
I'm back home in Queens in fifteen minutes, there is no traffic,
the new Manhattan skyline next to the Brooklyn/Queens
    Expressway,
the never-ending billowing smoke,
the empty space where the Twin Towers once stood.
    Not knowing what to do,
where to go,
what to do,
    I instinctually follow my routine,
my New York City Marathon training schedule,
driving to Flushing Meadows Park,
my refuge,
my oasis,
the Meadow Lake where I love to run,
I change into my running clothes
    running around my beautiful lake,
in the distance,
as Indian Summer sun warmly glistens
across sparkling waters,

as geese and ducks swim peacefully by, gray/black billowing
    smoke
darkens the sky, sirens still wailing,
I run,
I cry.
    With love from,
Hernán

Poza, H. (2001)
http://www.nycstories.com/places/911/8.html

Chapter 3

Brief Interventions with Traumatized Children and Families After September 11

Susan W. Coates,
Daniel S. Schechter, and
Elsa First

In this chapter, clinicians closely involved in the immediate response to September 11 reflect on their interventions and resulting implications for trauma theory, attachment, and shared mentalization. The authors report on their experience offering emergency psychiatric first aid at the Kids' Corner of the Family Assistance Center. This center at Pier 94 was set up by an ad hoc consortium of city, state, and private agencies in the wake of the World Trade Center bombings. This chapter explores some clinical insights that came from unstructured open-air interventions of the staff, and it explores strategies for emotional containment in a high-emergency situation. The most important finding was that children's posttraumatic reactions seemed to be inextricably tied up with the meanings that trauma, death, and loss had in the family system.

In this chapter, we reflect on our experiences in providing crisis interventions with children and families directly affected by September 11, as volunteer clinicians in a public disaster-relief setting. We hope to contribute to further discussion and reflection on the effects of this trauma on the most affected children of the greater New York region. We consider how we responded and why and what may be most helpful in preventing acute traumatic distress from deepening or rigidifying. We could not help but observe how the children's mutual or concurrent trauma, including traumatic bereavement, affected relatedness and attachment to their caregivers. Sometimes relationships helped protect against traumatization; in other cases, traumatization worked to put both parents and children more out of touch with each other. We discuss and illustrate this along with some related interventions. A special focus is on adults' difficulties in letting children know about the death of a family member and the resulting confusion children felt.

We need to describe the context of our work. The Family Assistance Center housed on Pier 94 was where our site, Kids' Corner, was set up by Desmond Heath of Disaster Psychiatry Outreach as a place of respite where children whose families had suffered could gather, play, and be free to respond in any way that they needed to in an atmosphere of understanding and support. It was originally set up at the armory where families had gone to list their missing, record identifying marks, and wait for news, at the beginning when many still hoped that the missing might be found injured and identified in hospitals or rescued from the ruins. But at the end of the day the hospital beds stood empty, emergency doctors faced the unprecedented ache of having no one to try to save, and it was soon evident Ground Zero was a vast gravesite.

The images of the planes' attack on the World Trade Center (WTC), the flames, and then the incredible swift fall of the towers was of course burned into our psyches, and we soon learned that the whole world had watched along with us in real time. Now more than a year has gone by. We now know that more than 3251 children lost parents in the attack (*In Memoriam: New York City 9/11/01*, 2002). The bereaved families and our communities bear this loss like a scar that will take generations to heal. Before describing our work site on Pier 94, we need to contextualize the work more broadly by noting briefly a few specific features of this disaster, which may have shaped the traumatic experiences that ensued and perhaps left their mark in ways not yet fully discernable. Some aspects of the temper of the city in the two months after 9/11 need brief mention also as part of the context of this work.

A Very Few Men Doing Great Evil

Stephen J. Gould (2002) noted that a novel element in this act of terrorism was that so few men, through the use of advanced technology and by targeting a landmark creation of advanced technology, could wreak such massive destruction. Gould's point is that a far larger mass of humankind remains good, although it may be hard to remember that after such destruction. We suggest that this feature—so much havoc wreaked by so few so efficiently—might especially stimulate destructive fantasy in children along with the general heightening of aggression, rage, and revenge to be expected after acts of violence.

Terrorism, the Uncanny, and the Rupture of Reality

The destruction of WTC was uniquely unbelievable in ways that many have tried to articulate. It was instant wisdom that the world had changed utterly. America's shock can be explained in part because our land has not been invaded for more than 200 years. Certainly some kind of idealized sense of protectedness, America's "mantle of safety" (Hamilton, 1989), had been breached.

We underscore, however, another aspect to the 9/11 traumatizing effect because we think it is worth considering its relevance in general. All acts of terrorism make the commonplace unsafe, unreliable. Such, for example, was the implicit aim of Hitler's policy of *Schrecklichkeit*, or gratuitous frightfulness. Making the ordinary unsafe is one result (if not necessarily always the explicit aim) of all terrorist acts, whatever the scale, and across all kinds of sponsorship, whether in overt state-sponsored genocide under cover of war, covert state-sponsored death squads, clandestine political terrorist organizations, or desperate indi viduals. When ordinary reality can no longer be relied on to be only what it seems, it becomes uncanny. Once reality is uncanny, it be- comes harder to tell reality from unreality. One six-year-old girl on the

Pier, from a West African immigrant family, told Elsa First of her new repetitive nightmares. The burden of the nightmares was that each time she thought she had woken up, the nightmare continued and she was told by the ghosts and monsters in the dream that her nightmare had come true. Ghosts and monsters were real. The boundaries between real and unreal falter when the unthinkable happens.

Contents usually sequestered in fantasy, dream, and nightmare had invaded reality on 9/11. Bragin (2002), citing Freud's "The Uncanny" (1917), has linked the traumatizing effects of extreme violence against civilians with the fact that the carrying out of horrific fantasy in reality attacks and undermines the victims' and bystanders' capacity for symbolization. The West African girl's nightmare, we suppose, represented anxieties about the possible failure of the capacity for reality testing.

Uncertainty Separations and Threatened Attachments

Those who escaped on 9/11 went through a period of several hours of not knowing exactly what was happening and the extent of the disaster and often were unsure whether they would survive. Radio, phone, and cell-phone communications were down. Many families spent many hours not sure where family members were and if they were safe. Parents raced to schools to bring children home. As the day of 9/11 wore on, families who could not locate relatives who worked in the WTC raced from hospital to hospital hoping to find their loved ones. The stories children told in the first weeks afterward all focused on when and how they were retrieved by a parent or how many hours it took until all family members were accounted for and reunited. (The loyalty of those teachers who saw them to safety before going to find their own children was also stressed in the narratives of younger children from downtown schools.) Separation anxiety and awareness of the vulnerability of human bonds were much heightened for a period. Families stayed home together; the majority of children under 12 slept in the parental bed or bedroom. People with young children considered leaving the city. For our purposes, it is significant that many parents felt they had to come to terms in a new way with not being able to protect their children's safety: parents felt undermined and humiliated in this loss of protective capacity.

Witnessing Agonies and Horrors

In the literature on disaster and trauma, witnessing the grotesque such as dismembered bodies is listed as a significant source of enduring traumatization, even for very young children (Gaensbauer, 2000). Children from the many downtown schools and colleges near the WTC directly witnessed the falling live bodies of those who jumped, some of them aflame, from the high floors; this made a profound impression on many children. Others briefly saw sights like a plaza awash in blood soon covered by rubble and never covered in the media. Adults were privy to last cell-phone calls. These secrets about private agonies slowly filtered into public consciousness, begging, it seemed, for containment at each step. The children of emergency medical service (EMS) workers and the other first responders, and of the volunteer construction workers who gradually cleared the site, overheard their parents' traumatic stories.

Reparative Drives

An immediate response to the terrorist attack was a widespread and astonishingly intense desire to rescue, help, heal, and console in some way. Volunteers and offers of support poured in from around the country and abroad. In New York City, lines to donate blood went around the blocks. Other lines of friends or relatives of families with missing members slowly circled the downtown hospitals bearing the homemade "missing posters" with photocopied snapshots and descriptions of the missing, identifying on what floor of the WTC they had worked. This procession was met by unknown neighbors bringing them water and food.

As it became clear there would be few survivors, the city's energy and reparative needs focused on the task—which took eight and a half months—of clearing the site at Ground Zero, driven first by the hope of finding survivors and then of finding identifiable remains. It is well known how difficult it was for the voluntary workers, firefighters, policemen, and EMS workers to leave that site where comrades had been lost, and which was so compellingly awesome; when shifts were done, many stayed or sneaked back to work overtime until past exhaustion. It was a 24-hour-a-day operation, lit after dusk by sports stadium lighting that kept vigil for the city even after the many neighborhood candlelight vigils, peace vigils, and memorials died down. Again, a small, impressive brigade of downtown volunteers organized a constant flow of support supplies for these workers, including specialized equipment and protective gear. The hard-to-bear uselessness of the medical professionals who had no one to help was given a name: peripheral syndrome (Pynoos, 2001). Mental health workers who succeeded in finding ways to be of use felt profoundly relieved. Many of us who were able to work on the Pier were also driven in our reparativeness and relieved to find a way to assuage helplessness, to work through our degree of shock and disbelief, and to channel hyperarousal and vigilance into attentive concern.

Complicated Bereavement, Ambiguous Loss

There were few bodies and few identifiable remains to bury. There were some reports of how some had died and how far down the stairs they had got, mostly reports about those who stayed or turned back to help others. For many families, there was the period from hours to days to weeks during which at least one person in the family held on to frail hopes. After weeks, this increasingly delusional hope was signaled publicly by processions of people still carrying "missing" posters. This was cruelly painful. Then, like a change of season, the "missing" posters turned in the consciousness of the city into memorials wherever they remained, on lampposts, walls, and the ubiquitous New York scaffolding. It was a relief to most New Yorkers to see those posters as signs of grief. The plywood walkway from the West Side Highway into Pier 94 was lined with posters of the missing, as if that was their last home. Inside the pier was a memorial wall the length of a school gym lined with posters of the missing, on which people wrote messages of farewell. It was known as the Walk of Bears because the floor beneath was lined with a row of teddy bears, which had been sent from Oklahoma by children affected by the Oklahoma City bombing.

We mention the problem of complicated bereavement because of what we found on the Pier when parents couldn't tell children about a death. The procession of those still hoping for news when most citizens had accepted that there would be no miraculous finds was like an enactment of a state of a confused, oscillating inability to begin grieving, for all the rest to see and bear in mind. In the children's confusion, we may have been seeing a reflection of still later stages of families' relinquishment of hope.

Pier 94

Pier 94 is a vast hangar-like structure on the Hudson River on the west side of Manhattan, which in other times could berth ocean liners or hold large commercial expositions. The Family Assistance Center was set up by Mayor Giuliani to expedite provision of services to families who had lost a family member, a job, or housing as a consequence of 9/11. Expedition included facilitating the obtaining of death certificates in the absence of a body, necessary for pursuit of emergency benefits and entitlements. Dozens of temporary booths housed federal state and city agencies such as the Federal Emergency Management Agency as well as the Red Cross Disaster Relief service and private agencies. Mental health workers made themselves available to the adults or accompanied them as they completed their grim business of providing forensic evidence for identifying remains. Later, mental health workers accompanied bereaved families who wished to do so on ferryboats to view the Ground Zero site, to facilitate grieving. There were translators and chaplains, cafeterias and lounges. Besides the Walk of Bears, there were other tributes: an immense cascading mobile of Japanese origami cranes symbolizing, as they have since Hiroshima, the wish for peace; and cards and drawings from foreign and U.S. schoolchildren.

Gretchen Buchenholtz (2002), from the Association to Benefit Children, described Pier 94 as "a utopia of comprehensive coordinated services." "It was a marvelous enactment of the will of the people." It was the "instinctive" response of people who knew how to respond with respect, compassion, caring, and love.

It was access and the facilitation of access to services, in Buchenholtz's analysis, that was distinctive and remarkable about the Pier. Ordinarily, the working poor, she noted, are discouraged from seeking the services they are entitled to because the bureaucratic requirements are punitively onerous. The experiment of Pier 94, she said, demonstrated that people would seek health care and mental health care if access were simplified.

One clinical psychologist, in an online bulletin to colleagues considering volunteering, wrote:

> There is a general feeling of safety and openness in the whole complex, which lends itself to people sharing their stories, feelings, and concerns. Some family members and affected people have been coming to the center every day. There is a sense of community that is powerful and rare for New York City.
>
> I think families and affected individuals have developed a positive transference to the whole Assistance Center; as a result, although therapists don't work in an ongoing way with one individual, there is a sense that one is continuing the therapeutic work of others who have gone before them [Ulrich, 2001].

This context is important because we think that it influenced the trust and confidence with which families approached us at Kids' Corner.

Kids' Corner: The Setting

Kids' Corner, at Pier 94, was located centrally and easily visible so that families could leave their children and easily check back in between visits to various Family Assistance agencies.

Parents also came to seek advice, talk about their predicaments around parenting while grieving, or be with their children in a place that offered respite from the stress of the full-time demands of children who were already distressed.

Kids' Corner was the size of a small classroom and had an adjoining family consultation area with comfortable sofas. It had a block building and toy area, equipped especially with toy fire engines, police cars, and rescue vehicles to promote group play. There was a crafts and painting table, which also promoted older children's working and talking together. We discovered it was especially meaningful and consoling for children to see their signed artwork mounted all around the walls of Kids' Corner, knowing that others similarly affected would see them. Snacks and children's books were always available, and there was a constantly replenished supply of donated teddy bears that could be taken home when a child left. The bears were much wanted and comforting.

Studies on Children's Response to Traumatic Disasters

In the past 10 years, researchers have begun to look more closely at the impact of disasters, natural and man-made, on both children and adults. (The category of man-made disasters in epidemiology includes the effects of wars, genocide, terrorism, and large-scale technological accidents and safety failures.) Researchers studying infancy and trauma have demonstrated in case reports and systematic studies that the classic triad of posttraumatic stress disorder (PTSD) symptoms—reexperiencing, numbing/avoidance, and hyperarousal—does occur in young children (Scheeringa and Zeanah, 1995; Zeanah and Scheeringa, 1996; Schechter and Tosyali, 2001; Schechter et al., 2001/2002; Scheeringa et al., 2001; Coates et al., 2002a, b; Schechter et al., in press).

It is well known that those closest and most exposed to a disaster are most at risk for PTSD, along with those personally bereaved. Studies of children's reactions to the Oklahoma City bombing and the September 11 attack on the WTC have found that those who lost a loved one, were closer to Ground Zero, or watched the disaster repeatedly on television, in addition to those who had experienced previous trauma, were at greatest risk for PTSD (Pfefferbaum et al., 1999; Marshall, 2001; Pfefferbaum, 2001; Pfefferbaum et al., 2001; Regehr et al., 2001; Galea et al., 2002).

Relationship with Parents as a Protective Factor

During the London blitz in World War II, Anna Freud made the now well-known observation that children sleeping in the London Underground air-raid shelters seemed protected from anxiety and fear so long as their mothers didn't show anxiety. Anna Freud and Dorothy Burlingham's (1943) psychoanalytic observational study *Children in War* is the classic statement of the protective role of parents in preventing traumatization of children in situations of grave threat:

> The war acquires comparatively little significance for children so long as it only threatens their lives, disturbs their material comfort, or cuts their food rations. It becomes enormously significant the moment it breaks up family life and uproots the

first emotional attachments of the child within the family group. London children, therefore, were on the whole much less upset by bombing than by evacuation to the country as a protection from it.

In several recent studies of children where the family and child were both evaluated, a significant relationship has been found between "poorer maternal or family functioning" and worse child outcomes (Cornely and Bromet, 1986; Laor et al., 1996, 1997; Yehuda, Halligan, and Grossman, 2001). In one study where effects were evaluated separately for ages three, four, and five (Laor et al., 1996, 1997), a strong relationship between family functioning and child outcomes was found in children age three and four but not at age five, suggesting that the younger the child the greater the protective or detrimental impact of the family. Scheeringa et al. (1995) attempted to identify the types of trauma that best predicted severity of PTSD in children under age four and found only one factor, "trauma that occurred when there were threats to the child's caregivers." In a follow-up study, Laor and colleagues (1997) attempted to identify the specific factors in the traumatized parent that predicted worse child outcome and found only one factor, maternal avoidance. Mothers who tried to avoid reminders of the trauma and who were in a numb emotional state that restricted their capacity for closeness were unable to help their children process the experience of trauma (Pynoos, Steinberg, and Wraith, 1995).

In a very recent study, the New York Academy of Medicine (Stuber, Galea, and Fairbrother, 2002) found that in the aftermath of September 11, children age six to 11 who had parents that were depressed were five to nine times more likely to have behavior problems. (The behavior of children younger than six has not yet been studied.) Even more striking are the findings that children whose parents did not know how their children were responding after September 11 were 11.1 times more likely to have behavior problems at ages six to 11 and 4.0 times more likely at ages 12 to 17. Parents who cannot keep their children's experience in mind after a traumatic event have more behaviorally disturbed children, and this effect is nearly three times greater in younger children than in adolescents. These findings provide further confirmation of the importance of reflective functioning in the parent as a protective factor for children under circumstances of adversity, as described by Fonagy and Target (this volume) and Slade (2002). These findings taken together also provide evidence of a growing consensus of the relational nature of trauma, especially in young children (Scheeringa and Zeanah, 2001).

Diagnostic Approaches to Trauma in Children

Whereas the DSM-IV distinguishes acute stress disorders, which emerge immediately after an event and last no more than four weeks, from more long-term PTSD (American Psychiatric Association, 1994), the 0-to-3 Diagnostic Classification that developed criteria especially for young children does not make this distinction.

The 0-to-3 diagnostic criteria for traumatic stress disorder (Zero to Three: National Center for Infants, Toddlers, and Families, 1994) include:

• Reexperiencing of the traumatic event as evidenced by posttraumatic play (i.e., compulsively driven play that represents a repetitive reenactment of the trauma), recurrent recollections of the traumatic event, repeated nightmares, distress at exposure to reminders of the trauma, and episodes with features of a flashback or dissociation.

• Numbing of responsiveness in a child or interference with developmental momentum, revealed by increased social withdrawal, restricted range of affect, temporary loss of previously acquired developmental skills, and a decrease or constriction in play.

• Symptoms of increased arousal, as revealed by night terrors, difficulty going to sleep, repeated night waking, significant attentional difficulties, hypervigilance, and exaggerated startle response.

• Symptoms, especially fears or aggression that were not present before the traumatic event.

Presentations of Trauma at Kids' Corner

Our contact with children was often a single visit, but the child's stay might have been for two to three hours because of the allowance for parents to drop off children while using the Assistance Center services. Some children were brought back over consecutive days or for several weekends in a row.

A range of traumatized and resilient responses was immediately visible at Kids' Corner. (Our observations date from the end of September through December 2001. By two weeks after September 11, the most intense trauma may have been somewhat metabolized.) Most impressive in the first weeks was the intensity with which many children wanted to make symbolic representations of the traumatic scene: countless paintings of the planes crashing into the WTC, the towers burning, and people leaping from windows, often shown aflame. Some paintings were compulsively repetitive, the mark of acute traumatization, but most, though somewhat driven and repetitive, were executed with a defiant zeal and liveliness, as if the children were aware they were struggling to cope creatively with their shock, disbelief, and perhaps their overstimulated aggression by putting it into imagery. Boys between ages seven and 11 would find their way to the paint table and ask, "You have red paint? You have black? White?" The white was to make gray. That was all they needed to set to work: red for flames, black for the towers, and gray for smoke. More despairing children covered pages over and over in black, unable yet to make images. Others painted nightmares. One by a nine-year-old boy, which typically condensed the WTC attack with fears for his own family, showed his apartment house melting like the WTC.

Younger children who weren't too depressed to play elaborated narratives with block towers and rescue vehicles. Some preadolescent children and young adolescents who were still stunned by the loss of a relative, especially when it had just been acknowledged by the family after a period of holding out hope, appeared numb, withdrawn, and unresponsive. Several of the withdrawn children were able to respond to therapy dogs who would roll over to get their bellies rubbed and allow the children to hug, pet, and stroke them. Once they were able to make contact with the dogs, a number of children became responsive to the staff.[1] Others of that age had already entered a grieving process and might have taken mental health workers to show them

---

[1]The Red Cross, the Society for the Prevention of Cruelty to Animals, and the Delta Society (a society that trains therapy dogs) teamed up to bring therapy dogs to help at the Family Assistance Center. Therapy dogs were sent from around the country and roamed the halls of Pier 94, making themselves available to be petted, hugged, and played with by children and adults.

their mother's or uncle's photo on the wall of missing posters, or write a note on the poster, or design a memorial collage.

One little girl whose father was killed on a high floor of the WTC had posted a written explanation alongside her memorial painting: "My picture is about my Daddy. My grandmother saw something in her room. She saw an angel. It looked like a butterfly. So that's what made me want to draw a butterfly. I think I will call it butterfly angel. I think the butterfly was Dad" (Buchenholtz, 2002). Here, a child was evidently struggling to understand death, creating a symbolic representation of her father's sudden disappearance and transformation and using cultural beliefs in the family to make it bearable.

Goals and Guidelines for
Brief Interventions After Disaster

We should note that we are reporting reactions that appeared in the first months after the trauma. Having the opportunity to intervene soon after the event, we hoped that such an early response could help contain overwhelming experiences so that the acute symptoms we saw wouldn't become organized later into chronic pathology. We understood the intense acute reactions of children and parents—repetition of the trauma, nightmares, and withdrawn states—as a sign of their disorganization and their difficulty in metabolizing the event and giving it symbolic representation.

At Kids' Corner, we tried to be available and responsive without being intrusive, guided by the hope that the presence of understanding adults would provide a safe space where, as a first step, children's overwhelming feelings of pain, shock, loss, anguish, anger, and fear could be expressed in a containing atmosphere. Often, we and other clinicians were providing ordinary human acknowledgment and recognition for very difficult experiences, and often with few words. Interventions on Pier 94 were of course frequently spontaneous, though clinically informed, responses to the moment.

Research has demonstrated that dogs are very useful in lowering stress levels in crises simply by being petted. Since the Oklahoma City bombing, pet therapy has been provided throughout the United States at disaster sites.

Reflecting on what we had been doing, we formulated some implicit principles and guidelines. The guidelines that emerged for us at Pier 94 were consonant with those developed by Robert Pynoos and his colleagues on trauma (Pynoos and Nader, 1988). Our later clinical vignettes exemplify some of this approach. The following guidelines apply to children:

• *Facilitate*. We attempted to facilitate children's symbolic expression in play and in art projects by being gently and supportively interested and available to observe, join play, or talk with them while they used art and crafts materials. Children who are still unable to play or who can only paint compulsively in black should not be urged upward to the next symbolic level; a companionable, tolerant, interested presence may be all it takes for the child to regain capacities for symbolization.

• *Listen*. Some children spontaneously want to talk with a sensitive outsider about what they or their parents and other family members were going through; others readily appreciate the offer to do so. Here, acknowledging the reality of trauma and loss is implicit in simply listening.

• *Clarify*. Children who wish to talk can be helped to make sense of their feelings and to find words to name emotions. Finding words promotes containment, the development of symbolic representation, and the capacity for self-regulation. Clarification of affects and events helps toward the restoration of a coherent narrative. We were careful to follow the child's lead and to avoid probing exploration, responding only to what the child spontaneously introduced, to support containment of overwhelming feelings.

• *Support the capacity to imagine repair, restoration, and constructive action*. Bob Pynoos (personal communication) described key moments in the crisis intervention after the bombing in Oklahoma City when he helped children to imagine reparative possibilities. When he ended a session with a child reliving trauma by telling about it or representing it, he found it could tend to retraumatize them. But, when he ended a session by helping the child imagine some way they might actively contribute to repairing or healing the damage, this worked to restore a sense of safety, agency, and hope. We tried to do this in play as well. We helped younger children to think about how their family and community would take care of them and encouraged older children to imagine a future in which they would have some agency.

• *Normalize feelings.* Children could be helped to normalize their feelings by letting them know that many other kids were having similar feelings. We understand children's and parents' acute stress reactions, intense reexperiencing of the event, nightmares, and frequently reported sense of psychic numbing as expectable responses to a horrifying disaster and to traumatic grief. Normalizing their reactions as a natural response to an extreme situation can help older children.

• *Support attachment bonds.* For children who were ready to do this, we supported the child's identification with or internalization of the attachment to the lost family member by actively facilitating the child's need to remember and talk about his or her lost loved one.

The following goals apply to parents:

• *Normalize parents' reactions.* We helped them, as we did older children and adolescents, to understand that they were not going crazy and that their fears, anxieties, and flashbacks were normal reactions to a severely traumatizing event.

• *Support children's surviving attachment relationships by helping parents understand their children's feelings and by facilitating parent–child communication.* We tried to help parents recognize how much their children understood the events all around them. We tried to help parents, family members, and friends be more accessible by answering children's questions directly and honestly without providing more information than children needed.

• *Help parents make sense of their children's perplexing and disturbing expressions and behavior.* For example, we worked with parents to help them understand and make meaning of the feelings being expressed through children's repetitive dramatic play, traumatized drawings, dreams, or nightmares, which parents often had difficulty making sense of and found upsetting. In this way, the adult's reflective function could be reengaged.

• *Help parents understand their children's experience.* Some parents were frightened or became angry with their children for their increased clinginess, tantrums, and aggression. Parents were afraid these reactions were signs of lasting damage and future pathology. It was hard for parents to see these reactions as expectable responses to a situation of great insecurity. Parents' anxiety or anger in turn made the children more frightened of losing them, and so more demanding or aggressive. We tried to stop this escalating cycle.

• *Help parents answer the questions their children raised both directly and indirectly, while protecting children from exposure to adult conversations.*

• *Encourage families to try to return to ordinary daily life and customary routines as soon as possible.*

• *Encourage parents to turn off the TV and not expose children to endless repetitions of images of the attack and the towers' collapse.*

Parents Who Could Not Bear to Have Their Children Know

In an effort to protect themselves and their children, many bereaved families could not bear at first to let their children know about the death of the other parent or a close relative. At Pier 94, we were soon impressed by how prevalent an issue this was and how difficult it was for bereaved parents to speak with their children about what had happened. During the period of hours, days, or even weeks when the loved one's death was not a certainty, accepting it could have seemed disloyal, as if maintaining hope might have helped keep the missing one alive. Even when a death was known or accepted, this "not knowing" was preserved for a while longer with children and even older adolescents. This may have been a way of adults' dealing with their own oscillations between shocked denial and grief.

The idea that children were too young to understand or needed to be protected in their innocence could serve denial. We speculated that "protecting the child's innocence" also could represent a need to construct an imaginary space of innocence, projected onto the child, as a way to defend against the adult's sense of violation.

Some adults of course were so traumatized by the enormity of the disaster that their own terror, traumatic grief, and some degree of dissociation made it very difficult to keep their children's minds in mind. It should be mentioned that in states of shock some parents may have dissociated and may not then have remembered their own initial reactions, which children witnessed.

A grieving child can be a constant reminder to the parent of his or her own loss. Parents may fear the child's pain will threaten their own fragile defenses. Parents not directly bereaved but significantly impacted by the WTC disaster also had difficulty realizing how much their young children were trying to make sense of events.

Many parents less tragically affected also had little idea of how much their children already knew about the terrorist attack. Some were unaware of the ways in which their children were alert to what was happening in their environment, how much their children had taken in from overheard conversations and constant exposure to TV. Finally, and most important, in the wake of trauma it was hard for many parents to realize how attuned their children were to their parents' mental states.

We became interested in the confusion that arose when parents had difficulty talking with their children about the attack or their losses. Confusion also arose from the children's limited developmental capacities and their own defenses. Finally, confusion arose when parents used denial in misguided protectiveness. We also speculated that "protecting the child's innocence" could represent a need to construct an imaginary space of innocence, projected onto the child, as a way to defend against the adult's sense of violation.

Parents for whom the terrorist attack revived significant earlier or recent trauma could have a hard time trusting ordinary processes of growth and healing in their children; parental preoccupation with the revived trauma could also be disjunctive for their young children.

Denial was a concern because of the literature on detrimental and sometimes devastating effects of denying a child the facts of a parent's death. Specialized studies of the effects of hiding the causes of a parent's death have been made, based on children of parents who committed suicide (Cain and Fast, 1972) and on children of Holocaust survivors (Laub and Auerhahn, 1993). These have shown that when parents cannot talk directly to their children about what happened, or deny what the child has already witnessed or pieced together, the child's confidence in the parent is eroded. Persistent pressure by parents to accept a story that conflicts with what the child has figured out on his or her own can lead not only to the development of confusion about knowing and not knowing but may lead to a sense of unreality. When children feel that they must comply with a parent's distorted reality, various characteristic symptoms may develop, which include transient selective mutism, general shyness, reticence to speak, inhibitions in learning, and dissociative splits (Cain and Fast, 1972).

Clinical Vignettes Illustrate Confusion in Young Children

The father of Ben, a two-year-old boy whose mother was lost in the WTC bombing, told us that his son's crying, sleeplessness, and apparently inconsolable anxiety about being separated from his mother haunted him. Ben's grandmother had told him that "Mommy got stuck on the subway and will be coming home as soon as they get it working again." Ben's father, however, said he wasn't sure that was the right thing to tell him. Expressing similar conflicts, an aunt who had lost her sister told her two-year-old nephew, Andy, that "Mommy is away on business . . . at a meeting." Both these toddlers knew that mommy was gone. Ben even remarked, "Mommy went up into the clouds with the smoke." He later said, "Mommy burned—I saw it." The adults, still in shock, could not take in what the children already knew. Andy showed his distress even if he did not verbalize his knowledge. His aunt reported, "Little Andy told me to get out of the room and threw a truck at me—he never did anything like that before."

The raw anxiety, rage, and despair of very young children often flew in the face of the adults' protective defenses that at this early stage were still dominated by shock and disbelief. Some adult caregivers found themselves irritated by the reminders coming from their young children and then felt guilty for being angry with them. Ben, told his mother was stuck on the subway, could not walk by a subway stop afterward without asking, "Mommy there?" This behavior brought his grandmother to tears, the father reported, adding sorrowfully, "My son is killing his grandmother." Neither could bear to be reminded of what had happened.

As long as two months after September 11, even older bereaved children remained confused about the fate of loved ones. Some seemed to know and not know at the same time. Dr. Coates sat with a 13-year-old girl, Bailey, whose father had died in the WTC. On the day that her mother was picking up a memorial urn filled with ashes retrieved at Ground Zero, she left Bailey at Kids' Corner. Announcements could be heard on the public-address speakers with information for survivors about where to pick up the memorial urns.

Coates said to Bailey, "This is a hard and sad day."

Bailey responded, "No it isn't. My dad is missing, but he is not dead."

Coates said, "Then you must be very worried about him."

Bailey said, "I have never been more worried in my life." She then began to draw a picture of a church with a graveyard beside it.

Her godmother, who was with her, said, "Why in the world are you drawing a church?"

Bailey maintained, "I just wanted to."

The godmother explained to Coates that Bailey had no idea of what happened and had not been told her dad was dead. Her need to ignore the message of Bailey's drawing was remarkable.

Bailey was evidently caught between trying to comply with her mother's and godmother's wish for her to not know about her father's death while simultaneously knowing about it in another part of her mind. In drawing the churchyard, she was perhaps trying to prepare herself to begin grieving, using the presence of the therapist to obtain the permission to mourn, which her family could not provide.

Confusion and Parent–Child Communication in Traumatic Loss of Safety and Threatened Loss of Attachment Figure: Maria

A more complex confusion can be seen in a three-year-old child's attempt to put together, from fragments that she was experiencing, a story of what happened to her father that made sense to her. A little Mexican girl, whom we shall call Maria, had settled at our play table with crayons and paper, while her father, Mr. P, waited to speak to a benefits counselor at an adjacent booth. He had lost his job as a cook because of the WTC attack. Maria was a wide-eyed girl with shoulder-length black hair, wearing a pink jumper. She spoke in an animated manner in Spanish. Her mother was at home with her younger brother. Mr. P later told us that Maria had been waking from nightmares, too frightened to sleep in her own bed. Like many New York City children, Maria had been sharing her parents' bed since 9/11.

Maria began to scrawl intently in bright overlapping reds, yellows, and black. She readily told us that she was drawing the buildings that "fell and burned," adding that she had seen this on television. (This family saw the WTC attacked again and again, initially unsure as to whether they were watching the death of Mr. P on the screen.) Maria told us that her father had escaped from the WTC, where he had worked, as the buildings collapsed. She emphasized that her father's lungs had been filled with smoke so that he could hardly breathe. While her father was running from the WTC to get home, burning pieces of the building fell on him, she added, and burned his arms: "He has marks from the fire on his arms!" A second drawing repeated the wild scrawl of bright fire with one addition, a thick black monolith—both a charred tower and a black void. Dr. Schechter did not interpret this to the child but supposed it represented not only a burnt tower but also an experience of the death and disappearance of the father.

Mr. P came over to check on his daughter while waiting for forms to be processed. Dr. Schechter then asked the father about the events his daughter had described. He was surprised. "I was not anywhere near the WTC," he said and added incredulously, "She told you I was there?" Mr. P had indeed been employed as a cook at Windows on the World (hence the old burn scars from splattered grease on his arms), but he had exchanged the breakfast shift with a colleague the week prior to the attack. On the morning of 9/11, while his daughter had stayed home with her mother, Mr. P went into Manhattan to run some errands but had not been near the WTC, though he had needed to walk across a bridge from Manhattan, closed to vehicles, to get home.

Dr. Schechter asked the father how he was doing. The father, a young man, slight and soft-spoken, wanted to downplay any troubles of his own. He was profoundly distressed by the loss of his coworkers at Windows on the World. He struggled with feeling responsible for having switched shifts and also for finding work at the WTC for some of his friends. His agonizing survivor guilt took the form of feeling obliged to vividly imagine how his friends had died: the fire, the smoke, and what they had felt. He also had nightmares from which he awakened several times a night, leaving him to ruminate alone over their deaths.

After the father spoke, Dr. Schechter exclaimed, "So your daughter is drawing your dreams!" Indeed, Mr. P appeared shocked that his daughter's drawings and fantasies (perhaps also her nightmares) so closely resembled his own nightmares; he had not discussed them with her. He went on: "Every night when I close my eyes, I see all my coworkers trapped in the smoke and burning up, and there's nothing I can do to save them." His eyes welled with tears as he said, "I guess I'm lucky. It could have been me there. I miss all of my friends and am sorry for the guy who took my place. I pray for his family." This conversation was carried on within earshot of Maria, sometimes intentionally including her.

After this, Maria turned to drawing a picture of her school, a low rectangle with many windows and doors. She emphasized that there were as many doors as windows, and counted them. Elsa First remarked that perhaps she meant that there were many ground-floor openings, many ways to get out of the school so that it would be safe if there were a fire. Elsa First asked if she meant that her preschool was safe. Yes, replied Maria. Elsa First commented that she was showing us her feelings about her school being a good safe place where the grownups thought about the children's safety, and father chimed in with pride about what a good school it was, how much Maria liked school, and how well she was doing there, thus joining the effort to reestablish some sense of adult-sponsored safety and of there being an imaginable future.

We think this vignette shows how a three-year-old girl pieced together a narrative from bits and pieces of reality and what she had picked up of the parents' psychic reality, including her mother's fear that the father had stopped at the WTC that day and especially the father's agonized preoccupations. The fantasy that father had been engulfed in smoke and flames evidently condensed her profound recognition of and sympathy with her father's survivor guilt with her pressing fear that she might have lost him—a form of intergenerational transmission of trauma. Contrary to her father's expectation, the opportunity to hear him share his emotional concerns as well as recounting the facts of his whereabouts on 9/11 seemed to be therapeutic for Maria.

Father and daughter both knew and did not know what was going on in the mind of the other. Each was attempting to make sense of the trauma in relative isolation. We can speculate that for both father and child strong affects of fear and anguish were at first regulated by mutual avoidance of communication. We can speculate that, were it not for the intervention, which showed that distressing affects could be communicated and helpfully managed and regulated through mutual understanding, which they began to recover through interaction with the clinicians, Maria's acute symptoms might have persisted.

In a subsequent phone call, the father reported the little girl's symptoms had subsided, though she still needed to sleep in her parents' bed. He also said that his own symptoms were better, he was receiving benefits, and he was hopeful that he might get another job. The father felt no further need for intervention.

What in this brief intervention may have helped Maria to move on? We think that the father realizing the extent of Maria's concern for him and attunement to him and Maria seeing her father take this in were most important for Maria, along with the clarifications of his where-abouts that day. For this father, his survivor guilt and agonized imaginings seemed somewhat normalized and detoxified after speaking with Dr. Schechter, so he no longer felt he had to conceal his pain. As the father and daughter each became able to understand what was going on in the other's mind, their anxiety was further reduced, and they were helped to move on.

Reactions of Children Who Were Told Directly About the Loss of Their Parent

In contrast to bereaved families who could not find words, some surviving parents valued letting their children, even quite young ones, know honestly and simply and as soon as they could that the other parent had died. They saw this as a way to keep the relationship between surviving parent and child trustworthy. In the following family, the mother let her children know that their dad had been killed in the Twin Towers collapse. She had even taken them to witness the site at Ground Zero, believing that by doing so, where and how their father had died could be real for them.

Though in a state of shock and traumatic bereavement, she was able to talk directly to her children, Debra, a girl of 12, and David, a boy of seven. She answered their questions and gave them reassurance that she would be there for them and that they would all find a way to go on. This allowed both children to talk about their experience very directly. Despite their shock and traumatic grief, they seemed to assume that we at Kids' Corner would also talk with them openly about their inner experience and feelings.

Dr. Coates met with both children at Kids' Corner two weeks after the WTC bombing, while their mother conferred about services. Dr. Coates spoke first with the 12-year-old, asking how she was doing. Debra said she was okay, but she was worried about her mom and her brother, who had been very angry. She said, "My brother is too young to understand that God is taking care of our dad, so he is having a lot of trouble."

She continued confiding for a short while, and then Dr. Coates turned to her seven-year-old brother David, who said, "Some people think you should not talk about what has happened, but I think you should."

Dr. Coates told him that she agreed with him. He then fell silent. Dr. Coates remarked, "This is a scary time. A lot of kids around here have some pretty big feelings; some are sad, and some are mad."

David said, "I do have big feelings. I am sad and mad, but that is not the biggest one. The horrible one is that I feel so guilty that I had a fight with my dad at the breakfast table."

Dr. Coates said, "All kids have fights with their moms and dads all the time, and they understand about that, and I am sure that your dad knows how much you love him."

David brightened up and said, "That's exactly what my mom said."

"You must have a pretty terrific mom," Dr. Coates said.

David told Dr. Coates that his dad had made enough money so that his mom could stay home and take care of him and didn't have to go to work. He then began to build towers with Lego blocks and knocked them down and rebuilt them over and over again. After a while, Dr. Coates asked him how he would like to see the WTC built up again, and he began to make one architectural plan after another.

He then said, "My dad loved New York City so much, but this is the first time I have ever been here, and I don't think I ever want to come back again."

Dr. Coates said, "I can really understand that, but maybe when you get older you might want to come discover why your dad loved New York so much."

David shook his head yes.

One of the large golden retrievers designated and provided on the Pier as therapy dogs happened to be brought to visit Kids' Corner just then, and David wanted to take the dog for a walk. David became very animated as he took the dog's leash. Dr. Coates joined him until they found his mother, who then went off with David and the golden retriever.

Dr. Coates tried to provide a space for David for his feelings to be known and recognized while supporting his loving attachment to his dad. An important question for Dr. Coates with David was how she could support his attachment in the face of the painful inevitability that his main experience of his father while growing up would be his father's absence. Dr. Coates, by attempting to imagine a future enlivening identification, suggested, in effect, that he might refind his father symbolically.

Conclusions: Plea for a Relational Diagnosis of Childhood PTSD

Our observations provide further support for theories that point to the relational nature of trauma in young children and highlight the protective element in parental reflective function. Where parents were unable to take in and keep in mind what their children were experiencing, children seemed to develop more stress-related symptoms, to struggle more with states of shut down or confusion, and perhaps transiently to feel unable to know what was real. At Pier 94, we attempted to provide recognition, acknowledgment, and containment for children's and their parents' overwhelming affect. We also tried to provide parents with the psychological space in which they could regain their sense of themselves as thoughtfully protective parents and begin to let themselves understand their children's experience. They could thus respond more sensitively to their children's needs for understanding and connection at a time of great fear, insecurity, and disruption. We hope that these observations will contribute to our collective efforts to develop effective ways of helping children during times of grave threat.

References

American Psychiatric Association (1994), *Diagnostic and Statistical Manual of Mental Disorders*, 4th ed. Washington, DC: American Psychiatric Association.

Bragin, M. (2002), Living in the nightmares of others: Case studies from the U.S. and Afghanistan. Presented at conference Terror and the Psychoanalytic Space: International Perspectives from Ground Zero, May 2002, New York City.

Buchenholtz, G. (2002), 9/11: A town hall meeting. A special edition of *New York Tonight*, NY1 television production, August 1.

Cain, A. C. & Fast, I. (1972), Children's disturbed reactions to parent suicide. In: *Survivors of Suicide*, ed. A. C. Cain. Springfield, IL: Charles Thomas.

Coates, S. W., Schechter, D. S., First, E., Anzieu-Premmercur, C., Steinberg, Z. & Hamilton, V. (2002a), Considerazioni in merito all'intervento di crisi con I bambini di New York City dopo l'attentato alle Torri Gemelle. *Infanzia E Adolescenza*, 49–62.

———— ———— ———— ———— ———— & ———— (2002), Reflexions sur l'intervention de crise aupres des enfants de New York après l'explosion du World Trade Center. *Psychotherapies*, 22:143–152.

Cornely, P. & Bromet, E. (1986), Prevalence of behavior problems in three-year-old children living near Three Mile Island: A comparative analysis. *J. Child Psychol. Psychiat.*, 27:489–498.

Freud, A. & Burlingham, D. (1943), *Children in War*. New York: Medical War Books.

Freud, S. (1917) The uncanny. *Standard Edition*, 17. London: Hogarth Press, 1955.

Gaensbauer, T. (2000), Psychotherapeutic treatment of traumatized infants and toddlers: A case report. *Clin. Child Psychol. Psychiat.*, 5:373–385.

Galea, S., Ahern, J., Resnick, H., Kilpatrick, D., Bucuvalas, M., Gold, M. J. & Vlahov, D. (2002), Psychological sequelae of the September 11 terrorist attacks in New York City. *New Engl. J. Med.*, 346:982–987.

Gould, S. J. (2002), *I Have Landed*. New York: Harmony Books.

Hamilton, V. (1989), The mantle of safety: Festschrift for Frances Tustin. *Winnicott Stud.*, 4:70–97.

In Memoriam: New York City 9/11/01 (2002), HBO documentary.

Laor, N., Wolmer, L., Mayes, L. C. & Gershon, A. (1997), Israeli preschool children under Scuds: A 30-month follow-up. *Amer. Acad. Child Adolesc. Psychiat.*, 36:349–356.

———— ———— ———— Golomb, A., Silverberg, D. S., Weizman, R. & Cohen, D. J. (1996), Israeli preschoolers under Scud missile attacks. *Arch. Gen. Psychiat.*, 53:416–423.

Laub, D. & Auerhahn, N. C. (1993), Knowing and not knowing massive psychic trauma: Forms of traumatic memory. *Internat. J. Psycho-Anal.*, 74:287–302.

Marshall, R. D. (2001), Coping mechanisms and post-traumatic stress reactions: Life after September 11, 2001, www.fathom.com.

Pfefferbaum, B. (2001), The impact of the Oklahoma City bombing on children in the community. *Mil. Med.*, 166:49–50.

_____ Nixon, S. J., Tivis, R. D., Doughty, D. E., Pynoos, R. S., Gurwitch, R. H. & Foy, D. W. (2001), Television exposure in children after a terrorist incident. *Psychiatry*, 64:202–211.

_____ _____ Tucker, P. M., Tivis, R. D., Moore, V. L., Gurwitch, R. H., Pynoos, R. S. & Geis, H. K. (1999), Posttraumatic stress responses in bereaved children after the Oklahoma City bombing. *J. Amer. Acad. Child Adolesc. Psychiat.*, 38:1372–1379.

Pynoss, R. S. (2001), Keynote address: Trauma and Attachment Conference on "When the Bough Broke," Columbia University, New York City, November 3.

_____ & Nader, K. (1988), Psychological first aid and treatment approach to children exposed to community violence: Research implications. *J. Traumatic Stress*, 1:445–473.

_____ Steinberg, A. M. & Wraith, R. (1995), A developmental model of childhood traumatic stress. In: *Risk, Disorder and Adaptation: Vol. 2, Developmental Psychopathology*, ed. D. Cicchetti & D. J Cohen. New York: Wiley.

Regehr, C., Hemsworth, D. & Hill, J. (2001), Individual predictors of posttraumatic distress: A structural equation model. *Can. J. Psychiat.*, 46:156–161.

Schechter, D. S., Coates, S. W. & First, E. (2001/2002), Observations from New York on young children's and their families' acute reactions to the World Trade Center attacks. *Bull. Zero to Three*, 22:9–13.

_____ _____ & _____ (in press), "Lessons in loss": Beobachtungen von den Reaktionen der Risiko-Kinder auf die Angriffe auf das World Trade Center. In: *Bindung und Trauma: Risiken und Schutzfaktoren in der kindlichen Entwicklung*, ed. K.-H. Brisch & T. Hellbruegge. Stuttgart, Germany: Klett-Cotta Verlag.

_____ & Tosyali, M. C. (2001), Posttraumatic stress disorder from infancy through adolescence: A review. In: *Anxiety Disorders in Children and Adolescents*, ed. C. A. Essau & F. Petermann. New York: Brunner-Routledge, pp. 285–322.

Scheeringa, M. S., Peebles, C. D., Cook, C. A. & Zeanah C. H. (2001), Toward establishing procedural, criterion, and discriminant validity for PTSD in early childhood. *J. Amer. Acad. Child Adolesc. Psychiat.*, 40:52–60.

_____ & Zeanah, C. H. (2001), A relational perspective on PTSD in early childhood. *J. Traumatic Stress*, 14:799–815.

_____ _____ Drell, M. J. & Larrieu, J. A. (1995), Two approaches to the diagnosis of posttraumatic stress disorder in infancy and early childhood. *J. Amer. Acad. Child Adolesc. Psychiat.*, 34:191–200.

Slade, A. (2002), Keeping the baby in mind: A critical factor in perinatal mental health. *Bull. Zero to Three*, June/July:10–16.

Stuber, J., Galea, G. & Fairbrother, F. (2002), The mental health of New York City families. Presented at Columbia University's Psychiatry Grand Rounds, September 11, New York City.

Ulrich, N. J. (2001), Internet communication. NYU Postdoctoral Program in Psychoanalysis and Psychotherapy members listserve, The Psychoanalytic Connection, October 18.

Yehuda, R., Halligan, S. L. & Grossman, R. (2001), Childhood trauma and risk for PTSD: Relationship to intergenerational effects of trauma, parental PTSD, and cortisol excretion. *Devel. Psychopathol.*, 13:733–753.

Zeanah, C. H. & Scheeringa, M. S. (1996), Evaluation of posttraumatic symptomatology in infants and young children exposed to violence. *Bull. Zero to Three*, 16:9–14.

Zero to Three: National Center for Infants, Toddlers, and Families (1994), *Diagnostic Classification: 0–3 (DC:0–3)*. Washington, DC: Zero to Three.

Chapter 4

Mental Health of
New York City Public School
Children After 9/11
An Epidemiologic Investigation

Christina W. Hoven,
Donald J. Mandell, and
Cristiane S. Duarte

*The following study of the impact of the World Trade Center
disaster on the mental health of the schoolchildren of New
York City is a remarkable story in its own right. Lower
Manhattan, site of the tragedy, while not a residential area,
is nonetheless rich in schools, and students travel there from
all areas of the city. Amid the general crisis atmosphere, the
authors of this study grasped that not only would major
funding have to be appropriated for mental health intervention with the schoolchildren near the Ground Zero area,
but also that the information needed to guide intervention
would have to be gathered on a much wider basis than the
immediate area of the attack. Based on a citywide sample,
the authors came to the stunning finding that in the wake
of the disaster major psychiatric disorders, including not
only posttraumatic stress disorder but also separation anxiety, depression, agoraphobia, and other disorders, could be
found in fully one fourth of the city's children.*

I n this chapter, we describe the New York City Board of Education (BOE) post-9/11 schools study, "Effects of the World Trade Center Attack on New York City Public School Students," which was carried out on a representative sample (N = 8266) of the city's 1.1 million public school children (Hoven, Duarte, Lucas, et al., 2002). We describe how this study came to be, its purposes and methodology, the problems and political issues encountered in launching such an ambitious study, the importance of its general findings to date, and how the study results highlight the need for increased mental health services and follow-up studies (Hoven, in press). It is hoped there will be an opportunity to conduct a longitudinal study soon so as to contribute maximally to the understanding of the effects of disaster-related risk on childhood psychopathology. Such a study could extend and rationalize further the influence of this study, conducted to help plan for more efficient and effective ameliorative services.

September 11 has become for the United States, and perhaps for the entire world, a new "day of infamy." School texts in American history frequently refer to the rifle fire at Lexington and Concord, Massachusetts in 1775 as "shots that rang 'round the world." That is clearly an exaggeration, for certainly it was not the case that the American Revolution affected people worldwide. The terrorist attacks of September 11, 2001, however, may indeed have had such universal reach. Reports continue to corroborate the fact that events on that day were emblazoned on children's minds throughout the world. For example, immediately after our May 1, 2002 report of the study findings were presented to the BOE and released by them to the press, a producer from LTN, the public television of Chile, asked for an interview because in a current school survey of Chilean children students reported, in overwhelming numbers, that they were experiencing nightmares from watching televised replays of the airplanes crashing into the World Trade Center (WTC). In a similar vein, a journalist from Japan, who also called for an interview, said that during a teaching assignment in Turkmenistan in the fall of 2001 she observed that schoolteachers there were unable to conduct regular classes for three weeks after 9/11, as children were preoccupied and unable to concentrate on their school work. Similar stories have come to us from around the world, including Armenia, Borneo, Egypt, France, and Zimbabwe, and assuredly more will follow. Whereas major disasters occur frequently throughout the world, in some places on a regular basis, rarely, if ever, do these occurrences have such a powerful impact beyond the national borders in which they happen (Wright et al., 1989; Cantor, Mares, and Oliver, 1993; Cantor and Nathanson, 1996; *L'etat du monde,* 2000; Pfefferbaum et al., 2000).

We have systematically studied New York City (NYC) public school children and can report on only our own survey results. Yet, in light of all the other reports of disasters, we cannot help but wonder how this disaster has been different from other disasters of equal or even greater magnitude in terms of loss of life and damage to property and infrastructure. What was it about September 11 that has caused it to have such universal reach? Why has it been accorded such great importance? Admittedly, the attacks caught the American public off guard. But so do most, if not all, disasters present some element of surprise, whether natural or the result of human intervention. The death toll alone certainly cannot account for such worldwide attention. Nor even the property damage. How can one compare 9/11 with, say, August 1945 and the bombings of Hiroshima and Nagasaki? Or to the human slaughter of 800,000 human beings in Rwanda over a period of just three months, one decade ago? It seems, to us an inescapable conclusion that the aftershock effects of the 9/11 terrorist attacks reach beyond death toll or property loss and are simply not measurable in those terms.

What then might account for such worldwide discomfiture? We propose that much of the modern sense of safety, built on confidence in carefully negotiated treaties and alliances, enormous buildup of military might, and sophisticated modern methods of warfare (including defense), which would be an effective deterrent to attack or war, was dashed on 9/11. What had been the posture and the political polemic for half a century was threatened when an organization, al Qaeda, demonstrated its ability to penetrate all that apparatus, to turn our own civilian planes into their agents of military destruction, and to topple the symbol of Western world capitalism, the World Trade Center. It was indeed a modern day enactment of the Biblical account of David and Goliath.

It became apparent soon after 9/11 that this event had a global effect that was similar, we suppose, to that felt by the small group of followers of the ancient Greek philosopher Pythagoras, who taught that numbers corresponded to actual physical points in space—that is, that they were real (Dantzig, 1930). On finding that in constructing a right triangle with sides of unit measure the hypotenuse could not be subdivided into an even number or even fractional units commensurable with these units, their philosophical world belief was shattered. It was for precisely this reason that the followers of Pythagoras called the measure of the hypotenuse, "the square root of two," an "irrational number." For much of the world, 9/11 became our new irrational number!

Further discussion and analysis of the modus operandi of terror can be found in chapter 12, by Herman, Aaron, and Susser, as well as in a number of recent publications and presentations (Frieden, 2002; Hoven, 2002; Sederer, 2002; Susser, Herman, and Aaron, 2002). As we view the situation, the goal of terrorists is, put simply, to create in the target population a general mental state of terror. This state of terror is intended to create ubiquitous panic, to be followed by generalized paranoia, leading ultimately to total paralysis. Panic, paranoia, paralysis. It was just such a total breakdown in the calm confidence and sense of security characterizing the pre-9/11 United States that al Qaeda had fervently wished for by simultaneously attacking the multiple targets of September 11. The great gasp that has been uttered all through the world is a good measure of how successful they were. What, we wondered, would be the effect on New York City's children and adolescents?

In many ways, NYC public school students demonstrated remarkable resilience and creativity in the aftermath of September 11. Perusing the web pages of individual schools in the months following the attack revealed a high level of student involvement, both in school and after school, in developing programs to address potential problems, like prejudicial action against some Middle Eastern members of the school community. We learned later from answers to our survey questions that some two thirds of students increased their reading of news magazines and Internet news regarding terrorism and its roots. These were not school assignments, and we cannot yet be sure how adaptive these activities were. This was not a period of apathy or paralysis for the youth of NYC.

Another BOE study demonstrated how the teachers and other school staff, at every level of the school system, became involved in assisting and comforting students, often taking on additional responsibilities on their students' behalf (Degnan, 2002). For example, food service managers saw to it that the same familiar personnel and same favorite hot meals went to students' new schools for those whose schools had to be closed following 9/11. The outpourings of warmth and concern from New Yorkers has done much to dispel that often cited view of New York as a place where people are uncaring, unconcerned, and unwilling to become involved.

That is not to say, however, that 9/11 left no scars—quite the contrary. Our epidemiologic study of one of New York City's most vulnerable populations, its public school children, demonstrates that 9/11 has indeed left significant scars on the minds of children and adolescents. As La Greca and others (1996) point out, the "costs" of disasters, for children in particular, "extend far beyond the money spent rebuilding homes and replacing possessions." Indeed, as we passed the one-year anniversary of the September 11 attacks and engaged in the ceremonies commemorating the heroes of that day, we simultaneously took comfort in the unveiling of plans for memorial areas and the rebuilding of sites that were destroyed. If, however, we repair only these material things and ignore the consequent costs of allowing to lie untreated the serious psychological wounds inflicted on our children, wounds that will in some individuals fester and grow, then we will have only ourselves to blame for the profound consequences of our shortsightedness (Pynoos et al., 1987; Baum and Davidson, 1990; Prinstein et al., 1996; Osofsky, 1997; Shaw, 2000; Hoven, in press).

Study Background

To confront the post-9/11 mental health problems of children, it is necessary first to identify the nature and scope of their problems. What is known from scientific studies of natural and human-made disasters, as well as from common sense, indicates that one should look first for elevated rates of posttraumatic stress disorder (PTSD) or PTSD-related symptoms in those living closest to the site of the disaster (Bromet, Hough, and Connell, 1984; Vogel and Vernberg, 1993; Pynoos, Steinberg, and Wraith, 1995; Earls, Smith, Reich, et al., 1998; Pfefferbaum et al., 1999; Schechter, Coates, and First, 2001).

Previous evidence from disaster studies also demonstrates that the negative effect diminishes with distance, in concentric circles, from the point of impact (Bromet, Hough, and Connell, 1984; Geiger, Michaels, and Rush, 1992; Pfefferbaum et al., 1999; Jacquez, 2000). Would the mental health sequelae of the WTC attack follow these established patterns within NYC? Would PTSD be the major psychological consequence of 9/11? Would there be a greater prevalence of mental health problems in children living or only attending school near Ground Zero? We weren't sure.

Time for planning and exploration of all the relevant issues was limited, as demands for an immediate mental health response came to the BOE from all corners: parents, teachers, administrators, and even students themselves. To its credit, the BOE effectively and courageously resisted political pressures to conduct a "quick-and-dirty" study, which could be used to justify a quick-fix solution through immediate allocation of newly available federal funds. Instead, the BOE leadership[1] acknowledged that there was neither solid comprehensive information in any BOE database that could identify the students affected by 9/11 nor an adequate child mental health disaster-response system in place to deal with potential service need. The lack of both presented an important challenge for the BOE. Fortunately, a multidisciplinary research team was assembled to lead the BOE effort to conduct a needs assessment.

Joining with Francine Goldstein, director of Student Support Services at the BOE, in an effort to meet this newly identified challenge was the Children's Mental Health Alliance, which in collaboration with the BOE set up the Partnership for the Recovery of the NYC Schools (a.k.a., the Partnership) with Dr. Pamela Cantor, a child psychiatrist, as its head. The Partnership, through an arrangement with Dr. Steven Marans at Yale University, immediately arranged for the training of teachers and counselors in how to address the crisis, starting first in the high-impact schools. To provide scientific oversight and to determine the current and possible long-term mental health needs of students consequent to 9/11, the Partnership enlisted Drs. Christina W. Hoven and J. Lawrence Aber, both of the Mailman School of Public Health, Columbia University, to collaborate with Dr. Michael Cohen,

---

[1]The leaders were Chancellor Harold Levy, Deputy Chancellor Dr. Judith Rizzo, Director of Student Support Services Ms. Francine Goldstein, Deputy Director of Student Support Services Mr. Vincent Giordano, and Deputy Director of Special Education Linda Weirnikoff.

who was already under contract with the BOE to conduct a post-9/11 study.[2]

The research team soon concluded that the shape and scope of pre-9/11 mental health pathology among NYC public school children was completely unknown and that, because there existed no accurate measure of the extent, distribution, and specificity of mental health problems in a representative NYC school-age population, the first logical step would be to establish such a baseline. The initial idea was to select a representative sample and then mount a longitudinal study, collecting future waves of data, so that the mental health sequelae of 9/11 could be understood from a developmental perspective. To initiate such a study at this troubled time (just months after 9/11), however, would require a lengthy process, beginning by identifying a randomly selected sample of participating students, gaining active consent to enroll them in a longitudinal study, accessing available student records, and so forth. Logical as such a process might be, the

---

[2]Dr. Hoven, the study's principal investigator, accepted responsibility for designing a study that would portray and profile the post-9/11 mental health status of NYC schoolchildren by determining the needs-assessment methodology, including the screening instrument and development of the sampling plan. Dr. Aber assumed the role of addressing policy matters and organized the solicitation of funds for services with the Partnership. Dr. Michael Cohen, the contract principal investigator, who was also a partner in the research, and his staff assumed responsibility for implementing the fieldwork, including all data collection. As with any large-scale investigation, this one too benefited from significant input from other individuals, most notably from Columbia University–New York State Psychiatric Institute: Dr. Cristiane S. Duarte and Professors Patricia Cohen, Renee Goodwin, Christopher P. Lucas, Donald J. Mandell, Ezra Susser, and Ping Wu, with statistical support from Drs. Fan Bin, Henian Chen, and Pat Zybert and Mr. Mark Davies and Mr. Steven Greenwald, with other support from Ms. Barbara Aaron, Mr. George J. Musa, and Ms. Judith Wicks. Individuals from Applied Research and Consulting (ARC), including Ms. Nellie Gregorian, Ms. Victoria Francis, Mr. Chris Bumcrot, and 50 field researchers, also provided significant input. This important study could not have been conducted without the outstanding leadership from other members of the BOE not previously identified, especially the superintendents, principals, teachers and, of course, the students, who in the final analysis contributed the most to advance the state of our knowledge through their generous study participation.

mood was not ripe for so slow a procedure. It would, perhaps, have been viewed as "Nero fiddling while Rome burns." Moreover, obtaining active consent (signed by parent/guardian) for all students (not just for 4th and 5th graders, with simple informed consent [parental notification] for 6th through 12th graders, as was eventually done in this study) would have lengthened the time needed to get into the field and undoubtedly would have brought about a lower compliance rate. Given the importance of representativeness, the highest compliance rate possible was a major objective; so, reluctantly, the idea of a longitudinal study was shelved, at least for this first study.

When we stepped back to consider carefully what was already known from available BOE data about students attending NYC public schools, including their potential exposure and possible travel patterns, we surmised that a traditional distance formula for study inclusion might not be appropriate for New York City. Furthermore, given both the enormity and wide media coverage of this disaster, the topography and complex transportation system of the city, and the daily mobility of both students and their working parents, we wondered if elevated post-9/11 rates of disorders other than PTSD might also be found in the school population. For example, we wondered about agoraphobia. With a school population exceeding 1.1 million students, of whom some 750,000 travel daily by subway, bus, and even boat, across bridges, through tunnels, and over waterways, might not the fear of crowds and of being in a confined space or aboard a vulnerable conveyance now be particularly terrifying? We wondered too about other anxiety-related disorders and about substance abuse; might these rates also be elevated after 9/11? In other words, we asked ourselves whether existing disaster literature should necessarily constrict the focus of the study we were planning; that is, should these previous study results limit our thinking in constructing a study design to assess mental health problems in NYC public school children following the WTC attack? We decided that they should not.

The team agreed that there was no compelling reason to assume that it could confidently make informed and precise projections about what could be found from a well-crafted, completely representative investigation without conducting such a study. As epidemiologists, we asked ourselves *who* might have been affected, *what* were the possible exposures, *when* and *for what duration* was an effect possible, *where* (i.e., at what realistic distance from the disaster) should we continue to assess outcomes, and *how* (i.e., which) disorders and other domains ought to be assessed. Because the goal, indeed the mandate from the BOE, was to provide information that could be used to guide the planning of mental health services, the team determined that only a full-scale epidemiologic investigation of the mental health status of all NYC public school children could yield the valid and reliable information on which a rational planning process should depend.

Not everyone agreed, however. Some said that the important thing, indeed the only necessary thing to do, was to survey students in the affected Ground Zero area schools and to see to it that appropriate mental health services were offered to those students. A few skeptics even suggested that little was to be gained from conducting any kind of needs assessment study. They questioned how an epidemiologic investigation such as what we had proposed (and ultimately conducted) would really help those who had been affected by the attack. Why, they asked, would anyone need to bother with a study and then wait for its results before designing ameliorative services? Inasmuch as everyone realized immediately (and intuitively) that following so catastrophic a disaster as 9/11 there was bound to be a need for mental health services for children attending schools in the area around Ground Zero, why not just spend all the money on service provision exclusively to these children? Why even look at the children in the Bronx or the other boroughs distant from the WTC?

Consider for a moment by what means one might actually carry out such a directive: distributing funds and services to those assumed to be the only ones in need. Is this a pragmatic plan? Could this plan be sensibly accomplished without first accurately determining who these individuals are, where they live, what services they need, and who is best positioned to render service? Consider just one of the many scenarios that characterized the Ground Zero school population after 9/11. Some schools in the area of the WTC were evacuated on 9/11, and many of the students enrolled were subsequently transferred or relocated to other schools, pending reopening of their own school. Also, many parents, in response to 9/11, immediately transferred their children out of Ground Zero area schools, in most instances bringing them back home to attend local schools, usually in other boroughs, or to public and private schools in suburban or vacation-home areas. In the absence of sound epidemiologic information revealing the true distribution of possible psychopathology among NYC public school students, money spent over and above that obviously required for crisis intervention in the Ground Zero area would most probably be money spent in the dark, with but little chance of ameliorating the long-term needs of the majority of children affected by 9/11, including some children attending Ground Zero schools on the day of the attacks.

The questions of skeptics do, however, provide a useful foil to demonstrate the rationale for choosing to conduct an epidemiologic study. They also highlight reasons for our thinking that many studies that have been launched in the aftermath of natural and human-influenced disasters may have failed to reveal all that they might have uncovered had they been planned from an epidemiologic perspective. It was our opinion that to acquire valid, reliable information on the mental health status and needs of NYC public school children only an epidemiologic investigation with a representative sample would suffice. Accordingly, to determine just how many children and adolescents attending NYC schools had mental health problems (either evident or subtle and hidden) potentially requiring professional mental health intervention, we proposed to the BOE that we conduct such an epidemiologic survey on a representative sample of all of New York City's public school children in grades 4 through 12. Within weeks after the formation of the Partnership, all concerned parties had committed to the idea of such a study and were poised to make a broad-based investigation happen, seeking approval from all appropriate Institutional Review Boards.[3]

---

[3]All aspects of this study were carried out in full compliance with multiple Institutional Review Board (IRB) approvals. The survey instrument (Hoven, Duarte, Mandell, et al., 2002) was reviewed by and approved by the New York City Board of Education IRB, which took particular care to ensure that all federal, state, and BOE guidelines regarding in-school assessments were met. Drs. Henry Solomon and Lori Mei were particularly diligent and helpful in thoughtfully and speedily reviewing and providing comments on all documents. The Columbia University–New York State Psychiatric Institute IRB also reviewed and approved all instruments and procedures, being particularly concerned about adequately protecting the rights of vulnerable subjects (students) and in this case the investigators, too, because there was no formal contractual relationship concerning this study and Columbia University, the primary research institution. Ms. Elizabeth Small demonstrated the highest level of professional commitment in facilitating the necessary transfer of

Sampling Design

The more than 1.1 million public school students in NYC attend almost 1200 schools administered by approximately 40 school districts, including autonomous districts for special education and special category programs, which are distributed across the five boroughs.[4] Whereas for the most part, elementary and middle school programs serve local residents, high schools and other special programs may be attended by residents from anywhere within the boundaries of NYC. In the borough of Manhattan alone (the site of the WTC), there are 65 high schools, some with special programs enrolling from 30 to 300 students and some with a general curriculum enrolling several thousand students, many of whom may travel from any of the five NYC boroughs to attend specialized high schools. In general, NYC schools vary in size from alternative schools, with fewer than 200 enrolled, to comprehensive high schools with some 4000 students. To obtain a meaningful sample from appropriate strata was therefore a formidable task, requiring careful planning and the assistance of the BOE and the Centers for Disease Control and Prevention.[5]

For reasons of proximity, the schools nearest the Ground Zero location (Stratum 1) were appropriately the first to be singled out for surveying. Children attending these schools were the most likely of any students in NYC to have seen or heard the impact of the planes hitting the WTC towers and witnessed bodies falling as people jumped from the inferno inside the WTC towers. They were most likely to have had to run for their lives, to have been enveloped in smoke, and to have been commingled with crowds running to get away. We, therefore, would attempt to sample all schools in this vicinity (see Figure 4–1).

---

information between different IRBs. In addition, the New York State Office of Mental Health, which had created a Special Review Committee for all World Trade Center Related Research, reviewed and approved all aspects of the participation of the Columbia University–New York State Psychiatric Institute investigators and staff.

[4] See the BOE Web site at www.nycenet.edu.

[5] The cooperative consultation of Dr. Victor Balaban and Dr. Bradford Woodruff of the Centers for Disease Control and Prevention (CDC), who made frequent trips to New York to consult on the planning of what was an elegant sample design, was critical.

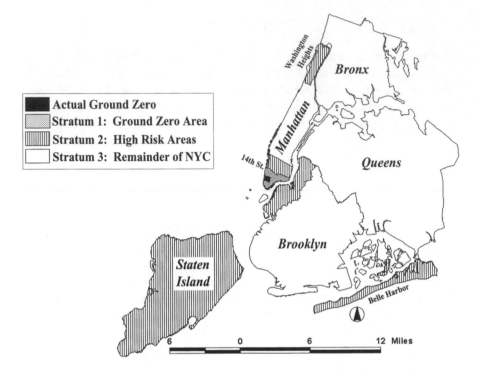

FIGURE 4-1. Student survey strata. Projection: State Plane, NAD83, Long Island. Source: U.S. Census. New York City Board of Education. Author: George J. Musa, Child Epidemiology Group, Columbia University School of Public Health.

Stratum 2, which we defined as "high-risk areas," consisted of the remaining schools south of 14th Street. Because of proximity to the WTC, students from this area could have also easily witnessed the impact of the attacking planes, seen the flames shooting out of the buildings, and directly experienced the clouds of dust and smoke. This stratum also included the area of Brooklyn along the East River, where schools had windows directly facing the WTC; all of Staten Island, where a disproportionate number of firefighters, police officers, and other rescue workers live and therefore the families would have suffered a high death rate; Belle Harbor–Rockaway, Queens, which experienced the American Airlines plane crash of flight 587 on November 12, 2001, which was thought at first to have been an extension of the 9/11 terror plot, as well as Washington Heights in northern Manhattan, where a number of those who died in the November 12 plane crash lived or where their family members resided.

Stratum 3 included schools in all the remaining areas of NYC.

Note that the sampling strategy we adopted for studying the NYC students was very different from that which had been envisioned originally. However, it was ultimately agreed by the BOE, all the investigators, and the CDC consultants that merely surveying students in schools that are (or were) situated in close proximity to the WTC would necessarily fail to capture a broad representation of all students potentially affected by the attack and fail to assess the effects felt by students who were not themselves in the eye of the attack but who nonetheless suffered loss of family or friends, the sting of stigma, or changed economic conditions. Consider the fact that the resident population of the downtown area surrounding the WTC corresponds only minimally with the population actually in the area on the morning of September 11, 2001. In fact, the area around the WTC is home to but a small portion of NYC residents; its population, according to the 2000 Census, is only 35,000, less than 0.5% of the NYC total population. The area surrounding the WTC is not a residential area, nor has it been for almost a century. At the moment of the 9/11 WTC attack, the number of persons at work, at school, or attending other functions or activities in the Ground Zero area exceeded the residential total by approximately 3000%—that is, 30 times the number of residents! It should be clear, therefore, that people who lost their lives, friends, family, businesses, or jobs were far more likely to have resided in areas outside Ground Zero. It follows also, therefore, that affected children would also have been likely to live and attend school outside the Ground Zero area.

The final sampling plan was designed to survey a representative sample of NYC schoolchildren, drawn from every borough, in every grade above grade 3, in every kind of school or special program, excluding the special education district. Moreover, the plan was designed to give every student in every kind of program an opportunity to be selected for participation, while guaranteeing that students attending schools proximate to the WTC and other high-risk areas were adequately oversampled. The ideal target sample was approximately 8000 children and adolescents, including approximately 900 per grade level. Our plan required selecting 100 schools, approximately 85 proportional to size, all schools in the Ground Zero area, and 400 randomly selected classrooms from among all these schools. When the data from oversampled strata (1 and 2) were combined with the rest of NYC (Stratum 3) and the appropriate weights were added to reflect the sampling design, the findings were expected to represent the entire NYC public school population.

Survey Instrument and Procedures

It was immediately obvious that we needed to develop a survey instrument that would not only effectively measure exposure and demographics but would also include valid diagnostic screens that could inform on the mental health status of the student respondents six months after 9/11. We also recognized the importance and necessity of tapping into a broad range of informative domains other than psychopathology.[6]

The full survey instrument included the following domains:

- Exposure: prior, direct, family, media.
- Loss and bereavement.
- Individual response.
- Probable psychiatric disorders.
- Impairment in day-to-day functioning.
- Health effects.
- School performance.
- Service need and utilization.
- Coping strategies.
- Ethnic-religious discrimination.
- Other risk factors.

---

[6]In addition to a tireless, dedicated team of uncompensated researchers at Columbia University Mailman School of Public Health, a number of other experts were willing to provide free ongoing consultation to the principal investigator (Hoven) as she developed the survey instrument, including Dr. Elissa Brown at New York University, Dr. Claude Chemtob at the Veterans Administration in Honolulu, Dr. Betty Pfefferbaum at the University of Oklahoma, and members of the National Child Traumatic Stress Network, especially Dr. Robert Pynoos and Dr. Alan Steinerg at UCLA.

- Fear of anthrax and bioterrorism.
- Perspective on the future.
- Demographics.

One of the key domains of our survey instrument (Hoven, Duarte, Mandell, et al., 2002) was the measurement of probable psychiatric disorder. Given the time constraints under which we had to work, administering the "gold standard" DISC-IV (American Psychiatric Association, 1994), Diagnostic Interview Schedule for Children (Shaffer et al., 2000) would have been impossible. However, the psychometric properties of the DISC Predictive Scales (DPS) and its fidelity to DISC-IV results made it an ideal choice for use in this study (Lucas et al., 2001). We decided to screen for eight of the common psychiatric disorders of children and adolescents: PTSD, major depressive disorder (MDD), generalized anxiety disorder (GAD), separation anxiety, panic, agoraphobia, conduct disorder, and, in grades 6 through 12, alcohol abuse/dependence. The DPS was embedded in the body of the survey protocol, allowing students an opportunity to respond to a variety of other measures both before and following diagnostic questions.

Although every effort was made to incorporate only valid and reliable measures, in many instances it was necessary to develop new measures for this challenging battery of assessments (e.g., fear of anthrax and bioterrorism, as well as stigma and prejudice, coping, etc.). The final instrument was designed to assess similar domains across each grade, but, because of time constraints, children in grades 4 and 5 received slightly shorter versions (Hoven, Duarte, Mandell, et al., 2002). Prior to implementation, a careful pilot study was carried out, and appropriate alterations in the protocol were made.

To accommodate the time allowed for the survey (45 minutes), each student protocol included a complete set of core items, but only two thirds of other noncore items. In grades 6 through 12, the interviews were randomly distributed. In grades 4 and 5, all students in each classroom received the same questionnaire. The survey was self-administered (in classrooms) by all students in grades 6 through 12. In grades 4 and 5, it was read aloud by ARC interviewers as the students marked their own answers. Two ARC social science research staff, who had been fully trained on the protocol and registered with the BOE, were available in each classroom to administer the instrument, with at least one adult available to respond to individual questions. In almost all cases, the teacher also remained in the classroom during the survey period.

The NYC BOE's IRB needed to exercise extreme caution before allowing any study to occur in the schools at this time. For example, it was felt that some questions asked in the standard DPS section on conduct disorder were too sensitive (i.e., possibly self-incriminating). To circumvent this objection, a greater number of substitute questions replaced the deleted ones, while preserving the psychometrics of the measure. Having Dr. Lucas, developer of the DPS, as a member of our research team greatly facilitated these necessary changes. Similarly, with only passive informed consent in grades 6 through 12, it was not possible to assess suicidal behavior. As this behavior is one of the most predictive items for MDD, multiple question substitutions had to be made to compensate for the loss of this item as well.

Main Findings and Challenges

We obtained a larger than projected sample, with a slight overrepresentation among the upper grades and fewer than projected numbers for the two lowest grades. This outcome is partly accounted for by the high (96%) compliance (agreement to participate) rate for those in grades 6 through 12 and the 69% compliance rate for those in grades 4 and 5. We assumed that the lower compliance for grades 4 and 5 was partially associated with the requirement that we obtain active consent for this age group.

The basic demographic profile (ethnicity and sex) of the obtained sample of 8266 students in grades 4 through 12 mirrored the demographic composition of the New York City public school population (see Figure 4-2). For the 1999–2000 school year, the distribution of students in all grades (K–12) was 35% African American, 38% Hispanic, 15% White (non-Hispanic), and 12% Asian, Pacific Islander, or other. On every critical measure taken from the U.S. Census, NYC Planning Department, and U.S. Labor Department, our surveyed sample corresponded well with the universe from which it was drawn.

We estimate that approximately 200,000 (27%) of NYC public school children met criteria for one or more of the probable psychiatric

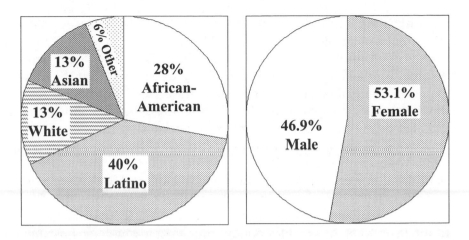

FIGURE 4–2. Ethnicity and sex of New York City school survey participants, grades 4 through 12 (N = 8266).

disorders assessed in this study, including problems with day-to-day functioning (functional impairment). The probable rates of disorders are 10.6% for PTSD, 8.1% for MDD, 10.3% for GAD, 12.3% for separation anxiety, 8.7% for panic, 14.8% for agoraphobia, 12.8% for conduct disorder, and 4.5% for alcohol abuse (grades 6–12).

Although no pre-9/11 NYC baseline prevalence rates exist with which to compare the rates we found, these new rates are elevated on each of the eight probable disorders assessed, when compared with pre-9/11 rates ascertained in other communities. Although the best child epidemiologic data available with which to compare are not based either on the same diagnostic instrument or on an NYC public school sample, they are useful. For example, agoraphobia was three times the expected rate, separation anxiety was twice the expected rate, PTSD was more than five times the expected rate (unpublished), and conduct disorder was two and a half times the expected rate (Shaffer et al., 1996).

This survey provides the first and most complete assessment of the mental health status of NYC public school children and adolescents. Because the study was conducted six months after 9/11, it was sufficiently removed in time to reflect persistent rather than simply ephemeral conditions. PTSD, because of the DSM-IV requirement for having a specific event (in this case, the 9/11 attacks) as a prerequisite for meeting criteria for the disorder, is the only disorder assessed in the study that can clearly be attributed to September 11.

In general, and as expected, girls had the highest rates of probable disorder and all children were more likely to be affected if they had experienced direct or family exposure to the attack. The findings from this investigation support the disaster literature that has shown that elevated rates of psychopathology are associated with various levels and types of exposure to a disaster (Bromet, Hough, and Connell, 1984; Vogel and Vernberg, 1993; La Greca et al., 1996). Perhaps most important, however, this study demonstrates that the elevated rates were identified at nearly similar levels among children throughout the city, not just among those who were at or near Ground Zero. This finding supports the need for conducting an epidemiologic investigation in an appropriately large geographic area in the aftermath of disaster.

What Was Learned from the Tragedy?

The former image of New York City, so poignantly portrayed and so widely accepted, was epitomized in the celebrated case of Kitty Genovese, who in the spring of 1964 ran screaming from an attacker at 3 a.m. in a Kew Gardens, Queens apartment complex, just yards away from a Long Island Railway parking lot. She failed to rouse any help, although one person even opened his window, yelled for the attacker to leave the victim alone, and then closed the window again, apparently to shut out the noise. She was repeatedly stabbed as she ran from doorway to doorway, eventually being raped after death, and then left there for hours, before the police were finally called (Gansberg, 1964). Professor Helen Benedict of Columbia University said of this situation: "Her case came to symbolize the corruption of modern city life, a life in which everyone is too frightened or too selfish to help another person."

The Kitty Genovese story and the image of urban unconcern have been reiterated many times over, in news media, psychology texts, and even on GRE exams. Fortunately, recent accounts of 9/11 heroism and samaritanism in New York City thoroughly contradict that previous image. Certainly, that characterization was not in effect on 9/11, either for New York City as a whole or at the Board of Education. Rather, in terms of preparedness and ability to respond adaptively to this most challenging of crises, both the city and the BOE receive very high marks. The world watched as Mayor Rudolph Giuliani masterfully led the city through this crisis, but out of sight the BOE, too, exercised appropriate leadership for its more than 1.1 million students and their teachers and staff. The students in schools in the Ground Zero area were safely evacuated and relocated to other schools, while classes throughout much of the city resumed a normal schedule immediately after the disaster. The central BOE provided principals and teachers guidance on addressing the needs of students, with explicit instructions and recommendations for reassuring students and their families that safety precautions were in place, guidelines for explaining factual details about the disaster, and, for those students who had to be evacuated, information on ways to reduce the impact from being transferred to a new school (Degnan, 2002).

Surely, however, we still know too little about how people will respond in times of crisis, and this is especially so for children and adolescents. Anna Freud once interviewed children who had been written about in news accounts for having been heroes—risking their lives to save others (Freud, 1969, 1992). She found that these real-life heroes seldom had had dreams about being heroes (unlike so many who dreamed of heroic deeds but almost never were so involved). Only future research will help elucidate how the images of 9/11 will play out in the lives and minds of NYC's children and adolescents.

The NYC BOE survey has already taught us that many well-established ideas about the aftermath of disasters on the local population's health and mental health may be in need of revision or modification, especially as they pertain to children (Burke et al., 1982; Eth and Pynoos, 1985). In many ways, 9/11 drew out much that was positive in New York and in our society. A cataclysmic event like 9/11 lays bare some of the meshlike social structure that underpins the complex urban society of a city. In this case, our data and other accounts indicate that there is a tension in children between vulnerability and resilience. Which children will exhibit which trait and why is something we would very much like to know more about. Perhaps analysis of data gleaned from this study, and from proposed follow-up investigations, will shed additional light on how children's microenvironments may either exacerbate vulnerability or support resilience.

Finally, we assumed that our study would be most useful for planning mental health services if it revealed associations between specific mental disorders and demographic or contextual factors. We believe the data generated are such that these analyses are now possible. Ancillary to the epidemiologic approach, the investigators are also currently attempting to use these data to better describe and understand the social world in which children and adolescents live, grow, and develop, based on currently available geographic and spatial methodologies.

At least in the case of NYC, we found higher than expected rates for a range of psychopathologies, and these high rates were found throughout all five boroughs, not just in the area nearest to the disaster site. We have been able from our data to map salient features of work and travel patterns of schoolchildren's parents to Ground Zero workplaces, as well as student travel routes to schools in the Ground Zero area, often far from their place of residence. The microenvironments in which children grow up and go to school are surely important in influencing risk factors for health and psychopathology (Sidel, 2002). Constructing such mosaic models might eventually be useful in extending the customary methods of epidemiologic analyses of risk. We suggest, therefore, that in future disaster work the application of spatial analysis tools and GIS (Geographic Information System)–associated techniques might prove useful in shedding more light on the nature of disaster-response differences (Dogan and Rokkan, 1969; Holly, 1998; Demers, 2000; Jacquez, 2000; Cromley and McLafferty, 2002). Consequently, we also recommend that appropriate geographic information be collected in future epidemiologic disaster investigations.

From our perspective, the NYC Board of Education Post-9/11 School Study has already proved to be a highly successful endeavor; first, because its findings have resulted in the allocation of additional resources for NYC child mental health services; and second, because ongoing analyses of the study data hold promise for further improving our understanding of childhood psychopathology after a traumatic experience. Although it is a profound loss not to have conducted this investigation with a longitudinal design, we believe this cross-sectional information will prove to be critically important to our understanding of postdisaster childhood psychopathology. We suggest that those persons interested in providing postdisaster services should always ask the basic epidemiologic questions that drove this investigation—who, what, when, where, and how—or possibly run the risk of failing to identify the affected.

Certainly, these meaningful outcomes have resulted from the extraordinary collaborative effort of the BOE, researchers, and the entire NYC community, which had the common goal of helping children to cope with the very difficult set of problems brought about by September 11. We are truly honored that we were able to provide sound information to help guide policy decisions to ameliorate children's emotional suffering. We hope our description of the complex process underlying the planning and implementation of such a large-scale study in the aftermath of an emergency will be useful for individuals having to face similar critical, unfortunate situations in the future.

References

American Psychiatric Association (1994), *Diagnostic and Statistical Manual of Mental Disorders,* 4th ed. Washington, DC: American Psychiatric Association.

Baum, A. & Davidson, L. (1990), Posttraumatic stress in children following natural and human-made trauma. In: *Handbook of Developmental Psychopathology,* ed. M. Lewis & S. Miller. New York: Plenum Press, pp. 251–259.

Bromet, E. J., Hough, L. & Connell, M. (1984), Mental health of children near the Three Mile Island reactor. *J. Prevent. Psychiat.,* 2:275–301.

Burke, J. D., Borus, J. F., Burns, B. J., Millstein, K. H. & Beasley, M. C. (1982), Changes in children's behavior after a natural disaster. *Amer. J. Psychiat.,* 139:1010–1014.

Cantor, J., Mares, M. L. & Oliver, M. B. (1993), Parents' and children's emotional reactions to TV coverage of the Gulf War. In: *Desert Storm and the Mass Media,* ed. B. S. Greenberg & W. Gantz. Cresskill, NJ: Hampton Press, pp. 325–340.

_____ & Nathanson, A. (1996), Children's fright reaction to television news. *J. Comm.,* 46:139–152.

Cromley, E. K. & McLafferty, S. L. (2002), *GIS and Public Health.* New York: Guilford Press.

Dantzig, T. (1930), *Numbers: The Language of Science.* Garden City, NY: Doubleday, 1956.

Degnan, N. (2002), Adherence to protocol in times of disaster. NYC Board of Education Web site: www.nycenet.edu.

Demers, M. N., ed. (2000), *Fundamentals of Geographic Information System,* 2nd ed. New York: Wiley.

Dogan, M. & Rokkan, S., eds. (1969), *Social Ecology*. Cambridge, MA: MIT Press.

Earls, F., Smith, E., Reich, W. & Jung, K. G. (1998), Investigating psycho-pathological consequences of a disaster in children: A pilot study incorporating a structured diagnostic interview. *J. Amer. Acad. Child Adolesc. Psychiat.*, 27:90–95.

Eth, S. & Pynoos, R. S. (1985), Developmental perspectives on psychic trauma in childhood. In: *Trauma and Its Wake*, ed. C. R. Filgery. New York: Brunner/Mazel, pp. 36–52.

Freud, A. (1969), Research at the Hamstead Child-Therapy Clinic and other papers 1956–1965. In: *Writings of Anna Freud, Vol. 5*. New York: International Universities Press, pp. 20–210.

_____ (1992), Freud on child heroes. In: *Harvard University Lectures*. Madison, CT: International Universities Press.

Frieden, T. (2002), The challenge of terror to the public's health. Presented at One Year After 9/11: What Have We Learned and Where Do We Go from Here? Conference of the New York Academy of Medicine, New York City, September 9.

Gansberg, M. (1964), 37 who saw murder didn't call the police. *New York Times*, March 27, pp. A1–A4, A38.

Geiger, H. J., Michaels, D. & Rush, D. (1992), Dead reckoning: A critical review of the Department of Energy's epidemiologic research. In: *Epidemiologic Research*. Washington, DC: Physicians for Social Responsibility.

Holly, H. L. (1998), Geography and mental health: A review. *Soc. Psychiat. Psychiatric Epidemiol.*, 33:535–542.

Hoven, C. W. (2002), Which options for community based services best meet children's needs? Children's Aid Society Launch of the Downstate Prevention Resource Center, New York City, October 11.

_____ (in press), Testimony to U.S. Senate Field Hearing (Chair, H. R. Clinton), Senate Health, Education, Labor and Pensions Committee, June 10, 2002, regarding the unmet mental health needs of New York City public school children as a result of the September 11th attacks on the World Trade Center. New York: U.S. Government Printing Office.

_____ Duarte, C. S., Lucas, C. P, Mandell, D. J., Cohen, M., Rosen, C., Wu, P., Musa, G. J. & Gregorian, N. (2002), *Effects of the World Trade Center Attack on NYC Public School Students–Initial Report to the New York City Board of Education*. New York: Columbia University Mailman School of Public Health–New York State Psychiatric Institute and Applied Research and Consulting, LLC.

_____ _____ Mandell, D., Musa, G., Wicks, J., Wu, P., Lucas, C. & Cohen, M. (2002), *WTC-NYC Child and Adolescent Questionnaire*. New York: Columbia University–New York State Psychiatric Institute.

Jacquez, G. M. (2000), Spatial analysis in epidemiology: Nascent science or a failure of GIS? *J. Geograph. Syst.*, 2:91–97.

La Greca, A. M., Silverman, W. S., Vernberg, E. M. & Prinstein, M. J. (1996), Posttraumatic stress symptoms in children after Hurricane Andrew: A prospective study. *J. Consult. Clin. Psychol.*, 64:712–723.

L'etat du monde: Annuaire economique geopolitique mondial 2000 (1999), Montreal, Canada: Editions la Decouverte & Editions du Boreal.

Lucas, C. P., Zhang, H., Fisher, P., Shaffer, D., Regier, D., Narrow, W., Bourdon, K., Dulcan, M., Canino, G., Rubio-Stipec, M., Lahey, B. & Friman, P. (2001), The DISC Predictive Scales (DPS): Efficiently predicting diagnoses. *J. Amer. Acad. Child Adolesc. Psychiat.*, 40:443–449.

Osofsky, J. D., ed. (1997), *Children in a Violent Society*. New York: Guilford Press.

Pfefferbaum, B., Nixon, S. J., Tivis, R. D., Doughty, D. E., Pynoos, R. S., Gurwitch, R. H. & Foy, D. (2000), Television exposure in children after a terrorist incident. *Psychiatry*, 64:202–211.

_____ _____ Tucker, P. M., Tivis, R. D., Moore, V. L., Gurwitch, R. H., Pynoos, R. S. & Geis, H. K. (1999), Posttraumatic stress responses in bereaved children after the Oklahoma City bombing. *J. Amer. Acad. Child Adolesc. Psychiat.*, 38:1372–1379.

Prinstein, M. J., La Greca, A. M., Vernberg, E. M. & Silverman, W. K. (1996), Children's coping assistance after a natural disaster. *J. Clin. Child Psychol.*, 25:463–475.

Pynoos, R. S., Frederick, C., Nader, K., Arroya, W., Steinberg, A., Eth, S., Nunez, F. & Fairbanks, L. (1987), Life threat and posttraumatic stress disorder in school-age children. *Arch. Gen. Psychiat.*, 44:1057–1063.

_____ Steinberg, A. & Wraith, R. (1995), A developmental model of childhood traumatic stress. In: *Developmental Psychopathology, Vol. 2: Risk, Disorder, and Adaptation,* ed. D. Cicchetti & D. Cohen. New York: Wiley, pp. 57–80.

Schechter, D. S., Coates, S. & First, E. (2001–2002), Observations of acute reactions of young children and their families to the World Trade Center attacks. *Bull. Zero to Three*, 22:9–13.

Sederer, L. (2002), Policy implications related to the psychological impact of terrorism. Presented at NGO Committee on Mental Health and WHO World Mental Health Day United Nations meeting: Addressing Global Issues on Violence and Mental Health, New York City, October 10.

Shaffer, D. Fisher, P., Dulcan, M. K., Davies, M., Piacentini, J., Schwab-Stone, M. E., Lahey, B. B., Bourdon, K., Jensen, P. S., Bird, H. R., Canino, G. & Regier, D. A. (1996), The NIMH Diagnostic Interview Schedule for Children Version 2.3 (DISC-2.3): Description, acceptability, prevalence rates, and performance in the MECA Study. *J. Amer. Acad. Child Adolesc. Psychiat.*, 35:865–877.

_____ _____ Lucas, C. P., Dulcan, M. K. & Schwab-Stone, M. E. (1996), NIMH Diagnostic Interview Schedule for Children Version IV (NIMH DISC-IV): Description, differences from previous versions, and reliability of some common diagnoses. *J. Amer. Acad. Child Adolesc. Psychiat.*, 39: 28–38.

Shaw, J. A. (2000), Children, adolescents and trauma. *Psychiat. Quart.*, 71: 227–243.

Sidel, V. (2002), The future of public health in New York City. Presented at the Second 9/11 Conference, New York City, March 14.

Susser, E. S., Herman, D. B. & Aaron, B. (2002), Combating the terror of terrorism. *Sci. Amer.*, 287:70–77.

Vogel, J. M. & Vernberg, E. M. (1993), Psychological responses of children to natural and human-made disasters: I. Children's psychological responses to disasters. *J. Clin. Child Psychol.*, 22:464–484.

Wright, J., Kunkel, D., Pinon, M. & Huston, A. (1989), How children reacted to televised coverage of the Space Shuttle disaster. *J. Comm.*, 39:27–45.

Chapter 5

Clinical Management of Subsyndromal Psychological Sequelae of the 9/11 Terror Attacks

Lawrence Amsel and
Randall D. Marshall

Contemporary psychiatric practice looks for the consequences of major trauma in terms of increased rates of established psychiatric diagnoses, most especially posttraumatic stress disorder. But one of the striking features of the World Trade Center disaster was the great variety of psychological responses that different individuals exhibited. Moreover, some of these responses were clinically highly salient and subjectively quite disabling, yet they could not be located within any standard nomenclature. This chapter examines this important and largely unappreciated phenomenon, the "subsyndromal" response to severe trauma, in a way that may immediately seem familiar to most New Yorkers on the basis of their own reactions and experiences with friends and relatives. An important point made by the authors in conclusion deserves special emphasis: as a consequence of the disaster, much of the residual stigma that once was associated with posttraumatic reactions has been removed.

T he terrorist attack on the World Trade Center Towers and the Pentagon is already the most widely documented such attack in history, and, from a mental health perspective, it is also the most promptly and thoroughly studied such event. National surveys were conducted within the first week following the attack (Schuster et al., 2001) and at regular intervals since then (Galea et al., 2002). These studies documented the increase in a wide range of symptoms following the attack. Numerous projects to examine longer term mental health consequences are also underway. Taken together, these studies will elucidate a multiplicity of issues relating to resilience versus risk factors for developing mental illness and will examine the effects of public health outreach efforts, crisis counseling, and clinical treatment.

Clinical services were made available to those affected by the attack at a level unprecedented in the history of mental health services. Whereas the epidemiologic studies documenting syndromal psychopathology have deservedly received a great deal of attention (see, for example, the chapter by Hoven, Mandell, and Duarte in this volume), the clinical experience of treating 9/11 related problems, especially subsyndromal problems, has not been as widely discussed.

It is becoming clear that, although many of those seeking clinical services after the 9/11 attack had DSM-IV diagnosable disorders, others presented with a great deal of personal distress but without a diagnosable disorder. For this latter group, appropriate support might mean the difference between a rapid recovery and the development of chronic psychological difficulties with potential functional deficits (Shalev, 1996). Paradoxically, while evidence-based treatments and good outcomes are well established for many psychiatric disorders, treatment for the subsyndromal patient may involve a greater professional challenge, as there are fewer evidentiary landmarks by which to steer (Macleod, 2000).

In this chapter, we focus on the understanding and treatment of persons presenting with troubling but subsyndromal psychological problems, as well as those who had a past diagnosable disorder and now present with psychological problems directly related to the 9/11 attacks. First, we give examples of the broad spectrum of problems that presented to our clinic after the 9/11 attacks and discuss why they posed a challenge to existing models of disaster-related mental health assessment and treatment. Second, we discuss how patients' perception of the meaning of this attack may have influenced the nature of their problems. Third, we review how an emerging model of adaptation might help us address this unique situation. Fourth, we apply this model to a few representative clinical vignettes. Finally, we propose a number of possible future directions for research in this area.

Living the New Reality:
Psychological Problems After 9/11

Most clinicians were trained to observe patients through the defined psychopathology lens of DSM-IV, which is usually focused on the individual life. The events of 9/11, however, have had a broader social, political, and economic impact on our patients and their well-being in ways that require a flexible response from clinicians. When patients presented with a well-defined posttraumatic stress disorder (PTSD) or major depression, we have drawn on the existing evidence-based treatments to address their disorder. Often, however, patients had more amorphous complaints not limited to traditionally classified symptoms. These individuals presented, instead, with a myriad of issues and struggles, as if the foundations of ordinary life had been fractured.

The terms *subsyndromal, subclinical,* and *subthreshold* are often used interchangeably, and the terminology carries the implication that subsyndromal problems, or subthreshold symptoms, will generally not be brought to clinical attention (Altshuler et al., 2002). As this event rippled through ever widening circles of relationships, communities, and social structures, however, patients presented with significant problems even when their symptoms were subthreshold. This has raised a number of interesting questions such as the following: Are syndromal descriptions insufficiently sensitive to capture important clinical phenomena? Are psychological responses after a terrorist attack different from other traumas and thus underdescribed in our nomenclature? Does an "exposure" to a traumatic event that takes place primarily through television lead to qualitatively different psychological responses? Did the supportive atmosphere and the highly publicized availability of clinical services reduce the stigma and other barriers to mental health services, resulting in help-seeking behaviors within a population that usually does not use these services? The answers to these questions will affect our approach to terror and disaster related mental health and may also throw light on the nature of help-seeking behavior for emotional problems in general.

Subthreshold Disorder Versus
Adjustment Disorder

The DSM-IV adjustment disorders identify psychological reactions to identifiable stressors occurring within 3 months of the onset of the event or events. They are characterized by "marked distress that is in excess of what would be expected given the nature of the stressor, or by significant impairment in social or occupational (academic) functioning." The implications of the use of this disorder are widely misunderstood. *The presence of an adjustment disorder does not imply psychopathology.* The disorder, rather, allows the study of impairment or "excessive" reactions to a wide range of psychosocial stressors, including community disaster. As defined, however, the determination of "excessive" is essentially probabilistic, and this presents serious difficulties after a major event such as 9/11.

The presence of impairment of functioning is simpler and probably more reliable to assess but raises equally difficult questions. Given the widespread "impairment of functioning" among New Yorkers in the weeks after 9/11, the diagnosis may have ceased to be meaningful. Of greater salience to our discussion is the question of whether any kind of clinical intervention might have accelerated recovery of functioning under these circumstances.

The distinction between a subthreshold disorder and an adjustment disorder is of primary importance as well. There would be considerable overlap, for example, between subthreshold PTSD, with insomnia, irritability, general anxiety, vigilance, and impaired concentration, and adjustment disorder with anxiety. The treatment implications of the two are theoretically distinct, however. Although there are no controlled trials investigating the treatment of subthreshold PTSD, we have assumed that a trauma-focused treatment is preferable, as opposed to a general supportive and anxiety-focused treatment for adjustment disorder. In addition, the public health model after community disaster advocates the promotion of normalization of symptomatology, utilization of existing support systems, and maintenance of basic self-care behaviors. None of these approaches is well studied.

As a result of the events of 9/11, people sought help from mental health practitioners for an enormous breadth and range of problems that directly affect their daily lives. Their expectations of receiving help from the mental health establishment have required us to stretch our purview and to consider the broad sociopolitical and economic ramifications of events such as this one. We have therefore begun to learn to draw on a multiplicity of perspectives when working with those people affected by the 9/11 attacks (Shalev, 1993).

To illustrate this point, we list examples of adjustment problems or subsyndromal disorders that have arisen in our clinical work and experience over the past year. We return to a more detailed discussion of a few of these cases later in this chapter.

- A man without prior psychological difficulties developed the unshakable conviction that in the near future New York City will be the target of a nuclear attack. These thoughts were prominent in his consciousness and highly demoralizing. However, he did not meet criteria for either major depression or PTSD.
- A woman had her childhood fundamentalist faith reawakened by her conviction that the end of the world was near. Rather than becoming hopeless, she became consumed with worry about the timely salvation of the souls of those around her (including her therapist). Her conviction, however, was nondelusional.
- A man who became unemployed because of the economic depression that followed the 9/11 attacks developed a highly uncharacteristic hatred for people of Middle Eastern descent that was ego dystonic and for him a therapeutic focus.
- A psychotherapist and administrator who changed his career focus after 9/11 to becoming a trauma specialist sought psychological help to manage the adjustment.
- An olive-skinned Puerto Rican taxi driver was forced to the side of the road by a white driver and threatened with the words, "It is because of you and your kind that all those people are dead."
- A psychotherapist took on so many WTC victims as patients and felt so guilty for asking a fee from them that he compromised his family's financial security. He sought therapy to deal with the conflict.
- An artist whose studio had been in lower Manhattan was no longer comfortable in that locale but could not leave for fear of losing her workspace and thus her artistic standing.

- A woman who watched the towers burn from an elevated subway in Brooklyn became incapacitated by the memories of her son-in-law, killed in a sporting accident two years earlier.
- A man without past psychological difficulties started looking out his apartment window and visualizing all the buildings ablaze (non-hallucinatory).
- A young "progressive" college professor suddenly found himself more in agreement with politically conservative thinkers and felt confused and angry about this radical shift in his belief system.

Many of these issues had not been a focus of attention in a trauma clinic that is traditionally oriented toward DSM-IV diagnoses and cognitive behavioral therapy (CBT) treatments. However they are the problems that many 9/11-traumatized patients have been bringing into our clinic and into their sessions. Thus our challenge has been to understand, in the broadest possible sense, how to best aid these patients.

The Iconography of Terrorism

Perhaps the breadth of these clinical problems should not come as a surprise. In their discussion of the personal consequences of 9/11, our patients have articulated not only their memories of the events of 9/11 but also the meaning they constructed for these events. These constructed meanings have profoundly affected our patients' view of the world and the future. It has become clear that these patients are not responding to the traumas of ordinary life, as horrific as those might be. Rather, these patients are responding specifically to the fact that this was a highly sophisticated and psychologically engineered terrorist attack that left many with an altered sense of basic safety. The epidemiologist Ezra Susser pointed out (personal communication, 2001) that terrorism, regardless of the weapons used, is not so much biological warfare as it is *psychological warfare*. Many of our patients have expressed similar insight from their own personal experiences.

Unlike conventional warfare, in which the targets are the military or industrial assets of a country, terrorism attacks the psychological well-being of a society, the wellspring of its human assets (Dershowitz,

2002). Psychological distress is not an incidental effect of terrorism. It is central to terrorism to devise attacks that are as psychologically damaging as possible. Thus, terrorist attacks use symbols and manipulate events in an attempt to induce particular meanings laden with fear, dread, anger, and shock. We refer to this as the *iconography of terrorism*. Some of the component elements of this iconography of terror included the following on 9/11:

- There was the element of surprise—that is, a lack of warning or of gradual escalation. The attack came literally out of the blue.
- The attack involved major symbols (the Pentagon and World Trade Center) of American pride and power, both military and economic; in particular, the World Trade Center was a symbol of America's international economic dominance and of Western capitalism.
- The attack targeted random civilians going about their ordinary daily routine, thus increasing identification with the victims and accentuating the ongoing danger.
- The dramatic and visually arresting attack took place in the media capital of the world and thus appeared to have been produced, designed, and directed to garner maximum television coverage and extensive broadcast repetition.
- The collapse of both towers magnified the impact even further, as it symbolized the helplessness of both the initial victims and the rescue workers, emphasizing that even the authorities who are supposed to protect civilians were vulnerable.
- Perhaps the most chilling aspect of the attack was the embedded message that the attackers had absolutely no qualms about the random destruction of thousands of lives, including their own.

There is also a technology of terrorism that aims at maximal disruption of the fundamental relationships in a society: its economic, social, and political structures. Part of the induced meaning of the attack is that the terrorist expresses a murderous rage at complacency to the terrorists' grievances. Complacency is thus the other important target for the terrorist. The terrorist seeks to disrupt the structures that sustain "business as usual," which, of course, are the very foundations of a stable culture. Examples of the way life before 9/11 has been disrupted are the following:

- The target was chosen because its destruction would necessarily lead to profound secondary economic consequences, both in New York City and throughout the country.
- The attack was designed to provoke an angry response from the American political leadership that might further polarize the international Islamic community against the United States.
- The attack was designed to fragment community cohesion in the United States owing to fear and anxiety about further threats and attacks.
- The implicit future threat has drained important U.S. resources in myriad attempts to increase security and stave off such further attacks.
- The clandestine nature of the "sleeper" cells of attackers and their assimilation into mainstream culture has induced greater government surveillance of the population and has created a situation in which civil liberties may be compromised in the interest of safety, further eroding community cohesion.
- The attacks may also have been intended to increase ethnic conflict as well as to polarize political positions.

Given the strategic iconography and technology of terrorism, with its dual targets being the human psyche and structures of social cohesion, one might expect to see psychological distress broadly distributed in the population and with a great deal of clinical variation. This is precisely the pattern borne out by the epidemiological research done so far.

Reactions to the World Trade Center attack across the United States were pervasive in the first five to seven days (Schuster et al., 2001). Symptoms of PTSD were assessed, and most affected adults would not have met full criteria for PTSD, but experienced manifestations of increased anxiety and vivid remembering. In the first week following the attacks, 44% of adults in this nationwide survey reported having at least one symptom, and even among those who lived more than 1000 miles away, 36% reported substantial stress reactions (Schuster et al., 2001). Moreover, across the nation, this powerful emotional reaction was mostly mediated by witnessing or learning of the disaster through the media. One to two months later, Galea et al. (2002) found that among residents of Manhattan, rates of individual symptoms remained very high, with intrusive memories at 27%, insomnia at 25%, jumpiness/startling easily at 24%, and a sense of foreshortened future at 21%. Two months after the attacks, Schlenger et al. (2002) found that similar rates of clinically significant psychological distress in New York (16.6%) remained high.

The questions then become: how do we conceptualize these resulting human responses, and how do we help our patients and ourselves to achieve a healthy integration in living with this newly revealed reality?

Meta-Adaptation After 9/11

To accommodate these broad clinical issues, we have been working on a framework to encompass both healthy and pathologic responses to trauma. The framework builds on Shalev's observation (2002) that a number of the early responses to trauma are healthy and reparative, but if they persist these same responses become symptoms (Shalev, 2002).

We begin with the commonplace observations that the hallmark of life is physiological adaptation to a physical environment and that the hallmark of psychological life is behavioral adaptation to a physical, social, and meaningful environment. In the language of systems or complexity theory, the adaptation of an organism can be thought of as an emergent property made up of multiple interdependent, interacting components working synergistically within an individual. An analogous phenomenon is a beehive, which seems in many ways to behave as if it were a single integrated and purposeful entity. Yet the hive is made up of thousands of individual bees each governed by its own functionality without "awareness" of how the interacting functions emerge as a unitary beehive able to adapt to a variety of environments (Huang et al., 1992).

Similarly, an adapted individual consists of multiple interacting biological and psychological functionalities that range from simple reflex circuits to subtle capacities of emotional intelligence needed to interpret social meaning. Examples of these functions include the autonomic fear response, conditioned learning mechanisms, a variety of memory systems, psychological defense mechanisms, belief schemata, and introjected object relations. We can think of a variety of these biopsychological components acting in concert to form a unitary adapted individual. Moreover, such an individual can, by virtue of this adaptation, tolerate a good deal of environmental change in the physical, social, or meaning realms.

Outside of a certain tolerance range the adaptation fails and the individual must readapt. That is, the individual must fundamentally reorganize the functioning of one or more component psychological modules, and, more important, their interrelationships. The capacity for readaptation to abrupt environmental change, or change in the meaning of the environment that is beyond the organism's initial tolerance, can be called "meta-adaptation." Meta-adaptation is challenged in the posttraumatic period. This concept is related to the notion of resilience and to Freud's dictum that mental health is defined by flexibility of response. It differs from psychoanalytic ideas, however, in that it recognizes two levels of adjustment, one that takes place within an existing adapted system and one that requires the individual to fundamentally change some aspect of his or her previously adapted selves. An analogy might be a wire spring, which under Hook's law is governed by its elasticity parameter and will generate an equilibrating force proportional to how much it has been stretched. If it were stretched beyond its tolerance, however, the structure would be deformed such that it would then be governed by a different elastic parameter.

This framework encompasses many important aspects of what is known about responses to trauma. Rothbaum and Foa (1992) noted that a defining characteristic of a traumatizing event is that it is unexpected, uncontrollable, or inescapable. In other words, a psychological trauma is defined as a stressor that is often outside of the usual range of adaptation. Those who witnessed the WTC collapse on television but were in no personal immediate danger may very well have experienced a change in their internal representation of the environment (its meaning) as "safe enough." For many, this change was so profound that it simply could not be accommodated by existing cognitive schema and belief structures and required a readaptation. This readaptation process may entail a great deal of psychological discomfort, accounting for Shalev's observation of the nearly universal experience of "symptoms" in the immediate posttraumatic period, as well as his observation that these "symptoms" are in fact effective coping responses that signify an active recovery process (Shalev, 1993).

If one's capacity for readaptation is adequate, these "symptoms" aid in the achievement of readaptation and subside as that readaptation coalesces. When readaptation does not succeed, the symptoms persist (as PTSD, depression, or subsyndromal symptoms), indicating that the individual has not achieved a reintegration and is no longer adapted to the environment as currently perceived.

As an example of how the 9/11 trauma required a readaptation of a common defense mechanism, consider the stigmatization and destigmatization of victims. Jack Rosenthal, Pulitzer Prize–winning journalist and president of the New York Times Foundation, noted in the *New York Times Magazine* editorial on the new language of 9/11 that "victim" was no longer a pejorative term. But why should it have ever been a pejorative term? Stigmatizing victims probably serves a defensive purpose of putting them into a class separate from the self, and thus protecting onlookers from a potentially frightening identification. Such identification could undermine the defensive illusion of being in control of one's fate—of being safe. Thus, stigmatization, while potentially cruel to the victims, may serve a psychologically protective function by keeping the onlookers emotionally isolated from the trauma. The events of 9/11 abruptly sheared away these fundamental defense mechanisms, as most people appear to have identified with the victims rather than stigmatizing them and thus were in need of alternative defenses that could keep them feeling safe. Unfortunately, such alternative defenses were not always available.

One of the authors first noticed this dual role of stigmatization when working in a military hospital during a war. As he walked through the hospital filled with severely wounded young men in the prime of their lives, he realized that in all his own previous hospital experiences he had unconsciously placed the patients in a separate category of "sick people," a category so separate that it protected one from potential membership. But in the military hospital with all the patients about his own age and just recently in good health, the isolating defense collapsed. After some difficult readaptation, different defenses became functional.

Other examples of readaptation abound. Many families left the New York area after 9/11. If there are no further attacks, this departure may come to be seen as a fearful overreaction; if there is a more catastrophic attack, their departure will certainly be seen as perspicacious. Is it sensible or paranoid to have gas masks at home? Is it healthy or avoidant to rarely watch the evening news? Is it foresighted or hypervigilant to *always* watch the evening news? Is it fiscally conservative or symptomatic of a foreshortened future to convert one's retirement investments in the stock market into cash? Of course, it is not up to us to make these decisions for our patients, but we also are not absolved of our responsibility to help them struggle with these issues.

A related phenomenon is that of overgeneralization (Foa and Kozak, 1986), that is, allowing a particular traumatic experience to influence largely unconscious views of the whole self, the whole world, or most of humanity. Extreme examples are found in the many persons we have encountered who out of fear did not leave their apartments for weeks or months after 9/11. The whole world became dangerous, except for the apparently magically protected interior of their living space. When exploring such issues, which touch on existential disintegrations, a psychologically supportive approach can be effective when combined with a rational discussion of probabilities. As in psychodynamic therapy, a general maxim is that an insight will have greater emotional impact if the patient arrives at it herself.

An additional complicating factor is that many patients we have seen have prior trauma histories. This is not surprising as psychological trauma is extremely common. In the National Comorbidity Study, 60.7% of men and 51.2% of women interviewed reported having experienced at least one major (criterion A) traumatic event in their lifetime (Kessler et al., 1999). It is a normal function of memory to activate associative networks linked to a particular emotional state. For example, when an individual is preoccupied by fear and anxiety, previously traumatizing or simply frightening experiences will be vividly brought to consciousness. An early dogma in the history of psychotherapy, now largely discredited, was that these prior traumas *explained* the current response to trauma, particularly if the trauma occurred at critical points in development. Although prior trauma often seems to play a powerful role in shaping the individual's current responses, we believe it is important to give equal emphasis, or even primary emphasis, to the adult's current response and the seriousness of the event. Otherwise, there is the potential pitfall of seeming to minimize the person's often very vivid emotional engagement with the current experience, and of seeming to imply it is an overreaction.

Thus, our therapeutic approach has been to attempt to help each individual achieve a coherent readaptation. There are no studies that address the question of differential response to distinct psychosocial approaches across a range of posttraumatic reactions, but our anecdotal experience suggests there are instances in which particular techniques are preferred.

To do this, we identify those psychological functions that have been adversely affected and then bring to bear therapeutic tools appropriate to this domain. These tools might range from medication to cognitive behavioral approaches to supportive, existential and psychodynamic interventions. In the case of distortion of risk appraisal after a new threat is introduced into awareness, an appropriate tool may be cognitive restructuring. This approach encourages patients to use their capacity for rational thinking and thus constitute a supportive technique in that it draws on existing healthy capacities to overcome emotional distress. Similarly, when the major disruptions appear to be in the realm of relationships, an approach like that of interpersonal psychotherapy, with its focus on role identity and role change, may be the most beneficial approach. However, for symptoms of avoidance, cognitive or psychodynamic approaches may not always suffice. Avoidance of reminders of the traumatic experience often involve overactivated autonomic fear responses to certain stimuli, and thus exposure techniques, medication, or both may be particularly helpful (Pitman et al., 1999).

As pointed out earlier, terrorism is particularly engineered to induce meanings and reactions that can cause great psychological and interpersonal disruptions in a society, and results in a broad range of clinical responses. By thinking of our patients as complex, adapted individuals with a capacity to readapt to new realities, we can bring to bear a multiplicity of specific therapies for each of the affected psychological domains and thereby help the individual attain a new and more comfortable integration. One possible additional benefit of such an approach would be the promotion of psychological flexibility and a capacity for meta-adaptation in the context of future adversity.

Clinical Vignettes

As the emerging symptoms are viewed as part of a readaptation, our goal with these patients is to conduct short-term therapeutic interventions that focus on reestablishing prior adaptations or helping patients achieve new forms of adaptation with the expectation that this action will simultaneously eliminate the concrete symptoms. Whenever possible, this goal involves uncovering the specific psychological components that, as a result of the traumatic challenge, are no longer functioning adequately, and working to repair or replace them. Some vignettes from our clinical experience will help to clarify this approach. For reasons of confidentiality and heuristic purposes, details have been altered to protect patient identity.

Sarah

Sarah is a 49-year-old woman. For a time, she and her husband lived in Bosnia, where her husband was involved in education and was politically active. The marriage grew strained, and Sarah returned to the United States with her two daughters, while her husband remained in Bosnia. The couple did not divorce, however, and Sarah held on to hopes of eventual reconciliation, even as the years passed. One morning, after not hearing from her husband for many months, Sarah received word that he had been murdered by political foes and that his body had been mutilated and thrown into a river. Although shocked and in grief, Sarah did not become overtly symptomatic. Instead, she focused on raising her children as she had been doing before. She obtained a number of newspaper clippings regarding the political murder of her husband, but she could not read them.

Two years later, on September 11, 2001, Sarah, on hearing of the WTC attacks, began crying uncontrollably. When she presented to the clinic she was able to identify the core of her sadness as focused on the fact that, like herself, so many families would have no body to bury. She came to realize that both concretely and metaphorically she had not buried her husband.

Using denial and distancing as a characteristic defense, Sarah had managed a tenuous adaptation to her husband's death. The events of 9/11, with their strong resonance to her own trauma, made it impossible to continue the denial and, simultaneously, made real grieving possible. Thus, we did not view her uncontrollable crying as a symptom needing reversal, but rather as a signal that some form of mourning might be possible. Still, it was clear that a normal grieving process was unlikely to unfold spontaneously. We adapted aspects of Foa's work on imaginal exposure to help Sarah deal with her internal images of her husband's brutal murder as well as in vivo exposures to the newspaper reports she had saved (Foa, 2000). Gradually, Sarah brought in the newspaper clippings and was able to tolerate them, which also allowed Sarah an emotionally constructive grieving process. Subsequently, Sarah was also able to read newspaper reports about 9/11, which she had been avoiding as well.

It became clear that after the death of her husband Sarah had managed an adaptation that was functional but quite brittle, as it was based on a profound level of emotional denial, manifested overtly by avoidance. From an adaptation perspective, denial and avoidance are two sides of the same coin, two psychological functions among many others that work together to maintain a particular adaptive style. In Sarah's case, we used exposure to break down the avoidance, without which the denial was unsustainable. Others may have focused on the denial as a way of approaching the avoidance. Regardless, the important goal for our work was that Sarah was finally able to adapt to the death of her husband in a stable fashion without gross denial or symptomatic avoidance.

Jim

Jim is a 49-year-old legal secretary without prior psychiatric history. On the morning of 9/11, hearing the news of a plane crash at the WTC, he and a number of coworkers went up to the roof of their midtown law office, from which they had an unimpeded view of the evolving catastrophe. Jim and his coworkers spent much of that day alternating between watching the events live from the roof and watching the television reports in the office. Subsequently, Jim presented to the clinic complaining that the joy had gone out of his life. He was utterly (but not delusionally) convinced that Manhattan would be destroyed in a thermonuclear attack. While deeply saddened by this, Jim continued to function normally. He did not have a major depression or PTSD. In fact, avoidance seemed to be absent, as Jim insisted that despite his conviction he would not move because he did not care to survive the destruction of New York. In discussing these beliefs with friends, coworkers, and the woman with whom he was involved, he found that most people actually agreed with his assessment of the potential danger but, somehow, it did not affect their daily thinking. They were inexplicably not obsessed with this possible (highly probable?) catastrophe.

When the law office moved many of its employees, including Jim, to the Bronx as a cost saving measure, he seriously considered quitting, despite his accumulated seniority and benefits that would be difficult to replace, simply because he did not want to spend his work hours outside of his "beloved" Manhattan. In one session, Jim pleaded for help: if only someone could convince him that he was wrong, that this destruction would not happen, he could then return to his previous feelings and would be the happiest man in the world. But of course, he hastened to add, he knew no one could convince him of that, because everyone recognized the potential risks. This reference to Manhattan as a "beloved" turned out to be the key to understanding Jim's pre-9/11 adaptation. Central to Jim's adaptation, central to his integrated identity, was his relationship to Manhattan and its cultural life. On one hand, Manhattan was an anthropomorphic other, an object with which he had a relationship. On the other hand, Jim felt his own identity to be largely defined by the cultural life of Manhattan in which he was a very active participant. Like an enmeshed couple, Jim could not imagine life without his beloved.

One can conjecture as to how Manhattan came to serve this role in Jim's overall adaptation. Jim's father was a strict man with a military background who made and lost a fortune. He was killed in a car crash when Jim was 12 years old and living in a small Midwestern town. Later, during the Vietnam conflict, Jim became an antiwar activist and felt further estrangement from his father's values. When a career in the arts did not materialize, the pragmatic part of Jim took a job that would pay the bills if not quench his passions, and he immersed himself in Manhattan's culture. Although he has enjoyed a number of long-term relationships with women, Jim never wished to marry or have children and felt quite complete and satisfied in the adaptation he had constructed, until 9/11 somehow made it unworkable.

Jim's lack of interest in surviving the nuclear destruction of Manhattan now became understandable, as he would lose both a significantly loved object and his own identity. In a sense, given this adaptation, it was not possible for Jim to "survive" the destruction of Manhattan. Jim's anthropomorphizing of Manhattan is not without precedent in the arts and even in complexity theory. Poets (Sandburg, Whitman) have long anthropomorphized cities (Chicago, Brooklyn). One of the fathers of complexity theory, John Holland, in citing examples of what he calls Complex Adaptive System (CAS), also includes the city (Holland, 1992). For Holland, it is an entity made up of the thousands of interacting parts (agents) that function as a unity, and though it is capable of huge changes in the interest of adapting, it maintains its identity. Thus, it shares important structural properties with living things. Given the vulnerability of flesh and blood objects in Jim's world, taking an immortal city as a primary attachment object was an adaptation that, although having serious limitations, seemed to have "worked" for Jim until 9/11.

Given the centrality of relationships in Jim's experience of 9/11, we adapted aspects of short-term interpersonal psychotherapy (IPT) as manualized by Markowitz (1999) to help Jim work through these role transitions. Our goal therefore was to help Jim to de-anthropomorphize Manhattan and see its cultural heritage as something already internalized that could not be taken away by a thermonuclear blast. Jim needed to see himself as already containing this beloved culture within himself like a memorized book in *Fahrenheit 451*. Another important goal was to help him feel safe to form deeper attachments with others. Perhaps since the mortality of Manhattan had become apparent, this would become possible.

Again we expected the presenting symptom, that, is the rumination on a future attack, to resolve simultaneously with the establishment of a new adaptation, in this case an IPT realignment of relationships and roles. It was not at all clear at the start that this was the right approach, however. We had begun by trying to work with imaginal exposure, only to find that focusing on the events of 9/11 did not help with Jim's ruminations about the future.

Monica

Monica is a 50-year-old divorced bookkeeper. On the morning of 9/11, she was on her usual commute to Manhattan. She was riding the elevated portion of the Brooklyn subway from which the burning towers were clearly visible. Like the others in that subway car she did not go into the city that day. In the months that followed, she found it more difficult to get to work or to do her job at work. Gradually she found herself avoiding subways and elevators, at least in tall buildings. Although she was able to find alternative means of transportation, she found the work less satisfying and had difficulty completing tasks.

After losing her job, she presented to the clinic asking for help with her phobic avoidance of subways and elevators.

A program of in vivo exposure was initiated, and Monica responded well, doing her assigned exposure homework and successfully reducing her phobic anxieties. As the work proceeded, Monica revealed that a few years prior to 9/11 her son-in-law, with whom she was very close, had died in a rock-climbing accident. Monica's daughter had been anxious about the particularly dangerous climbs that her husband chose, and he had agreed because of their two young daughters that this would be his last such climb.

Monica began to speak of how closely identified she felt with those families that had lost young married men, leaving widows and small children behind. She also began to be aware of some resentment for the amount of emotional and financial help that these families were getting, while her daughter was struggling and barely managing. Monica also became aware that she had been furious at her son-in-law for taking risks when he had a wife and small children to care for. She connected her phobic avoidance with not wanting to "take risks" as he had done. Monica came to see that she had never adapted to the death of her son-in-law in a stable fashion, that she had simply tried to "be strong" for her daughter and grandchildren. After 9/11, this temporary fix no longer gave her a sense of safety, and she no longer believed she could protect her family from harm by working hard and being careful. Instead, work had become a source of frustration and a reminder of her own professional shortcomings.

In addition to the phobic exposure, we adapted an imaginal exposure from Kathy Shear's work on complex grief (Shear et al., 2001). Our expectation was that if Monica could go back to where her grieving had been derailed and do the psychological work needed, she would be on her way to an adaptation to this loss. Thus, for Monica, classic in vivo exposure was able to reduce her acute, physiological response to the phobic objects, namely subways and elevators, and this in turn opened up the other issues in which her adaptation had failed her and made them available for further therapeutic intervention.

Mary

Mary is a 30-year-old married woman who lives in Florida and gave birth to her first child, a girl, three months before 9/11. A few days after

9/11, Mary presented in a distraught state at the Family Resource Center in New York with her infant in her arms. A week earlier, her husband had come to New York on business. She believed that one of his appointments involved the World Trade Center, and she had not heard from him since 9/11. Mary was frantic with anxiety for her husband.

Although there was great concern for Mary's plight, there was something about Mary's story that did not feel quite right. She had no identification with her, claiming it had been lost in her hasty bus trip to New York, and she could not give any usable contact information for family or friends in Florida. Yet she appeared truly distressed, and gave no sign of being psychotic and no indication of malingering or of wanting anything from the various governmental and social agencies. She simply was terrified about the fate of her husband and wanted desperately to find him alive. She was also obviously a caring and responsible mother, who despite her ordeal was spending most of her time and energy appropriately caring for her infant girl.

Eventually, with the help of the police department, we were able to trace her family in Florida. As she had said, she lived with her mother and husband in a modest neighborhood. Three days previously, Mary had disappeared with the baby, and the mother and husband had not heard from her. They had reported her as missing to the police and were sitting by the phone distraught, hoping to hear news of her whereabouts. Mary had been psychiatrically stable for an extended period, they explained, but had a history of bipolar disorder and had manic episodes in the past. On reinterview, it became clear that Mary was telling the truth, at least as she knew it. Mary had the unshakeable delusion that it was her husband, not herself, who was "missing." Later, when he came from Florida to take her home, she was immensely relieved that he had somehow survived. Mary responded to a brief hospitalization. With medication, she came out of what appeared to be a brief and circumscribed manic delusion induced by the events of 9/11.

We saw Mary in consultation at the time of her initial presentation. Her bipolar disorder was clearly not a subsyndromal condition, yet we include her in this series of cases because her story illustrates so poignantly how people well adapted despite their chronic mental illness might be affected by a trauma such as 9/11. Her case thus fits with our model of disrupted adaptations. We speculate that her capacity for grandiosity, though dormant, had led to Mary's experience of the news reports on 9/11 as necessarily including herself. The news reports seemed to have induced a delusion of reference. Mary was vulnerable to "leaky boundaries," and as she heard all the reports of distraught spouses seeking their loved ones, the story became her own. Moreover, in a sort of projective identification, she actually made the story of the missing spouse into a reality. These sorts of behaviors have been described as constituents of "manic defense" as part of a complex psychological process of adaptation to chronic mood disorder and its effects on role and relationships (Janowsky et al., 1970).

Future Directions for Research and Treatment

The research already available on the assessment and treatment of posttraumatic psychological sequelae has focused on syndromal cases of depression, PTSD, or other anxiety disorders. Less is known about the evaluation and treatment of subsyndromal conditions that are responsible for a great deal of suffering and dysfunction. Thus, despite great progress, there are many gaps in our knowledge. Most important, the community and government must support efforts to create evidence-based assessments and treatments for these patients.

Epidemiologic studies rely on the existence of a valid and reliable system for making diagnoses. The creation of the DSM and ICD has made possible worldwide study of psychiatric disorder. However, this model is based on the assumption that psychopathology can be identified as a syndrome—that is, that a cluster of signs, symptoms, and behaviors define a categorical entity with sharp boundaries.

A consequence of reliance on a categorical model is that persons with symptoms that fall short of full criteria are neglected. Yet, subsyndromal PTSD and other subsyndromal sequelae of trauma are important phenomena in their own right, and have received less attention than they deserved. These clinical phenomena may occur as primary responses to trauma or may occur in people who have partially recovered from full PTSD, either through treatment or through spontaneous improvement. Nevertheless, subthreshold PTSD appears to be associated with impairment and risk of suicide (Marshall et al., 2001). Even persons with a DSM diagnosis may, as a result of trauma, develop subsyndromal symptoms in another area. A recently studied example is schizophrenic patients who have developed anxiety symptoms as a result of secondary traumatization (Kennedy, 2002).

Unfortunately, current research technicalities may actually play a role in these persons being neglected. For example, the National Comorbidity Study was unable to address the question of partial PTSD because in the branching questionnaire the diagnostic module for PTSD was abandoned if at any point in the interview the individual did not meet criteria for the particular symptom cluster being evaluated. Although this procedure aids in the efficient assessment of a wide range of psychiatric disorders, it also has costs in ignoring important subsyndromal cases.

It is possible that overall rates of full PTSD will decrease over time but that many people will be left with subthreshold symptoms such as hypervigilance, insomnia, irritability, or emotional numbing. Research is therefore sorely needed in this area if we are to be prepared for potential future incidents (Marshall et al., 2002).

As we have argued throughout this chapter, assessment of a much broader set of consequences would be particularly useful, including nonpathological reactions, behavioral changes made as a result of 9/11, and changes in cognitive schema and worldviews. How many persons left the New York area after 9/11? Did parents have their children change schools? How many people changed their television viewing habits? Did many persons become more, or less, religious? How widespread and long-lived was a new emphasis on family and community? How many became more socially conscious? In other words, what is the process of readaptation? When does it work, and when does it not work?

The issue of resilience after psychological trauma, or, as we have called it, meta-adaptation, is also timely and important. Because the majority of people directly exposed to the attacks did not develop PTSD, the field could learn much from the study of their character traits, coping, healthy defenses, resilience factors, and perhaps even biological features.

All crises are a combination of danger and opportunity. The dangers following the 9/11 attacks are clear, but there have also been opportunities for restructuring the delivery of mental health services to the public, and for destigmatizing these services. The general public's acceptance of the idea that emotional stress was a normal part of coping with the trauma of 9/11, the nonjudgmental recognition that people who were seriously affected by 9/11 may need professional mental health services, and the acknowledgment of mental health professionals as integral recovery workers in our country's healing process, all point in a hopeful direction.

Acknowledgments

This work was supported in part by National Institute of Mental Health Grant MH01412, The New York Times Foundation, and The Atlantic Philanthropies.

References

Altshuler, L. L., Gitlin, M. J., Mintz, J., Leight, K. L. & Frye, M. A. (2002), Subsyndromal depression is associated with functional impairment in patients with bipolar disorder. *J. Clin. Psychiat.*, 63:807–811.

Dershowitz, A. M. (2002), *Why Terrorism Works.* New Haven, CT: Yale University Press.

Foa, E. B. (2000), Psychosocial treatment of posttraumatic stress disorder. *J. Clin. Psychiat.*, 61:43–48.

_____ & Kozak, M. J. (1986), Emotional processing of fear: Exposure to corrective information. *Psychol. Bull.*, 99:20–35.

Galea, S., Ahern, J., Resnick, H., Kilpatrick, D., Bucuvalas, M., Gold, J. & Vlahov, D. (2002), Psychological sequelae of the September 11 terrorist attacks in New York City. *New Engl. J. Med.*, 346:982–987.

_____ Resnick, H., Ahern, J., Gold, J., Bucuvalas, M., Kilpatrick, D., Stuber, J. & Vlahov, D. (2002), Posttraumatic stress disorder in Manhattan, New York City, after the September 11th terrorist attacks. *J. Urban Health,* 79:340–353.

Holland, J. H. (1992), *Adaptation in Natural and Artificial Systems,* 2d ed. Cambridge, MA: MIT Press.

Huang, Z. Y. & Robinson, G. E. (1992), Honeybee colony integration: Worker–worker interactions mediate hormonally regulated plasticity in division of labor. *Proc. Natl. Acad. Sci.*, 89:11726–11729.

Janowsky, D. S., Leff, M. & Epstein, R. S. (1970), Playing the manic game: Interpersonal maneuvers of the acutely manic patient. *Arch. Gen. Psychiat.*, 22:252–261.

Kennedy, B. L., Dhaliwal, N., Pedley, L., Sahner, C., Greenberg, R. & Manshadi, M. S. (2002), Post-traumatic stress disorder in subjects with schizophrenia and bipolar disorder. *J. Ky. Med. Assn.*, 100:395–399.

Kessler, R. C., Sonnega, A. M., Bromet, E., Hughes, M., Nelson, C. B. & Breslau, N. (1999), Epidemiologic risk factors for trauma and PTSD. In: *Risk Factors for Posttraumatic Stress Disorder*, ed. R. Yehuda. Washington, DC: American Psychiatric Press.

Macleod, A. D. (2000), Psychiatric casualties of World War II. *New Zeal. Med. J.*, 113:248–250.

Markowitz, J. C. (1999), Developments in interpersonal psychotherapy. *Can. J. Psychiat.*, 44:556–561.

Marshall, R. D., Galea, S. & Kilpatrick, D. (2002), Response to Schlenger and North. *J. Amer. Med. Assn.*, 288:2683–2684.

_____ Olfson, M., Hellman, F., Blanco, C., Guardino, M. & Struening, E. (2001), Comorbidity, impairment, and suicidality in subthreshold PTSD. *Amer. J. Psychiat.*, 158:1467–1473.

Pitman, R. K., Orr, S. P., Shalev, A. Y., Metzger, L. J. & Mellman, T. A. (1999), Psychophysiological alterations in post-traumatic stress disorder. *Semin. Clin. Neuropsychiat.*, 4:234–241.

Rothbaum, B. O., Foa, E. B., Riggs, D. S., Murdock, T. & Walsh, W. (1992), A prospective examination of post-traumatic stress disorder in rape victims. *J. Traumatic Stress*, 5:455–475.

Schlenger, W. E., Caddell, J. M., Ebert, L., Jordan, B. K., Rourke, K. M., Wilson, D., Thalji, L., Dennis, J. M., Fairband, J. A. & Kulka, R. A. (2002), Psychological reactions to terrorist attacks: Findings from the national study of Americans' reactions to September 11. *J. Amer. Med. Assn.*, 288:581–588.

Schuster, M. A., Stein, B. D., Jaycox, L. H., Collins, R. L., Marshall, G. N., Elliott, M. N., Zhou, A. J., Kanouse, D. E., Morrison, J. L. & Berry, S. H. (2001), A national survey of stress reactions after the September 11, 2001 terrorist attacks. *New Engl. J. Med.*, 345:1507–1512.

Shalev, A. Y. (2002) Acute stress reactions in adults. *Biol. Psychiat.*, 51:532–543.

_____ Galai, T. & Eth, S. (1993), Levels of trauma: A multidimensional approach to the treatment of PTSD. *Psychiatry*, 56:166–177.

_____ Peri, T., Canetti, L. & Schreiber, S. (1996), Predictors of PTSD in injured trauma survivors: A prospective study. *Amer. J. Psychiat.*, 153:219–225.

Shear, M. K., Frank, E., Foa, E., Cherry, C., Reynolds, C. F., Vander Bilt, J. & Masters, S. (2001), Traumatic grief treatment: A pilot study. *Amer. J. Psychiat.*, 158:1506–1508.

Chapter 6

Evolution of the Interpersonal Interpretive Function

Clues for Effective Preventive Intervention in Early Childhood

Peter Fonagy and Mary Target

In trying to elucidate the range of responses to trauma, from diagnosable psychiatric syndromes like posttraumatic stress disorder to subclinical reactions, the clinician must ask himself: What is lost? What is not working? These questions in turn raise the theoretically important issue of why and how some people respond better to traumatic situations than do others. Since the pioneering work of Anna Freud and Dorothy Burlingham studying children during the London Blitz in World War II, an impressive body of knowledge has arisen that suggests not only that the child's attachment relationships function as the decisive buffer to trauma in childhood but also that a secure attachment history in childhood provides the best prophylaxis against the future vicissitudes of adult traumatization.

The culmination of this tradition has come in the work of Peter Fonagy, Mary Target, and their colleagues at the Anna Freud Centre in London over the past decade. They have produced an impressive body of work, based on clinical and nonclinical populations, that shows how the attachment relationship facilitates or compromises the child's growing ability to be flexibly aware of his or her own mind and the mind of others. Articulation of the roots of this ability in an expanded attachment framework, in turn, has allowed them to redefine the psychological nature of the resilience to trauma. In this current contribution, Fonagy and Target seek to answer the decisive questions as to what is lost in traumatization and what is required for it to be regained.

99

The events of September 11 showed all of us the importance of equipping our youngsters to cope with a world far more dangerous than most of us had to encounter during our own development. Talk of prevention and resilience may have been a counsel of perfection in the past, but if psychological problems are not to reach epidemic proportions among children who are now confronted by terror and loss, we must come up with ways of protecting them that go beyond armed guards on airplanes.

This chapter was begun as a scholarly treatise that showed how Bowlby's assumptions about the evolutionary functions of early attachment might be extended to later stages of development. But in the wake of September 11, it became self-evident that one now must either say something of consequence or keep quiet. We have therefore focused this contribution on how secure early attachment may influence our capacity to adapt to interpersonal danger and reduce its impact on the mind.

Attachment and Trauma

Attachment theory and research offer a useful framework for understanding the impact of trauma.[1] Trauma triggers the attachment system, inhibiting exploration and activating affectional bonds (Bowlby, 1969). We feel distressed, and we want to be hugged. Even in New Yorkers, September 11 triggered the need to belong to a community. Crisis brings our ultimate interdependency into focus and challenges most those whose capacity for relationship is weakest. It is generally accepted that a history of secure attachment will increase the chances of responding to trauma in relatively adaptive ways. Why should this be?

Classical attachment theory contends that templates of relationships are established in infancy and are enacted in later development (Main, 1991; Crittenden, 1994; Sroufe, 1996; Bretherton and Munholland, 1999). Traumatic experiences activate and interact with such early relationship patterns. A child of parental disharmony or divorce whose attachments have been disrupted, whose sense of security has

---

[1] The best contemporary treatment of this theme may be found in Jon Allen's (2001) brilliant book, *Interpersonal Trauma and Serious Mental Disorder.*

been undermined, often expects to be rejected. This inclines the child to turn away from those who can help. Such a child might dismiss a helper in much the same way as the infant in the strange situation feels she cannot afford to turn for comfort to the caregiver.

Although classical attachment theory can help to explain the persistence of sometimes apparently self-defeating ways of behaving, it is not a satisfactory frame of reference for intervention or prevention. Modern attachment theory has gone a long way beyond identifying the basic patterns of attachment (Fonagy, 2001a). Psychological and biological research has identified important developmental functions of attachment beyond physical protection (Belsky, 1999; Polan and Hofer, 1999). Stress regulation (Cicchetti and Walker, 2001), the establishment of attentional mechanisms (Posner and Rothbart, 2000)—particularly effortful control—and the development of mentalizing capacities (Fonagy, in press) are perhaps the most important. The disorganization of attachment undermines these basic psychological capacities. Thus, disruption of early affectional bonds not only sets up maladaptive attachment patterns but also undermines a range of capabilities vital to normal social development. The absence or impairment of these three overlapping psychological capacities, which are acquired in the context of attachment relationships, decreases resilience in the face of trauma.

Stress regulation, the establishment of attentional mechanisms, and the development of mentalizing capacities may be usefully considered under a single heading as components of the *interpersonal interpretive function* (IIF; Fonagy, 2001b), a term inspired by the work of the philosopher Bogdan (1997, 2001). The capacity for "interpretation," which Bogdan (1997) defined as "organisms making sense of each other in contexts where this matters biologically," becomes uniquely human when others are engaged "psychologically in sharing experiences, information and affects." The capacity to make sense of each other requires the intentional stance: "treating the object whose behavior you want to predict as a rational agent with beliefs and desires" (Dennett, 1987). To be able to adopt this stance, the individual needs a symbolic representational system for mental states and also needs to be able to selectively activate states of mind in line with particular intentions (attentional control).

The IIF, which provides the individual with the crucial capacity for interpretation in psychological terms, develops out of complex psychological processes engendered by close proximity in infancy to another human being, the primary object. Unlike Bowlby's internal working model (Bowlby, 1980) or representations of object relationships (e.g., Kernberg, 1980), however, the IIF does not contain representations of experiences and is not a repository of personal encounters with the caregiver. It is best thought of as a mechanism for processing and responding to new experiences, much like Bion's (1962) alpha function.

Our suggestions are that the IIF is the inheritor of the quality of early object relations (the security of the infant–caregiver bond), a key mediator of individual differences in coping with trauma, and itself involved in trauma in that some or all aspects of IIF are susceptible to inhibition or decoupling following trauma. We further maintain that the common effects of trauma may in some instances be understood as the reemergence of primitive mental functions that were superseded by the IIF and that recovery from trauma in part involves rebuilding the IIF, just as protection comes from its robust establishment in earlier development.

The Three Components of the IIF as Inheritors of a Secure Attachment History and the Capacity to Withstand Trauma

A secure early relationship leaves the infant with a better coordinated set of biological mechanisms for the regulation of the stress response. We have known this from primate studies for some time (e.g., Sanchez, Ladd, and Plotsky, 2001), but more recent developmental studies have demonstrated close associations between the experience of sensitive caregiving and the efficient functioning of the hypothalamic–pituitary–adrenocortical (HPA) axis (Bremner and Vermetten, 2001; DeBellis, 2001; Gunnar et al., 2001). It is not surprising then that children with secure attachment relationships should be able to regulate their emotional arousal better in the face of stress or trauma (Kochanska, 2001).

The second path from early attachment to resilience in the face of trauma is via selective attention mechanisms (Broadbent, 1958). Trauma inevitably requires the mind to focus on current imperatives while it is still attempting to process unthinkable experience, refocusing away from the immediate past in order to cope with the present (Allen, 2001). Posner and Rothbart have termed the ability to inhibit a dominant response to perform a subdominant response "effortful control by attention" (Posner and Rothbart, 2000). We have suggested that early attachment equips children with this capacity, which is an internalization of the mother's ability to divert the child's attention from something immediate to something else (Fonagy, 2001a).

The third component of resilience shaped within attachment relationships is mentalization, or reflective function (Fonagy and Target, 1997). We focus here on this third component. Being able to understand human behavior in terms of thoughts and feelings empowers self-regulation in the face of trauma. What a difference it makes if a boy is able to attribute his withdrawn mother's sadness to her hopelessness about things she has been trying to do, not to his failure or to her not loving him! But this capacity to understand human behavior as organized by thoughts, feelings, wishes, beliefs, and desires is gradually acquired, and even then not consistently available (Target and Fonagy, 1996).

Good mentalization is associated with secure attachment history. We assume that a secure attachment relationship is one in which the parent is able to adopt a mentalizing stance toward a not-yet-mentalizing infant, to think about him in terms of his thoughts, feelings, and desires, and in terms of her own feelings about him and his mental state (Fonagy et al., 1991). A direct test of this hypothesis was provided by Elizabeth Meins and colleagues (Meins et al., 2001). They analyzed the content of mothers' speech in interaction with their six-month-old children and coded the number of comments the mother made on the infant's mental states (knowledge, desires, thought, and interest), of comments on the infant's mental processes ("Are you wondering about . . .?"), and of comments about what the infant might think the mother thinks ("You think I don't know you hid your vegetables!"). The proportion of such "appropriate mind-related comments," if in line with the immediate history of the interaction and not cutting across the child's apparent intentions, was highly significantly associated with attachment security in the child six months later.

The psychological self, with its awareness of mental states, does not emerge from a process of introspection. A child's awareness of the mental world arises intersubjectively, through a process of having been thought about (Fonagy et al., 1995). His awareness of his feelings and thoughts comes through the recognition of these states by the caregiver (Gergely and Watson, 1996). Extending this concept somewhat, and following many object relations theories as well as philosophers of mind, we consider the psychological self to be a reinternalization of one's thoughts and feelings as they have been perceived and understood by the other (Fonagy et al., 2002). These internalizations come to *represent* the primary self-state. What we are aware of as our thoughts and feelings are at root our parents' perceptions of rudiments of these, in infancy and beyond.

We assume that the robustness of our second-order representations of mental states depends on the caregiver's ability to reflect the infant's mental states, particularly his affect states, which are internalizations of the caregiver's mirroring displays. For this internalization to be effective, two conditions must be met: contingency and markedness (Gergely and Watson, 1999; Gergely, 2001).

By contingency, we simply mean that the caregiver's response accurately matches the infant's internal state. By markedness, we mean the caregiver's capacity to incorporate into her expression a clear indication that she is not expressing her own feelings, but those of the baby. If her attempt at mirroring is not contingent, if it does not match the infant's primary experience, we have argued that there will be a tendency toward the establishment of a narcissistic false-self–like structure where representations of internal states correspond to nothing real. If the infant perceives the caregiver's contingent mirroring as an expression of her own feelings—that is, if it is not marked as something that corresponds to his affect—then a predisposition to experiencing self-states externally is established. At the extreme, this latter pattern corresponds to borderline personality pathology. In either case, children who have limited experience of early marked, contingent mirroring that appears characteristic of secure mother–infant dyads (Koós and Gergely, 2001) will later be at risk of losing their capacity to mentalize in the face of trauma.

Secure attachment relationships greatly increase the chance of seeing the interpersonal world in mental-state terms (Fonagy, 1997; Fonagy, Redfern, and Charman, 1997). We have reason to anticipate that good reflective capacity might moderate the impact of trauma. For example, we have found that mothers in a relatively high stress (deprived) group characterized by single-parent families, parental criminality, unemployment, overcrowding, and psychiatric illness were far more likely to have securely attached infants if their reflective function was high (Fonagy et al., 1994). Reflective function protects.

Impact of Trauma on the IIF

Trauma commonly brings about a partial and temporary collapse of interpretive function. We have both clinical and experimental evidence for this. The disorganizing effects of trauma on attention and stress regulation are well known and hardly need going over again (Allen, 2001). The capacity for mentalization is undermined in a significant proportion of individuals who have experienced trauma. Maltreated toddlers have difficulty in learning to use internal-state words (Cicchetti and Beeghly, 1987; Beeghly and Cicchetti, 1994). Young adults who have been maltreated experience greater difficulty with reading the mind in the eyes test, a relatively simple measure of mentalization (Fonagy, Stein, and White, 2001).

The collapse of mentalization in the face of trauma entails a loss of awareness of the relationship between internal and external reality (Fonagy and Target, 2000). Where the ability to mentalize is lost, forms of psychic reality that antedate the achievement of mentalization in normal development reemerge. We assume that, before the child experiences his mind as truly representational, internal reality has a dual character (Fonagy and Target, 1996; Target and Fonagy, 1996). On one hand, the two-year-old assumes that everything in his mind exists in the physical world and that everything in the physical world must also be in his mind. This is the mode of psychic equivalence. It is most likely to reemerge if the caregiver's mirroring was insufficiently marked, so that second-order representations of feelings remain confused with their actuality. It is apparent when the traumatized child starts fearing his own mind, not wanting to think. Flashbacks are terrifying as they are memories experienced in the mode of psychic equivalence.

On the other hand, the child allows himself to imagine a world with the proviso that it must be completely separated from physical reality. This alternative mode of functioning is equally devoid of mentalization. We have called this the pretend mode. The heir of the pretend mode of psychic reality is dissociation in the wake of trauma. In dissociated thinking, nothing can be linked to anything. The principle of the pretend mode, in which fantasy is cut off from the real world, is extended so that nothing has implications for anything else (Fonagy and Target, 2000). The compulsive search for meaning is a common reaction to the sense of emptiness that the pretend mode generates. We have speculated that this reaction is more likely to arise in individuals whose experience of mirroring failed to correspond to their inner experience, and therefore lacked "realness" and contingency. The most characteristic feature of traumatization is the oscillation between these two modes of experiencing internal reality.

When trauma undermines mentalization, the consequences can be tragic. We all heard various individuals in the media, following the events of September 11, speaking with uncontained rage about "the enemy," "evil," and so on. While one empathizes with their rage, it may be dangerous to assume that the enemy is mindless, inhuman, and incapable of responding intelligently to what is presented to them. These sorts of black-and-white, stereotyped reactions to acute trauma, in which the other is thought of as having no mind and, one might say, no soul, may be understood in a number of ways. It may be biologically adaptive to react to an emergency with a fight or flight response. Such a reaction simplifies the situation, leaving no room for conceiving of mental states either in oneself or in the other. Alternatively, it is possible that trauma floods information-processing capacities; in an overwhelming situation, conceiving of mental states is a luxury that has to be jettisoned in the face of death. One way to understand the aims of terrorism might even be as a wish on the part of the aggressors to deprive their victims of the capacity to mentalize, thus undermining interpersonal interaction and generating social confusion.

We favor the view that the loss of reflective function is principally defensive. Trauma frequently involves being harmed and rendered helpless by another person. It may be too painful and terrifying to picture the aggressor's murderousness, hatred, or contempt. This is particularly so when their imagined thoughts are experienced concretely, in the mode of psychic equivalence. Similarly, internal conflict is reduced by not having to focus on the destructive response provoked in oneself. It reduces guilt about violence if the enemy is seen as inhuman.

Reflective function is more likely to be inhibited in those whose capacity to mentalize was not well established in the first place (Fonagy,

Target, and Gergely, 2000). Nevertheless, the same individuals can respond to trauma by precisely the opposite of this inhibition, redoubling their efforts to understand why things have happened. This may carry its own costs, with some children focusing on the internal world of the other at the expense of attention to their own mental states. Such vigilance is a common adaptation among physically maltreated youngsters (e.g., van der Kolk, 1993).

Interpersonal trauma is inevitably disorganizing. By definition it defies understanding. For some, the response can be a paralyzing effort after meaning which cannot be discovered, and this endless search may in fact inhibit effective action. A similar compulsive search for psychological meaning was perhaps discernible in obsessive watching of the television coverage of the events of September 11, where the same clips were repeatedly searched for illumination. Yet perhaps this very repetitiveness paradoxically stripped those extraordinary images of meaning, just as repeating a word aloud eventually renders it nonsensical. Something in the determined pursuit of understanding distances the re-presentation of the traumatic experience from reality, moving it closer to a state of dissociation.

When in infancy mirroring fails, when the parent's perception is inaccurate or unmarked, or both, the child internalizes a noncontingent mental state as part of a representation within the psychological self. These internalizations sit within the self without being connected to it by a set of meanings. We have called the resulting incoherence within the self-structure an "alien self" (Fonagy and Target, 2000). Such incoherencies in self structure are not only features of profoundly neglected children. Even the most sensitive caregiver is insensitive to the child's state of mind more than 50% of the time. Thus, we all have alien parts to our self-structure. The coherence of the self, as many have noted, is somewhat illusory. This illusion is normally maintained by the continuous narrative commentary on behavior that mentalization provides, which fills in the gaps and weaves our experiences together so that they make sense. In the absence of a robust mentalizing capacity, with disorganized patterns of attachment, the fragmentation of the self-structure is clearly revealed.

But when trauma inhibits mentalization, the self is suddenly experienced as incoherent. There are parts within that feel like the self, yet also feel substantively different, sometimes even persecutory. The only way the child can deal with this is by constantly externalizing these alien parts of the self-structure into the other, so that he can feel whole. At the simplest level, the world then becomes terrifying because the persecutory parts are experienced as outside. At a more complex level, it is felt essential that the alien experiences are owned by another mind, so that another mind is in control of these parts of the self. Thus, children who before the trauma were well-behaved and controlled suddenly become coercive and controlling. They appear so because their attempts at control are crude. They may appear to have lost a previous level of subtlety of relating based on an awareness of their own and others' feelings. So the child may be contemptuous, provoking rage in the object, a rage that had originally been internalized in infancy from the insensitivity of the caregiver and that becomes experienced as alien and intolerable following the trauma.

A brief vignette from Mary Target's work may help to illustrate these ideas. Callum is a five-year-old boy, the younger of two siblings, whose mother suffers from severe obsessional neurosis. Before September 11, she had dreamed of a plane crashing into the World Trade Center, where one of her rivals in the financial world was based. As well as her anxiety disorder, Callum's mother harbors brooding grievances of sometimes paranoid intensity. When Callum's mother brought him to the clinic as a baby, it was obvious that she had great difficulty in understanding his feelings. She tended to avoid contact with him, particularly if he was distressed or demanding, which made her extremely impatient and exacerbated her symptoms. Callum had developed into a rather withdrawn, "good" child, wary of his mother's moods and preferring to be in the neighbors' house. The family moved to New York shortly before the twin towers were struck. Callum's mother became frantic, convinced that her fantasies had spilled over into physical reality and that she was about to destroy the world. Callum also became anxious, expressing this through disobedience and rages. After a week, this settled into a different pattern in which Callum bullied and tormented his mother, broke favorite possessions, and ordered her to serve him. He demanded to sleep in her bed and to be spoon-fed by her, she felt, to torture and punish her. She shouted at him and hit him, telling him that she hated him and wished she had never had any children. She felt he was just manipulating her to be in control, not because he really needed what he was forcing out of her. She felt she had to "submit" and that he had taken control of her life.

Callum's reaction reflects his partial loss of reflective function following the trauma, not so much the trauma of the events (he was kept away from all coverage of the disaster, and they lived outside Manhattan) but the traumatizing effect of his mother's reactions to these. His fantasies, like his mother's, became real, and he was thrown back developmentally, once again experiencing his mind in a mode of psychic equivalence. We can imagine that his representations of his mental states were not firmly established to start with and that his mother's unmarked mirroring predisposed him to confuse the mental and the real. Also in this mode, he became once again vulnerable to experiencing his mother's feelings as his own, and the noncontingent, alien part of his self came to be colonized by the mother's nearly delusional anxieties and sense of responsibility for the events. His apparently coercive, manipulative behavior reflects his inability to contain the incoherence of his self-structure. Callum's need for close-ness to his mother is not simply motivated by anxiety but also by the need for a vehicle to contain the alien part of himself. We assume that inside Callum's self-structure was a rather vacuous, intolerant figure that Callum's mother now needed to become in order to reassure him that this state of mind was no longer inside him. So Callum is bullying and tormenting to create rage.

Callum's ways of controlling his object are rudimentary; they lack subtlety. This is a clue to his limited mentalizing capacities, but, if Callum were more able to conceive of mental states, he would not be so troubled by the alien parts of his self. As it is, he only has rudimen-tary schemata for both his own and his mother's thoughts and feelings. By becoming a vehicle for his unwanted states of mind, Callum's mother saves him. Unfortunately, in doing so, in becoming angry and punitive, she is in the worst possible state to restore Callum's mental-izing function, because she can no longer be in touch with his mental world. At moments like these, traumatized families may need input from the outside, even if this is little more than sensitive descriptions of what has happened to them.

Recovery of Mentalization

Normally, after trauma, mentalization is gradually restored in a natural process of reexperiencing a social matrix. We even argue that the attachment system is activated by trauma precisely to recreate the mental closeness to others on which a recovery of reflective function depends. Only in a minority is the psychological self so poorly established that the two primitive modes of experiencing the internal world persist. The persistence of trauma is the result of experiencing the events of the trauma in an unmentalized way. The effective therapeutic approaches for treating victims of trauma have in common the provision of a secure framework to support the recovery of the child's mentalizing capacity. Even behavior therapies, using exposure treatments, work to reinforce the representational nature of the child's mental experience (e.g., Foa and Kozak, 1986). Exposure teaches the child that there is no one-to-one correspondence between his anxiety and the physical world, that the isomorphism of psychic equivalence is an illusion. When they actually experience the situation, it is not as bad as they expected.

Ideally, these ideas should infuse our advice to parents, particularly in relation to the early phases of child-rearing. Understanding the child as an intentional being, offering the experience of a mind that has the child's mind in mind, is the ultimate source of protection against the mind's vulnerability to being overwhelmed by the force of the concreteness of the experiences it is capable of generating. For some people who are deprived of this early experience, especially if this deprivation is followed by further brutalization, a propensity for interpersonal violence is created. For others, we see a continuing vulnerability to trauma. In either case, to protect ourselves from the threat posed by our mastery of the physical world—biological and nuclear weapons, for instance—we *must* address the problem of our collective weakness in containing and processing mental experiences.

Acknowledgments

This chapter was first presented at the "When the Bough Broke: Perspectives on Trauma from Psychoanalysis, Attachment Theory, and Developmental Psychobiology" conference of the Center for Psychoanalytic Training and Research and the Sackler Institute for Developmental Psychobiology, Department of Psychiatry, Columbia University, November 3, 2001.

References

Allen, J. G. (2001), *Interpersonal Trauma and Serious Mental Disorder*. Chichester, England: Wiley.

Beeghly, M. & Cicchetti, D. (1994), Child maltreatment, attachment, and the self system: Emergence of an internal state lexicon in toddlers at high social risk. *Devel. Psychopathol*, 6:5–30.

Belsky, J. (1999), Modern evolutionary theory and patterns of attachment. In: *Handbook of Attachment*, ed. J. Cassidy & P. R. Shaver. New York: Guilford Press, pp. 141–161.

Bion, W. R. (1962), *Learning from Experience*. London: Heinemann.

Bogdan, R. J. (1997), *Interpreting Minds*. Cambridge, MA: MIT Press.

_____ (2001), *Minding Minds*. Cambridge, MA: MIT Press.

Bowlby, J. (1969), *Attachment and Loss, Vol. 1*. London: Hogarth Press.

_____ (1980), *Attachment and Loss, Vol. 3*. London: Hogarth Press.

Bremner, J. D. & Vermetten, E. (2001), Stress and development: Behavioral and biological consequences. *Devel. Psychopathol*, 13:473–489.

Bretherton, K. & Munholland, K. A. (1999), Internal working models in attachment relationships: A construct revisited. In: *Handbook of Attachment*, ed. J. Cassidy & P. R. Shaver. New York: Guilford Press, pp. 89–114.

Broadbent, D. E. (1958), *Perception and Communication*. London: Pergamon.

Cicchetti, D. & Beeghly, M. (1987), Symbolic development in maltreated youngsters: An organizational perspective. In: *New Directions for Child Development, Vol. 36: Atypical Symbolic Development*, ed. D. Cicchetti & M. Beeghly. San Francisco: Jossey-Bass, pp. 5–29.

_____ & Walker, E. F. (2001), Stress and development: Biological and psychological consequences [editorial]. *Devel. Psychopathol.*, 13:413–418.

Crittenden, P. M. (1994), Peering into the black box: An exploratory treatise on the development of self in young children. In: *Rochester Symposium on Developmental Psychopathology, Vol 5: Disorders and Dysfunctions of the Self*, ed. D. Cicchetti & S. L. Toth. Rochester, NY: University of Rochester Press, pp. 79–148.

DeBellis, M. D. (2001), Developmental traumatology: The psychobiological development of maltreated children and its implications for research, treatment, and policy. *Devel. Psychopathol.*, 13:539–564.

Dennett, D. (1987), *The Intentional Stance*. Cambridge, MA: MIT Press.

Fonagy, P. (1997), Attachment and theory of mind: Overlapping constructs? *Assn. Child Psychol. Psychiat. Occasional Papers*, 14:31–40.

_____ (2001a), Early intervention and the development of self-regulation. Presented at meeting of the Australian Association for Infant Mental Health, Perth, Australia, August 30.

_____ (2001b), The human genome and the representational world: The role of early mother–infant interaction in creating an interpersonal interpretive mechanism. *Bull. Menn. Clin.*, 65:427–448.

_____ (in press), The development of psychopathology from infancy to adulthood: The mysterious unfolding of disturbance in time. *Infant Mental Health J.*

_____ Gergely, G., Jurist, E. & Target, M. (2002), *Affect Regulation and Mentalization.* New York: Other Press.

_____ Redfern, S. & Charman, T. (1997), The relationship between belief-desire reasoning and a projective measure of attachment security (SAT). *Brit. J. Devel. Psychol.*, 15:51–61.

_____ Steele, H., Moran, G., Steele, M. & Higgitt, A. (1991), The capacity for understanding mental states: The reflective self in parent and child and its significance for security of attachment. *Infant Mental Health J.*, 13: 200–217.

_____ _____ Steele, H., Higgitt, A. & Target, M. (1994), Theory and practice of resilience. *Child Psychol. Psychiat.*, 35:231–257.

_____ _____ _____ Leigh, T., Kennedy, R., Mattoon, G. & Target, M. (1995), Attachment, the reflective self, and borderline states: The predictive specificity of the Adult Attachment Interview and pathological emotional development. In: *Attachment Theory*, ed. S. Goldberg, R. Muir & J. Kerr. Hillsdale, NJ: The Analytic Press, pp. 233–278.

_____ Stein, H. & White, R. (2001), Dopamine receptor polymorphism and susceptibility to sexual, physical, and psychological abuse: Preliminary results of a longitudinal study of maltreatment. Presented at 10th biannual meeting of the Society for Research in Child Development, Minneapolis, MN, April 21.

_____ & Target, M. (1996), Playing with reality I: Theory of mind and the normal development of psychic reality. *Internat. J. Psycho-Anal.*, 77: 217–233.

_____ & _____ (1997), Attachment and reflective function: Their role in self-organization. *Devel. Psychopathol.*, 9:679–700.

_____ & _____ (2000), Playing with reality III: The persistence of dual psychic reality in borderline patients. *Internat. J. Psycho-Anal.*, 81:853–874.

_____ _____ & Gergely, G. (2000), Attachment and borderline personality disorder: A theory and some evidence. *Psychiat. Clin. North Amer.*, 23:103–122.

Foa, E. B. & Kozak, M. J. (1986), Emotional processing of fear: Exposure to corrective information. *Psychol. Bull.*, 99:20–35.

Gergely, G. (2001), The development of understanding of self and agency. In: *Handbook of Childhood Cognitive Development*, ed. U. Goshwami. Oxford, England: Blackwell.

_____ & Watson, J. (1996), The social biofeedback model of parental affect-mirroring. *Internat. J. Psycho-Anal.*, 77:1181–1212.

_____ & _____ (1999), Early social-emotional development: Contingency perception and the social biofeedback model. In: *Early Social Cognition*, ed. P. Rochat. Mahwah, NJ: Lawrence Erlbaum Associates, pp. 101–137.

Gunnar, M. R., Morison, S. J., Chisholm, K. C. & Schuder, M. (2001), Salivary cortisol levels in children adopted from Romanian orphanages. *Devel. Psychopathol.*, 13:611–628.

Kernberg, O. F. (1980), *Internal World and External Reality*. New York: Aronson.

Kochanska, G. (2001), Emotional development in children with different attachment histories: The first three years. *Child Devel.*, 72:474–490.

Koós, O. & Gergely, G. (2001), The "flickering switch" hypothesis: A contingency-based approach to the etiology of disorganized attachment in infancy. In: *Contingency Perception and Attachment in Infancy, Special Issue of the Bulletin of the Menninger Clinic*, ed. J. Allen, P. Fonagy & G. Gergely. New York: Guilford Press, pp. 397–410.

Main, M. (1991), Metacognitive knowledge, metacognitive monitoring, and singular (coherent) vs. multiple (incoherent) model of attachment: Findings and directions for future research. In: *Attachment Across the Life Cycle*, ed. C. M. Parkes, J. Stevenson-Hinde & P. Marris. London: Tavistock/Routledge, pp. 127–159.

Meins, E., Ferryhough, C., Fradley, E. & Tuckey, M. (2001), Rethinking maternal sensitivity: Mothers' comments on infants' mental processes predict security of attachment at 12 months. *J. Child Psychol. Psychiat.*, 42:637–648.

Polan, H. J. & Hofer, M. (1999), Psychobiological origins of infant attachment and separation responses. In: *Handbook of Attachment*, ed. J. Cassidy & P. R. Shaver. New York: Guilford Press, pp. 162–180.

Posner, M. I. & Rothbart, M. K. (2000), Developing mechanisms of self-regulation. *Devel. Psychopathol.*, 12:427–441.

Sanchez, M. M., Ladd, C. O. & Plotsky, P. M. (2001), Early adverse experience as a developmental risk factor for later psychopathology: Evidence from rodent and primate models. *Devel. Psychopathol.*, 13: 419–449.

Sroufe, L. A. (1996), *Emotional Development*. New York: Cambridge University Press.

Target, M. & Fonagy, P. (1996), Playing with reality II: The development of psychic reality from a theoretical perspective. *Internat. J. Psycho-Anal.*, 77:459–479.

van der Kolk, B. A. (1993), Childhood trauma and psychiatric illness. Presented at Commonwealth of Massachusetts Department of Mental Health Conference on Post-Traumatic Stress Disorder in Serious Mental Health, Boston, MA.

Chapter 7

Intergenerational Communication of Maternal Violent Trauma

Understanding the Interplay of
Reflective Functioning and
Posttraumatic Psychopathology

Daniel S. Schechter

*How does one intervene with a mother who in the wake of
9/11 and her own history of violent traumatization begins
to see her eight-year-old son as a second Osama bin Laden?
If research now shows that a secure attachment bond is the
best protection against traumatization, the question arises
as to the ways in which an insecure or disorganized attachment relationship raises the risks of traumatization for the
child. Even more pressing clinically is the situation where
the primary caretaker, far from being able to provide a
secure base for the child, is already laboring under the
burden of his or her own history of severe traumatization.*

*This chapter is a major contribution to the under-
standing of the phenomenon of the intergenerational transmission of trauma. First articulated as a phenomenon by
Selma Fraiberg and her colleagues nearly three decades
ago, the intergenerational transmission of trauma is here
subjected to systematic research that clarifies the factors as
to whether violence and trauma in the parent's background
are repeated in the next generation. In addition, Schechter
uses the research to fashion a form of mother–child brief
intervention that seems to have significant potential for
reducing one of the decisive mediating variables—negative
maternal attributions.*

To contemplate "what evil lurks in the hearts of men" is something that most of us do not like to do. Perhaps this is why *The Shadow*, the detective radio program, was so popular during the 1930s and 1940s—the darkest period of the 20th century: The idea that the radio program's hero, the Shadow, *knows* was a great comfort to many Americans during World War II. Indeed, it might be of some consolation to us in the wake of September 11, to understand what evil lurked in the hearts of those al Qaeda terrorists—those who would live among us, then take over our passenger planes and use them to assault our city, destroy New York City's two tallest buildings, and damage the Pentagon. What was going on in the minds of those hateful men who would obliterate the lives and damage the families of thousands of innocent civilians and—as if that were not enough—terrorize our minds? I literally shudder to think.

Most of us do not go about our lives expecting such diabolical treatment from our fellow men. Most of us, as Peter Fonagy describes elsewhere in this volume, are disorganized and disoriented by the interpersonal trauma, the psychological attack on each of us by terrorists who meant to harm every American's sense of safety. For those who might have sought to escape their venom, it was injected into the living rooms of most of our homes through the all too vivid barrage of flashbacks on television and in newspaper and magazine photos.

Despite most of us feeling shocked, for some individuals—those who have known hatred and violence in their own lives, especially as enacted by people on whom they most depended for protection and nurturance—the attacks of 9/11 confirmed their darkest expectations. In fact, for many parents with histories of interpersonal violent trauma such as child abuse and domestic-violence exposure, I have found that the events of 9/11 unfortunately resonated with the familiar violence of their past, reactivating posttraumatic stress symptoms. Some parents indeed have come to expect the hatred and violence with which they are familiar in themselves and anticipate in their children.

In the following vignette, a traumatized mother compares her eight-year-old son to Osama bin Laden on 9/11.

Mrs. Y, a 43-year-old real estate agent, brought her son, Fred, to my private practice initially at age six with the complaint of his severe separation anxiety and preoccupation with fears of his mother's death.

Mrs. Y and Fred came through two years of treatment with promising results: Mrs. Y and Fred were better able to understand Fred's intense fears of loss as relating to his mother's violent temper, often activated by her alcohol abuse, as well as his own frightened and enraged reaction to her. Not only had Mrs. Y hurled an end table across the living room at his father and bloodied his nose, but also she had many times lost her temper at little Fred and called him a "screaming monster" who could be a "tyrant . . . just like his father." Mrs. Y described Fred's temperament as "sweet and shy" with everyone except her; he could be "manipulative and controlling" with her and "not say he was sorry for hurting her feelings" when he would say that he hated her during a tantrum.

Fred described his mother during bouts of her "vein-popping screaming" at him as, "turning into all mouth and teeth like a pit bull that's going to bite. . . . Her eyes are closed or her brain is closed—she doesn't see me when she yells like that."

In the early phase of the therapy, during and between sessions, Fred drew countless pictures of pit bulls, wolves, lions, vipers, and tyrannosauruses (Figure 7–1). At first, he depicted those animals as out of control, wild, and lunging for the necks of their victims; then, after some months

FIGURE 7–1. "Hungry lions and hyenas trying to make a kill."

of our work together, he rendered them still as looming and rageful but better contained, either on leashes or in cages (Figure 7–2).

While with his angry mother, Fred clearly feared for his life; yet without her, he feared her death as well as his. Through intensive work individually, with the family, between Mrs. Y and her therapist, and between Mrs. Y and her psychiatrist (she began medication to address her irritability), Fred's symptoms subsided. He simultaneously stopped drawing pictures of vicious carnivores as frequently, choosing instead to portray friendly dogs, hamsters, or human figures interacting with and affecting each other. he also drew pictures of his mother and himself yelling, rather than one simply victimizing each other (Figure 7–3). His capacity to tell a complex story involving the thoughts and feelings of each figure in the drawings increased concomitantly.

Mrs. Y, born into an Egyptian-Jewish family, had experienced physical abuse and domestic violence at the hands of her alcoholic father. He had apparently served in the allied campaign in North Africa toward the end of World War II but never discussed the details of his military service with his family. Mrs. Y never felt sufficient nurturance or protection from her depressed and anxious mother. Mrs. Y had suffered from posttraumatic stress disorder (PTSD) and depressive symptoms for years, which significantly subsided with the aforementioned combined treatment.

On the morning of September 11, Mrs. Y walked her four-year-old son, Larry, to his preschool in Soho, less than a mile north of the World

FIGURE 7–2. "Pit bull on a leash."

FIGURE 7–3. "My mother and me."

Trade Center, only to see the attacks in their entirety. Shaken and panicked, she grabbed Larry and took a cab immediately to Fred's school and brought him home as well.

At home, Mrs. Y, glued to the newscast on the small television in the kitchen, cried alone while the boys played with blocks and paper airplanes in the living room. Mr. Y, a banking executive preoccupied with upcoming deadlines, had decided to stay at work in Midtown as long as possible after hearing that the city was being shut down—despite Mrs. Y's pleading that he return home as soon as possible. Mrs. Y felt exasperated by what she understood to be her husband's lack of support of her and their children's needs.

Meanwhile, Fred, who had been most often the object of Mrs. Y's attacks as a younger child, watched as Larry built up towers of blocks and then toppled them with the paper airplanes.

Fred, who had not seen the World Trade Center attacks, panicked and yelled at his little brother with increasing desperation to stop the play. Fred began to cry as Larry continued to play obliviously. The boys got into a fight. Mrs. Y, frazzled and comforted only by a glass of wine she was not supposed to have, began to have trouble hearing the newscast. She stormed out of the kitchen and hovered over the two boys seated next to the chaos of blocks and crumpled paper airplanes, and screamed, "Who are you, Osama bin Laden now destroying the city here? The world's falling apart, and you're playing terrorist?! Look at this mess!" Larry blamed Fred for the noise. Fred squeezed a block tightly in his hand and dissolved into a puddle of tears. He threw the block at his brother before disappearing into his room and refusing to eat dinner. His father later went into Fred's room to tell Fred that he had upset his mother by not coming to dinner.

The family returned to my office the following week, noting a resurgence of symptoms in Fred: severe separation anxiety, queasiness, nightmares, refusal to eat meat, fear of riding in elevators (causing Mrs. Y to walk up six flights of stairs in their apartment building), and new fears that Osama bin Laden, who Fred heard was living in a cave, was hiding out in New York City underground garages. Every time he passed a possible Osama hideout, including the garage under his own apartment building, he became acutely anxious. Moreover, Mrs. Y reported seeing the burning towers every time she closed her eyes, nightmares, avoidance of "tall buildings and Islamic cab drivers," fear of imminent apocalypse, palpitations and being startled when planes flew overhead or sirens sounded, as well as troubled sleep and increased irritability. Although Larry did have some difficulty sleeping, with nightmares and preoccupation with what he had seen and with his mother's reaction, he, unlike Fred, did not develop a sustained syndrome. Mr. Y did not develop distressing symptoms, yet became preoccupied with watching feature films about war, which Mrs. Y avoided.

During that first session back, when I asked Mrs. Y what had gone on in her mind when she was unable to see how frightened Fred was of Larry's play and Mrs. Y's response to it on 9/11, she replied, "I think Fred has a way of bringing out my father in me—the hot-blooded Mediterranean part. His father can do it, and Fred can do it. It's like Fred brings out the Arab in me! When I get freaked out like on 9/11 or drunk like on 9/11 . . . that happens before I know it. I mean I was thinking this is World War III, like Pearl Harbor all over again, and the play just seemed insensitive to me at the time. Now I see that they were trying to work out their feelings."

In this second treatment, Fred did not spontaneously talk about the events of September 11 in the world or in his home, even though we began in an open-ended way so as to see where he would begin. He asked if he could draw a picture but chose to draw "an Einstein equation" that his father had taught him: $E = mc^2$ (Figure 7–4). He did not, however, understand what the equation meant, except that his father had told him that: "This was the equation that helped build

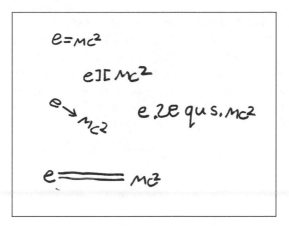

FIGURE 7–4. "Einstein equation."

FIGURE 7–5. "Before and after the planes hit
the twin towers."

bombs." When I directed him to remember what had happened on
September 11, Fred said, "I don't want to talk about that." I said, "I know
this makes you nervous to talk about it. Suppose you draw for me what
upset you so much that day with Larry and Mommy?" Fred agreed and
drew "before" and "after" pictures of his brother's construction of the
towers with a paper airplane approaching and "a big mess" afterward
(Figure 7–5). This drawing enabled us to focus on what he was feeling
while his brother reenacted the attacks and then when his mother came
into the room in a rage.

Over time, after individual and family sessions, as we created caves with blocks and had police dogs sniff out Osama, Fred's symptoms abated. He put Osama on trial and, when it came to sentencing, commanded that he not be put to death but live the rest of his life in a dog's cage under the ground, guarded by crocodiles and piranhas (Figure 7-6). Fred also began to draw pictures of kamikaze planes he had seen in a World War II movie (Figure 7-7). He took special pleasure in destroying the pictures before the planes reached their destination. I commented to Fred on how good it felt to let his anger

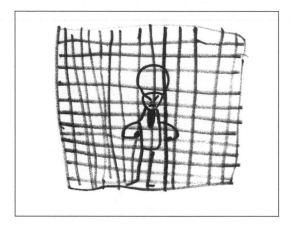

FIGURE 7-6. "Osama in a jail-cage."

FIGURE 7-7. "Kamikaze plane dropping a bomb before crashing."

loose and make the bombs, but also then to destroy them, so as to restore order. He looked at me and smiled. We had done these activities together within the safety of the treatment.

On realizing the effect of her own history of violent trauma on her relationship with Fred before and after September 11, Mrs. Y was moved to tears. She said several times during the treatment, "I don't want him to have to go through the craziness that I lived through with my family when I was growing up."

Most parents who have histories of child maltreatment or family violence exposure like Mrs. Y do not want their children to suffer these same adverse experiences. Research has shown, however, that one to two thirds of parents who are physically and sexually abused nevertheless maltreat their own children (Oliver, 1993). These percentages do not include children of abused parents who, because of disturbances in the ability of the traumatized parent to protect the child, end up maltreated by someone else.

The only epidemiologic study to date that explores the intergenerational transmission of domestic violence shows that one third of boys who have been exposed to domestic violence perpetrate acts of family violence as adult men (Martin et al., 2002). This percentage does not include those violence-exposed males who go on to be victimized and does not consider females like Mrs. Y. Hundreds of thousands of children who yearly experience interpersonal violent trauma (e.g., physical and sexual abuse and domestic-violence exposure) in the United States have the potential to have children who are similarly traumatized (U.S. Department of Health and Human Services, 2000, 2002; Martin et al., 2002).

Intergenerational transmission of violent trauma is clearly an immensely important and understudied public health problem. Because individuals like Mrs. Y, who have prior trauma histories or PTSD (or both), have been shown to be more vulnerable to sustained traumatic effects following large-scale violence (Schuster et al., 2001; Coates, this volume) such as terrorist attacks, the risk of intergenerational transmission of violent trauma, PTSD, and other trauma-related psychopathology (e.g., substance abuse relapses and major depression) is even greater now (Stuber, Galea, and Fairbrother, 2002). This has been demonstrated following other episodes of large-scale political violence and terrorism. In the cases of the Scud missile attacks on Israel during the Gulf War and the Oklahoma City bombing, caregivers' anxiety and distress, such as that associated with PTSD, were potent determinants of children's social-emotional disturbances even years following these disasters (Pfefferbaum et al., 1999; Laor, Wolmer, and Cohen, 2001).

What leads parents, often despite their best intentions, to expose their children, directly or indirectly, to adverse experiences similar to those they experienced?

Although individual risk factors for intergenerational transmission of trauma have been identified—for example, attachment disorganization (Lyons-Ruth, Bronfman, and Parsons, 1999a), parental frightening-frightened behavior (Schuengel, Bakersman-Kraneburg, and Van, 1999), and parental dissociative behavior (Egeland and Susman-Stillman, 1996)—no studies have demonstrated the psychological mechanisms by which maternal traumatic history, attachment, psychopathology, physiology, and behavior are linked together. This linkage is essential to the development and targeting of interventions to interrupt cycles of family violence and abuse.

Traumatically stressed caregivers, I hypothesize—based on my clinical observations (Schechter, in press)—are compelled to communicate their experiences of violence in an effort to regulate their own affect and physiology. They therefore skew the focus of joint attention to their traumatic experience(s) at the expense of mutual regulation and flexibility in the relationship with their young child.

A striking example of this occurred during a videotaped interaction session with a 17-month-old girl and her mother, who had brought the toddler in with the complaint that the little girl was trying to kill herself. The mother, who had an extensive history of sexual and physical abuse as well as domestic-violence exposure, introduced an adult male doll to the child and twirled the figure enticingly before the child's face, even though her daughter was interested in other toys. Just when the little girl became interested in the daddy doll and began to mouth the toy while looking at mother's face, mother said in a lulling tone, "You like him, don't you?" before abruptly yanking the doll from the child's mouth and saying, "But not in the mouth!" This interaction was repeated three or more times in 20 minutes of play; the observers viewed the act as inhibiting the child's exploration. Later, during the same session, as the child became distressed following a separation–reunion, mother smiled and took a stuffed gorilla and loomed it into the girl's face so abruptly that the little girl covered her eyes defensively and became more agitated.

When the traumatized caregiver–child dyad enters the clinical setting, the dyad as a complex, dynamic system then communicates its *coconstructed, developing variation* of the caregiver's original traumatic experience(s) to the therapist-observer, in an effort to find meaning and containment of mounting negative affect. The coconstructed, developing variation can be seen in the aforementioned clinical example. The mother communicated interest in and conflict over the male father-doll and the gorilla and communicated the excitement, frustration, fear, and distress associated with the mother's original childhood abuse, which did involve forced oral penetration. This new distress, however, which caused the toddler and mother to feel frightened and helpless, was not sexual abuse but only one variation on the mother's memory of her abusive experiences.

I have therefore hypothesized that violent traumatic experience is communicated intergenerationally within and by the caregiver–child relationship, both via action and language. This intergenerational communication of violent traumatic experience begins with everyday interactions between caregivers and children, involving spoken language and nonverbal behavior, possibly from birth on.

I focus here on mothers' use of spoken language about their very young children, who are not yet able to regulate their emotions or think about intentionality. In other words, as Peter Fonagy has described elsewhere in this volume, these children will not yet have developed the capacity to mentalize, an intrinsic part of what he calls the Interpersonal Interpretive Function (IIF). The clinical and attachment literature has supported the notion that maternal attributions toward her child—as markers for maternal perception—are the links between maternal mental representations and maternal behavior with her child (Zeanah and Zeanah, 1989; Benoit, Parker, and Zeanah, 1997; Lieberman, 1997, 1999).

In the first clinical vignette, Mrs. Y compared her son to terrorist Osama bin Laden and described him as "a screaming monster, manipulative and controlling," "a tyrant . . . just like his father." But she also referred to him as "sweet and shy." Another case of a single inner-city Hispanic mother was similar in that respect. She had a history of severe physical and sexual abuse, beginning in early childhood, at the hands of her stepfather. This mom came to our hospital-based

Infant–Family Service with her three-year-old son, complaining that he was hitting, kicking, and biting her. As her anxious son was sitting perfectly still beside her keeping her in his peripheral gaze in the waiting room, she said, "You know those kids that shot up those people in Columbine? Well, my son here is going to be the next one of them if you don't do something about it. He is an evil child, and I do not want him to keep on that way and grow up to be a murderer or a rapist."

Based on clinical observations by my research team (Schechter, 2002, in press), we have noted that distress of the child under four years of age, who has not yet developed the capacity to regulate his or her own emotions, often becomes a posttraumatic reminder for caregivers who have memories of their helplessness, horror, and outrage during a violent assault or memories of violent perpetrators who also had extreme difficulty modulating their negative affect and hostile aggression. The caregivers often have low frustration tolerance, and, like the young child, have deficits, likely defensively based, as Fonagy describes in functioning of their IIF, and again, specifically their capacity for mentalization, which is operationalized as "reflective functioning" (Fonagy et al., 1995). These traumatized caregivers, in other words, cannot think in a heated moment about what might be going on in their own mind or in that of the other person, or these caregivers have faced memories of their own helplessness, horror, and outrage during a violent assault.

One striking finding in the recent four-month follow-up of the random-digit-dial study of 475 New York City parents with children ages four through 17, was that children of parents who said that they were unaware of their children's response to the events of 9/11, were 11.1 times more likely to have behavioral problems (Stuber et al., 2002). Might this mean that the children of parents who were unable to think about what might have been going on in their own children's minds after 9/11 (because they were themselves so traumatized) became the most emotionally and behaviorally dysregulated?

Clinical reports have described how, when confronted with child distress, caregivers with childhood histories of overwhelming violent trauma lose the capacity to reflect on what might be going on in the mind of their young child or in their own mind and may even enact behavior with their child that conforms to their perception of that *child-as-threat* (Fraiberg, Adelson, and Shapiro, 1975; Lieberman, 1997;

Schechter et al., in press). The child, in turn, finds this frightening, disorganizing, and disorienting.

The Parent–Child Interaction Project

We designed a study with the overall aim of identifying the mechanism(s) by which maternal violent traumatic experience, in the context of a mother's other relational experience, might influence her perception, as marked by attributions toward her child and her behavior with her child. Toward this aim, we had two essential objectives.

First, we wanted to understand the relationship of the severity of maternal violent-trauma history during her childhood to maternal mental functioning, the latter both in terms of attachment as marked by mentalization or "reflective functioning" (Fonagy et al., 1997) and trauma-related psychopathology. Second, we wanted to understand how these factors (i.e., trauma severity, psychopathology, and reflective capacity) might impact on a negative and distorted maternal perception of her child, as marked by attributions both before and after single-session video feedback, using the principles of a standard infant–parent psychotherapy known as interaction guidance (McDonough, 1995).

To understand the relationship of the severity of maternal violent-trauma history to other variables, we defined interpersonal experiences of violent trauma clearly and conservatively, using a semistructured, clinician-administered questionnaire (Marshall et al., 1998). We considered that a subject had been physically abused during childhood if she reported that, before age 16, she had been hit by a caregiver with an object or hit and injured, in excess of what would be considered simple corporal punishment. A subject was considered to have been sexually abused during childhood if she reported that, before age 16, she had been fondled, placed in any form of genital contact, or penetrated by an individual at greater advantage due to power, size, or age. We considered a subject to have been exposed to domestic violence if she reported that, before age 16, she witnessed physical violence between household members involving a caregiver or other adult household member. We also measured experience of physical and sexual assault during adulthood (i.e., after age 16).

We then derived a "trauma-severity score" by adding together weighted factors such as age of onset, comorbidity of trauma, duration, frequency, proximity of relation to the perpetrator(s), and degree of injury. Maternal mental functioning was measured both in terms of current and lifetime symptomatology as well as degree of mentalization, operationalized as "reflective functioning." Reflective functioning (RF) is defined as the ability to think about possible intentions, thoughts, and feelings in one's own and in the other's mind (Slade, 2000).

RF has been empirically linked to maternal mental state with respect to attachment as well as to maternal sensitivity (Slade, 2002, in press). Developmentally, RF generally emerges during the fifth year of life, which is consistent with the development of theory of mind.

RF can be measured through coding of adult narrative on a scale of 0 to 9 (Fonagy et al., 1997). Originally developed for use in coding narratives from the Adult Attachment Interview, Slade et al. (2000) adapted the scale for use with maternal narratives on a parent-perception instrument. RF can be coded from 20 to 30 minutes of transcribed videotaped narrative. In this study, narratives in response to situations that called for pondering the thinking of self and other (i.e., noncontent items) on the "Working Model of the Child Interview," a standard parental-perception instrument (Zeanah and Benoit, 1995), were used to code RF.

The following mother's response to the clinician's probe, "What do you think is going on in your son's mind?" would be consistent with a low score (1): "I don't know. He's crazy."

By contrast, the following mother's response would be consistent with a high score (9): "I can't be sure, but I think that my son J is feeling frightened . . . because he knows that I don't leave him in a strange place. Maybe he also picks up on my feeling guilty that I am leaving him behind, because my feelings made me less available to him when he needed me to reassure him."

In terms of psychiatric symptomatology based on self-report, I focused on overall current psychiatric symptoms via the Basic Symptom Inventory (Derogatis and Melisaratos, 1983), depression via the Beck Depression Inventory (Beck, Rial, and Rickels, 1974), dissociative symptoms via the Hopkins Dissociative Symptom Inventory (Briere and Runtz, 1990) and posttraumatic stress symptoms via the Posttraumatic Stress Symptom Checklist–Short Version (Weathers et al., 1996). I also measured current and lifetime posttraumatic stress symptoms and disorder (continuously and categorically) based on clinician rating according to DSM-IV criteria via the Structured Clinical Interview for the DSM-IV (First et al., 1995).

To pursue my second objective, namely to understand factors predictive of negative and distorted maternal attributions before and after single-session video feedback, I operationalized negativity and distortion of maternal attributions and created a simple continuous measure of these two dimensions.

Whereas most mothers, when asked to give five adjectives that describe their young child's personality, as a content item on the Working Model of the Child Interview, will respond with adjectives such as *cute, playful, bright, loving, sweet,* the violence-exposed mothers more often tended to describe their children as *violent, controlling, mean, very strong, adultlike.* Again, these violent-trauma–associated attributions are given to the child who is perceived ambivalently as a threat. *Mean* and *badly behaved* we considered highly negative attributions. *Very strong* and *adultlike,* though not necessarily negative, were rated as "distorted," given that these adjectives represent an inflation of capacities not usually associated with very young children. *Violent* was rated both highly negative and distorted.

To rate these attributions, I devised a simple measure called the Maternal Attributions Rating Scale (MARS), consisting of a five-point Likert scale for each dimension: negativity and distortion. Along the scale, four Ph.D.-level clinicians and researchers with specialization in early childhood were able to rate five-adjective sets at baseline, after parent–child interaction involving separation–reunion and then after single-session video feedback. The four raters were naive to any clinical details or histories of the subjects beyond the age of the children in months. We achieved highly significant reliability among raters, along both dimensions.

Hypothetical Model

The study was designed to test the hypothetical model depicted in Figure 7–8. In the white box is a simplified version of the traumatized mother's mind, and to the right of that image is the prereflective young child in distress. This distressed child may represent one of a variety of possible posttraumatic triggers for the violence-exposed mother; others include ongoing domestic violence and other violent events, including the terrorist attacks of September 11, for those who were direct witnesses or who lost a loved one. These posttraumatic triggers are filtered through the mother's prior relational experience,

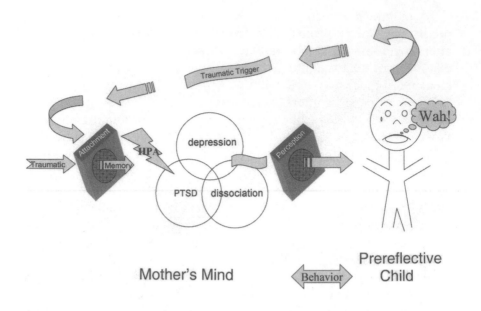

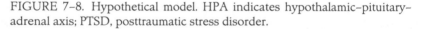

FIGURE 7–8. Hypothetical model. HPA indicates hypothalamic–pituitary–adrenal axis; PTSD, posttraumatic stress disorder.

operationalized as maternal mental state with respect to attachment, the latter marked in the study by RF.

I hypothesized that the security of attachment, positively correlated to RF, has the potential to buffer the individual from pathogenic effects of violent traumatic experience, depending on the severity of the trauma. The lower the RF and the greater the trauma, we expected, the greater impact on the physiologic stress-response system, otherwise known as the limbic (i.e., amygdala driven) hypothalamic–pituitary–adrenal axis, as marked by salivary cortisol level. The greater the stress, the more likely trauma-related psychopathology would be activated, including PTSD, dissociation, and depression. I furthermore hypothesized that maternal psychopathology, along with a history of violent trauma and insecurity of attachment, would adversely affect maternal perception.

The more negative and distorted the maternal perception, the more maternal behavior would reflect a fight ("frightening") or flight ("frightened") response to child cues, I hypothesized, leading paradoxically to increased child distress and behavioral disorganization. This vicious parent–child cycle is analogous to what Mechthild Papousek (2000)

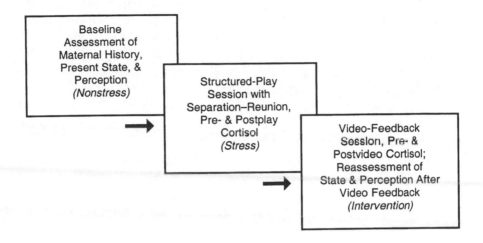

FIGURE 7-9. Three-visit protocol.

terms *Teufelkreis* ("devil's cycle"), spinning the parent–child system into greater disarray over time.

Testing

To test the hypothetical model, my research team and I studied an inner-city clinical sample at identified high risk for familial violence and maltreatment, using repeated measures according to the protocol described in Figure 7–9.

All biological mothers (66) and their children—ages eight to 50 months, who were registered or presented for evaluation at the Infant–Family Service, a hospital-based mental health clinic for very young children (ages zero to five years) and their families, between January 2000 and December 2001—were offered the opportunity to participate in the study. Families are referred to this clinical service by medical and mental health professionals, day care centers, and community social service agencies because of concerns about potential child abuse, neglect, or family violence. Entry criteria include a complaint by the mother or others, involving concern about potential or actual violence or disruptive behavior in self, child, or other household member.

Of those 66 contacted, 21 (32%) refused to participate, did not follow up in the clinic before signing informed consent, or were found on psychiatric screening not to meet entry criteria because of presence of psychotic symptoms, substance use, or not being a primary care-giver for most of their child's life. Forty-five mothers signed the consent form; one of these subsequently disclosed that she was the child's grandmother and not the biological mother, and one mother did not return after the first visit. The 43 remaining participant-mothers ranged in age from 19 to 45, with a mean age of 30. Their participating children ranged in age from eight to 50 months, with a mean age of 32 months. The sample included 88% Hispanics, largely of Dominican or Puerto Rican nationality, and thus 59% were immigrants. Those of American birth and similar descent made up 29% of the sample. An additional 12% were African American. Fifty-one percent of the sample was on public assistance; 52% had less than a high-school education; 67% were single mothers. This ethnic distribution approximates that found in the neighborhoods surrounding the medical center.

In their survey study of 475 New York City parents and their children four months after initial assessment following September 11, Stuber et al. (2002) found that children of single parents were 7.7 times more likely to suffer behavior problems and that inner-city Latino and African American children were 2.6 to 3.1 times more likely. Therefore, my study population was among the most vulnerable to the adverse effects from the terrorist attacks on the World Trade Center, as well as from the crash of flight 587 en route to the Dominican Republic, which occurred just more than two months after 9/11.

All 43 mothers in the sample shared in common a chief complaint involving violent, aggressive, or disruptive behavior of their preschool-age child or of another household member. Forty-one (95%) stated that they had had exposure to interpersonal violent trauma in childhood, adulthood, or both. (That is, they experienced physical or sexual abuse or domestic violence during childhood or physical or sexual assault in adulthood, or any combination of those experiences.) The remaining two mothers were excluded from this study, leaving a remaining N of 41.

Thirty-nine (95%) of these remaining 41 mothers reported clear histories of physical or sexual abuse or domestic violence (or any combination) before age 16. This very high rate of violent trauma we attributed, at least in part, to referral bias—the clinic was identified as serving families with young children at risk for abuse and neglect.

Most mothers in this victimized sample had experienced two or more of those forms of trauma. Of the 41 traumatized mothers, 88% stated that they had been physically abused; 76% stated that they had been physically abused by their own primary caregivers, often their mothers; 44% stated that they had been physically abused beginning before age five. Fifty-four percent of the traumatized mothers had experienced childhood sexual abuse, with 29% before age 10. Sixty-one percent of the traumatized mothers had been exposed to domestic violence during childhood. Twenty-nine (71%) of the 41 traumatized mothers reported clear histories of physical or sexual assault (or both) after age 16.

Additional factors that would support a description of this particular sample as "high risk" included high rates of maternal report of her young child being one of the three biggest current stressors in her life (59%), involvement in a child protective services investigation (39%), filing of restraining orders (32%), report of child's father being violent (39%), report of mother (self) being violent (37%), attempted suicide (34%), and lack of any perceived social supports (20%).

The PTSD rates in this sample were therefore quite high. Conservatively, we considered that a mother had current PTSD only if she self-rated as having current PTSD on the Posttraumatic Stress Symptom Checklist–Short Version in addition to having been rated by the clinician as having current PTSD on the Structured Clinical Interview for the DSM-IV (SCID). Even so, 24 (59%) of 41 met criteria for current PTSD, and 37 (90%) of 41 met criteria for lifetime PTSD on the SCID.

Findings

The sample showed a wide range of variability on measures of trauma severity and severity of current and lifetime psychopathology, but less so on the measure of reflective functioning. Although the reflective functioning scale ranges from 0 to 9 (Slade et al., 2000), the sample of 41 traumatized mothers had RF scores only from 0 to 5, with a mean of 3.2. Nevertheless, within this abbreviated low range there was substantial variability and within-group differences.

Severity of maternal violent-trauma history was positively and significantly correlated with overall psychiatric symptoms, as well as current and lifetime posttraumatic stress symptoms—particularly in the avoidance cluster. No significant relationship was found, however, between trauma severity and either depressive or dissociative symptoms.

Interestingly, we found no significant relationship between severity of maternal violent-trauma history and either degree of reflective functioning or negativity/distortion of maternal attributions.

We did find that both maternal trauma-related psychopathology as well as level of reflective functioning independently and synergistically predicted the degree of distortion and negativity of maternal attributions. There was no significant relationship between maternal RF and any form of psychopathology measured.

The degree of current depressive and posttraumatic stress symptoms— particularly the avoidance symptom cluster, in the context of lifetime PTSD, for the overwhelming majority of the sample—was positively and significantly correlated with the degree of distortion of maternal attributions. Similarly, the degree of current depressive symptoms alone, in the context of lifetime PTSD, was significantly and positively correlated with the degree of negativity of maternal attributions.

The degree of RF was negatively and significantly correlated with the degree of distortion and similarly but less significantly (i.e., at a trend level) correlated with the degree of negativity.

In a multiple-regression model considering predictors of degree of distortion of maternal attributions, the number of lifetime PTSD avoidance-cluster symptoms and the level of RF contributed synergistically and accounted for 18% of the variance.

Single-Session Video Feedback

Mothers were asked to return after the parent–child interaction assessment visit for a video-feedback session, which was videotaped using a split screen so as to observe the mother's facial expression in response to watching herself and her child on videotape. The video-feedback session took place two to four weeks after the observed play paradigm. The tapes were reviewed by the principal investigator, and four 30-second excerpts were picked. Before feedback, the mother was asked what she remembered as positive and negative interactions from the play. The clinician showed the optimal interactive moment (i.e., the most mutual joy, spontaneity, or joint attention) first. The mother was then asked for five descriptors of the child's personality (i.e., attributions).

The clinician then asked the mother what changed from those given during the previous two visits. The separation/reunion/play moments were then shown, followed by a similar interview. After each moment, the mother was asked, "What happened? What was going on in your/ your child's/the interviewer's mind? Does it remind you of anything?"

We hypothesized that, for traumatized mothers, the presence of the reflective clinician while watching the videotaped excerpts would lead to a reduction in the degree of negativity and distortion of maternal attributions toward the child, because the mother would be in a condition that supports her own affect regulation. In this less stressed condition, we expected that traumatized mothers would be better able to use their reflective capacity.

Several authors have described the use of video feedback in a supportive setting to promote behavioral change among "difficult-to-reach" caregivers who are preoccupied, dissociative, or otherwise resistant to parent–infant psychodynamic psychotherapy (Muir, 1992; McDonough, 1995; Cohen et al., 1999, 2002; Papousek, 2000; Zelenko and Benham, 2000; Beebe, in press). In a very brief intervention involving video feedback with high-risk dyads, Van den Boom (1994), Juffer and colleagues (Juffer, Hoksbergen, et al., 1997; Juffer, van Ijzendoorn, and Bakermans-Kranenburg, 1997), and Cohen and colleagues (Cohen, 2002; Cohen et al., 1999) have shown remarkable change that is sustained over time.

However, little to no empirical research has focused on mechanisms of psychic change afforded by the use of video feedback or on how use of video feedback can help to elucidate mechanisms of intergenerational communication of violent trauma.

I now describe changes in maternal attributions that we noted via repeated measures across visits as well as within the single session of video feedback.

Changes Across Visits

Measuring degrees of negativity and distortion of maternal attributions as described, I found that over the three experimental visits— baseline assessment, parent–child interaction, and single-session video feedback—both degrees of negativity and distortion of maternal attributions decreased significantly. In the case of negativity, significant reduction occurred only after the single session of video feedback.

Again, we found that higher reflective functioning was significantly and positively correlated with greater reduction of negativity, whereas an increased number of PTSD avoidance-cluster symptoms as well as depressive symptoms was negatively correlated with change. When we placed RF and PTSD avoidance into a multiple-regression model to predict degree of decrease of negativity, after controlling for baseline effects through analysis of regressed change, these two factors alone accounted independently and significantly for 21% of the variance.

These results imply that security of maternal attachment experience as marked by RF measured at the time of initial assessment not only serves as a protective factor with respect to violent trauma but also is associated with greater capacity to change during an intervention. Conversely, greater severity/number of avoidant symptoms related to PTSD mark greater risk and mitigate against change.

Further research is necessary to replicate these findings as well as to extend them by understanding what is necessary to sustain change as well as by understanding the relationship of change of perception to change of behavior.

Furthermore, we have presented results from only one form of perception measure, which relies on single-adjective or adjective-phrase attributions made at one time-point. Although this method has advantages because of its simplicity, it cannot capture the complexity of the context in which a mother might use a given descriptor and cannot capture the individual meaning of a given attribution to a given mother.

Despite these caveats, the results from this pilot study are compelling. One question remaining for clinicians who work over hundreds and thousands of sessions to effect change is: What permits any change over the course of such a brief intervention?

Change Within the Video-Feedback Session

The most elegant answer to this question comes from the participant mothers of our study. The following is an excerpt from a video-feedback session that highlights the importance of the traumatized, post-traumatically avoidant mother seeing her child's facial expression in the presence of the reflective therapist.

Ms. V is a 30-year-old unmarried mother of five children, ages three to nine. She has a history of domestic-violence exposure and physical abuse by her psychiatrically ill mother during childhood, as well as a history of physical assault and witnessing as an adult the murder of her boyfriend. She described her three-year-old son Kevin's personality with the following descriptors: *loving, caring, independent* (despite the complaint of severe separation anxiety), *moody, wants things his way.*

Both at the time of the initial interview and one year later, Ms. V described Kevin as reminding her of her own physically abusive mother. Listen to the following descriptions she used for describing her mother, one year after her aforementioned description of her son: *complicated and moody, helpful, controlling, a lot like Kevin, set in her ways.*

Ms. V suffers from marked current and lifetime PTSD and dissociative symptoms. Consider the following four brief video excerpts.

In the first excerpt, a separation episode from the mother–child interaction visit, Kevin tried to follow Ms. V out of the room as she tried to appease him, and he would not let her leave. Clearly distressed, he withdrew from the approaching stranger/research assistant who tried to calm him and collapsed at his mother's feet in a daze. Mother meanwhile stood back giggling and smiling anxiously.

In the second episode, Ms. V saw the beginning of the interview from the third visit, but before video feedback. She stated that what was most memorable from the previous visit is that she was asked to leave the room but could not, because as she put it, "Kevin would not let go of [her] leg."

She interpreted this "upset" as a sign of "trying to get away with something . . . trying to have things *his* way . . . and of feeling angry." In response to the question of how she was feeling at the time, Ms. V stated that she had been feeling "stressed."

In the third excerpt, Ms. V watched the video feedback of the separation as we were able to see her facial affect in response, via a mirror placed next to the television screen. Ms. V watched intently as Kevin grew increasingly distressed in the video. Her smile while watching faded, and she became serious and introspective. Following the video feedback, Ms. V stated, "I think he was scared. . . . Oh my God! That was a scary moment for him. He probably thought that I was leaving and wouldn't come back." In response to the question of how she was feeling at the time, Ms. V stated that she had not liked the idea of having to leave the room and had feared Kevin would cry.

In the final excerpt, Ms. V said that what allowed her to change her mind following the single-session video-feedback intervention was seeing the expression on Kevin's face that showed her that he was anxious.

When Ms. V, feeling stressed, anxiously laughed as her child collapsed with dread at the door, she was unable to see, feel, or contain her child's anxiety. Karlen Lyons-Ruth and colleagues (Lyons-Ruth, Bronfman, and Parsons, 1999a; Lyons-Ruth and Jacobvitz, 1999) have described this in their work on disorganized attachment. When a caregiver's self-regulation overrides mutual regulation while under stress, the child is left with a sense of loss and confusion. This is a result of the "ruptured bond" produced by trauma, which Myron Hofer, citing Bowlby, has described elegantly in his consideration of the effects of the London Blitz at macroprocess to microprocess levels of physiologic regulation in the context of recent attachment research (Hofer, this volume).

Ms. V, confronted with her child's negative affect as traumatic trigger, could only see her angry, abusive, controlling mother. On review of this excerpt, while jointly attending to her child with a reflective therapist, Ms. V could allow herself to join with her child and feel for his pain. She cannot only hear his cries, to paraphrase Selma Fraiberg (Fraiberg et al., 1975). Ms. V can see Kevin's face, and in so doing, assume a competent maternal role.

Summary

Ms. V's violent traumatic exposure with her own mother demanded to be told both to child and therapist via action and language in the course of routine separations and play, until it could be integrated, explicitly verbalized, and felt during video feedback. Kevin contributed to the variation of Ms. V's original trauma with her abusive, abandoning mother.

We are now beginning to look at maternal behavior more closely. Our preliminary analysis of maternal behavior data from the Atypical Maternal Behavior Instrument (AMBIANCE; Lyons-Ruth et al., 1999b) has found that 76% of the traumatized mothers display predominantly disrupted maternal communication. Exposure to any form of psychotherapy was significantly associated with a lower level of disrupted maternal communication. Thus, our pilot data provide strong support for looking more carefully at the interplay of reflective functioning and posttraumatic psychopathology as these factors affect maternal interactive behavior (i.e., that marked by disrupted maternal communication on the AMBIANCE) as the next important step. We now plan to take this next step with a carefully matched comparison group. This work is particularly exciting because it puts us on a pathway to developing effective evidence-based intervention strategies that will help break the cycles of intergenerational violence and violent trauma that have denied so many children a sense of safety in their bodies and minds, in their relationships, and—now particularly after September 11, in their world.

Acknowledgments

Portions of this chapter are based on a collaborative research effort involving the following individuals: Daniel S. Schechter, Charles H. Zeanah, Jr., Susan A. Brunelli, Michael M. Myers, Susan W. Coates, Michael R. Liebowitz, Randall D. Marshall, John F. Grienenberger, Tammy Kaminer, Patricia Baca, and Myron A. Hofer. I also acknowledge the grant support of the International Psychoanalytical Association Research Advisory Board, the American Academy of Child and Adolescent Psychiatry Pilot Research Award, the Lionel Ovesey Fund, and the Sackler Institute for Developmental Psychobiology at Columbia University.

References

Beck, A. T., Rial, W. Y. & Rickels, K. (1974), Short form of depression inventory: Cross-validation. *Psychol. Rep.*, 34:1184–1186.

Beebe, B. (2002), Brief mother–infant treatment: Psychoanalytically informed videofeedback. *Infant Ment. Health J.*

Benoit, D., Parker, K. C. & Zeanah, C. H. (1997), Mothers' representations of their infants assessed prenatally: Stability and association with infants' attachment classifications. *J. Child Psychol. Psychiat.*, 38:307–313.

Briere, J. & Runtz, M. (1990), Augmenting Hopkins SCL scales to measure dissociative symptoms: Data from two nonclinical samples. *J. Pers. Assess.*, 55:376–379.

Cohen, N. J., Lojkasek, M., Muir, E., Muir, R. & Parker, C. J. (2002), Six-month follow-up of two mother–infant psychotherapies: Convergence of therapeutic outcomes. *Infant Ment. Health J.*, 23:361–380.

———— Muir, E., Lojkasek, M., Muir, R., Parker, C. J., Barwick, M. & Brown, M. (1999), Watch, wait, and wonder. Testing the effectiveness of a new approach to mother–infant psychotherapy. *Infant Ment. Health J.*, 20: 429–451.

Derogatis, L. R. & Melisaratos, N. (1983), The Brief Symptom Inventory: An introductory report. *Psychol. Med.*, 13:595–605.

Egeland, B. & Susman-Stillman, A. (1996), Dissociation as a mediator of child abuse across generations. *Child Abuse Negl.*, 20:1123–1132.

First, M. B., Spitzer, R. L., Gibbon, M. & Williams, J. B. (1995), *Structured Clinical Interview for DSM-IV Axis I disorders.* Washington, DC: American Psychiatric Press.

Fonagy, P., Steele, M., Steele, H., Leigh, T., Kennedy, R., Mattoon, G. & Target, M. (1995), Attachment, the reflective self, and borderline states: The predictive specificity of the Adult Attachment Interview and pathological emotional development. In: *Attachment theory,* ed. S. Goldberg, R. Muir & J. Kerr. Hillsdale, NJ: The Analytic Press, pp. 233–278.

———— Target, M., Steele, M. & Steele, H. (1997), The development of violence and crime as it relates to security of attachment. In: *Children in a Violent Society,* ed. J. D. Osofsky. New York: Guilford Press, pp. 150–177.

Fraiberg, S., Adelson, E. & Shapiro, V. (1975), Ghosts in the nursery. A psychoanalytic approach to the problems of impaired infant–mother relationships. *J. Amer. Acad. Child Psychiat.*, 14:387–421.

Juffer, F., Hoksbergen, R. A., Riksen-Walraven, J. M. & Kohnstamm, G. A. (1997), Early intervention in adoptive families: Supporting maternal sensitive responsiveness, infant–mother attachment, and infant competence. *J. Child Psychol. Psychiat.*, 38:1039–1050.

———— van Ijzendoorn, M. H. & Bakermans-Kranenburg, M. J. (1997), Intervention in transmission of insecure attachment: A case study. *Psychol. Rep.*, 80:531–543.

Laor, N., Wolmer, L. & Cohen, D. J. (2001), Mothers' functioning and children's symptoms 5 years after a Scud missile attack. *Amer. J. Psychiat.*, 158:1020–1026.

Lieberman, A. F. (1997), Toddlers' internalization of maternal attributions as a factor in quality of attachment. In: *Attachment and Psychopathology,* ed. L. Atkinson & K. J. Zucker. New York: Guilford Press.

———— (1999), Negative maternal attributions: Effects on toddlers' sense of self. *Psychoanal. Inq.*, 19:737–756.

Lyons-Ruth, K., Bronfman, E. & Parsons, E. (1999a), Atypical attachment in infancy and early childhood among children at developmental risk: IV.

Maternal frightened, frightening, or atypical behavior and disorganized infant attachment patterns. *Monogr. Soc. Res. Child Devel.*, 64:67–96.

———— ———— & ———— (1999b), Maternal frightened, frightening, or atypical behavior and disorganized infant attachment patterns. *Monogr. Soc. Res. Child Devel.*, 64:67–96.

———— & Jacobvitz, D. (1999), Attachment disorganization: Unresolved loss, relational violence, and lapses in behavioral and attentional strategies. In: *Handbook of Attachment,* ed. J. Cassidy & P. R. Shaver. New York: Guilford Press, pp. 520–555.

Marshall, R. D., Schneier, F. R., Fallon, B. A., Knight, C. B., Abbate, L. A., Goetz, D., Campeas, R. & Liebowitz, M. R. (1998), An open trial of paroxetine in patients with noncombat-related, chronic posttraumatic stress disorder. *J. Clin. Psychopharmacol.*, 18:10–18.

Martin, S. L., Moracco, K. E., Garro, J., Tsui, A. O., Kupper, L. L., Chase, J. L. & Campbell, J. C. (2002), Domestic violence across generations: Findings from northern India. *Internat. J. Epidemiol.*, 31:560–572.

McDonough, S. C. (1995), Promoting positive early parent–infant relationships through interaction guidance. *Child Adolesc. Clin. North Amer.*, 4: 661–672.

Muir, E. (1992), Promoting positive early parent–infant relationships through interaction guidance. *Infant Ment. Health J.*, 13:319–328.

Oliver, J. E. (1993), Intergenerational transmission of child abuse: Rates, research, and clinical implications. *Amer. J. Psychiat.*, 150:1315–1324.

Papousek, M. (2000), Der Gebrauch von Video Feedback in der Eltern-Kind Beratung und Psychotherapie [Use of video feedback in parent–infant counseling and psychotherapy]. *Prax Kinderpsychol. Kinderpsychiatr.*, 49: 611–627.

Pfefferbaum, B., Nixon, S. J., Tucker, P. M., Tivis, R. D., Moore, V. L., Gurwitch, R. H., Pynoos, R. S. & Geis, H. K. (1999), Posttraumatic stress responses in bereaved children after the Oklahoma City bombing. *J. Amer. Acad. Child Adolesc. Psychiat.*, 38:1372–1379.

Schechter, D. S. (in press), Intergenerational communication of violent traumatic experience within and by the dyad: The case of a mother and her toddler. *J. Infant Child Adolesc. Psychother.*

———— Brunelli, S. A., Cunningham, N., Brown, J. & Baca, P. (in press), Mother–daughter relationships and child sexual abuse: A pilot study of 35 mothers and daughters (ages 1–9 years). *Bull. Menn. Clin.*

———— Coates, S. W. & First, E. (2002), Observations of acute reactions of young children and their families to the World Trade Center attacks. *Bull. Zero to Three*, 22:9–13.

Schuengel, C., Bakermans-Kranenburg, M. J. & Van, I. M. H. (1999), Frightening maternal behavior linking unresolved loss and disorganized infant attachment. *J. Consult. Clin. Psychol.*, 67:54–63.

Schuster, M. A., Stein, B. D., Jaycox, L., Collins, R. L., Marshall, G. N., Elliott, M. N., Zhou, A. J., Kanouse, D. E., Morrison, J. L. & Berry, S. H. (2001), A national survey of stress reactions after the September 11, 2001 terrorist attacks. *N. Engl. J. Med.*, 345:1507–1512.

Slade, A. (2000), The development and organization of attachment: Implications for psychoanalysis. *J. Amer. Psychoanal. Assn.*, 48:1147–1174.

_____ (2002), Keeping the baby in mind: A critical factor in perinatal mental health. *Bull. Zero to Three*, 22:10–16.

_____ (in press), Holding the baby in mind: A discussion of Joseph Lichtenberg's paper. *Psychoanal. Inq.*

_____ Bernbach, E., Grienenberger, J., Levy, D. & Locker, A. (2000), *Addendum to Reflective Functioning Scoring Manual.* New York: City University of New York, Department of Psychology.

Stuber, J., Galea, G. & Fairbrother, F. (2002), The mental health of New York City families after September 11, 2001. Presented at Columbia University Child Psychiatry Grand Rounds, New York State Psychiatric Institute, New York City, September 11.

U.S. Department of Health and Human Services (2000), *Child Maltreatment 2000: Reports from the States to the National Child Abuse and Neglect Data System.* Washington, DC: U.S. Government Printing Office.

_____ (2002), *In Harm's Way: Domestic Violence and Child Maltreatment.* Washington, DC: U.S. Government Printing Office.

Van den Boom, D. C. (1994), The influence of temperament and mothering on attachment and exploration: An experimental manipulation of sensitive responsiveness among lower-class mothers with irritable infants. *Child Devel.*, 65:1457–1477.

Weathers, F. W., Litz, B. T., Keane, T. M., Herman, D. S., Steinberg, H. R., Huska, J. A. & Kraemer, H. C. (1996), The utility of the SCL-90-R for the diagnosis of war-zone related posttraumatic stress disorder. *J. Trauma Stress*, 9:111–128.

Zeanah, C. H. & Benoit, D. (1995), Clinical applications of a parent perception interview in infant mental health. *Child Adolesc. Psychiat. Clin. North Amer.*, 4:539–554.

_____ & Zeanah, P. D. (1989), Intergenerational transmission of maltreatment: Insights from attachment theory and research. *Psychiatry*, 52: 177–196.

Zelenko, M. & Benham, A. (2000), Videotaping as a therapeutic tool in psychodynamic infant–parent therapy. *Infant Ment. Health J.*, 21:192–203.

Chapter 8

Relational Mourning in a Mother and Her Three-Year-Old After September 11

Adrienne Harris

This moving clinical account of a mother who lost her husband in the World Trade Center is a remarkable illustration of how a parent can help her children adapt to an irreparable loss. The creative ways in which this mother copes with her own trauma while simultaneously helping her children negotiate theirs makes for a humanly stirring and a clinically illuminating demonstration of the operation of attachment-related capabilities, like reflective functioning, in a real-life tragedy. The reader grasps how the mother's spontaneous strategies for helping her children will enable them to keep the internal representation of their father alive for years to come. Not only a contribution to our understanding of how loss can be made bearable, this narrative also alerts the clinician to the relational fabric entailed in the kind of successful mourning that allows an individual to create and keep a sense of attachment to a memory.

Life dealt Pam, the mother of three- and one-year-old girls,[1] a tragic and shocking blow when her husband was killed on September 11. I tell Pam's clinical story to open up a consideration of the powerful, hard work that underlies a family's grieving, a process I am calling *relational mourning*. Like many clinicians, I have often listened to an adult patient giving a history that has, at its core, some significant early loss of a parent. Very frequently, all representation of that parent disappeared, and all too often the surviving, grief-stricken parent "disappeared" emotionally as well. The depression in the surviving parent feels to the child like another abandonment.

The material I present here is about the extraordinary challenges and difficulties in mourning and accepting death, for adults and children. My case illustrates that the potential for working through the extreme developmental challenges of grieving is enabled by exceptional capacities in the parent. This is a study of a process of mourning in children and their mother, a woman deeply committed to their fullest survival and emotional well-being. It is also a clinical story, an account of the containment and complex affective entrainments[2] I established with Pam in the context of shared trauma. New to therapy but very psychologically minded, Pam drew on me as a steadying partner who could reflect and help her contain her pain while she was beginning to find and make meaning in the wake of a stunning and unexpected loss. I think it is also important that I was a therapeutic partner who was also shaken by fears and the effects of a traumatic shock, though at a less acute and threatening level.

As Rees so eloquently notes in her chapter in this volume, both partners in clinical dyads were in deep shock in those post-9/11 weeks and months. For clinicians and patients, early losses and anxieties, any prior vulnerability, and trauma were conjured up by the intense amalgam of experiences we code as 9/11. This context, so multilayered, so public, and yet so uniquely individual, deeply affected my

---

[1] I have changed the names of the parents and children here.

[2] The term *entrainment* comes from the infancy work of Sander (2002) and describes the patterns of resonance, coherence, and multilevel mirroring that characterize early dyadic systems. These archaic patterns of mutual attunement can arise in new dyads. They are deep aspects of the processes of mutual recognition (Benjamin, 1998) and are aspects of what can be established in a therapeutic alliance (Beebe and Lachmann, 2002).

clinical capacities in ways that were sometimes enhancing and sometimes compromising. Like many clinicians, I was working under unusual conditions of arousal, vigilance, dissociation, and aliveness.

The loss of a parent is obviously a crisis for an entire family system. Death and loss always present cognitive and emotional challenges, requiring a significant developmental leap. The severity of this developmental demand is captured in the distinction Freud (1917) made between mourning and melancholia. In melancholy, remnants of denial and continuing idealization of the lost love remain in a kind of haunting. Mourning is, most agonizingly, the work to accept death's finality and to metabolize the experience of loving and losing a significant person into a deep loving and loveable aspect of the self. Mourning, in these terms, is a kind of double loss. Finally, Freud argued, in the resolution of an act of mourning, even the vitality of the memorialized other is absorbed into the self. Only then is the mourner free to love again, though not without some lingering melancholic strain.

Melancholy has the odd effect of foreclosing acceptance of loss, maintaining the bereaved person in a suspended state unable to invest love and attachment in new experiences and relationships. In melancholic grieving, the lost love is memorialized but also kept "alive" imaginatively and in fantasy. Abraham and Torok (1994) capture this process in what they term the "fantasy of the exquisite corpse," the potent conviction that the lost other is perfectly preserved somewhere, waiting to be found. These fantasies bind the mourner into a sometimes endlessly self-berating transitional state, tied to the living dead, as Green describes in the case of the "dead mother" (Green, 1970).

What is required of a person to represent the lost object as lost? This is deep psychic work, entailing a thought process utterly dependent on emotional capacities in oneself and one's surrounding communities or family. There is a complex interweaving of melancholy and mourning, a continuing shift between acceptance and denial, an interweaving of fantasy and reality. Melancholic preoccupations, nostalgia, and ghostly sweet presences enrich psychic life. They are necessary and creative respites for the grueling ordeal of mourning. In the case I will be describing, certain kinds of melancholic preoccupations, suspending reality for imaginative longing, were particularly crucial in Pam's young children for their developing capacities to absorb loss.

We are learning from studies of children with separation anxieties and traumatic loss how dependent their own reactions are to the reactions of their parents, in particular the parental capacities to be containing of intense and terrifying affects (Bowlby, 1960; Cain and Fast, 1972; Fonagy and Target, 2000, this volume; Coates, this volume; Schachter, this volume). Pam had the daunting task of both protecting her children from emotional flooding and from the anxieties that they might lose her to depression. She had to reach out and create means of expression for their feelings, while in great emotional agony herself. When Green wrote about the "dead mother," he made clear that he was speaking of a mother not actually dead but dead to her child because, caught up in a bereavement, her vitality was reserved for and channeled toward the lost object. Pam needed to allow a deep engagement with her lost husband in a way that safely included her children, all the while firmly embedding them in a living world with her.

There is the triple consciousness of processing what is lost, what endures, and what thrives. There is the task of coordinating witnessing for others and making space for those aspects of loss that arise in that part of the self Winnicott termed *incommunicado*—private but not isolated. There is the need to balance concern for self and for others. It is these dimensions of grief that lead me to use the term *relational mourning.*

Fonagy and Target (this volume) point out the complex situation for families who suffered losses on September 11. On one hand, secure attachment can profoundly help any child in the process of stress regulation. Yet the rupture of a powerfully felt strong attachment is devastating. It is paradoxically as though strong attachment is both an abiding strength and a place of deep vulnerability. This has consequences for thought and feeling. From much evidence, we know that secure attachment is an important substrate for reflective mentalization. Fonagy (1997) and Fonagy and Target (1996, 1997, 2000) conceptualize the overriding function of an interpersonal interpretive mechanism as a capacity in the adult that will greatly influence the child's capacity to develop this function as well. The emergence of this capacity will enable the maintenance of focus on one's own subjective experiences, as well as the thoughts and feelings of others. This work requires what Fonagy and Target term an *intentional stance,* or being able to imagine the "aboutness" of another's experience. The child must be seen not solely as object but as subject, and this is the precondition of the child's own development of the capacity to mentalize. It depends on conditions of fundamental respect for the other's point of view, and an ability to understand an experience that is different from one's own. These capacities seem deeply connected to strong and secure experiences of attachment (Fonagy and Target, 1997; Beebe and Lachmann, 2002).

Relational psychoanalysts (Mitchell, 2000), focused on the intersubjective dimensions of experiences in various dyads, would render this process of mentalization as the cocreation of self and self and other. Speaking of the process of discovering the subjectivity in the other, Benjamin (1998) has been theorizing the emergence of mutual recognition in the context of keeping a delicate balance between drawing on a parental object and recognizing that parent's individual subjectivity. This is a bidirectional process making great demands for complex integrations of contradictory feelings and experiences as an ongoing evolution in child and parent.

All these processes become profoundly at risk under conditions of traumatic loss. The clinical and personal quandaries might be phrased as follows: there is a challenge to grow dramatically in capacities to integrate thought and feeling in a situation that threatens thought and feeling at every level. Grief is inherently a self-absorbing process, so the particular challenge for a parent is to be able to understand children's experience at a moment when one's own needs are so intense. In this clinical case, I believe I have been witnessing and helping in the negotiation of traumatic loss by the containing adult and the children under very fortuitous conditions. Pam, in her adult character, shows so many signs of her own history of secure attachments, and her children came into this shocking situation after solid, good beginnings. It makes a great difference.

I want particularly to draw on Coates and colleagues' work at the Kids' Corner at Pier 94, where they interacted with and supported children and families who had lost a family member in the World Trade Center attack (see their chapter in this volume). What emerges from their observations and interventions is the complexity of knowing and not knowing about the fate and death of someone in one's family. Coates and her coworkers describe many striking examples of children's acute capacities to sense and understand what had happened to that lost parent. These capacities for imagination and reflection and curiosity were not always recognized by the survivors. The opportunity to represent and give voice to losses and their quite unique and complex meanings needs a context. Parental mourning can shape the potential for integration or dissociation, as a child explores feelings, questions, and stray fantasies, however odd or unsettling.

Bowlby's (1960) very important and initially controversial thinking on this matter is relevant here. He wanted psychoanalysts to see that many of the experiences of mourning—depression, rage, and separation anxiety—are normative. He also wanted to illuminate the deep experience of loss that children are capable of registering. He felt the need to educate parents and mental health workers on the requirements for care and relief of children experiencing grief in the wake of separations and sudden traumatic losses. It is a lesson we are still absorbing and developing (see Frankiel, 1995, for an exploration of work on object loss and on children's mourning).

Clinical Material

I have been working for almost a year with Pam, the mother of three-year-old Sarah and one-year-old Catherine. The family lost its husband and father, Chris, who worked on a high floor in the second tower. Coming into therapy a month after 9/11, Pam was concerned with how to shape things for her children and to find a living experience in which she could hold the memory of her husband and the father of her children for herself and her family.

The work of Myron Hofer (1984, 1996, this volume) on the biological consequences of bereavement and separation shows very dramatically that the sudden violent loss of a parent and spouse is shocking to a family at deep somatic and biological levels. As he traces the disruption of what he terms *hidden regulators* of human, particularly parent–child, interactions, Hofer's work seems particularly relevant in this case, where the loss was in a new and young family with a breast-feeding infant still in her parent's bedroom and an active toddler learning the routines of preschool and practicing separations. Nursing and sleep cycles, separations and reunions were evolving and enmeshing at deep physiological levels in this closely knit foursome. Ruptured rhythms in the subtle ecosystem of living, breathing, sleeping, and eating are part of the massive reaction to loss. These disruptions become part of the procedural memory of traumatic loss within the family and in all the individuals.

In the clinical material that follows, I track Pam's work to mourn while simultaneously trying to steady her children, particularly her older daughter. This mother allowed and facilitated mourning in many modalities—pictures, music and song, physical activities of play and sports, stories and joint narratives built with her child.

The work Pam did was attuned to the developmental levels of the children, but she also understood that they would have to make big developmental leaps to even begin to metabolize and find ways to cope with this traumatic change. I have thought of her determination to have her children survive well and her commitment that they not be damaged irreparably by the death of their father as, in part, a deep identification with her determined, active husband.

Chris had spoken to her from the second tower twice after the first plane hit. He told her that others were leaving his floor and that he was staying. She remembers urging him to "run." After the second tower was hit, she was never able to reach him on the phone again. Her initial shock response was to pack a suitcase with his clothing and to have a neighbor take a picture of her and the girls that might be shown to him if he were in a hospital.

Fantasy and reality ran alongside each other. Melancholic imagining and hard-core acceptance of death go hand in hand. In a very few days, she accepted that the fantasy she had harbored to make matters bearable, a fantasy that Chris had been injured and had lost memory and speech and would be found somewhere on a hospital gurney, was an empty hope. She describes the unpacking of that suitcase as excruciatingly hard.

The act of unpacking, she thought, was perhaps the first concrete action in which she truly acknowledged to herself that he was dead. But this first representation of a death remained, for a while, quite shaky. She did not want phone calls in the first weeks because she could not protect herself from the thought that it was him.

This is a somewhat religious family, and so the first way Pam represented and spoke with her children about the loss of their father was to draw on her background creating a "heaven" in their shared fantasies, a place where he could be "alive" in the family's imaginations. Interestingly, heaven was imagined as a place up high. This seemed to me important, not only to carry the memory that the husband was on a very high floor but also to capture his function as overseeing and protecting.

Three-year-old Sarah has taken to this idea very intensely. She holds up pictures she is drawing for him to see. She sings to him. She speaks to him. On her mother's birthday, she announced the news of this birthday to her father. Chris was a young father, deeply enthusiastic, with an active hands-on involvement with his children. He expected to meet his child after her first day at school. Sarah often speaks to him during her walk there. He spent the last night of his life at Yankee Stadium with Sarah, waiting to see if the rain would lift and Roger Clemens would get his 20th win. This was an important game, and he wanted to be with his family. When Pam told me this anecdote, it was in the context of describing a man who was confident and enthusiastic about developing a rich family life. Sports, travel, and outings were all experiences that he lived actively and intensely with his young children.

Throughout the first year since Chris's death, Sarah and her mother talked about him, the mother both eliciting and scaffolding memories. Sarah had little shards of memory of her father that came up spontaneously. Pam elaborated on these details to create narratives and storylines, drawing on the natural forms of conversation that parents and children use, as complex symbolic language comes online developmentally (Locke, 1993). Katherine Nelson (1985) used the term *scripts* to describe the little scenes and stories that parents build with children to expand the child's knowledge and repertoire.

This communicative pattern was used to help Sarah (and Pam) hold reliable and replicable narratives about Chris. Many daily events required a discussion of his presence and participation. Only then could he be represented as absent. The family made adventurous summer trips, and Pam and Sarah revisited that last summer experience in conversations. Sarah could produce some details of narrative—"Daddy went for coffee across the street"—and her mother could then elaborate and expand on her child's experience. Taking that element, Pam would extend the story, describing walks, outings, and activities the family did together, noting how Chris's morning coffee was woven into the family's day. Pam is making narrative memories, scenes that could be held in mind for both herself and Sarah. For Sarah, memories of Chris are strengthened and solidified, and simultaneously the loss of her father was established as a fact for her.

As Rees suggests, a current emotional climate enters narrative memory, making both new memories and altering old emotional memories. Representations are woven in narratives and systems of meaning, what Kurt Fischer has termed a *constructive web* (Fischer et al., 1997), and clearly this has had enormously vital emotional resonance for Pam and Sarah. It must also be a very complex experience for Sarah in that in these conversations and storytelling she is with her mother, who is both animated and revived by these memories but simultaneously saddened by them. The presence of a child to care for can be an opportunity to craft lovely memories. It also occasions many moments of searing pain.

Pictures have been very much part of the way Pam was to build and facilitate the complex representation of a father that was lost but whose influence and presence continue. From the beginning, this vision of a father who was competent, loved competence in others, and lived with enthusiasm and determination was an influence Pam was interested in preserving for her and the girls. Pam has been worried about how to bring her youngest child, Catherine, into this process. How would she and Catherine create the shared experience of remembering, loving, and losing? She has put many pictures of Chris around the apartment, and certainly he was spoken of freely and frequently. As Catherine grew over this year and began to speak, pointing at her dad's photo and saying "Dad" became part of the experience of learning language. Pam found a picture of the baby taken, on a summer family outing, from the front seat of the car. Seeing how much this child looks like her father, she writes on the picture, "This is what your father saw when he looked at you." This particular representation of a father to a child who has such slender direct experience of her father seems very interesting to me.

Pam, in a sense, offered a vision to her youngest child of a father who held her in mind, a vision of a parent who could recognize her, who thought about her. I see this as an effort to provide this child with an experience of being mentalized, thought about, and known. This is the core of reflective functioning. Pam maintained for herself and the children the experience of parents collaborating for their children. With each developmental milestone, Pam evoked the delight the father would have been feeling for both children: "Daddy would be so proud of you." It is an evocation of the way Chris felt about his children and a creative envisioning of a protective and observant parent.

One day very early on in the fall, Sarah was in her bath. Perhaps because Chris was so actively involved in her care, including bathing, this was a setting where bodily memories of her father's presence were conjured up. She asked Pam her repeated question. "When is he coming home?" Pam answered simply but with tears in her eyes that he can't come home, that he has been injured and has died. She also says how much she wishes he could be with them. Sarah then began to sing and clap and made up a song about "Daddy not coming back." For Pam, it was a very complex moment. Was Sarah defending against her mother's affect? Was this an anxious mastery? Did songs at bath time particularly evoke her father for Sarah so that she held him alive in her play while singing about his absence? I was impressed, as I have been much of the time in this treatment, by this mother's ability to tolerate and support all the modalities her child needed to absorb this new reality.

One evening, Sarah asks her mother if there is a door in heaven. Pam, with some private uncertainty, says, "Yes, there could be." The child then says, "Well, if there is a door, couldn't Daddy open it and run out?" Had Sarah held in mind her mother's alarmed command on the phone to her husband to run? To follow Coates's thinking on this matter (this volume), children are astute registers of experiences, particularly ones in which a beloved parent is deeply affected. I wondered if Sarah had held that quite intense affect-laden expression and integrated the detail with what she knew of her athletic vital father. He is represented even in heaven as she experienced him.

But later Sarah sees a dead squirrel on the road and asks what is the matter with it. The concepts of "dead," "heaven," and "injured" come up again. How will she parse out these competing representations? Was her father dead like that squirrel? Pam tells me that when she speaks to the child she is trying to be careful with verb tenses. What is to be spoken of as past and what as ongoing? How subtle these representations are! Mother and child are beginning to coordinate experiences that were initially mapped quite distinctly. Animals, running, father, husband: how are these schemes to be integrated with dying, with dead animals, with falling towers?

These representations have elements that can barely be tolerated as joined up, integrated ideas. This is cognitive work, of course, but there are crucial and intense emotional and social braces that must undergird these thoughts. The conception or representation of Daddy—

husband and father—is very complexly held as living and not living, injured and whole, remembered and missing. There is a representation of a continuing father who loved, encouraged, protected. Robert Pynoos (2001), discussing the impact on a child of violent loss of a parent, describes the ripping off of a parental shield, a protective capacity. Hamilton (1989) has written of the loss of the "mantle of safety," what we know to be a crucial ingredient of psychic functioning. Indeed, this mantle is a crucial ingredient of the very capacity to think, reflect, and feel.

As weeks go by, Pam is clearly taking up that protective role herself, using memory and representation to make a protective shield for herself and offering it to the children. Often, the image of parental care appears in the family, in Pam's dreams and in the children's actions, as an arm wrapped around a shoulder. Sarah puts her arm around her sister one day at lunch when Pam is tearful. "Mommy, Catherine and I miss Daddy, but we are not crying." Note the adult way she talks as well as the protection she offers her younger sister, an act that both identifies with her parents and perhaps vicariously soothes her by soothing her sister.

For Pam, it is important to represent both love and loss, and so she acknowledges that she is crying and in simple terms she says why. She is crying, she says, because she misses Daddy. Later, while taking a walk, she cries in the street. Then she imagines Chris holding her hand and then putting his arm around her. Often in her fantasies of him, he is encouraging her, telling her he is proud of her. This is calming. Later in a session, as she wept and told me these experiences, she remembered the girls holding hands in the backseat of the van on a family outing. In this fantasy, her husband is driving and she feels soothed.

There are complex layers of protection and containment operating. One of my containing functions, I believe, has been to tolerate myself and help Pam tolerate the deep contradictions and rapid shifts in her states. One minute she is a deeply competent parent, the next minute she could feel numbed and bereft. She felt genuinely grateful for the outpourings of help, and she could resent and feel swamped by these gestures. She could be angry at the indifference in the world or the smooth ease of intact families. She was shopping in a supermarket late one evening, walking through the aisles weeping. She noticed someone looking at her, and she shouted angrily, "I am crying because my husband died, okay?" We decided that under the circumstances it was all right to shout in Gristede's. People have doubtless shouted in the grocery store before. Perhaps she will be shouting there or somewhere else again. We are making complex representational spaces, jointly imagined scenes and narratives, in which a kaleidoscope of feelings and wishes and thoughts can coexist.

More and more, Pam is the competent protector, literally and figuratively. She is the driver in the front seat. After a difficult day and troubled sleep, she had a first dream in which Chris appears. In the dream, he said to her, "Who will we give the crib to?" She reminded him whom it belongs to. In our session, she associated the girls growing to the question of who will disassemble the crib. But the dream was set in the future when the one-year-old will have outgrown her crib. This is a future she could only sometimes carry her husband into, especially with Catherine, who was not old enough to have a narrative memory of her dad. There was also hidden in the dream the thought that there will be no more babies, and although this had been their plan, that idea then carried her grief and sense of loss.

The opportunity for the children to know and remember their father is encouraged but not pressured. Pam is sensitive to the children's pacing. This is a family that grieves and lives. Children go on play dates, spend weekends with family and friends. They have lessons and do sports. Pam had determined to spend these early years with a young family primarily at home, and she now orchestrates those old plans with the needs for some more child care and more time for herself. Sarah has learned to ride a bike this year and to do cannonballs at the lake near the family vacation home. The youngest child, who was still breast-feeding on September 11, is becoming an active toddler, so there are time-outs and plenty of moments of exasperation.

Pam has the normal exhaustion of a mother of young children. But her exhaustion is also shaped by extreme psychological demands. Pam was recounting a particularly ragged week for herself and the children, and as we went over her experiences it was clear that part of the raggedness came from the acute pain of emptying a chest of drawers that held Chris's clothing. This project brought her back to a more intimate connection with his body, stirring up a lot of memory and sadness. My role here is as protector and guide. At times, I function as an arm draped over her shoulder, a supportive voice in her head, helping her to make a space for herself, for the unique and delicate

feelings that can arise, almost without warning, from the many expected and unexpected tasks of mourning.

There have been limits in Pam's processing. I have noticed that certain
doors are shut in Pam, and I have felt them shut in me. We have rarely
talked about the circumstances of her husband's death, of what happened
after the second plane hit, an event she saw on the television but cannot
yet represent or easily integrate with other representations of him. She
could sometimes hold a terrible sense of his fear, imagining how terrified
he must have been at the end. But she has not very frequently pursued
or allowed herself to dwell on a more detailed fantasy.

Around the circumstances of death, Pam is using dissociation
adaptively. Part of this is the particular context of the September 11
deaths. There has been a great deal of public discussion of vaporized
bodies, of dismemberment. Pam and her family had to decide about
samples for DNA testing. Thinking about the fate of Chris's body,
which has never been recovered, has required extreme measures of
coping, measures that require knowing and not knowing, feeling and
repressing. I have often felt my work with Pam is in supporting her
own unique pace and emerging representations.

One influence on my thinking here has been Kurt Fisher's dynamic-
skills theory (Fischer et al., 1997; Fischer and Bidell, 1998; Fischer and
Watson, 2002). Along with Fonagy's theory of reflective functioning
and the conception of knowing another mind and being mentalized
as a key aspect to psychic growth, I find Fischer's work on the need to
integrate representation and emotion and action very useful. He also
authored a particularly key idea in regard to psychopathology. He
suggests we think not of arrest or fixation or immaturity but of unique
configurations of skills and adaptations. Dissociation and negotiating
the complex organizations of fragmented internal worlds are skilled
emotional processes. In a family's mourning, dissociation can be a
crucial survival skill.

Pam's process of mourning has its own time lines and moves along
multiple narrative sequences. As 2002 unfolded, each first post-9/11
encounter with birthdays, anniversaries, and holidays brought a shocking revival of acute grief. Opening a family summer house made Pam
feel that Chris had been barely gone a week. And paradoxically, as Pam
moved into the world and developed some new work projects, those
experiences opened new aspects of loss. There was a stretching future,

sometimes terrifyingly empty, sometimes a matter of curiosity, and there was a shrinking, foreshortened past.

In the early months, Pam missed her husband in the quotidian work of child care—an extra pair of hands loading the van or shepherding children to their activities. Later she had to integrate the experiences of loss into other life projects. Getting dressed in business clothes going to a meeting, she registered her husband's absence as a dinner companion, as someone to meet up with after work, as a lover. There has been the ever more exacting cognitive/emotional demand to integrate the representation of the way she has been coping, managing, and enduring and even, reluctantly, representations of coming to life as a woman with a body. These experiences have to be held together with ongoing pain and her ever deepening sense of loss. The mental mappings become more complex.

At Christmas when the time came to hang up stockings, Sarah wanted to include one for her father. She and Pam imagined the scene: tree, stockings, presents. In the morning when they speak of the stockings, Sarah asks, "Will there be presents for Daddy?" Pam decides to say no. She explains again that he is in heaven and is not able to be with them. Then she asks if Sarah thinks Daddy has a stocking in heaven. Sarah says no.

One interesting question here is which fantasy is tolerable and which is not. Was Sarah becoming more able to integrate the reality of her father's loss? Does the closing of imaginative space by her mother who says, in effect, that there will not be presents for Daddy shut down the child? Did Sarah feel a moment of loss that eclipsed fantasy, a moment when sadness and pain broke through along with reality? Pam and Sarah had made a transitional space in which the father could participate in this ritual. Had that space collapsed for the child? Or was the image of stockings in heaven too abstract for Sarah to represent? One aspect of this experience I found important is that Sarah was allowed to explore her own mind, to have an experience different than her mother. She did not have to comply or feel taken over by what Pam was conjuring up or interpreting.

Several months later, Sarah goes with her sister to the door to the family apartment after hearing sounds in the hallway. She says to the neighbor she meets, who is going to work, "Catherine thinks when there is noise in the hallway that Daddy is coming back. I know he isn't because he was in World Trade Two." Pam scoops up the children and hopes ruefully that her neighbor would not be freaked out. She felt a little embarrassed; but as she and I work in session on this powerful episode, we talk about splitting and dissociating as a kind of helpful skill, managing the tempo of acceptance and working through. We talked first about the division in Sarah of the parts that know and the parts that don't know. Pam had felt some embarrassment regarding her neighbor, an embarrassment she sometimes felt about her too-public widowhood generally.

One aspect of mourning that is worth thinking about here is the odd ways that shame can accrue to loss. Pam has had some worries about how she is seen, what people make of her experience and the children's. Our work has been to support and contain her intuitive capacities to let the children feel and speak. She and I talk about the individuality of mourning, the deep privacy of personal grief, its unique forms and meanings. Often we try to hold together the incredible contradictions in this experience. Sarah may have projected a hope she fears is babyish into her little sister and kept for herself what she feels is a more grown-up experience. Pam, at the end of this particular session, says, "But that is me, too. I have those thoughts; I have that split in me."

Dissociation is a skill, Fischer argues. Splitting is a crucial aspect of the psychic work of mourning. Bearing absolute loss must be done in doses, particularly in the experience with children whose narrative memories of the lost parent must be simultaneously built and grieved. Insight and reality are won and lost hour by hour, day by day.

Pam has accepted and organized these contradictory states that Sarah oscillates in and out of. But part of this reflective capacity is to see the continuing aspects of denial and disbelief and the slow pace of accepting reality. Loss remains known and not known, held and resisted by her and Sarah. Pam lives in a kind of double consciousness. One feature of the shifting is that even adaptive dissociation occurs in Pam's experience of time.

Sometimes there has seemed to be no future, only an endless repeating numb present. A rich past has been approached with longing and with pain, but it has been a past also used to bear the present. Sometimes, for Pam, the future has seemed long and endlessly empty. There have been glimpses of potentials to come, an unknown future that could be interesting. Pam's body state and body ego have sometimes felt to her static and sometimes living and vital. Bromberg's

(1999) work on shifting self-states and dissociation seems relevant here. Pam has had the particularly arduous task of standing in the spaces, between and within starkly distinct and conflictual self-spaces.

Throughout the work with Pam, I have been very mindful of the thin line between the living and the dead that exists in the representations of loss in early stages. In an early dream, Pam was set to walk down a nearby street. Her husband appears to tell her not to walk there. When I ask her about this street, she tells me it is very desolate and even dangerous. We talk about her sense of having, in her husband, a guide through a desolate path. This reminds her of an experience in her local playground. She had arranged a play date and then had gone with a father and his child to have pizza. The playground stirs up sadness and anger. She watches other children having fathers to play with, particularly the kind of roughhouse play she associates with her husband. Anger has not been prominent in Pam's experiences, having emerged most usually in the context of watching or interacting with people or families whose lives have gone on relatively undisturbed. She has been angry at feeling caught up in a historical event she wanted no part of.

At the restaurant, surrounded by intact families, Pam feels tearful and imagines Chris sitting close talking quietly into her ear, comforting her. She imagines his arm around her shoulder. Her tears fall, and she sees that the father sitting with her is discomfited. She looks away but does not banish the fantasy or her feelings. This makes me think of Loewald's deep sense of the interweaving of fantasy and reality. In the process of mourning, there is (perhaps always to some degree) the simultaneous need for acceptance and creative denial. Chris "lives" as a voice in her ear, a presence at her shoulder; at the same time, he is dead and she is grieving.

Around the six-month anniversary, Pam has a drink with a neighboring fireman. She wants to ask about the conditions of death by smoke inhalation. So a door is opening, as she begins to try to represent the circumstances of her husband's death. What the fireman tells her brings some relief: he describes loss of consciousness and a process of dying that is more peaceful and contained than the fantasies or images of burning, falling, pulverized, and crushed bodies. Pam had begun to worry about the details of her husband's last hours. She had been most haunted by what she imagined to be his fear in those last moments. The idea that loss of consciousness precedes death by smoke inhalation relieved her. At the same time, she is aware of some denial. She approaches these matters at her own pace.

As they are enjoying some wine, one of the men leans back and raises his arm behind his head. Pam tells me she felt a rush, a suddenly unexpected and startling twinge of pleasure. She gasps inwardly: flesh, male arm, muscle. (She and I are laughing when she tells me this.) Then she walks back to her own apartment, smiling, a little buzzed. Inside, she sees a picture of her husband and is immediately sobbing. She later describes "tumbled feelings." Sitting in the session, our eyes fill with tears.

Pam is moving through complex contradictory representational states in which there are unsettling presences and absences. There is a body dying and disappearing, and there is her own continuing body with its renewing appetites and engagements. There is a fascinating trajectory here. Pam has been feeling more power and steadiness, which allows her to begin to imagine her husband's bodily death. This opening is followed by arousal to a new living body, and then she moves back to grief. Weeping can quickly follow laughter, in her daily life and in our sessions.

As the process has evolved, there has been increasingly nuanced appreciation of sameness and difference between Pam's experience and the children's. After the family had been out hearing some music, Sarah was jumping around playing "air guitar" and making up a country-and-western–type song about her daddy. It led Pam to say that she "really, really" missed her husband and that she "really, really" loved him. She was picking up on the words of the song Sarah was inventing. Her daughter paused and then responded: "I don't *really, really* miss Daddy. I *really* miss Daddy. But I love you, and you didn't die." Pam was startled but attentive, capable of imagining that Sarah was coming to her own way of feeling and thinking.

That Pam supported this difference is yet another sign to me of her ability to get beyond the self-absorption of grief. She can make mental space for this new idea Sarah was beginning to develop. Sarah articulated something distinct in her experience, something she connected to the continuing availability of her mother. Different perspectives and subjectivities were dawning here, and Pam made space for this new evolution. Perhaps here the developing mentalization will be unique to Sarah and will depend on her mother's ability to hold her own and her daughter's distinct mind and feelings in active representation.

In doing this work, I think mostly of my capacity to create a setting for such affect-laden thought, the hard work of mourning. I think of my task as one of mentalization, keeping in mind the unquenchable pain of losing a beloved partner. But to aid another's grief means that the containing analyst revisits, holds, and suspends her own experience and knowledge of mourning. When Pam would try to explain the sometimes confusing experience of not wanting to talk to old friends or see people in social settings, I knew what she was talking about. There is, in conditions of difficult mourning, the dread at the sight of a new, even though friendly, loving face because each meeting entails a retelling and a revisiting of loss. Pam also voiced the dilemma that many grieving people know: that sometimes condolences are masking requests for help or at least requests to hear that the mourner's suffering is passing.

Mourning, I try to convey to Pam, is in part a matter of pacing. When a friend says to her, "Your world did not end," Pam and I talk together about how this is true and not true. There has often been great difficulty in simply representing how she is at any moment in time. She is fine. She is not fine. Her world did not end, but a planned world of that foursome did end. A new family goes on. And Pam has gone on or, as she says, "endured." Like many grieving people, she fears the end of sadness, another loss of connection to Chris. She needs to allow for multiple representations of systems, roles, and relationships that are often not synchronous. She has been living in multiple time lines, along multiple narratives, inhabiting multiple psychic spaces.

As you might imagine, I am often tearful in sessions. The "skills" of grieving are enabled by someone else creating space for one's thoughts. The challenge for me was to hold both my history and revived memories of sudden, unexpected loss and attend to the specific and unique experience Pam was having in all its contradictions and unquenchable anguish. I am aware how much my colleagues in our trauma study group hold open a complex landscape and constructive web for me that helps me in what I can offer Pam. A capacity like grieving with its strange asynchronies, gaps, and novel integrations takes collective work as well as individual emotional and cognitive labor.

In our theories and culture, we often speak of closure and working through grief, and we see protracted and ongoing grief as somehow pathological. But regarding the longevity and unfolding of grief, perhaps we need to make more distinctions. A supervisee describes a patient about whom she frequently feels so hopeless. A woman in early middle age remains suspended and remote from almost any personal, intimate life. Her interior world seems haunted and hidden. Her father died suddenly and unexpectedly when she was very little, and from that moment his name was never mentioned, and all pictures disappeared. She never saw a picture of herself with her father until she was an adult. A father disappeared, his memory was occluded, and the child's exhausting mental labor to keep a secret, cryptlike space for this lost father came at the expense of living. At the core of this patient's life has been a pervasive belief that the loss of the father did not matter to her mother. There are multiple abandonments here.

Recently, Pam provided me with a different example of the long-term carrying of loss. She met an old friend, a woman in early middle age. The woman approached Pam to offer condolences and to tell her that she too had lost her father when she was very young—about age three, as Sarah was. Pam watched her friend's face and said to her that what she had just seen so relieved her. The woman's face lit up when she said "my father," and for Pam that meant that love for a father could survive over a lifetime. She was thinking of her daughter, but this had meaning for her continuing love as well. To her surprise, her friend wept, agreeing that something in that phrase "my father" and those memories continued to be deeply important to her. Pam felt given to in that encounter, but it is equally clear that the other woman received a gift, an opportunity for recognition, unexpected but deeply welcome.

I know that I have helped Pam cherish and value this ability to let another's feelings come to life even when experiencing great pain herself. But she is wonderfully endowed with such capacities. Only scant months after 9/11, Pam was part of an arranged outing with other widows and their families. She engaged a somber little boy in conversation, talking about traveling into New York. Pam asked if he had done that kind of thing with his dad. His face opened in the first smile she had seen, and he told her something he and his father had done. "So that's a nice memory," she said and the boy's face was, even if briefly, beaming and alive.

Writing this, I have just remembered a chance meeting after many years with a friend whose daughter had drowned tragically at the age of 10. My friend has had an effective career and an ongoing life with family. As we were catching up, she spoke of her daughter, "There is not a day that I do not think about her. But I have had a life." Margaret Little (1985) said it very emphatically, "Mourning is for life." Then I remember Pam's voice quoting Chris: "Life is for the living." This is the tension that as clinicians, as parents, and as citizens we must try to hold.

Acknowledgments

I am indebted to a study group coconvened by Elizabeth Young-Bruehl and Peter Neubauer after 9/11. This group includes colleagues Susan Coates and Dan Schachter from the Columbia Psychoanalytic Parent Infant Program (PIP); Ken Corbett, Virginia Goldner, and Ruth Stein from the journal *Studies in Gender and Sexuality;* Ellen Rees from Columbia Psychoanalytic; Sam Heschkowitz from the Psychoanalytic Association of New York; and Murray Schwartz from the University of Massachusetts.

References

Abraham, N. & Torok, M. (1994), *The Shell and the Kernel.* Chicago: University of Chicago Press.
Beebe, B. & Lachmann, F. (2002), *Infant Research and Adult Treatment.* Hillsdale, NJ: The Analytic Press.
Benjamin, J. (1988), *The Bonds of Love.* New York: Pantheon.
_____ (2001), *Shadow of the Other.* New York: Routledge.
Bowlby, J. (1960), Grief and mourning in infancy and early childhood. *The Psychoanalytic Study of the Child,* 15:9–52. New Haven, CT: Yale University Press.
Bromberg, P. (1999), *Standing in the Spaces.* Hillsdale, NJ: The Analytic Press.
Cain, A. & Fast, I. (1972), Children's disturbed reactions to parent suicide. In: *Survivors of Suicide,* ed. A. Cain. Springfield, IL: Thomas.
Fischer, K., Ayoub, C., Singh, I., Noam, G., Andronicki, M. & Raya, P. (1997), Psychopathology as adaptive development along distinctive pathways. *Devel. Psychopathol.,* 9:749–779.
_____ & Bidell, T. (1998), Dynamic development of psychological structures of action and thought. In: *Handbook of Child Psychology, Vol. 1,* 5th ed., ed. R. Lerner. New York: Wiley.
_____ & Watson, M. (2002), Dynamic development of socioemotional roles and distortions in families: The case of the Oedipus conflict. In: *Risk and Development,* ed. G. Roeper & G. Noam. Frankfurt, Germany: Suhrkamp.

Fonagy, P. (1997), Attachment and theory of mind: Overlapping constructs? *Assn. Child Psychol. Psychiat. Occasional Papers,* 14:31–40.

_____ & Target, M. (1996), Playing with reality I: Theory of mind and the normal development of psychic reality. *Internat. J. Psycho-Anal.,* 77: 217–233.

_____ & _____ (1997), Attachment and reflective function: Their role in self-organization. *Devel. Psychopathol.,* 9:679–700.

_____ & _____ (2000), Playing with reality III: The persistence of dual psychic reality in borderline patients. *Internat. J. Psycho-Anal.,* 81:853–874.

Frankiel, R. (1995), *Essential Papers in Object Loss.* New York: New York University Press.

Freud, S. (1917), Mourning and melancholia [1915]. *Standard Edition,* 14: 243–258. London: Hogarth Press, 1957.

Green, A. (1970), The dead mother. In: *On Private Madness.* London: Hogarth Press.

Hamilton, V. (1989), The mantle of safety: Festschrift for Frances Tustin. *Winnicott Stud.,* 4:70–97.

Hofer, M. (1984), Relationships as regulators: A psychobiologic perspective on bereavement. *Psychosom. Med.,* 46:183–197.

_____ (1996), On the nature and consequence of early loss. *Psychosom. Med.,* 58:570–581.

Little, M. (1985), Working with Winnicott where psychotic anxieties predominate. *Free Assn.,* 5:1–19.

Locke, J. (1993), *The Child's Path to Spoken Language.* Cambridge, MA: Harvard University Press.

Mitchell, S. (2000), *Relationality.* Hillsdale, NJ: The Analytic Press.

Nelson, K. (1985), *Making Sense: The Acquisition of Shared Meaning.* New York: Academic Press.

Pynoos, R. (2001, November), Paper presented at the conference "When the Bough Broke," Columbia University, New York.

Sander, L. (2002), Thinking differently: Principles of process in living systems and the specificity of being known. *Psychoanal. Dial.,* 12:11–42.

Chapter 9

Some Clinical Observations After September 11
Awakening the Past?

Ellen Rees

This chapter illustrates an important phenomenon that can determine how a person reacts to sudden trauma, namely the presence of previous traumas whose emotional significance has been kept out of awareness. Rees describes how, in two high-functioning patients being seen in intensive treatment, the trauma of 9/11 may have suddenly brought back to life memories of previous major traumatizations that had heretofore lain sequestered in quasi-dissociation; that is, the traumatic events had been known about cognitively but possessed little emotional content. Rees thus reports an important experiment in nature insofar as the existence of the ongoing alliance enabled a closer monitoring of the processes involved than otherwise would have been possible. The experience of terror was required as a trigger for feelings associated with the childhood memory. In terms of internal psychological processes, Rees articulates how the combination of fresh trauma and old memory creates a new memory of what happened in the past, one that is emotionally laden.

When Michael heard that the towers had been attacked, he felt terrified and alone. He thought, "The city is a powder keg," and felt trapped in Manhattan. He grabbed his dog and held him close to his chest. Later, Michael woke up in the bathtub and was to awaken there several times.

He hadn't done this since age 12 in the weeks after the flood. At that time, he saw a 30-foot wall of water looming over the roof of his grandmother's house. It came down the valley, and each time the lightning flashed he could see water flying by and hear people screaming. People were killed, and the "missing" list changed each day as the bodies were found. It rained nine inches in two hours without warning, and the water came rushing down from the hills, washing everything away. It took months to clean up. A classmate had gotten into a tub to save herself, but the tub broke apart, and she drowned. A little girl with her was saved, and told the story.

Michael does not remember how he felt that night. He remembers only that he wanted to hold his little brother. He held him against his chest and didn't want to let him go. Shortly thereafter, he started waking up in the bathtub.

Michael experienced sudden trauma during the flood and during the terrorist attack. How are we to understand the relationship between Michael's reactions to the two events? Are we to consider his fantasies about being trapped on an island surrounded by water (Manhattan) to be determined by his earlier fear of being trapped in a house surrounded by rising water? Are we to think that his waking in the bathtub has meaning in relation to his classmate's drowning? Are Michael's reactions *forms of remembering* the trauma surrounding the flood? How do the old trauma and the new join to create experience that oscillates in time? The atrocities of September 11 have given us another opportunity to learn.

The clinical material I present explores the relationship between trauma in adulthood and residue of trauma from earlier life. It has been disguised to protect privacy, but I have tried to accurately represent the clinical phenomena. I focus on the experience of the terrorist attack as it apparently affected memory and defense in the therapeutic process (Kate and Harry). I also present data obtained by interview (Michael and Diana).

Kate and Harry have been doing analytic work for many years—Kate in psychoanalysis and Harry in analytically oriented psychotherapy.

They each had conscious memories of childhood trauma, but their memories did not include the expected feelings. Certain intense feelings had remained out of awareness during treatment, despite my best efforts. Kate and Harry are high functioning and capable of mounting successful defenses against an awareness of feelings associated with trauma. I believed that Kate and Harry feared reliving deeply disturbing emotional experiences in the transference because they unconsciously expected to be retraumatized.

To my surprise, Kate and Harry suddenly appeared to gain conscious access to memories of feelings associated with childhood trauma or, more precisely, that they associated to traumatic experiences in childhood, in the weeks following the terrorist attack. The availability of these emotions and the fantasies that accompanied them changed the quality of the therapeutic process. The old defenses against an awareness of the transference seemed to vanish, for a time. The transference relationship was more alive emotionally, and fantasy was more available.

The new emotional intensity lasted about three months, then gradually faded. Even after these emotions receded from awareness, however, conscious memories of childhood trauma remained altered. An emotional dimension seemed to have been restored or added to the narrative form of the memory that had always been available in consciousness. The narrative memory continued to be remembered with emotion, at times. More usually, the narrative memory was remembered in close association with the *memory* of "awakened" feeling. The newly found emotional context for memories and fantasy experiences that had been remembered without emotion deepened self-understanding and altered the conscious experience of the self, retrospectively and in the present. In each case, the experience contributed to progress in the analytic work and was probably made possible by the analytic work that had been done.

These clinical experiences intrigued me, and I have tried to understand them. I have been helped in my efforts by members of a study group formed to study the impact of September 11.[1] I am writing from

---

[1] This group was organized at the request of Peter Neubauer and is funded by the Viola Bernard Foundation. It is chaired by Elisabeth Young-Bruehl, and our members include Susan Coates, Kenneth Corbett, Virginia Goldner, Adrienne Harris, Samuel Herschkowitz, Murray Schwartz, Daniel Schechter,

the point of view of a psychoanalyst in the tradition of ego psychology and object relations. My clinical experience with trauma has been limited to the kinds of trauma experienced by my patients and to the nature of the analytic work that we do together. The clinical observations I have made are in particular contexts with particular kinds of people.

My data will be most useful if I describe clinical characteristics that may help place them. Kate, Harry, and Diana do not meet DSM-IV criteria for posttraumatic stress disorder (PTSD); Michael may (American Psychiatric Association, 1994). All but Michael have not experienced flashbacks, intrusive images or memories, or recurrent dreams of their traumatic experiences during adulthood. They are not aware of being unduly distressed by narrative memories of trauma nor are they preoccupied with these memories. Kate, Harry, and Diana have repressed intense feelings and fantasies surrounding trauma. I am not able to say what Michael's defenses have been. They all show evidence of persistent hyperarousal, but this has more the quality of a trait than a state (Perry et al., 1996). Kate, Harry, and Diana are among those who have been considered analyzable, and their treatments have been intense and fruitful.

The clinical features I highlight for Kate and Harry are conscious memories of childhood trauma accompanied by what I had understood to be a particularly tenacious repression of emotions associated with trauma. I am using the word *trauma* to describe the psychic experience of being overwhelmed or flooded so that the capacity of the mind to process is altered. This "terrifying too-muchness" (Shengold, 1979) interferes with the capacity to think, feel, and remember. The mind, brain, and body and the experience of the self, the other, and the world are changed in finding ways to respond and to recover (Laub and Auerbahn, 1993; van der Kolk, 1994; Nadel and Jacobs, 1996; Perry et al., 1996).

The processes that contributed to Kate's and Harry's lack of awareness of emotions associated with their traumatic experiences were complex. For each, sudden shocks and losses were combined with ongoing or cumulative experiences of trauma in a family life that had

and Ruth Stein. I am particularly indebted to Susan Coates, Adrienne Harris, and David Olds for their ideas and their invaluable editorial help.

been essentially loving and stable. The experiencing of trauma was elaborated over years of childhood development in a changing interpersonal environment so that the interweaving of fantasy and the reworking in thinking, understanding, and memory were extensive and rich. Conscious narrative memories helped Kate and Harry to make sense of themselves and their experiences, to defend themselves and to recover. As such, they are creative constructions. The clinical phenomena that have intrigued me have to do with the fate of emotions that were part of the fabric of traumatic experience. It now seems to me that although Kate and Harry had not appeared to use dissociative mechanisms, dissociated aspects of experience were present and had contributed to the tenacity of defense.

For me, the hyperarousal, intense affect, emotional numbing, and transient states of dissociation that followed the attack provided a forceful reminder of the state of mind during trauma and started me thinking about dissociation and the representation of the various dimensions of trauma.

The literature on trauma in the various disciplines is vast. Many psychoanalysts have been studying the relationship between states of mind and conflict. I discuss the ideas of only a very few. I have selected these from among the contributions of so many because they have been particularly helpful in furthering my own thinking.

Clinical Material

Kate

Kate was getting back into the swing of things in her analysis after the summer break. Her summer had been glorious. She had been running in the park and was describing her feelings about being back in New York on such a beautiful September morning. Within hours, two planes hit the World Trade Center. Kate came to her hour the next day feeling numb. She described what had happened after leaving me the day before. When she got home, a friend called to tell her that a plane had flown into one of the towers. She turned on the television as the second tower was hit. Her first impulse was to call her husband even though she knew he was safe. Her need for contact with him became urgent as the news of the plane hitting the Pentagon came on the screen and she knew we were being attacked. She watched the slow, eerie, silent approach of the planes and the towers being hit, shown over and over on CNN. She told me that strangely her feelings had been for the buildings. The towers with gaping holes smoking but still standing had provided some relief. She had wanted them to withstand the blow. It seemed at first they would. Then she felt stunned. Later, she would begin to feel terrified.

Kate and I both felt emotionally numbed for two weeks following the attack, particularly during the first week. We worked, but not in the usual state of mind. I felt a peculiar absence of emotionality except when Kate's associations touched the events of September 11; then, for moments, I could feel a more active process interfering with my thinking. Kate described what sounded like similar experiences. (A shared experience of trauma raises the very interesting question of the impact of a changed state of mind in the analyst.) During the second week, Kate had flashes of intense feeling alternating with numbing. When she heard a story about a child whose father had been killed, dancing around singing "My daddy's dead. My daddy's dead," Kate had a fantasy of tearing bin Laden apart with her bare hands. By the third week, she realized she was terrified. She expected another attack and told me she would attack again soon if she were a terrorist. She did not think another attack could be prevented. It could happen any moment and take any form. She felt in danger.

Kate has been in analysis for many years. Her analysis has been intense, but Kate had not remembered certain feelings or wishes that later came to life in the wake of the attack. These feelings made sense of childhood fantasies and memories that had been remembered without emotion before and during her analysis. Kate's father went off to war when she was two. Her mother had to work while he was away, so Kate was left in the care of a baby-sitter. When her father came home, Kate was four, and she remembered being especially happy then until he left home suddenly when she was six. Kate remembered her mother saying that her father would not be living with them anymore because she and Kate's father were not compatible. Kate hid behind her dresser and would not come out.

Earlier in her analysis, Kate had dreamt of a tree being split in two by a bolt of lightning. She had associated to a tree in the front yard of the house in which she had lived when her father returned. She had played in that tree often. Kate did not remember how she felt when her father suddenly left. She knew she had loved him and that he had remained very important to her. She had not known where he was for some time. She still has a card she had written to him after he left. In it, she had written, "I would write to you if I knew your address." She remembered his coming to her new house to take back his tools and his seashells. These had been her special toys. She remembered scenes, not feelings. At the end of analytic hours during the time these memories were active, Kate became anxious. On one occasion, she described a flash fantasy of being sawed in two by an electric table saw. The fantasy was accompanied by a visual image but was isolated from her anxiety. She linked the fantasy to having her session with me come to an end and to her father's leaving.

Kate's fantasy seemed to me to represent an elaboration of her memory of an emotional and psychological state associated with her father's leaving. She had felt sawed in two. The emergence of this fantasy in the context of remembering a feeling and a state of mind illustrates one of the questions that occurred to me in thinking about Kate's "remembering" after September 11. How are the fragments of past experience in the form of affects, sensations, and ego states woven together with newly constructed imagery and fantasy and then linked to memories of childhood experience and fantasies in narrative form in consciousness? How will we understand the mixing of the old and the new in the construction of memory in conscious experience?

Even though it is well known to psychoanalysts, clinicians, and researchers that memory is newly constructed in remembering, there is debate about whether memories encoded during trauma are more indelible or less malleable and therefore influence mental functions differently (Brenneis, 1994; van der Kolk and Fisler, 1995; Brenneis, 1996; Le Doux, 1996; Bremner, 2001).

I am put in mind of Freud's description of affect in dreams. He begins his discussion in chapter 6 of "The Interpretation of Dreams" (1900):

A shrewd observation made by Stricker (1879) has drawn our attention to the fact that expression of affect in dreams cannot be dealt with in the same contemptuous fashion in which, after waking, we are accustomed to dismiss their *content*. "If I am afraid of robbers in a dream, the robbers, it is true, are imaginary but the fear is real" [p. 460].

The sudden and unexpected attack on two buildings in her home city, while she was feeling happy and secure, created emotional conditions that I think resembled Kate's feelings and state of mind when she was told about her father's leaving. In an instant, everything seemed to change. Her sense of a future that was pleasantly unfolding was abruptly replaced by a sense of a future that could not be counted on. She felt uncertain and unsafe. Without her knowing, others had planned actions for reasons she could only partly comprehend, and her life had been altered violently. Fathers were missing and their families did not know where they were or if they were coming back.

Kate had worked hard in analysis to understand and mitigate the impact of her father's absence while he was away at war and of his later departure from the family. She had worked through many aspects of this traumatic absence and loss and its residues in feelings about herself, conflict and fantasy, in the present. Not surprisingly, however, she had remembered very few of her feelings as a child. Our understanding and analytic work had been with her intense feelings of love and attachment and her feelings about separation in her transference with me.

After September 11, we had a new context. Kate was terrified that something might be happening and she would not know about it. She was surprised at an unfamiliar, intense wish to be protected. Because I was traumatized by the shocking attack as well, I suspect that Kate did not have the usual sense of my containing presence. My own hyperarousal, intensity of feeling, and distraction when planes would fly overhead were part of my state of mind for many weeks. This very likely contributed to the Kate's wish for protection. Ordinarily, Kate thought of herself as adventurous and unafraid, and she rarely thought of asking for help. Her reluctance to rely on others had been an important theme in her analysis. After September 11, she listened for the fighter jets and was reassured when they roared overhead. She felt comforted by seeing the American flag flying and pinned and pasted seemingly everywhere. It seemed to represent the presence of something larger and stronger than she was.

Kate remembered a song on a record she had played over and over after her father left. It was about an Indian boy who got lost while out riding alone and signaled, "Run father, run father!" with his drum. She had remembered this song earlier in her analysis, but even then she had not remembered this desperate *feeling* that she wanted to be protected. She realized that this feeling had been missing in her experience of herself.

Kate began to think about memories and fantasies from the times her father was gone. They came to mind in the context of her wish for protection and her feeling that she needed protection in the present. Kate felt that she "knew" the feelings belonged with the memories. This linking of her current feeling with her memories created a new sense of awareness and self-understanding that affected both the present and the past. Kate felt a "missing piece" had been put into place, which seemed to alter her experience of *her memory of herself* as a child, in a profound way.

Kate also experienced an urgent need to protect her most important possessions. Most of the things she wished to protect had been given to her by her husband or by her father. She worried that if there were to be another attack, she would have to leave these precious things behind. She imagined realizing that she could not retrieve them. She felt their loss in fantasy. She moved her special things and anything irreplaceable to a place that she believed was safe. A fantasy she remembered having as a child took on new meaning and emotional texture. In this fantasy, Kate pictured herself alone in the world. All the people had vanished, and she did not know where they had gone or why. She was afraid that all the knowledge of the world would be lost, and she set out to preserve all the books. She dug a big hole and imagined herself collecting them. She would keep them safe underground so they would be there when the people came back. In her fantasy, Kate worked diligently but calmly. She only worried about the loss of precious history.

Kate's feelings while moving her irreplaceable possessions were very different. She was anxious while away from home lest she not be able to go back for them, should something happen suddenly. She imagined she would never forget losing them, would always feel bereft without them. She imagined her own safety necessitating that she not be encumbered trying to take them with her.

Kate thought again about a childhood fantasy from the time her father was away at war. She had worried that her father might be wounded and without help. She had imagined being there and trying to drag or carry him to safety. She had planned to do this the way the Indians did. She knew they dragged things on a travois, two poles with a platform for loads, trailing behind their horses. She had been given a book about North American Indians with a picture of this. She remembered her fantasy of being shipwrecked at sea and having to drag her mother to shore. In this fantasy, she imagined running out of strength and having to leave her mother behind in order to save herself. These fantasies took on new vitality. The attack seemed to have an emotional context similar to the one in which she had created them.

Kate began to understand more vividly why mastery had been so crucial to her. She *felt* her need for mastery as she compulsively watched CNN at intervals during the day so she would not be caught unaware again. She realized why on September 11 she had thought first of the buildings being lost and not the people in them. She now understood more fully that it had been much easier for her to think about losing irreplaceable things and knowledge than irreplaceable people. Kate felt she had gotten back an aspect of herself that she might never have known.

Because we are considering that the terrorist attack might have created psychological, emotional, and physiological conditions that were close enough to Kate's experience as a child that a resonance with memory might have been established, it is important to understand the original situation of trauma as best we can. Kate fantasized and dreamt of losing her father as a sudden bolt of lightning. She fantasized being sawed or rent in two. But her father's leaving the family was not her first loss. Earlier in her life, her father was suddenly called to war and was gone for two years. Kate knew he was in danger. When he returned, Kate introduced herself as if he would not know her, but it was she who did not know him. When Kate's father went to war, Kate's mother was suddenly without her husband and was worried about his safety. Kate was suddenly with a baby-sitter for the first time. Kate had her first sudden loss at the age of two when capacities for separation and individuation were still developing. The loss of her father was accompanied by a sudden change in her mother's state of mind and by the more prolonged separation from her mother necessitated by her mother's work. Consequently, Kate's loss also involved a significant change in the availability and tone and rhythm of her relationship with her mother, and probably in her perception of her mother. Kate's father's presence was maintained for her during these years through his letters, read to her by her mother, and by her mother's efforts to maintain his presence.[2] When Kate's father returned, he was a virtual stranger to Kate, and her feelings must have been suitably complex. The war had been traumatic for her father, and he had nightmares from which he would awaken feeling trapped and trying to escape. So Kate was sensitized to separation and loss when her father again left the family unexpectedly, and she didn't see him for some time or know where he was, and when Kate's mother again went to work and slowly became depressed. Both times, Kate lost the father and the mother she had known. One significant resemblance of the past and present contexts was the experience of sudden loss during a time of happiness and security. The reunion with her father after the war, although fraught with ambivalence and conflict, had provided a return of happiness and security.

Harry

I begin my discussion of Harry with a dream he had during the last week of September. In this dream, Harry got into an elevator, but when he pushed the button the elevator started going down instead of up. When the door opened, everything was dark. His mother's face loomed in the darkness, and he screamed. Harry felt horrified and terrified. His mother had a crazed look.

Harry's mother had her first of many psychotic episodes when Harry was seven years old. During these episodes, she talked to Harry about her delusional fears and involved him in acting in response to them. Harry tried to help his mother. He was the oldest and felt responsible. Harry's father was often absent and finally left the family.

Harry's treatment, an analytically oriented psychotherapy, had been shaped by his need to remain in control. Harry had not been able to risk the flying apart that he imagined would happen if he relaxed his guard, and I had not been able to help him give up this defense. Harry had learned to be prepared and had stoically trained himself to bear painful experience. Harry remembered his experience as a child but without feeling. His intellect and his capacities for mastery had served him well.

---

[2]In this volume, Adrienne Harris movingly discusses the importance of such efforts as she describes a mother's efforts to help her daughter mourn the loss of her father on September 11.

Almost immediately after the terrorist attack, Harry seemed different. He did not talk about his feelings about the terrorist attack, but
his dream heralded a change in the therapeutic process. In associating
to his dream, Harry said he had not been aware how much his mother
had terrified him. The look in her eyes when she was crazy had
horrified him, and he felt horrified while remembering. His new
awareness was quickly expressed in the transference, and Harry began
to worry that I might be dangerous. He remembered thinking that his
mother had wanted him to share her delusional experiences and had
tried to convince him that he did. He had been terrified and had looked
for signs that she was right. Harry never knew what he would find when
he came home from school or when he woke in the morning. He had
looked in his mother's eyes and tried to read her state of mind.

After his dream, Harry feared that I was involving him in a process
that would do him harm. Things in his head might blow apart and not
come back together. He had dream after dream of being menaced. In
these dreams, when he tried to defend himself someone got badly
injured. Harry worried he had exerted too much force and that he was
dangerous. He felt as if he might explode. Harry remembered childhood fantasies of smashing his hand with a rock. He remembered
feeling unbearable tension. He imagined that smashing his hand
would have brought relief.

Harry remembered his mother as creative, lively, and loving before
she became ill. His mother's psychotic episodes were sporadic, and
she would seem back to herself in between, but the change in her
worsened over time. When she was psychotic, she was absorbed in her
delusions, and Harry was left very much alone, except when his mother
needed his assistance. He believed her when she described that she
was in danger and that he might be as well. Harry's mother was
frightened, and he was terrified of her and of the things she feared.
Even so, her version of reality was at odds with Harry's sense of the
world and with his mother's sense of the world when she was not ill.
He watched to see if things were getting better or worse. His hopes to
have the mother he remembered back were dashed again and again
just when she seemed to be better. Harry began to feel hopeless about
the possibility of change for the better and braced himself for changes
for the worse.

Early in his treatment, Harry seemed not to be aware that his mother
had been psychotic. However, in transference dreams, I was portrayed

as crazy and menacing. Harry understood this intellectually but kept his distance for many years. In the months before the terrorist attack, Harry was allowing transference fantasies more regularly. He was becoming aware that he wanted me to be aware of his needs. He could not yet imagine that his needs would influence me in any way. Harry had described a terrifying childhood during the years of his treatment, but he had not mentioned feeling terrified before September 11. He had not remembered feeling so.

What Changed After September 11?

How can we understand the apparent "awakening" of memories of past emotional experience, a change in a seemingly intractable defense against such awareness? Did the feelings and fantasies that were aroused in Kate and Harry by the terrorist attack "awaken" memories of similar feelings and fantasies from childhood so that they were more available to consciousness? Did a state of mind in the present affect the availability of memories of past trauma? Did feeling shocked and terrified recruit memories to make the present experience comprehensible? Did a changed state of mind in the analyst play a role? The terrible events of September 11 have raised questions we will be thinking about for years. Because this was a shared experience, we have an unusual opportunity to use our shared expertise in understanding the impact of what has happened. We can think together from multiple points of view using our different frames of reference.

Historical Context

The study of trauma and memories of trauma has a long and rich history (van der Kolk and van der Hart, 1989; Terr, 1991; van der Kolk, Herron, and Hostetler, 1994). Freud and Breuer were interested in the relationship between memories of trauma and the formation of hysterical symptoms. As do researchers today, Freud and Breuer studied the influence of affect and states of mind on the remembering and forgetting of trauma. Breuer was particularly interested in the affect of fright, the effects of hyperexcitability of the nervous system and in hypnoid states. He thought that altered states of consciousness, states of autohypnosis that could be precipitated by emotional shock or states of reverie, had the power to bring about a splitting of the mind. Mental activity that occurred during such a state was split off from the normal state of consciousness and so was not remembered. Freud pursued his interest in psychological defense and gave birth to psychoanalysis with its cornerstone, the theory of repression.

The diverging interests of Breuer and Freud can be thought of as containing the roots of two traditions in the thinking about memories of trauma. The psychoanalytic tradition, following Freud, has been primarily interested in motivated forgetting in a context of psychological conflict and in the nature, function, and vicissitudes of wishes, fantasies, and psychological defense. The focus has been on psychic reality and the dynamic unconscious. Although there has been a tendency within the psychoanalytic tradition to view dissociation and repression as processes that are central to different models of mental functioning, the trauma model and the conflict model, there have been psychoanalysts who have been interested in the nature and functioning of dissociation in the psychoanalytic situation and who have studied the relationship between repression and dissociation in the psychoanalytic dyad (Bromberg, 1998). The predominant tradition in the research community and the related disciplines has been to study trauma and the memory of it in terms of the structure and functioning of the mind and, more recently, the brain. This tradition has continued to explore phenomena that interested Breuer: states of mind, states of arousal, and splits in consciousness or mind (dissociation).

The different points of view in these traditions may be able to enrich one another. Yovell has contributed to this effort (Yovell, 2000). Yovell makes the crucial point that "psychoanalytic theory can and should go beyond our current neurobiological understanding of the mind, but it must never contradict it. Therefore, psychoanalytic theory should be continuously reexamined and revised, to insure its coherence with emerging neurobiological research findings." The reciprocal point is that the research and academic communities can benefit from more than a century of clinical observation by psychoanalysts and other clinicians. How might we understand what happened to Kate and Harry after September 11 using insights from the two traditions?

States of Mind *and* Psychological Defense

Kate and Harry had conscious memories of their traumatic experiences. These memories were in narrative form and in an autobiographical context. Their autobiographical memory, although forming a coherent narrative, was only partial. Kate's memories of her father's leaving had the quality of screen memories, and her memories of her father's years at home were fragmentary. These fragments were exclusively of happy experiences with him. These observations suggest the influence of fantasy as well as defense. Harry had relatively detailed memory of his daily life with his mother, but his memory did not include fantasies that emerged after September 11, nor did it include experiences accompanied by feelings of apprehension and dread, let alone terror and horror. Kate and Harry had been able to keep feelings and fantasies associated with childhood trauma out of awareness in their lives and treatments. The terrorist attack came suddenly and shattered a sense of basic safety. Terrible sights and devastating loss were everywhere. Kate and I were shocked and numb. Harry said nothing about how he felt about the attack but began remembering feeling horrified and terrified with his mother.

The almost universal human response to overwhelming experiences combines hyperarousal and psychic numbing. Hyperarousal is accompanied by hypermnesia and hyperreactivity to stimuli. Psychic numbing is accompanied by amnesia, avoidance, and anhedonia (van der Kolk, 1994). These responses fade over time in those who do not develop PTSD but may leave residues that affect reactivity, affectivity, ego functioning, memory, neurotic symptoms, character, and psychosomatic conditions. The response to trauma includes the release of stress neurohormones, cortisol, epinephrine, norepinephrine, vasopressin, oxytocin, and endogenous opioids. These neurohormones interact and mutually regulate one another (McGaugh, 1990; McEwen, 1995) and have been found to impact memory systems in the hippocampus and the amygdala (van der Kolk, 1994; Nadel and Jacobs, 1996). There is growing evidence that neuronal change and damage may also occur (McEwen, 1995; Perry et al., 1996). The trauma is experienced subjectively, elaborated in fantasy and dreams, drawn into conflict, defended against, and repeated in action. Each of these levels of function and organization from body to brain to mind is affected by trauma and each makes a contribution to the response to trauma.

Kate, Harry, and I were in an altered state of mind. It has long been hypothesized and demonstrated clinically and experimentally that recall of traumatic experiences can be triggered by exposure to sensory, affective or cognitive elements that were present during trauma (Breuer and Freud, 1893–1895; van der Kolk and van der Hart, 1989; van der Kolk and Fisler, 1995). Pierre Janet thought that patients had to be in the same *state of consciousness* as they were at the time of the trauma in order to remember it. It was only in the same state of consciousness that affective, cognitive, and visceral elements of traumatic memories that were not integrated with narrative elements could be accessed. Because extreme affects like terror could not be accommodated by existing cognitive schema, they could not be processed conceptually and so were split off from ordinary consciousness (van der Kolk and van der Hart, 1989).

Breuer and Freud (1893) described the emergence of an attack of hysteria in a similar vein:

> An attack will occur spontaneously, just as memories do in normal people; it is, however, possible to provoke one, just as any memory can be aroused in accordance with the laws of association. It can be provoked either by stimulation of a hysterogenic zone or by a new experience which sets it going owing to a similarity with the pathogenic experience. We hope to be able to show that these two kinds of determinant, though they appear to be so unlike, do not differ in essentials, but that in both a hyperaesthetic memory is touched on [p. 16].

They noted that memories of trauma had a different quality than ordinary memories. They "possess remarkable sensory force," and when they return they act "with all the affective strength of new experiences." They could be provoked by *body experiences* or *subjective experiences* that were associated with the memory or by *new experiences that resembled the traumatic situation*.

Janet, Freud, and Breuer were thinking in ways that were remarkably similar to the thinking of many researchers today. In discussing amnesia for traumatic events, van der Kolk and Fisler (1995) state:

Generally, recall is triggered by exposure to sensory or affective stimuli that match sensory or affective elements associated with the trauma. It is generally accepted that the memory system is made up of networks of related information: activation of one aspect facilitates the recall of associated memories.³ Affect seems to be a critical cue for the retrieval of information along these associative pathways [p. 509].

Le Doux (1996) points out that the better the match between the current emotional state and the emotional state stored as part of memory, the better the likelihood of remembering. He drew on evidence for *contextual* fear conditioning. A context is made up of all the elements that are present at the time of danger. A context can stimulate memory. The conscious experience of a context associated with trauma is encoded in a network. Freud and Breuer had described a similar notion, simultaneity. Le Doux (1996) further points out that the *emotional implications* of an emotional experience are part of the context. Consequently, his model allows for a consideration of the impact of fantasy and meaning as contextual stimuli.

State of mind and body, affect, sensory cues, contextual configuration, and emotional meaning can be triggers that act as stimuli for memories of trauma. Kate described an altered state of consciousness that had the quality of dissociation. She also described hypervigilance, hyperarousal, emotional numbing, an expectation of further attack, and fear. Her conscious fantasies were about loss and the possibility of even more devastating attack and surprise. She fantasized coping strategies. We can only infer the changes in Harry's state of mind from his dreams, fantasies, and change in the transference to include the new themes of horror, terror, and unbearable tension accompanied by self-destructive fantasy and fantasies of exploding or flying apart.

I think it is possible that the *then present reality* of the terrorist attack *with its attendant fantasies* became a situation of danger that was accompanied by a *state of mind, by affects, and by emotional meaning and fantasy* that triggered memories of trauma. The terrorist attack created an unusual context that could be *experienced* and interpreted

---

³These authors cite Collins and Loftus (1975) and Leichtman, Ceci, and Ornstein (1992).

in accordance with personal meaning, fantasy, and past experience. I believe the intensity of the affects and the nature of accompanying fantasies came closer to matching the experience of a child who is confronted with a radically changed, terrifying, and horrifying mother or a sudden and devastating loss of a father than had the transference context. The affects of terror and horror, the context of loss and sudden change in expectation about the present and the future, and the uncertainty about basic safety all had the potential to act as stimuli that could resonate with aspects of memories of trauma. The terror attack provided sufficient stimuli of emotional memories to overcome Kate and Harry's capacities for repression or created conditions that allowed access to dissociated mental contents (or both). This new experience, possibly interpreted as so like the old, "awakened" emotional memory that could then be integrated or associated with conscious autobiographical memories. Psychoanalysts have described such phenomena as *deferred action, après coup,* or *Nachträglichkeit.*

The work of Le Doux (1996) illustrates how we might understand aspects of the functioning of memory in Kate and Harry. A memory system that involves the amygdala is thought to evaluate the emotional significance of experience—or, as Nadel and Jacobs (1996) put it, "to remember the goodness and badness of things." An important function of the amygdala is to detect danger and to respond to threat. The amygdala is thought to be part of a system that mediates the experience of fear and that generates responses conditioned by fear in the past. Sights and sounds and other contextual elements that were present during past danger become learned triggers of the fear system. As Le Doux (1996) explains, "Trigger stimuli can be real or imagined, concrete or abstract, allowing a great range of external (environmental) or internal (mental) conditions to serve as *conditioned stimuli.* . . . Fear conditioning is quick and long-lasting. There is no forgetting when it comes to fear conditioning." Fear conditioning promotes survival when experienced danger threatens again.

Ordinarily, experiences are registered relatively independently and in parallel in a number of memory systems (Schacter, 1992; Nadel and Jacobs, 1996). Kate and Harry had narrative memory of aspects of trauma. The declarative or explicit memory system encodes memory that is available to consciousness. This memory system is thought to involve the hippocampus that contributes temporal and spatial dimensions to conscious memories so that they can be experienced in an autobiographical context (Nadel and Jacobs, 1996). Kate and Harry experienced trauma at an age when the hippocampus has developed and is functioning (O'Keefe and Nadel, 1978). They both could envision themselves in time and place, as they remembered their traumatic experiences. However, during trauma, the encoding of memories can be altered because the high levels of circulating stress hormones affect memory storage, and can affect the functioning of the amygdala and the hippocampus differently. High levels of cortisol can activate the amygdala but can inhibit hippocampal functioning (Le Doux, 1996; Nadel and Jacobs, 1996; Bremner, 2001). Consequently, it is not unusual for experiences of trauma to be remembered as fragments, sensations, feelings, or images that do not have a context in space and time (van der Kolk and Fisler, 1995). We may eventually know enough about these memory systems to consider possible implications for the psychoanalytic concepts of primary and secondary process.

Le Doux makes a distinction between emotional memories and memories of emotions. Emotional memory is thought to be a kind of implicit memory (Schacter, 1992). Implicit memory operates outside of awareness and is thought to encode important aspects of experience that have not been symbolized, such as actions (skills and habits), perceptions (priming), sensations, and affects. Emotional memory of danger involves an encoding of features of the context in which the danger occurred. For the attack on September 11, for example, a feature could be a particularly clear sunny day, especially with light characteristic of September. Emotional memories activate body responses that prepare for defensive actions. These body responses include affects, the release of stress hormones, and body changes that allow for fight or flight. Emotional memories do not require conscious awareness to trigger responses, although the responses to these memories, feelings, hyperarousal, sensations, images, and urges to act can be known consciously. Memories of emotions are declarative memories. They are conscious memories of emotional events that do not activate body responses unless the connection between the hippocampus and the amygdala is also activated. Kate's and Harry's few memories of their emotions during trauma before September 11 were primarily memories of emotions. These memories have a descriptive quality and do not carry the color or force of emotion. This is the kind of memory we might describe as isolated from affect.

The absence of emotional memories of trauma or their expression in intrusive imagery, sensation, affect, or behavior suggest that Kate and Harry were able to keep emotional memories out of awareness using psychological defenses before September 11. Each, however, had ample evidence of reactions to trauma embedded in character and represented in fantasy.

Le Doux (1996) suggests a mechanism that allows memories of emotion to be given an emotional coloring. This mechanism may help explain the changes in memory of past trauma that I observed in Kate and Harry after the terrorist attack. If emotional memories are activated at the same time as memories of emotion, a new autobiographical memory can be created. The emotional arousal *in the present* combines with the memory of the emotional situation in the past so that a *new memory* of the past event is created. This new memory includes the *memory* of emotional arousal, affect, sensation, imagery, or urges to act that were experienced in the present. An emotionally toned memory of emotion has been constructed in consciousness and then in working memory. If the new memory is consolidated in long-term memory, it will be available in an ongoing way, as happened with Kate and Harry.

Le Doux's model gives us another way of understanding how new experience finds the trauma in the old, deferred action, and how old trauma is reshaped in the present experience, *après coup,* or *Nachträglichkeit.*

Clinical Material (Interview)

I believe the following vignette contributes to a consideration of the conditions or stimuli that may trigger memories of emotional aspects of trauma. All her life, Diana had had moments when she would suddenly feel as if all her life energy were being drained out. She felt like a shell of her former self. She described an occasion when this feeling came over her with great intensity while she was reading Guntrip's account of his analyses with Fairbairn and Winnicott (Guntrip, 1975). The context in memory for Diana's feeling was unable to be reached during two analyses.

The content of Guntrip's paper is part of the context for Diana's reaction, so I relate here what I think are the essential elements, from Diana's perspective. Guntrip seems to be describing the sudden breakthrough of repression of memories associated with early trauma in relation to significant life events. Guntrip had amnesia of a severe early trauma that persisted during his two analyses and, according to Guntrip, was never adequately analyzed. After spending much of his life trying and failing to reach these memories that he felt were crucial for his self-understanding and self-analysis, he gained access to them in his 70s only a few years before he died. This was in the context of current trauma that had similar meaning to the original trauma.

Guntrip sought analysis in order to resolve the impact of his younger brother's death. Percy died when Guntrip was three and a half. He developed a mysterious illness after his brother's death and almost died himself. The mysterious illness recurred three times in his life, and each time it recurred he was threatened with the loss of a man who represented his brother. When Fairbairn, Guntrip's first analyst, developed a serious flu during Guntrip's analysis, Guntrip again developed the exhaustion that he had come to call the "Percyillness."

Guntrip was not able to understand the meaning of his brother's death and the depth of the threat that it represented until after he had terminated his analysis with Winnicott. The memories that helped him understand the trauma that surrounded his brother's death were represented in a series of dreams. The dreams occurred at the time of Guntrip's retirement (one kind of loss), which he took to preserve his health, and upon hearing of Winnicott's death (another kind of loss). Using his dreams, Guntrip came to believe that the core of his problem lay in his feeling that his depressed and unavailable mother could not keep her children alive. Guntrip believed that his mother let his brother die by refusing to breast-feed him. After Percy died, Guntrip felt he had to struggle to keep himself alive and to feel alive. It was this constellation that Diana felt resonated with her memories.

Diana's brother Mathew was born when she was five to a mother who was depressed after his birth and who told Diana that she had to raise him. Mathew was sickly, requiring multiple hospitalizations during his first year for a constant fever and a noisy rattle in his chest. Diana remembers being afraid that he might die. She felt anxious during much of her childhood about her ability to keep him alive. (He died in an accident in his late adolescence.)

Approximately during her brother's first year, Diana walked home from school by herself one day and saw blood all over the street. She immediately thought that her dog had been run over by a car and, returning home, discovered that this was true. Her mother had let her dog out without a leash and her dog had been hit and killed by a car. Diana developed an intense grief reaction to this loss and began to believe that her mother could not keep anyone alive.

Some 10 years after her brother's death when she was in her mid-30s, Diana felt both *shock* and *recognition* after reading Guntrip's paper and was overcome with grief, once again. She read it over and over compulsively. In trying to understand her reaction, Diana linked the paper to her feeling that "I was losing my vital force; all my energy was being drained away." She thought this feeling expressed her fear that her mother couldn't keep anyone alive, and she feared that she could not as well. As she put these pieces together, the feeling of losing all her vital energy began to make sense, and she felt relieved. Guntrip's traumatic memories came very close to Diana's in content and in the quality and intensity of affect.

Guntrip's paper was thus a suitable stimulus for activating Diana's memory with intense feeling. Once the emotional memory was available in consciousness, it was linked to narrative forms of memory and fantasy. The grief over the loss of her brother had been associated with a fantasy that all her life force was being drained out of her, or became linked to that fantasy after reading Guntrip. This fantasy had been or was then elaborated to include the fantasy that her mother could not keep anyone alive so that she too might die or ought to die because she could not keep her brother alive.

Kate, Diana, and, apparently, Guntrip had the sense that they had reached a memory associated with early trauma, which promoted a feeling that a missing piece of themselves was falling into place. These memories had somehow remained unavailable during many years of analysis. These experiences of "remembering," complex as they may be to understand, have led me to think about the limitations of the transference relationship as a setting for reliving or remembering *some* emotional aspects of trauma. Analysts have been thinking about various kinds of limitations for a century or more and experimenting with techniques to address these. It may be that for an analysand with good ego strength who is able to keep emotional memories of trauma out of awareness, the relationship with the analyst does not always trigger, or allow for the emergence of, emotional memories or memories of emotions of the kind and intensity associated with childhood trauma. The benign presence of the analyst or therapist establishes a situation of safety that encourages the unfolding of fantasy, the tolerating of affects, and the moderating of shame and self-criticism, but it may be just this benign presence and the predictability of the relationship with the analyst that is *not* a "match" with memories encoded during fear and danger or traumatic loss. Transference fantasy, in the context of a trusted relationship with an analyst, who is perceived to be *not* the fantasy, may not always be enough. The dread of reexperiencing the traumatic state and the feelings and fantasies associated with it is well founded from the point of view of the child who experienced it. The wish to protect the self and to protect the analyst is very powerful. It may take an *unusual* stimulus to penetrate psychological defense or to alter neuropsychological processes or conditions that are contributing to keeping the memory out of awareness in our healthier patients.

Summary

I have presented post–September 11 clinical observations that led me to think about the relationship between trauma in adulthood and residues of trauma from earlier in life. It is unusual for an adult in our culture to experience a sudden and unexpected intentional attack that threatens bodily integrity and ruptures the sense of security in an ongoing way. When this occurs, the present reality, with its attendant fantasies, becomes a situation of danger. The state of mind and the affects that are generated under these extreme conditions may impact memories of trauma and allow them to come to consciousness. Hyperarousal, states of mind, and configurations or schema may activate and be a context for emotional memory that has been unavailable in the transference. The horrors of the terrorist attack gave us another opportunity to observe the interaction between state phenomena and psychological defense.

Concluding Thoughts

The study of trauma and memories of trauma offers an opportunity to bring together once again the clinical and research traditions of psychoanalysis, psychiatry, psychology, and the cognitive sciences and neurosciences. The psychoanalytic point of view contributes an intimate familiarity with the nature and functioning of psychic reality and fantasy as these influence experience, perception, and memory. In their daily work, psychoanalysts are immersed in the vicissitudes of motivated forgetting and remembering. They offer themselves as participants in remembering, using the phenomenon of transference and so have seen and experienced the impact of the past on the present, in its many forms. The research traditions contribute long experience with the study of the development, capacities, functions, and states of mind, brain, and body as they interact with each other and with the environment. Freud and Breuer began with a common interest in the impact of trauma on conscious awareness, states of mind, memory, and symptom formation. Their diverging emphases and interests set us on a path of conceptual polarities that have hindered collaboration among disciplines until relatively recently.

The terrible events on September 11 have put before us the effects of shock, hyperarousal, terror, horror, and catastrophic loss. For some of us, dissociation, numbing, hypervigilance, and intrusive images are experiences, not ideas about experiences. We have been given a glimpse of the "terrifying too-muchness" and overstimulation of a child who is actually overwhelmed during trauma and has to resort to "massive and mind-distorting defenses in order to continue to think and feel" (Shengold, 1967, 1979). How are we going to describe what we have seen and experienced? How will we combine our knowledge about states of the body, brain, and mind with our knowledge about meaning, motivation, fantasy, and defense? These are the challenges we have before us. Sadly, for many children, this tragedy is the trauma that may painfully reemerge later in their lives.

References

American Psychiatric Association (1994), *Diagnostic and Statistical Manual of Mental Disorders*, 4th ed. Washington, DC: American Psychiatric Association.

Bremner, J. D. (2001), A biological model for delayed recall of childhood abuse. *J. Aggress. Maltreat. Trauma*, 4:165–183.

Brenneis, C. B. (1994), Can early childhood trauma be reconstructed from dreams? On the relation of dreams to trauma. *Psychoanal. Psychol.*, 11: 429–447.

_____ (1996), Memory systems and the psychoanalytic retrieval of memories of trauma. *J. Amer. Psychoanal. Assn.*, 44:1165–1187.

Breuer, J. & Freud, S. (1893–1895), Studies on hysteria. *Standard Edition*, 2:1–309. London: Hogarth Press, 1955.

Bromberg, P. M. (1998), *Standing in the Spaces*. Hillsdale, NJ: The Analytic Press.

Collins, A. M. & Loftus, E. F. (1975), A spreading activation theory of semantic processing. *Psychol. Bull.*, 82:207–228.

Freud, S. (1900), The interpretation of dreams. *Standard Edition*, 5:339–625. London: Hogarth Press, 1953.

Guntrip, H. (1975), My experience of analysis with Fairbairn and Winnicott: How complete a result does a psychoanalytic therapy achieve? *Internat. Rev. Psycho-Anal.*, 2:145–156.

Laub, D. & Auerbahn, N. C. (1993), Knowing and not knowing massive psychic trauma: Forms of traumatic memory. *Internat. J. Psycho-Anal.*, 74:287–302.

Le Doux, J. (1996), *The Emotional Brain*. New York: Simon & Schuster.

Leichtman, M. D., Ceci, S. & Ornstein, P. A. (1992), The influence of affect on memory: Mechanism and development. In: *Handbook of Emotion and Memory*, ed. S. A. Christianson. Hillsdale, NJ: Lawrence Erlbaum Associates.

McEwen, B. (1995), Stressful experience, brain, and emotions: Developmental, genetic, and hormonal influences. In: *The Cognitive Neurosciences*, ed. M. Gazzaniga. Cambridge, MA: MIT Press, pp. 1117–1135.

McGaugh, J. L. (1990), Significance and remembrance: The role of neuromodulatory systems. *Psychol. Sci.*, 1:15–25.

Nadel, L. & Jacobs, W. J. (1996), The role of the hippocampus in PTSD and phobia. In: *The Hippocampus: Functions and Clinical Relevance*, ed. N. Kato. Amsterdam: Elsevier Science, pp. 455–463.

O'Keefe, J. & Nadel, L. (1978), *The Hippocampus as a Cognitive Map*. Oxford, England: Clarendon Press.

Perry, B. D., Pollard, R. A., Blakley, T. L., Baker, W. L. & Vigilante, D. (1996), Childhood trauma, the neurobiology of adaptation and use-dependent development of the brain: How states become traits. *Infant Ment. Health J.*, 16:271–291.

Schacter, D. (1992), Understanding implicit memory: A cognitive science approach. *Amer. Psychol.*, April:559–569.

Shengold, L. (1967), The effects of overstimulation: Rat people. *Internat. J. Psycho-Anal.*, 48:403–415.

_____ (1979), Child abuse and deprivation soul murder. *J. Amer. Psycho-anal. Assn.*, 27:533–559.

Terr, L. C. (1991), Childhood traumas: An outline and overview. *Amer. J. Psychiat.*, 148:10–20.

van der Kolk, B. A. (1994), The body keeps score: Memory and the evolving psychobiology of posttraumatic stress. *Harvard Rev. Psychiat.*, 1:253–265.

_____ & Fisler, R. (1995), Dissociation and the fragmentary nature of traumatic memories: Overview and exploratory study. *J. Traumatic Stress*, 8:505–525.

_____ Herron, N. & Hostetler, A. (1994), The history of trauma in psychiatry. *Psychiat. Clin. North Amer.*, 17:583–600.

_____ & van der Hart, O. (1989), Pierre Janet and the breakdown of adaptation in psychological trauma. *Amer. J. Psychiat.*, 146:1530–1540.

Yovell, Y. (2000), From hysteria to posttraumatic stress disorder: Psychoanalysis and the neurobiology of traumatic memory. *Neuropsychoanalysis*, 2: 1–18.

Chapter 10

The Emerging Neurobiology of Attachment and Separation

How Parents Shape Their Infant's Brain and Behavior

Myron A. Hofer

Myron Hofer's decades-long work, using an animal model, on the biological subsystems entailed in the attachment bond has provided an empirical basis for all modern conceptualizations of the way the attachment bond functions in earliest life. Through Hofer's work, we now understand that the attachment bond comprises multiple subsystems, whereby the maternal partner shapes and regulates the physiologic, neurophysiologic, and psychological functioning of the offspring. If one asks what exactly is lost when one is separated from an attachment figure, one has to go to Hofer's work. Put another way, his work provides an indispensable basis for understanding why separation can be a trauma.

In this communication, Hofer not only reprises his previous research findings vis-à-vis the effects of separation on the basic systems of stress management, but he also offers an important new conceptualization of a mechanism whereby certain positive maternal behaviors may enhance the chances that infants will repeat those behaviors in mothering the next generation.

Our own feelings revolt against the idea of infants living under the condition of air raid danger and underground sleeping.... A child of one [to] four years of age will shake and tremble with the anxiety of its mother.... The primitive animal tie between mother and baby ... [making] one being out of the two, is the basis for the development of this type of air raid anxiety in children....

[But] London children were on the whole much less upset by the bombing than by the evacuation to the country as a protection against it [pp. 37, 44].

—Freud and Burlingham,
War and Children, 1943

These observations made more than a half century ago could be considered to mark the beginning of the field now called *attachment.* The unprecedented trauma that the repeated Nazi air raids inflicted on the civilian population of London attracted the attention of the public to several unexpected aspects of the responses of young children to these events and their consequences. From our present perspective, it is hard for us to understand the surprise people expressed to find that children were much more distressed by evacuation to safe homes in the countryside than by the collapse of buildings around them when they were with their mothers. This buffering effect of maternal presence was unexpected to many, as was the degree to which the development of air-raid anxiety in children reflected the anxiety level of the child's mother.

It is ironic that the present book is appearing in the aftermath of another unprecedented form of mass trauma inflicted on an urban civilian population. As it was in 1943, we cannot predict what new insights and fields of study may emerge from September 11, 2001. We are in the early stages of a new appreciation for the biological origins of the human response to psychological trauma and are caught up in a wave of neuroscience research that is already giving us a new level of understanding of the role of early social relationships in that response.

Why Separation Is Traumatic

The first quotation at the beginning of this chapter, from Anna Freud and Burlingham in 1943, shows the authors' intuitive understanding that a "primitive animal tie" exists between mother and baby, but it was not until 25 years later that John Bowlby's evolutionary synthesis (1969) and Harry Harlow's early deprivation studies in monkeys (Harlow and Harlow, 1965) made the possibility of studying the biology of attachment a reality. In Bowlby and Harlow's work, as well as in the clinical observations of Freud and Burlingham a generation before, it was maternal separation that revealed the existence of a deeper layer of processes within the apparently simple interactions of mother and infant. Bowlby and Harlow viewed these processes as primarily psychological. Physiological responses of the infant to separation, in their conception, represented "rupture" of a psychological "bond" that was formed as part of the integrated psychophysiological organization of a unitary attachment system. More recent research, however, has revealed a network of simple behavioral and biological processes that underlie these psychological constructs generally used to define and understand early social relationships.

Experiments in our laboratory have shown that infant rats have complex and lasting responses to maternal separation similar to primates, in a number of different physiological and behavioral systems. A number of years ago, we found that the slower developing components (Bowlby's "despair" phase) were *not* an integrated psychophysiological response, as had been supposed, but the result of a novel mechanism. As separation continued, each of the individual systems of the infant rat responded to the absence of one or another of the components of the infant's previous interaction with its mother. Providing one of these components to a separated pup (e.g., maternal warmth) maintained the level of brain biogenic amine function underlying the pup's general activity level (Stone, Bonnet, and Hofer, 1976; Hofer, 1980) but had no effect on other systems (e.g., the pup's cardiac rate). Heart rate fell 40% after 18 hours of separation, regardless of whether supplemental heat was provided (Hofer, 1971). The heart rate, normally maintained by sympathetic tone, we found was regulated by maternal provision of milk to neural receptors in the lining of the pup's stomach (Hofer and Weiner, 1975).

By studying a number of additional systems, such as those controlling sleep–wake states (Hofer, 1976), activity level (Hofer, 1975), sucking pattern (Brake et al., 1982), and blood pressure (Shear, Brunelli, and Hofer, 1983), we concluded that in maternal separation all these regulatory components of the mother–infant interaction are withdrawn at once. This widespread loss creates a pattern of increases or decreases in level of function of the infant's systems, depending upon whether the particular system had been up- or down-regulated by the previous mother–infant interaction. We called these *hidden regulators* because they were not evident when simply observing the mother–infant interaction.

Other investigators, using this approach, have since discovered other maternal regulatory systems of the same sort. For example, removal of the dam from rat pups was found to produce a rapid (30 minutes) fall in the pup's growth hormone (GH) levels, and vigorous tactile stroking of maternally separated pups (mimicking maternal licking) prevented the fall in GH (Kuhn and Schanberg, 1991). Brain substrates for this effect were then investigated, and it now appears that GH levels are normally maintained by maternal licking, acting through serotonin (5HT) 2A and 2C receptor modulation of the balance between growth hormone–releasing factor (GHRF) and somatostatin (SS) that together act on the anterior pituitary release of GH (Katz et al., 1996). The withdrawal of maternal licking by separation allows GHRF to fall and SS to rise, resulting in a precipitate fall in GH.

Human Implications of Maternal Regulators

There are several biological similarities between this maternal deprivation effect in rats and the growth retardation that occurs in some variants of human reactive attachment disorders of infancy. Applying this new knowledge about the regulation of GH to low–birth-weight prematurely born babies, Tiffany Field and coworkers joined the Schanberg group (Field et al., 1986). They used a combination of stroking and limb movement, administered three times a day for 15 minutes each time and continued throughout their two weeks of hospitalization. This intervention increased weight gain, head circumference, and behavior-development test scores in relation to a randomly chosen control group, with beneficial effects discernible many months later. Clearly, early regulators are effective in humans, and over time periods as long as several weeks.

We began to understand the infant's separation response as one of loss of a number of individual regulatory processes that were hidden within the interactions of the previous relationship, with individual components of the interaction regulating specific physiological and behavioral systems. An important implication of this finding is that these ongoing regulatory interactions could shape the development of the infant's brain and behavior, throughout the preweaning period when mother and infant remained in close proximity. We could then think of the mother–infant interaction as a regulator of normal infant development, variations in the intensity and patterning of the mother–infant interactions gradually shaping infant behavior and physiology. These processes go beyond the adaptive evolutionary role of attachment as a protection against predators, as proposed by Bowlby. Regulatory effects of early interactions are likely to have evolved because of their capacity to shape the adaptive capabilities of the infant in accordance with the prior experience of the mother, as reflected in her maternal behavior toward her infant. Such a mechanism for intergenerational transmission of traits would provide a preadaptation for the next generation in the rapidly changing ecological conditions as mammals evolved (see later discussion).

How Infants Learn to Stay Close to Mothers

These regulatory interactions and their roles in separation responses and in shaping development all depend on the existence of a behavioral system through which the newborn maintains proximity to its mother. Bowlby was uncertain about exactly how such a system developed in mammals and hypothesized that some learning mechanism must exist that is similar to the phenomenon of imprinting in birds, made famous by Konrad Lorenz (1966). We are now beginning to gain an understanding of how such a specific proximity-maintenance system develops in animals and humans at the level of basic learning mechanisms and the brain systems mediating them.

These studies revealed for the first time that within two to three days after birth, neonatal rat pups could learn to discriminate, prefer, approach, and maintain proximity to an odor that had been associated with forms of stimulation that naturally occurred within the early mother–infant interaction (Sullivan, Hofer, and Brake, 1986b). Random presentations of the two stimuli (odor and reward) had no such effect, a control procedure that identified the change in behavior as due to associative conditioning and not some nonspecific effect of repeated stimulation. Because the learning required only two or three paired presentations and because the preference was retained for many days, it seemed to qualify as the long-sought "imprinting-like process" that is likely to be central to attachment in slow-developing mammals. Indeed, a human analogue of this process was found by Sullivan and others (1991), who showed that when human newborns were presented with a novel odor and then were rubbed along their torsos to simulate maternal care, the next day they became activated and turned their head preferentially toward that odor. This suggests that rapid learning of orientation to olfactory cues is an evolutionarily conserved process in mammalian newborns.

Attachment to Abusive Caretakers

Clinical observations have taught us that not only does attachment occur to supportive caretakers but also that children can suffer considerable abuse while remaining strongly attached to the abusive caretaker. Although it may initially appear to be counterproductive from an evolutionary perspective to form and maintain an attachment to an abusive caretaker, it may be better for a slow-developing mammalian infant to have a bad caretaker than no caretaker. This aspect of human attachment can also be modeled in the infant rat. During the first postnatal week, we found that a surprisingly broad spectrum of stimuli can function as reinforcers to produce an odor preference in rat pups (Sullivan et al., 1986; Sullivan, Hofer, and Brake, 1986). These stimuli range from apparently rewarding ones such as milk and access to the mother (Brake et al., 1982; Pedersen, Williams, and Blass, 1982; Alberts and May, 1984; Wilson and Sullivan, 1994) to apparently aversive stimuli such as moderate shock and tailpinch (Sullivan, Hofer, and Brake, 1986; Camp and Rudy, 1988), stimuli that elicit escape responses from the pups. Threshold to shock (Stehouwer and Campbell, 1978) and behavioral response (Emerich et al., 1985) to shock does not change between the ages of nine and 11 weeks. As pups mature and reach an age when leaving the nest becomes more likely, olfactory learning comes to more closely resemble learning in adults. Specifically, odor aversions are easily learned by two-week-olds, and acquisition of odor preferences are limited to odors paired with stimuli of positive value (Sullivan and Wilson, 1995).

Thus, the odor learning that underlies early attachment in the rat appears to take place in response to a very broad range of contingent events while pups are confined to the nest but becomes more selective at a time in development when pups begin leaving the nest and encountering novel odors not associated with the mother. Unique learning capabilities facilitating infant attachment appear throughout the animal kingdom and may have evolved to ensure that altricial animals easily form a repertoire of proximity-seeking behaviors, regardless of the specific qualities of the treatment they receive from the primary caretaker. It is certainly beneficial for pups not to learn an aversion to their mother's odor or inhibit approach responses to nest odors; instead, pups need to exhibit approach behaviors to procure the mother's milk, warmth, and protection.

A similar phenomenon exists in avian species. Specifically, experiencing an aversive shock during exposure to an imprinting object strengthens the following response. For example, in a series of classic experiments by Hess (1962) and Salzen (1970), recently hatched chicks were shocked (3 mA for 0.5 seconds) while presented with a surrogate mother. The next day, chicks that were shocked showed a significantly stronger following response than chicks that were not shocked. With striking similarity to the infant rat, similar pairings in older chicks resulted in a subsequent aversion to the surrogate mother. Additional mammalian species where similar phenomenon have been documented include nonhuman primates (Harlow and Harlow, 1965), dogs (Fisher, 1955, cited in Rajecki, Lamb, and Obmascher, 1978), and humans (Helfer, Kempe, and Krugman, 1997).

In rats, early attachment-related odors appear to retain value into adulthood, although the role of the odor in modifying behavior appears to change with development. Work done independently in the labs of Celia Moore (Moore, Jordan, and Wong, 1996) and Elliot Blass (Fillion and Blass, 1986) demonstrated that adult male rats exhibited enhanced sexual performance when exposed to the natural and artificial odors learned in infancy.

Brain Substrates for Early Attachment Learning

This rapid learning has been traced to focal odor-specific areas in the olfactory bulb where specific cell types alter their firing rates in response to the specific odor as a result of the learning experience (Sullivan et al., 1990; Wilson and Sullivan, 1994). This altered firing rate is the result of activation of norepinephrine (NE) pathways leading from the locus coeruleus. Indeed, the behavioral learning can be driven by stimulation of the locus or NE injection in the olfactory bulb in association with the novel odor, rather than the association of maternal interaction with the novel odor.

Recent evidence has shown that associations based on traumatic levels of stimulation in the first week are dependent on endogenous opioid receptor pathways, whereas positive associations are not (Sullivan et al., 2000). When aversion develops in response to intense stimulation after the first 10 days, the amygdala becomes involved in mediation of the response, which had not been the case before. Thus, two differences have been found in the neural mediation of traumatic early learning, as opposed to positive reinforcement of the same behavior.

Parallel Processes in Maternal Attachment to Infants

Successful mother–infant interactions require the reciprocal responding of both individuals. Human mothers rapidly learn about their baby's characteristics and can identify their baby's cry, odor, and facial features within hours of birth (Porter, Cernoch, and McLaughlin, 1983; Eidelman and Kaitz, 1992; Kaitz et al., 1992). An animal model for this rapid learning has received considerable attention (Brennan and Keverne, 1997; Fleming, O'Day, and Kraemer, 1999). Indeed, there are interesting parallels between the early attachment behavior of infants and the attachment behavior of the newly parturient mother. In rats and sheep, a temporally restricted period of postpartum olfactory learning in the mother involving NE facilitates the mother's learning about her young (Levy et al., 1990; Moffat, Suh, and Fleming, 1993). It is possible that mammalian mothers and pups use similar neural circuitry to form their reciprocal attachment.

From Physiological Regulation to Mental Representation

In humans, the early learning processes and the widespread regulatory interactions just described are also the first experiences out of which mental representations and their associated emotions arise. So far as we understand the process for the human, experiences made up of the infant's individual acts, parental responses, sensory impressions, and associated affects are laid down in memory during and after early parent–infant interactions (Stern, 1985; Gergeley and Watson, 1999). These individual units of experience are integrated into something like a network of attributes in memory, invested with associated affect, and result in the formation of what Bowlby referred to as an "internal working model" of the relationship.

It seems likely that these mental structures combine the infant's newly developing capacities to anticipate events and to respond to symbolic cues with the earlier biological functions of the "hidden" regulatory interactions, through processes similar to the functional links involved in the classical conditioning of physiologic responses. In this way, our concept of the "mental representation" can be thought to link together into a functional network within the child's brain, the learned patterns of behavior and the physiological response systems previously regulated by the mother–infant interaction. We can thus envisage the development of self-regulation of the behavioral and physiological systems underlying motivation and affect, gradually supplanting the sensorimotor, thermal, and nutrient-regulatory systems found in the interactions of younger infants with their mothers. This would link biological systems with internal-object representation and would account for the remarkable upheavals of biological as well as psychological systems that take place in adult humans in response to cues signaling impending separation or in response to losses established simply upon hearing of a death, for example, by telephone (Hofer, 1984, 1996).

Mother–infant relationships that differ in quality and that necessarily involve different levels and patterns of behavioral and physiological regulation in a variety of systems will be reflected in the nature of the mental representations present in different children as they grow up. The emotions aroused during early crying responses to separation, during the profound state changes associated with the prolonged loss of all maternal regulators and during the reunion of a separated infant with its mother, are apparently intense. These emotional states have commanded our attention; they are what everyone intuitively recognizes about attachment and separation and what we feel about the people we are close to. As inner experiences, these occur at a different level of psychobiological organization than the changes in autonomic, endocrine, and neurophysiological systems we have been able to study in rats and monkeys, as well as in younger human infants. Hidden regulators thus form a developmental as well as a conceptual bridge between the tangible and the intangible in our understanding of attachment.

Maternal Regulation of Development

The actions of maternal regulators of infant biology and behavior are not limited to the mediation of responses to maternal separation previously discussed. They exert their regulatory effects continuously, throughout the preweaning period and even beyond. A good illustration is the recent discovery of a major role of the mother–infant interaction in the development of the hypothalamic–pituitary–adrenocortical (HPA) axis during the preweaning period. It has been long known that in the rat from postnatal days four to 14 the pups' HPA response to isolation and to mild stressors like saline injections is less intense than in the newborn or weaning periods, a stage known as the *stress-hyporesponsive period* (Levine, 1994). A similar period in the first year of human infants has been documented by Gunnar and Donzella (2002). Surprisingly, it was recently found that this developmental stage in rats is not the product of an intrinsic developmental program but the result of hidden regulators at work within the ongoing mother–infant interaction. First, it was found that nine- to 12-day-old pups' basal corticosterone (CORT) level and the magnitude of the pituitary adrenocorticotrophic hormone (ACTH) and CORT response to isolation were increased five-fold after 24 hours of maternal separation (Stanton, Gutierrez, and Levine, 1988). Next, by utilizing our concept of hidden regulators, Suchecki, Rosenfeld, and Levine (1993) attempted to prevent these separation-induced changes by supplying various components of the mother–infant interaction. They found that repeated stroking of the separated infants for as little as three one-minute periods prevented the increase in ACTH response and that providing milk by cheek cannula during separation prevented the separation-induced blunting of the adrenal CORT response to ACTH.

Thus, the mother–infant interaction normally reduces infant HPA responses, and maternal separation reverses this hyporesponsive state. Tracing these regulatory effects back to brain systems, Levine's group has more recently found that stroking (representing maternal licking) regulates the intensity of neural responses in the paraventricular nucleus of the hypothalamus and the expression of the gene for production of corticotropin-releasing hormone (CRH) receptors in the amygdala and other limbic system sites as well (van Oers et al., 1998). It is intraorally administered milk, however, that regulates glucocorticoid receptor gene expression in the CA1 region of the hippocampus and corticosterone release from the adrenal cortex in response to pituitary adrenocorticotrophic hormone.

Through this anatomical and molecular neuromodulator analysis, Levine and colleagues (Suchecki et al., 1993) discovered that maternal licking and milk delivery during suckling independently exert a prolonged attenuating effect on the responsiveness of the HPA axis. This maternal regulatory effect, once established in the first few postnatal days, continues throughout most of the nursing period, finally declining as weaning occurs from day 15 to day 21. This regulatory effect is achieved by increasing the inhibitory feedback of CORT on the pituitary, through increased numbers of hippocampal glucocorticoid receptors, and by decreasing the hypothalamic stimulation of CRH and ACTH output. These maternal regulatory effects on the pup's brain can be rapidly reversed and stress responsiveness restored by maternal separation.

Early Shaping of Adult Stress Responses

These preweaning studies on brain mechanisms underlying maternal regulation of HPA axis function suggested that qualitative differences in the patterns of early mother–infant interaction could have long-term effects on HPA responses to stress in adults, similar to those we had discovered for adult blood pressure in spontaneously hypertensive rats (Myers et al., 1989). Meaney and his colleagues used the maternal-behavior-observational approach developed in those studies to directly test this implication of the discovery of maternal regulators (Liu et al., 1997). They found that dams in their colony that were observed naturally to have high levels of licking, grooming, and the high-arched-back nursing position (LG/ABN) produced pups that were later found to be less fearful in a variety of behavioral tests and to show lower than normal HPA axis responsivity to restraint stress as adults than the offspring of dams that naturally showed the lowest levels of these early interactions.

To show that these differences in adult offspring were not simply reflections of a different genetic constitution in the two groups, Meaney and his colleagues (Liu et al., 1997) handled daily the infants of the low-LG/ABN group, an early intervention that is known to increase levels of the mother's concurrent LG/ABN behaviors. By doing so, he showed that the adult behavior and HPA-axis responses of the offspring also changed to closely resemble the patterns that naturally occurred in the previously studied high-LG/ABN group.

Intergenerational Transmission of Maternal Effects

These results showed that an intervention that alters the mother–infant interaction pattern also changes the adult fear behavior and physiological-response characteristics of the offspring. One of the observations that currently occupies researchers in the attachment area is how mothers in one generation can pass on to their adult-female offspring the attachment pattern they experienced as infants. The experiment just described provided a chance to find out if this trans-generational effect occurs in nonprimate species and to explore how it comes about. By allowing the offspring of the handled litters to rear another generation, this time without handling and under normal laboratory conditions, Meaney and his colleagues went on to find that the mother–infant interaction shown by these normally reared prog-eny resembled the one their mothers had been induced to have by handling when they were infants (high LG/ABN) rather than the one characteristic of their grandmothers before the handling intervention (low LG/ABN) (Francis et al., 1999). Furthermore, the unmanipulated pups in these litters also went on to show the adult behaviors and hormonal stress patterns typical of offspring of high-LG/ABN litters.

What could be the basis for the transmission of maternal behavior from one generation to the next? A recent paper by the same group (Champage et al., 2001) showed that females that were more respon-sive to pups had higher levels of oxytocin in an area of the brain known to be central in mediating maternal behavior, the medial preoptic area, but also in other related areas. More directly, giving a drug to mother on the third postpartum day that blocked her oxytocin receptors completely eliminated the differences between high- and low-LG/ABN mothers. Thus, we can infer that the neural-substrate precursors for maternal behavior in the infant can be shaped by the infant's interaction with its mother so that in adulthood it will show patterns of maternal behavior that reflect this early experience and that may in turn shape the development of maternal behavior in its offspring.

These experiments show the intergenerational transmission of mother–infant interaction patterns and the developmental effects of these interaction patterns on adult behavior and physiology. They provide an animal model for the neurobiological analysis of mechanisms underlying environmental effects on the transgenerational patterns of mothering described by Schechter and by Teicher in this volume, and they provide an experimental verification of one of the central tenets of present-day human attachment research.

Summary and Perspective

I have described how recent research is beginning to deepen our understanding of the traumatic effects of maternal separation, the nature of the bond that keeps the infant close to its mother, and how different patterns or qualities of mother–infant interactions shape the development of the infant so as to alter both behavior and psychological responses to stress in adulthood. It has become evident that an "enduring social bond" (to use Bowlby's term) can be formed in laboratory animals and that we can now begin to understand that bond in terms of separate processes that can be delineated as they work independently, serially, or in parallel to produce the familiar behavioral signs of attachment. The discovery of these component processes allows us to begin to understand what makes up the "glue" that holds the infant to the mother. The discovery of regulatory interactions within the mother–infant relationship allows us to escape the circularity of the traditional attachment model, in which the response to separation is attributed to disruption of a social bond, the existence of which is inferred from the presence of that same separation response. Beginning before birth and continuing in the newborn period, novel processes of associative learning have been discovered that allow us for the first time to identify and understand the mysterious "imprinting-like process" that Bowlby envisioned as the altricial mammalian equivalent of avian imprinting. And, we can begin to see how one of the consequences of these early learning processes, acting within repeated regulatory interactions of the first relationship, provide a novel source of experiences for the formation of the mental representation of the infant–mother relationship.

At present, there is widespread use of the concept of regulation as inherent in human mother–infant interaction. The word is generally used in two ways: First, it refers to the graded effects of different patterns of interaction on the emotional responses of the infant, the so-called regulation of affect (Schore, 1994). Second, it refers to how the behaviors initiated by the infant and mother, their responses to each other, or both, regulate the interaction itself, its tempo or rhythm (hence its "quality") or the distance (both psychological and physical) between the members of the dyad (e.g., Gergeley and Watson, 1999). The word *regulation*, however, is also used extensively in the literature on molecular genetic, cellular, and electrophysiological brain processes so that it is a useful conceptual link across wide differences in the level of organization at which developmental processes are studied.

The discovery of regulatory interactions and the effects of their withdrawal allow us to understand not only the responses in young organisms of limited cognitive-emotional capacity to separation but also the familiar experienced emotions and memories that can be verbally described to us by older children and adults. It is not that rat pups respond to loss of regulatory processes while human infants respond with emotions of love, sadness, anger, and grief. Human infants, as they mature, can respond at the symbolic level *as well as* at the level of the behavioral and physiological processes of the regulatory interactions. The two levels appear to be organized as parallel and complementary response systems. Even *adult* humans continue to respond in important ways at the sensorimotor-physiologic level in their social interactions, separations, and losses, continuing a process begun in infancy. A good example of this is the mutual regulation of menstrual synchrony among close female friends, an effect that takes place out of conscious awareness and has recently been found to be mediated at least in part by a pheromonal cue (Stern and McClintock, 1998). Other examples may well include the role of social interactions in entraining circadian physiological rhythms, the disorganizing effects of sensory deprivation, and the remarkable therapeutic effects of social support on the course of medical illness (Hofer, 1984). Thus, adult love, grief, and bereavement may well contain elements of the simpler regulatory processes that we can clearly see in the attachment responses of infant animals to separation from their social companions.

This is perhaps the most challenging area for future research: to find out how to apply what we have learned in basic brain and behavior studies to the human condition. Studies on other animals cannot be used to define human nature, but many of the principles and new ways to approach the mother–infant interaction described in this chapter can be useful in studies of the human mother–infant relationship. We must take into account obvious differences between species, such as the primacy of olfaction and tactile senses in the newborn rat as contrasted to the wider range of senses available to the human newborn.

A role for nonverbal features of the early mother–infant interaction in the specification of lasting mental representations of maternal behavior in the adult is a central hypothesis of clinical attachment theory. It would be difficult to confirm clinically this useful idea with any degree of certainty. But the transgenerational effects on maternal behavior and the HPA axis, described in this chapter, can be a research model for understanding the psychobiological mechanisms for this important effect. Prospective clinical studies from infancy to childhood would be most interesting and could reveal which residues of particular early interactions can be related to which later characteristics of the stories, play, or social relationships of older children, and eventually the parental behavior of adults.

Our understanding of the evolutionary survival value of remaining close to the mother has been expanded to include the many pathways available for regulation of the development of the infant's physiological and behavioral systems, even the regulation of the development of its adult maternal behavior, by the early interactions of the infant with its caregiver. The first relationship thus provides an opportunity for the mother to shape the developing physiology, brain systems and behavior of her offspring, through her patterned interactions with her infant. Behavioral adaptations to environmental change occurring in the life of the mother can thus lead to "anticipatory" biological and behavioral changes in the offspring—a novel evolutionary mechanism that may form a bridge between biological and cultural evolution.

Acknowledgments

The research described in this chapter was supported by grants from the National Institute of Mental Health and by the Sackler Institute for Developmental Psychobiology at Columbia University.

Thanks to MIT Press for permission to use excerpts from my chapter with Regina Sullivan from the 2001 *Handbook of Developmental Cognitive Neuroscience*, edited by C. A. Nelson and M. Luciana, pp. 599–616.

References

Alberts, J. R. & May, B. (1984), Nonnutritive, thermotactile induction of filial huddling in rat pups. *Devel. Psychobiol.*, 17:161–181.

Bowlby, J. (1969), *Attachment and Loss, Vol. 1*. New York: Basic Books.

Brake, S. C., Sager, D. J., Sullivan, R. & Hofer, M. A. (1982), The role of intraoral and gastrointestinal cues in the control of sucking and milk consumption in rat pups. *Devel. Psychobiol.*, 15:529–541.

Brennen, P. A. & Keverne E. B. (1997), Neural mechanisms of mammalian olfactory learning. *Prog. Neurobiol.*, 51:457–451.

Camp, L. L. & Rudy, J. W. (1988), Changes in the categorization of appetitive and aversive events during postnatal development of the rat. *Devel. Psychobiol.*, 21:25–42.

Champagne, F., Diori, J., Sharma, S. & Meaney M. (2001), Naturally occurring variations in maternal behavior in the rat are associated with differences in estrogen-inducible central oxytocin receptors. *Proc. Natl. Acad. Sci.*, 98:12736–12741.

Eidelman, A. I. & Kaitz, M. (1992), Olfactory recognition: A genetic or learned capacity? *Devel. Behav. Pediat.*, 13:126–127.

Emerich, D. F., Scalzo, F. M., Enters, E. K., Spear, N. & Spear, L. (1985), Effects of 6-hydroxydopamine–induced catecholamine depletion on shock-precipitated wall climbing of infant rat pups. *Devel. Psychobiol.*, 18:215–227.

Field, T. M., Schanberg, S. M., Scafidid, F., Bauer, C. R., Vega-Lahr, N., Garcia, R., Nystrom, J. & Kuhn, C. M. (1986), Tactile/kinesthetic stimulation effects on preterm neonates. *Pediatrics*, 77:654–658.

Fillion, T. J. & Blass, E. M. (1986), Infantile experience with suckling odors determines adult sexual behavior in male rats. *Science*, 231:729–731.

Fleming, A. S., O'Day, E. H. & Kraemer, G. W. (1999), Neurobiology of mother–infant interactions: Experience and central nervous system plasticity across development and generations. *Neurosci. Biobehav. Rev.*, 23: 673–685.

Francis, D., Diorio, J., Liu, D. & Meaney, M. J. (1999), Nongenomic transmission across generations of maternal behavior and stress responses in the rat. *Science*, 286:1155–1158.

Freud, A. & Burlingham, D. (1943), *War and Children*. New York: Medical War Books.

Gergeley, G. & Watson, J. S. (1999), Early social-emotional development: Contingency, perception and the social biofeedback model. In: *Early Social Cognition*, ed. P. Rochat. Mahwah, NJ: Lawrence Erlbaum Associates, pp. 101–136.

Gunnar, M. R. & Donzella, B. (2002), Social regulation of cortisol levels in early human development. *Psychoneuroendocrinology*, 27:199–220.

Harlow, H. F. & Harlow, M. K. (1965), The affectional systems. In: *Behavior of Nonhuman Primates, Vol. 2*, ed. A. Schrier, H. F. Harlow & F. Stollnitz. New York: Academic Press.

Helfer, M. E., Kempe, R. S. & Krugman, R. D. (1997), *The Battered Child*. Chicago: University of Chicago Press.

Hess, E. H. (1962), Ethology: An approach to the complete analysis of behavior. In: *New Directions in Psychology*, ed. R. Brown, E. Galanter, E. H. Hess & G. Mandler. New York: Holt, Rinehart & Winston.

Hofer, M. A. (1971), Cardiac rate regulated by nutritional factor in young rats. *Science*, 172:1039–1041.

———— (1975), Studies on how early maternal separation produces behavioral change in young rats. *Psychosom. Med.*, 37:245–264.

———— (1976), The organization of sleep and wakefulness after maternal separation in young rats. *Devel. Psychobiol.*, 9:189–205.

———— (1980), The effects of reserpine and amphetamine on the development of hyperactivity in maternally deprived rat pups. *Psychosom. Med.*, 42:513–520.

———— (1984), Relationships as regulators: A psychobiological perspective on bereavement. *Psychosom. Med.*, 46:183–197.

———— (1996), On the nature and consequences of early loss. *Psychosom. Med.*, 58:570–581.

———— & Weiner, H. (1975), Physiological mechanisms for cardiac control by nutritional intake after early maternal separation in the young rat. *Psychosom. Med.*, 37:8–24.

Kaitz, M., Lapidot, P. & Bronner, R. (1992), Parturient women can recognize their infants by touch. *Devel. Psychobiol.*, 1:35–39.

Katz, L. M., Nathan, L., Kuhn, C. M. & Schanberg, S. M. (1996), Inhibition of GH in maternal separation may be mediated through altered serotonergic activity at $5HT_{2A}$ and $5HT_{2C}$ receptors. *Psychoneuroendocrinology*, 21:219–235.

Kuhn, C. M. & Schanberg, S. M. (1991), Stimulation in infancy and brain development. In: *Psychopathology and the Brain*, ed. B. J. Carroll. New York: Raven Press.

Levine, A. (1994), The ontogeny of the hypothalamic–pituitary–adrenal axis: The influence of maternal factors. *Ann. N. Y. Acad. Sci.*, 746:275–293.

Levy, F., Gervais, R., Kindermann, U., Orgeur, P. & Pikeytty, V. (1990), Importance of ß-adrenergic receptors in the olfactory bulb of sheep for recognition of lambs. *Behav. Neurosci.*, 104:464–469.

Liu, D., Diorio, J., Tannenbaum, B., Caldji, C., Francis, D., Freedman, A., Sharma, S., Pearson, D., Plotsky, P. M. & Meaney, M. J. (1997), Maternal care, hippocampal glucocorticoid receptors, and hypothalamic–pituitary–adrenal responses to stress. *Science*, 277:1659–1661.

Lorenz, K. (1996), *On Aggression*. New York: Harcourt, Brace & World.

Moffat, S. D. Suh, E. J. & Fleming, A. (1993), Noradrenergic involvement in the consolidation of maternal experience in postpartum rats. *Physiol. Behav.*, 53:805–811.

Moore, C. L., Jordan, L. & Wong, L. (1996), Early olfactory experience, novelty and choice of sexual partner by male rats. *Physiol. Behav.*, 60:1361–1367.

Myers, M. M., Brunelli, S. A., Squire, R., Shindeldecker, R. & Hofer, M. A. (1989), Maternal behavior of SHR rats and its relationship to offspring blood pressure. *Devel. Psychobiol.*, 22:29–53.

Pedersen, P., Williams, C. L. & Blass, E. M. (1982), Activation and odor conditioning of suckling behavior in 3-day-old albino rats. *J. Exp. Psychol.*, 8:329–341.

Porter, M. J., Cernoch, J. M. & McLaughlin, F. J. (1983), Maternal recognition of neonates through olfactory cues. *Physiol. Behav.*, 30:151–154.

Rajecki, D. W, Lamb, M. E. & Obmascher, P. (1978), Toward a general theory of infantile attachment: A comparative review of aspects of the social bond. *Behav. Brain Sci.*, 3:417–464.

Salzen, E. A. (1970), Imprinting and environmental learning. In: *Development and Evolution of Behavior*, ed. L. R. Aronson, E. Tobach, D. S. Lehrman & J. Rosensblatt. San Francisco: Freeman.

Schore, A. N. (1994), *Affect Regulation and the Origin of the Self*. Hillsdale, NJ: Lawrence Erlbaum Associates.

Shear, M. K., Brunelli, S. A. & Hofer, M. A. (1983), The effects of maternal deprivation and of refeeding on the blood pressure of infant rats. *Psychosom. Med.*, 45:3–9.

Stanton, M. D., Gutierrez, Y. R. & Levine, S. (1988), Maternal deprivation potentiates pituitary–adrenal stress responses in infant rats. *Behav. Neurosci.*, 102:692–700.

Stehouwer, D. J. & Campbell, B. A. (1978), Habituation of the forelimb-withdrawal response in neonatal rats. *J. Exp. Psychol.*, 4:104–119.

Stern, D. N. (1985), *The Interpersonal World of the Infant.* New York: Basic Books.

Stern, K. & McClintock, M. K. (1998), Regulation of ovulation by human pheromones. *Nature,* 392:177–179.

Stone, E., Bonnet, K. & Hofer, M. A. (1976), Survival and development of maternally deprived rat pups: Role of body temperature. *Psychosom. Med.,* 38:242–249.

Suchecki, D., Rosenfeld, P. & Levine, S. (1993), Maternal regulation of the hypothalamic–pituitary–adrenal axis in the infant rat: The roles of feeding and stroking. *Devel. Brain Res.,* 75:185–192.

Sullivan, R. M., Brake, S. C., Hofer, M. A. & Williams, C. L. (1986), Huddling and independent feeding of neonatal rats can be facilitated by a conditioned change in behavioral state. *Devel. Psychobiol.,* 19:625–635.

_____ Hofer, M. A. & Brake, S. C. (1986), Olfactory-guided orientation in neonatal rats is enhanced by a conditioned change in behavioral state. *Devel. Psychobiol.,* 19:615–623.

_____ Landers, M., Yeager, B. & Wilson, D. A. (2000), Good memories of bad events in infancy. *Nature,* 407:38–39.

_____ Taborsky-Barba, S., Mendoza, R., Itano, A., Leon, M., Cotman, C., Payne, T. F. & Lott, I. (1991), Olfactory classical conditioning in neonates. *Pediatrics,* 87:511–518.

_____ & Wilson, D. A. (1995), Dissociation of behavioral and neural correlates of early associative learning. *Devel. Psychobiol.,* 28:213–219.

_____ _____ Wong, R., Correa, A. & Leon, M. (1990), Modified behavioral olfactory bulb responses to maternal odors in preweanling rats. *Devel. Brain Res.,* 53:243–247.

van Oers, H. J. J., de Kloet, E. R., Whelan, T. & Levine, S. (1998), Maternal deprivation effect on the infant's neural stress markers is reversed by tactile stimulation and feeding but not by suppressing corticosterone. *J. Neurosci.,* 18:10171–10179.

Wilson, D. A. & Sullivan, R. M. (1994), Neurobiology of associative learning in the neonate: Early olfactory learning. *Behav. Neural Biol.,* 61:1–18.

Chapter 11

Neurobiological Effects of Childhood Stress and Trauma

Martin H. Teicher, Ann Polcari,
Susan L. Andersen, Carl M. Anderson, and
Carryl Navalta

It is misleading to think of the effects of severe physical or sexual abuse (or both) in childhood exclusively in terms of posttraumatic stress disorder (PTSD). Almost two thirds of children with documented abuse, severe enough to warrant removal from the home, do not show PTSD but instead a variety of other psychiatric syndromes. In terms of understanding these diverse reactions, ranging from dissociative identity disorder and borderline personality disorder to depression, substance abuse, and attention-deficit/hyperactivity disorder, research indicates that fundamental alterations of the stress-management systems of the brain and body seem to be involved.

This chapter reviews current knowledge about these basic systemic changes secondary to early trauma and severe stress while offering an intriguing reconceptualization of their significance. The authors argue that though extremely costly socially and physiologically, and potentially leading to maladaptive strategies in a benign social world, the altered functioning of brain and body, seen in severely abused children, is potentially valuable in fostering survival in a hostile and abusive world.

The potential for the young to be exposed to malevolent stressors is ever present. Recent terrorist events, child abductions, and plague scares are just a few of the threats looming in our society. For many unfortunate children, threats loom in their homes, where exposure to traumatic stress occurs at the hands of abusive or neglectful parents. Such early severe stress may leave an indelible imprint on the structure and function of the brain (Teicher, 1989). The limits of exposure to traumatic stress that produces major brain effects are unknown. Trauma exposure can be acute or chronic—for example, very traumatic episodic events such as sexual abuse outside the home, or a chronic home atmosphere of degrading verbal abuse. Trauma exposure can take one form or, more likely, can occur in concert with other experiences. For example, emotional maltreatment often occurs with physical or sexual abuse. It is unclear how much of the variance researchers have attributed to physical or sexual abuse alone actually stems from a persistent atmosphere of emotional adversity or fear rather than certain specific events.

By design, the human brain is meant to be formed into its final arrangement by the effects of early experience (Jacobson, 1991). The developing mammalian brain is a rich neural network whose primary task is to acquire new information and develop skills. This rich network performs inefficiently and slowly, at great metabolic expenditure, and requires long periods of deep sleep (Feinberg, 1982). At a certain stage of development, excess and redundant connections are sculpted to speed performance of acquired skills and reduce metabolic demands and sleep requirements while sacrificing a certain degree of plasticity. Because the brain is designed to develop in this fashion, it is intrinsically shaped by early experience, and the consequence of stressful or deleterious experience may be enduring and irreversible. This chapter reviews what is currently known about how early stress and trauma exposure is associated with alterations in brain development and, in turn, how these alterations effect an individual's moods, cognitive ability, capacity to form healthy attachments, capacity to endure stress, and ability to control aggressive impulses.

The Stress Cascade Model

When viewed narrowly, early severe stress simply evokes a cascade of neurohumeral and neurotransmitter effects that produce enduring deleterious alterations in brain function. In this perspective, excessive stress can be seen as a noxious agent that interferes with the organized progression of brain development, producing a somewhat altered and impaired brain (Teicher, 1989; Ito et al., 1993; Teicher et al., 1993; Schiffer, Teicher, and Papanicolaou, 1995; Teicher et al., 1997; Ito et al., 1998). Indeed, research shows that a cascade of alterations is likely to occur following exposure to intense stress prior to onset of puberty. First, exposure to stress early in life activates stress-response systems and fundamentally alters their molecular organization to modify their sensitivity. Second, exposure of the developing brain to stress hormones interferes with normal growth and development of neurotransmitters and synaptic connections to stress. Different brain regions have different windows of vulnerability depending on their maturational state, genetics, gender, timing, rate of development, and the presence or absence of certain neuron receptors. Third, enduring functional consequences occur that include reduced left-hemisphere development, decreased left–right hemisphere integration, increased electrical irritability within limbic-system circuits, and diminished functional activity of the cerebellar vermis. Fourth, there are associated neuropsychiatric consequences and vulnerabilities, which lead to an enhanced risk for the development of posttraumatic stress disorder (PTSD), dissociative identity disorder (DID), borderline personality disorder (BPD), depression, and substance abuse. Within this frame, the consequences observed with early exposure to stress are due to developmental insult (Teicher, 1989, 1994; Teicher et al., 1994; Teicher et al., 1996; Teicher et al., 2001). This point of view is also articulated by several other authors (e.g., Bremner et al., 1997; Anisman et al., 1998; Perry and Pollard, 1998; De Bellis, Baum, et al., 1999; De Bellis, Keshavan, et al., 1999; Glaser, 2000; Kaufman et al., 2000; McEwen, 2000a).

The Developmental Adaptation to Stress Pathway

A thoughtful reevaluation of the cascade model questions whether the brain's complexity and ability to adapt have been underestimated (Teicher, 2000). The brain is designed to be shaped by experience, and severe stress has often been a routine component of early experience throughout the history of our species. It seems unlikely that changes in brain development brought on by exposure to early stress are simply forms of damage occurring in a brain unable to cope with the cascade of stress responses. Rather, the developing brain more likely copes adaptively to exposure to early stress by following this cascade as part of an alternative developmental pathway. Hence, neurobiological differences that scientists have observed are natural and selected modifications in brain structure and function triggered by exposure to certain forms and levels of stress during key periods of development. These modifications in development allow the individual to cope with high levels of stress or deprivation, which he may expect to encounter throughout the rest of his life. In this fashion, the brain selects an alternative developmental pathway that best matches its wiring and configuration to the environment that, based on early experience, it expects to survive and reproduce in.

If an individual is born into a malevolent and stress filled world, it will be crucial for his survival and reproductive success to maintain a state of vigilance and suspiciousness that will enable him to readily detect danger. He will need to have the potential to mobilize an intense fight–flight response, to react aggressively to challenge without undue hesitation, and to produce a robust stress response to facilitate survival.

In this sense, all of the observed brain changes in response to stress are adaptations to facilitate survival and reproductive success. Alterations in the amygdala and limbic irritability may foster fight–flight responses and aggressive defense. Hippocampal alterations may foster a more robust corticosteroid response. Further, hippocampal abnormalities may facilitate emergence of dissociation as an intrapsychic defense mechanism. Diminished left-hemisphere maturation, reduced corpus-callosum size, and attenuated left–right hemisphere integration may markedly augment an individual's capacity to rapidly and dramatically shift into an intense, angry, aggressive state when threatened with danger or loss. Diminished development of the cerebellar vermis may be crucial for the maintenance of this state of limbic irritability, hyperarousal, and sympathetic activation.

Exposure to early stress produces a lifelong increase in levels of vasopressin mRNA and diminished levels of oxytocin mRNA in the hypothalamus (Liu et al., 1997). Recent research suggests that oxytocin is a critical factor in affiliative love, maintenance of monogamous relationships, and normal nonsexual social interactions (Witt, Winslow, and Insel, 1992; Carter, DeVries, and Getz, 1995; Pedersen,

1997; Carter, 1998; Ostrowski, 1998; Uvnas-Moberg, 1998). Vasopressin is a powerful stress hormone that enables us to cope with blood loss or dehydration, whereas oxytocin produces an antistress response (Uvnas-Moberg, 1998). Both hormones may also function in the regulation of sexual response, with vasopressin generally enhancing sexual arousal and oxytocin accompanying climax and release (Carmichael et al., 1994). Theoretically, altered levels of vasopressin and oxytocin could predispose mammals to suffer from enhanced sexual arousal, diminished capacity for sexual fulfillment, and deficient commitment to a single partner. This in turn could foster promiscuity, which may adaptively facilitate reproductive success in times of danger.

These alterations are not optimal for survival and reproductive success in a more benign environment, however. As McEwen (2000a, b) has recently articulated, there is a severe cost associated with glucocorticoid and catecholamine stress responses. In the short run, they are essential for adaptation, homeostasis, and survival (allostasis). Over longer time intervals, they exact a cost (allostatic load) that can accelerate disease processes. In his view, early childhood stress and trauma increase allostatic load and lead individuals into social isolation, hostility, depression, and substance abuse and foster the emergence of extreme obesity and cardiovascular disease (McEwen, 2000b).

Effects of the Early Stress Response on Mental Health

There is a close fit between the effects of early maltreatment related to brain development and the array of psychiatric symptoms observed in individuals with a history of childhood abuse. What we have learned from the child-abuse research can be applied to our understanding of the developmental effects of other adversities. First, we describe the clinical findings; later, we summarize the research evidence of the effects on the brain, from the molecular to the functional levels.

Posttraumatic Stress Disorder

Most children exposed to traumatic events never develop PTSD. Deblinger and others (1989) found that only 6.9% of psychiatrically hospitalized children with physical abuse and 20.7% with sexual-abuse history met diagnostic criteria for PTSD. Famularo and colleagues (1996) found that only 35% of severely maltreated and psychologically traumatized children who were removed from parental custody due to the trauma actually met strict criteria for PTSD. Widom (1999) reported a 37.5% lifetime prevalence for emergence of PTSD for victims of substantiated childhood abuse and neglect. This is not necessarily a matter of resilience. Kiser and others (1991) found that abused children and adolescents who did not develop PTSD actually exhibited more anxiety, depression, externalizing behaviors, and overall problems than children who did. Similarly, Glod and colleagues (1997) found that abused, psychiatrically hospitalized children without PTSD had more agitated and disrupted sleep than abused children with PTSD. These findings suggest that PTSD criteria formulated and validated in adults does not necessarily adequately describe the psychiatric impact of exposure to childhood trauma and does not necessarily identify children most adversely affected by trauma.

Early childhood trauma may put an individual at greater risk of developing PTSD in response to another traumatic event later in life (Schaaf and McCanne, 1998; Brewin, Andrews, and Valentine, 2000). This enhanced risk may be related to corticotropin-releasing factor (CRF) neuronal overactivity (Heim et al., 1997). Subsequent exposure to infrequent specific traumas may sensitize the CRF-receptor system and enhance feedback and circadian regulation of cortisol, providing the neuroendocrine underpinnings for PTSD (Yehuda et al., 1996). Molecular alterations within the amygdala and locus coeruleus may produce limbic irritability or kindling, induce sympathetic hyperarousal (Villarreal and King, 2001), enhance fear or startle reactions (Rauch et al., 2000), augment fight–flight responses (Lee et al., 1998), and lead to the emergence of intrusive memories (Grillon, Southwick, and Charney, 1996), which are other components of PTSD. Further, adverse effects of early stress on hippocampal development may facilitate the emergence of the dissociative and amnesic components of PTSD (Teicher et al., 1996).

Dissociative Identity Disorder

DID may be a more extreme degree of attenuated hemispheric integration. Flor-Henry and others (1990) reported that patients with DID had an extreme degree of left-hemisphere activation. Perhaps some personality shifts may be associated with activation and transition to a right-hemisphere dominant mode. Abnormal hippocampal development may facilitate the generation of dissociative states, which may be triggered or exacerbated by the presence of limbic irritability (Mesulam, 1981; Schenk and Bear, 1981). Although significant neurological and electroencephalogram (EEG) abnormalities are not usually observed in patients with multiple personality disorder, Coons and colleagues (1988) reported 23% of their population had abnormal EEGs with paroxysmal spike and sharp waves.

Borderline Personality Disorder

Diminished left–right hemisphere integration and smaller corpus callosums in patients with a history of childhood abuse suggest an intriguing explaination for the emergence of BPD (Teicher, 1994; Teicher, Feldman, et al., 2002). With less well-integrated hemispheres, patients with BPD may shift rapidly from a logical and possibly overvaluing left-hemisphere state to a highly negative, critical, and emotional right-hemisphere state. This seems consistent with the theory that early problems of mother–child interaction undercut the integration of left- and right-hemispheric function (Muller, 1992). Very inconsistent behavior of a parent (e.g., sometimes loving, sometimes abusing) might generate an irreconcilable mental image in a young child. Instead of reaching an integrated view, the child would form two diametrically opposite views—storing the positive view in the left hemisphere, the negative view in the right. These mental images, and their associated positive and negative worldviews, may remain unintegrated, and the hemispheres remain autonomous, as the child grows up. This polarized hemispheric dominance could cause a person to see significant others as overly positive in one state and as resoundingly negative in another.

Further, limbic electrical irritability may be responsible for problems with aggression, and abnormal electrical activity has been associated with increased risk of suicide and self-destructive behavior (Struve, Klein, and Saraf, 1972). Previous research has suggested a possible relationship between temporal-lobe–limbic-system dysfunction and BPD (Andrulonis et al., 1981; Snyder and Pitts, 1984; Cowdry, Pickar, and Davies, 1985). Snyder and Pitts (1984) found that patients with BPD had a higher incidence of EEG abnormalities than a contrast group of dysthymic patients. Similarly, Cowdry and colleagues (1985) found that many patients with BPD had a definite sharp-wave abnormality on EEG. Self-destructive behavior, mood fluctuations, and susceptibility to brief psychotic states are consistent with stress-induced alterations in dopamine and serotonin levels in the amygdala and nucleus accumbens (Teicher, Andersen, and Hostetter, 1995; Matthews et al., 2001).

Depression

Heightened risk for depression may be a consequence of reduced activity of the left frontal lobes (Bench et al., 1993; Passero, Nardini, and Battistini, 1995). If so, the stunted development of the left hemisphere related to trauma or abuse could easily enhance the risk of developing depression. Depression has also been associated with dysregulation of cortisol. Heim and colleagues (2001) have hypothesized that early life stress sensitizes the anterior pituitary to the effects of subsequent stress exposure. Exposure to frequent nonspecific stress may result in dysregulation of cortisol rhythms and emergence of symptoms of depression (Yehuda et al., 1996).

Substance Abuse

Early stress or maltreatment is an important risk factor for the later development of substance abuse (Simpson et al., 1994; Ellason, Ross, and Fuchs, 1996; Ellason et al., 1996; Wilsnack et al., 1997; De Bellis, Clark, et al., 2000). Early traumatic stress may enhance risk for later substance abuse by fostering limbic irritability and inadequate cerebellar vermis development (Anderson et al., 2001).

Attention-Deficit/Hyperactivity Disorder

There may be an association between childhood abuse and emergence of symptoms of attention-deficit/hyperactivity disorder (ADHD). Pynoos and others (1997) found a strong association between exposure to childhood trauma (playground sniper attack) and emergence of new-onset symptoms of ADHD. Putnam (1993) also reported a relatively high prevalence of ADHD symptoms in prepubertal children with a history of sexual abuse. Glod and Teicher (1996) found that one third of children with a history of severe abuse meet diagnostic criteria ADHD, although they were objectively less hyperactive then children with classic ADHD. Very early childhood abuse was particularly likely to be associated with emergence of ADHD-like behavior problems, and abuse later in childhood was associated with emergence of depression (Glod and Teicher, 1996). Early abuse may produce brain changes that mimic key aspects of ADHD.

The Molecular and Cellular Stress Response

An understanding of the neurobiological effects of childhood stress and trauma must begin with an understanding of the enduring impact of experiences on the developing brain. There are three major components to the stress-response system. One component involves the hippocampus and the hypothalamic–pituitary–adrenal (HPA) axis and is intimately involved in the feedback regulation of cortisol, a stress hormone that mobilizes energy stores, potentiates the release of adrenaline, increases cardiovascular tone, and inhibits growth, immune, and inflammatory responses (Sapolsky and Meaney, 1986). The second component involves the amygdala, locus coeruleus, adrenal gland, and sympathetic nervous system. This is the noradrenergic and adrenaline response to stress, which is crucial for enhancing and directing blood flow, increasing awareness, and mobilizing a fight or flight response. A third, and less explored, stress-response system involves the vasopressin–oxytocin peptide prohormone family. Vasopressin is predominantly involved in fluid retention during stress due to hemorrhage or severe fluid deprivation, though vasopressin and oxytocin also trigger the release of ACTH from the pituitary gland. Stress exerts effects on brain development via the concerted activation of the multiple components of the stress response. For instance, both norepinephrine and vasopressin synergistically potentiate the excitatory effects of glutamate on N-methyl D-aspartate (NMDA) receptors (Joels and Urban, 1984; Yang, Wang, and Cynader, 1996).

Normally, the developing mammalian brain is protected from exposure to high levels of exogenous cortiosteroids. There is a developmental time frame called the *stress hyporesponsive period* in which basal corticosteroid levels are low and a variety of stressors fail to elicit a strong corticosteroid response, presumably to protect the brain from the effects of exposure (Sapolsky and Meaney, 1986). Certain stressors, however, can effectively elicit a stress hormone response (Levine, Johnson, and Gonzalez, 1985; Kuhn, Pauk, and Schanber, 1990; Lau et al., 1992; Plotsky and Meaney, 1993), and this can set into motion a large number of effects on neural division, differentiation, and myelination.

Early stress produces enduring changes in the molecular organization of the stress response systems (Meaney et al., 1996). Animal studies have shown it programs and primes the mammalian brain to be more fearful and to have an enhanced noradrenergic, corticosteroid, and vasopressin response to stress.

Functional Consequences of the Stress Response

Preclinical and clinical researchers have studied the effects of early stress and trauma on the development of vulnerable brain regions. The most susceptible regions are those that develop slowly during the postnatal period, have a high density of glucocorticoid receptors, and continue to generate new neurons after birth, including the hippocampus, amydala, corpus callosum, frontal cortex, and cerebellar vermis.

Hippocampus

The hippocampus has long been known to play a critical role in memory storage and retrieval (Pinchus and Tucker, 1978) and is thought to be a critical region for the generation of dissociative states (Mesulam, 1981). The hippocampus plays a dominant role in the physiology of anxiety (Gray, 1983; Reiman et al., 1986; Teicher, 1988). Anxiety states may arise from excess noradrenergic influences on the hippocampus ascending from the locus coeruleus in the brain stem. In addition, the septal area and hippocampus may be crucial components of inhibiting inappropriate behavior (Depue and Spoont, 1986).

Serotonergic projections from the median raphe nuclei to the hippo-campus presumably play an important role in establishing an individual's overall level of behavioral inhibition (Depue and Spoont, 1986).

The hippocampus may be especially vulnerable to the damages of stress, as it develops slowly after birth (Gould and Tanapat, 1999) and has many glucorticoid receptors (Sapolsky, McEwen, and Rainbow, 1983; Patel et al., 2000). Exposure to stress corticosteroids can markedly alter pyramidal cell development and survival (Sapolsky, Armanini, et al., 1990; Sapolsky, Uno, et al., 1990). Imaging studies of the hippocampus are inconclusive. Bremner and colleagues (1997) and Stein (1997) have reported reduced hippocampal volume in adults with a history of childhood abuse and current PTSD. However, De Bellis, Keshavan, and colleagues (1999), in a sample of maltreated children, and Teicher, Andersen, and colleagues (2002), in a sample of maltreated college students, failed to find any hippocampal differences.

Amygdala

The interconnecting amygdaloid nuclei have been strongly implicated in fear conditioning and in the control of aggressive, oral, and sexual behaviors (Pinchus and Tucker, 1978). Episodic dyscontrol and impulsive violence in man may be due to irritable foci in the amygdaloid nuclei (Pinchus and Tucker, 1978). The amygdala is thought to play a crucial role in triggering flight or fight responses (Lee et al., 1998). Excessive amygdala activation has been proposed to play a crucial role in the development of PTSD (Grillon et al., 1996; Rauch et al., 1996; Shin et al., 1997; Rauch et al., 2000; Villarreal and King, 2001).

The amygdala nuclei are some of the most sensitive structures in the brain for the emergence of kindling, an important occurrence in which repeated intermittent stimulation produces greater and greater alteration in neuronal excitability that may eventually result in seizures (Goddard, McIntrye, and Leech, 1969; Post, Rubinow, and Ballenger, 1984). Even in the absence of overt seizure activity, however, kindling results in long term alterations in neuronal excitability that can have a major impact on behavioral control (Post et al., 1984). A positive association between paroxysmal EEG disturbances and suicidal ideation and attempts and assaultive-destructive behavior has been observed (Struve et al., 1972).

Seizures are often localized to limbic structures in the temporal lobe. Amygdaloid damage has been observed in a significant percentage of patients with temporal-lobe epilepsy (TLE; Kalviainen et al., 1997; Salmenpera et al., 2001). Teicher's initial studies on the potential impact of childhood abuse on the brain focused on the emergence of limbic-system dysfunction (irritability) as likely sequelae to abnormalities in amygdala or hippocampal development. The Limbic System Checklist-33 (LSCL-33) was devised to rate the occurrence of symptoms that often emerge during temporal-lobe seizures (e.g., perceptual distortions, brief hallucinatory events, motor automatisms, and dissociative phenomenon), with the postulation that stress effects or kindling of limbic structures may produce these symptoms (Teicher et al., 1993). Adult outpatients with self-reported history of physical or sexual abuse had increased LSCL-33 scores that were dramatically elevated in patients who had experienced multiple forms of abuse (Teicher et al., 1993). Ito and others (1993) found psychiatrically hospitalized children with a history of abuse had a twofold increase incidence of clinically significant EEG abnormalities, mostly frontotemporal spikes, sharp waves, or paroxysmal slowing, predominantly within the left hemisphere. There was also a strong association between the presence of EEG abnormalities and history of self-destructive or violent behaviors.

Imaging studies by Bremner and colleagues (1997), Stein (1997), and De Bellis, Keshavan, and colleagues (1999) failed to find any differences in amygdala volume in abuse survivors with PTSD, as compared to controls. Interestingly, although Teicher and colleagues did not find a reduction in hippocampal volume in young adults with a history of childhood abuse, they did find a significant reduction in the size of the left amygdala. Left-amygdala size correlated inversely with self-report ratings of depression and irritability (Teicher, Andersen, et al., 2002). Reduced amygdala size had previously been reported in depressed adults (Sheline et al., 1999). Teicher's sample differed from the previous studies in their low incidence of PTSD or psychopathology despite their substantial history of abuse. Because amygdala overactivation maybe a critical factor in PTSD (Villarreal and King, 2001), there is an alternative explanation. A smaller amygdala may provide protection from the emergence of PTSD following childhood trauma or may facilitate recovery from PTSD.

Corpus Callosum

The two hemispheres are connected through the corpus callosum and the anterior and posterior commissures. Delayed myelination of the corpus callosum enables the two hemispheres to develop relatively independently, with functions hemisphere specific. Usually, the left hemisphere is specialized for the perception and expression of language and is logical and analytical. The left hemisphere is also slightly more intricate in its development, and it usually dominates in a variety of tasks. The right hemisphere appears to play a pivotal role in the perception and expression of emotion, particularly negative emotion (Hirschman and Safer, 1982; Silberman and Weingartner, 1986; Borod, 1992; Tomarken et al., 1992; Ross, Thompson, and Yenkosky, 1997).

The two hemispheres need to interact closely to ensure optimal function (Liederman, 1998). Early experience can exert marked effect on lateralization in laboratory animals (Camp, Robinson, and Becker, 1984; Denenberg and Yutzey, 1985; Bulman-Fleming, Wainwright, and Collins, 1992). Cynader and others (1981) have shown that the normal bidirectional flow of information from the left and right hemispheres through the corpus callosum can be affected by early experience. Teicher and colleagues have shown that early stress affects the degree of left–right hemispheric integration (Teicher, 1994; Schiffer et al., 1995; Teicher et al., 1996). Schiffer and others (1995) used EEG auditory-evoked potentials to study laterality and hemispheric integration of memory in well-functioning adults with a history of childhood abuse. They found that early maltreatment was associated with increased hemispheric laterality and decreased hemispheric integration.

Neurotransmitter systems are lateralized in both rats and man (Rosen et al., 1984; Arato et al., 1991; Arora and Meltzer, 1991). The degree and direction of these hemispheric differences may have important behavioral consequences. For example, rats with right greater than left asymmetries in serotonin and dopamine projections to the amygdala and prefrontal cortex, respectively, were much more highly correlated with levels of anxiety then actual transmitter levels (Andersen and Teicher, 1999). Early stress alters development of monamine neurotransmitters and affects their degree of laterality (Jones et al., 1992; Andersen et al., 1999).

The corpus callosum is vulnerable to early exposure to excessive levels of stress hormones, which suppress glial cell division critical for myelination (Lauder, 1983). Handled male rats had significantly greater width of their corpus callosum than nonhandled male controls, specifically in the middle portions (Berrebi et al., 1988). Sanchez and colleagues (2000) found that the rearing of male monkeys in an isolating environment reduced the development of the corpus callosum, and diminished size was associated with defects in certain learning tasks.

Reduced size of the corpus callosum has been associated with diminished communication between the hemispheres (Yazgan et al., 1995). Teicher and others (1997) measured magnetic resonance imaging (MRI) scans of child psychiatric inpatients with a substantiated history of abuse or neglect compared to controls, and found a marked reduction in the size of the middle portions of the corpus callosum, particularly boys. De Bellis, Keshavan, and colleagues (1999) showed that reduced corpus-callosum size was the most prominent MRI finding in a group of children with a history of abuse and PTSD, especially in males. Teicher found that the corpus callosum of boys is particularly vulnerable to the effects of neglect, whereas the corpus callosum of girls appears to be more vulnerable to the adverse effects of sexual abuse (Teicher et al., 2000).

Cerebellar Vermis

The cerebellum occupies only 10% to 20% of brain volume, but it contains more than half of all neurons in the brain (Williams and Herrup, 1988). The cerebellar vermis is the midline structure within the cerebellum with structural and functional interconnections to many key brain regions.

Abnormalities in the cerebellar vermis may be involved in a wide array of psychiatric symptoms, as it seems to have modulating or mediating functions in attention, language, cognition, and affect (Schmahmann, 1991, 2000; Allen et al., 1997; Riva and Giorgi, 2000).

The vermis is likely to be very sensitive to the effects of early maltreatment. Like the hippocampus, the vermis has a protracted period of postnatal development and may produce granule cells postnatally (Altman and Bayer, 1997). The vermis also has the highest density of glucocorticoid receptors during development, exceeding that of the hippocampus (Lawson et al., 1992) and may be particularly vulnerable to the effects of stress hormones (Ferguson and Holson, 1999).

Anderson and colleagues (2002) studied the association between activity in the vermis and symptoms of limbic irritability. Vermal activation was assessed using T2 relaxometry, a novel functional MRI (fMRI) procedure that provides an indirect index of basal cerebral blood volume. Unlike bold fMRI, this technique does not utilize an activation procedure and provides an index of relative blood volume that correlates well with assessment of resting cerebral blood volume using dynamic susceptibility contrast mapping (Anderson et al., 2002). The researchers found a correlation between activity in the vermis and degree of limbic irritability on the LSCL-33 in both healthy young adult controls and young adults with a history of repeated sexual abuse. At any level of limbic symptomatology, however, there was a marked decrease in relative perfusion of the vermis in the individuals with the abuse history. This is indicative of a functional impairment in the activity of the vermis. The vermis is known to play an important role in modulating limbic irritability, and vermal stimulation is highly effective in suppressing limbic seizure activity (Maiti and Snider, 1975; Snider and Maiti, 1975; Heath, 1977; Cooper and Upton, 1985).

The vermis, through the fastigial nuclei, also regulates brain blood flow and exerts a robust neuroprotective effect on the neocortex and hippocampus (Golanov, Liu, and Reis, 1998; Reis et al., 1998; Glickstein, Golanov, and Reis, 1999). Stress-related damage to the vermis could compromise this process, making the hippocampus more vulnerable.

Cerebral Cortex

The prefrontal cortex has the most delayed development of any brain region. Major projections to the prefrontal cortex barely start to myelinate until adolescence, and this process continues into the third decade (Alexander and Goldman, 1978; Fuster, 1980; Weinberger, 1987). Early in its development, stress can exert a widespread effect, but as the prefrontal cortex matures, response to stress becomes more restrictive due to the inhibitory influence of the prefrontal cortex on other regions (Lyss et al., 1999; Andersen et al., 2000; Brake et al., 2000). Although cortical development is difficult to measure, EEG coherence findings in children with a history of abuse demonstrated that left-hemisphere cortex development lagged substantially behind the left hemisphere of healthy controls (Teicher et al., 1997; Ito et al., 1998). Using specialized MRI technology, De Bellis, Keshavan, and colleagues (2000) found a significant reduction in the ratio of N-acetylaspartate (NAA) to creatinine in the abused children with PTSD, suggesting that early maltreatment results in cortical neuronal loss or dysfunction (Duncan et al., 1996).

Reversibility of the Consequences of the Stress Response

The brain is designed to be shaped by experience and adapt to ensure survival. As a result, the brain prepares to cope with the future by selecting a developmental pathway that best matches its wiring to the environmental challenges, including early experiences, that the individual will face. In the absence of exposure to intense stress, an individual will develop in a manner that is less aggressive and more emotionally stable, social, empathic, and well integrated. In contrast, stress exposure exerts negative consequences on emotional well-being. Currently, there is no formula for the amount and degree of exposure to adversity that produces these negative consequences for an individual. Without argument, however, efforts to reduce exposure to severe stress early in life would have far-reaching individual and societal benefits.

We still know little about how plastic the brain is in children following early trauma. From other fields of research, we know that the immature brain is able to compensate, by increasing processing efficiency or by other structures taking over for the affected brain area, much better than the mature brain. The degree of plasticity that is observed is greatly influenced by the point in development when trauma occurred via the influencing of selective brain regions based on maturational state.

Anatomical changes in the corpus callosum may never be reversed, but interhemispheric processing may be able to compensate by becoming more efficient. Effects of trauma on hippocampal loss may someday be able to be minimized by enhanced neurogenesis (Gould et al., 2000) or dendritic branching of already existing neurons

(McEwen, 2000b). Growth factors, environmental enrichment (Johannsson and Belichenko, 2002), or pharmacological agents (Magarinos, Deslandes, and McEwen, 1999) may increase dendritic branching in the hippocampus. Agents, including tianeptine and adinazolam, have been shown to restore stress-induced loss of dendritic spines in the hippocampus in animals (Magarinos et al., 1999; McEwen, 2000b), and this is emerging as an important area of research. Although these treatments will never be a panacea, they offer hope as we continue to live in a world filled with abusive relationships and unpredictable terror.

Acknowledgments

The work described in this chapter was supported by National Institute of Mental Health Grants RO1 MH43743 and MH53636 to Martin H. Teicher. Carl M. Anderson was supported by a special supplement to MH53636.

References

Alexander, G. E. & Goldman, P. S. (1978), Functional development of the dorsolateral prefrontal cortex: An analysis utilizing reversible cryogenic depression. *Brain Res.*, 143:233–249.

Allen, G., Buxton, R. B., Wong, E. C. & Courchesne, E. (1997), Attentional activation of the cerebellum independent of motor involvement. *Science*, 275:1940–1943.

Altman, J. & Bayer, S. A. (1997), *Development of the Cerebellar System in Relation to Its Evolution, Structure, and Functions*. Boca Raton, FL: CRC Press.

Andersen, S. L., Lyss, P. J., Dumont, N. L. & Teicher, M. H. (1999), Enduring neurochemical effects of early maternal separation on limbic structures. *Ann. N. Y. Acad. Sci.*, 877:756–759.

———— & Teicher, M. H. (1999), Serotonin laterality in amygdala predicts performance in the elevated plus maze in rats. *Neuroreport*, 10:3497–3500.

———— Thompson, A. T., Rutstein, M., Hostetter, J. C. & Teicher, M. H. (2000), Dopamine receptor pruning in prefrontal cortex during the periadolescent period in rats. *Synapse*, 37:167–169

Anderson, C. M., Teicher, M. H., Polcari, A. & Renshaw, P. F. (2002), Abnormal T2 relaxation time in the cerebellar vermis of adults sexually abused in childhood: Potential role of the vermis in stress enhanced risk for drug abuse. *Psychoneuroendocrinology*, 27:231–244.

Andrulonis, P. A., Glueck, B. C., Stroebel, C. F., Vogel, N. G., Shapiro, A. L. & Aldridge, D. M. (1981), Organic brain dysfunction and the borderline syndrome. *Psychiat. Clin. North. Amer.*, 4:47–66.

Anisman, H., Zaharia, M. D., Meaney, M. J. & Merali, Z. (1998), Do early-life events permanently alter behavioral and hormonal responses to stressors? *Internat. J. Devel. Neurosci.*, 16:149–164.

Arato, M., Frecska, E., Tekes, K. & MacCrimmon, D. J. (1991), Serotonergic interhemispheric asymmetry: Gender difference in the orbital cortex. *Acta Psychiat. Scand.*, 84:110–111.

Arora, R. C. & Meltzer, H. Y. (1991), Laterality and 3H-imipramine binding: Studies in the frontal cortex of normal controls and suicide victims. *Biol. Psychiat.*, 29:1016–1022.

Bench, C. J., Friston, K. J., Brown, R. G., Frackowiak, R. S. & Dolan, R. J. (1993), Regional cerebral blood flow in depression measured by positron emission tomography: The relationship with clinical dimensions. *Psychol. Med.*, 23:579–590.

Berrebi, A. S., Fitch, R. H., Ralphe, D. L., Denenberg, J. O., Friedrich, V. L., Jr. & Denenberg, V. H. (1988), Corpus callosum: Region-specific effects of sex, early experience and age. *Brain Res.*, 438:216–224.

Borod, J. C. (1992), Interhemispheric and intrahemispheric control of emotion: A focus on unilateral brain damage. *J. Consult. Clin. Psychol.*, 60: 339–348.

Brake, W. G., Flores, G., Francis, D., Meaney, M. J., Srivastava, L. K. & Gratton, A. (2000), Enhanced nucleus accumbens dopamine and plasma corticosterone stress responses in adult rats with neonatal excitotoxic lesions to the medial prefrontal cortex. *Neuroscience*, 96:687–695.

Bremner, J. D., Randall, P., Vermetten, E., Staib, L., Bronen, R. A., Mazure, C., Capelli, S., McCarthy, G., Innis, R. B. & Charney, D. S. (1997), Magnetic resonance imaging–based measurement of hippocampal volume in post-traumatic stress disorder related to childhood physical and sexual abuse–A preliminary report. *Biol. Psychiat.*, 41:23–32.

Brewin, C. R., Andrews, B. & Valentine, J. D. (2000), Meta-analysis of risk factors for posttraumatic stress disorder in trauma-exposed adults. *J. Consult. Clin. Psychol.*, 68:748–766.

Bulman-Fleming, B., Wainwright, P. E. & Collins, R. L. (1992), The effects of early life experience on callosal development and functional lateralization in pigmented BALB/c mice. *Behav. Brain Res.*, 50:31–42.

Camp, D. M., Robinson, T. E. & Becker, J. B. (1984), Sex differences in the effects of early experience on the development of behavioral and brain asymmetries in rats. *Physiol. Behav.*, 33:433–439.

Carmichael, M. S., Warburton, V. L., Dixen, J. & Davidson, J. M. (1994), Relationships among cardiovascular, muscular, and oxytocin responses during human sexual activity. *Arch. Sex Behav.*, 23:59–79.

Carter, C. S. (1998), Neuroendocrine perspectives on social attachment and love. *Psychoneuroendocrinology*, 23:779–818.

_____ DeVries, A. C. & Getz, L. L. (1995), Physiological substrates of mammalian monogamy: The prairie vole model. *Neurosci. Biobehav. Rev.*, 19:303–314.

Coons, P. M., Bowman, E. S. & Milstein, V. (1988), Multiple personality disorder: A clinical investigation of 50 cases. *J. Nerv. Ment. Dis.*, 176: 519–527.

Cooper, I. S. & Upton, A. R. (1985), Therapeutic implications of modulation of metabolism and functional activity of cerebral cortex by chronic stimulation of cerebellum and thalamus. *Biol. Psychiat.*, 20:811–813.

Cowdry, R. W., Pickar, D. & Davies, R. (1985), Symptoms and EEG findings in the borderline syndrome. *Internat. J. Psychiat. Med.*, 15:201–211.

Cynader, M., Lepore, F. & Guillemot, J. P. (1981), Inter-hemispheric competition during postnatal development. *Nature*, 290:139–140.

De Bellis, M. D., Baum, A. S., Birmaher, B., Keshavan, M. S., Eccard, C. H., Boring, A. M., Jenkins, F. J. & Ryan, N. D. (1999), Developmental traumatology, Part I: Biological stress systems. *Biol. Psychiat.*, 45:1259–1270.

_____ Clark, D. B., Beers, S. R., Soloff, P. H., Boring, A. M., Hall, J., Kersh, A. & Keshavan, M. S. (2000), Hippocampal volume in adolescent-onset alcohol use disorders. *Amer. J. Psychiat.*, 157:737–744.

_____ Keshavan, M. S., Clark, D. B., Casey, B. J., Giedd, J. N., Boring, A. M., Frustici, K. & Ryan, N. D. (1999), Developmental traumatology, Part II: Brain development. *Biol. Psychiat.*, 45:1271–1284.

_____ _____ Spencer, S. & Hall, J. (2000), N-acetylaspartate concentration in the anterior cingulate of maltreated children and adolescents with PTSD. *Amer. J. Psychiat.*, 157:1175–1177.

Deblinger, E., McLeer, S. V., Atkins, M. S., Ralphe, D. & Foa, E. (1989), Post-traumatic stress in sexually abused, physically abused, and non-abused children. *Child Abuse Negl.*, 13:403–408.

Denenberg, V. H. & Yutzey, D. A. (1985), Hemispheric laterality, behavioral asymmetry, and the effects of early experience in rats. In: *Cerebral Lateralization in Nonhuman Species*, ed. S. D. Glick. Orlando, FL: Academic Press, pp. 109–133.

Depue, R. A. & Spoont, M. R. (1986), Conceptualizing a serotonin trait: A behavioral dimension of constraint. *Ann. N. Y. Acad. Sci.*, 487:47–62.

Duncan, R. D., Saunders, B. E., Kilpatrick, D. G., Hanson, R. F. & Resnick, H. S. (1996), Childhood physical assault as a risk factor for PTSD, depression, and substance abuse: Findings from a national survey. *Amer. J. Orthopsychiat.*, 66:437–448.

Ellason, J. W., Ross, C. A. & Fuchs, D. L. (1996), Lifetime axis I and II comorbidity and childhood trauma history in dissociative identity disorder. *Psychiatry*, 59:255–266.

_____ _____ Sainton, K. & Mayran, L. W. (1996), Axis I and II comorbidity and childhood trauma history in chemical dependency. *Bull. Menn. Clin.*, 60:39–51.

Famularo, R., Fenton, T., Kinscherff, R. & Augustyn, M. (1996), Psychiatric comorbidity in childhood posttraumatic stress disorder. *Child Abuse Negl.*, 20:953–961.

Feinberg, I. (1982), Schizophrenia: Caused by a fault in programmed synaptic elimination during adolescence? *J. Psychiat. Res.*, 17:319–334.

Ferguson, S. A. & Holson, R. R. (1999), Neonatal dexamethasone on day 7 in rats causes mild hyperactivity and cerebellar stunting. *Neurotoxicol. Teratol.*, 21:71–76.

Flor-Henry, P., Tomer, R., Kumpula, I., Koles, Z. J. & Yeudall, L. T. (1990), Neurophysiological and neuropsychological study of two cases of multiple personality syndrome and comparison with chronic hysteria. *Internat. J. Psychophysiol.*, 10:151–161.

Fuster, J. (1980), *The Prefrontal Cortex.* New York: Raven Press.

Glaser, D. (2000), Child abuse and neglect and the brain—A review. *J. Child Psychol. Psychiat.*, 41:97–116.

Glickstein, S. B., Golanov, E. V. & Reis, D. J. (1999), Intrinsic neurons of fastigial nucleus mediate neurogenic neuroprotection against excitotoxic and ischemic neuronal injury in rat. *J. Neurosci.*, 19:4142–4154.

Glod, C. A. & Teicher, M. H. (1996), Relationship between early abuse, posttraumatic stress disorder, and activity levels in prepubertal children. *J. Amer. Acad. Child Adolesc. Psychiat.*, 35:1384–1393.

_____ _____ Hartman, C. R. & Harakal, T. (1997), Increased nocturnal activity and impaired sleep maintenance in abused children. *J. Amer. Acad. Child Adolesc. Psychiat.*, 36:1236–1243.

Goddard, C. V., McIntrye, D. C. & Leech, C. K. (1969), A permanent change in brain functioning resulting from daily electrical stimulation. *Exp. Neurol.*, 25:295–330.

Golanov, E. V., Liu, F. & Reis, D. J. (1998), Stimulation of cerebellum protects hippocampal neurons from global ischemia. *Neuroreport*, 9:819–824.

Gould, E. & Tanapat, P. (1999), Stress and hippocampal neurogenesis. *Biol. Psychiat.*, 46:1472–1479.

_____ _____ Rydel, T. & Hastings, N. (2000), Regulation of hippocampal neurogenesis in adulthood. *Biol. Psychiat.* 48:715–720.

Gray, J. A. (1983), A theory of anxiety: The role of the limbic system. *Encephale*, 9:161B–166B.

Grillon, C., Southwick, S. M. & Charney, D. S. (1996), The psychobiological basis of posttraumatic stress disorder. *Mol. Psychiat.*, 1:278–297.

Heath, R. G. (1977), Modulation of emotion with a brain pacemaker. Treatment for intractable psychiatric illness. *J. Nerv. Ment. Dis.*, 165:300–317.

Heim, C., Newport, D. J., Bonsall, R., Miller, A. H. & Nemeroff, C. B. (2001), Altered pituitary–adrenal axis responses to provocative challenge tests in adult survivors of childhood abuse. *Amer. J. Psychiat.*, 158:575–581.

———— Owens, M. J., Plotsky, P. M. & Nemeroff, C. B. (1997), The role of early adverse life events in the etiology of depression and posttraumatic stress disorder. In: *Psychobiology of Posttraumatic Stress Disorder, Vol. 821*, ed. R. Yehuda, A. C. McFarlane, et al. New York: New York Academy of Science, pp. 194–207.

Hirschman, R. S. & Safer, M. A. (1982), Hemisphere differences in perceiving positive and negative emotions. *Cortex*, 18:569–580.

Ito, Y., Teicher, M. H., Glod, C. A. & Ackerman, E. (1998), Preliminary evidence for aberrant cortical development in abused children: A quantitative EEG study. *J. Neuropsychiat. Clin. Neurosci.*, 10:298–307.

———— ———— ———— Harper, D., Magnus, E. & Gelbard, H. A. (1993), Increased prevalence of electrophysiological abnormalities in children with psychological, physical, and sexual abuse. *J. Neuropsychiat. Clin. Neurosci.*, 5:401–408.

Jacobson, M. (1991), *Developmental Neurobiology*. New York: Plenum Press.

Joels, M. & Urban, I. J. (1984), Arginine-vasopressin enhances the responses of lateral septal neurons in the rat to excitatory amino acids and fimbria-fornix stimuli. *Brain Res.*, 311:201–209.

Johansson, B. B. & Belichenko, P. V. (2002), Neuronal plasticity and dendritic spines: Effect of environmental enrichment on intact and postischemic rat brain. *J. Cereb. Blood Flow Metab.*, 22:89–96.

Jones, G. H., Hernandez, T. D., Kendall, D. A., Marsden, C. A. & Robbins, T. W. (1992), Dopaminergic and serotonergic function following isolation rearing in rats: Study of behavioral responses and postmortem and in vivo neurochemistry. *Pharmacol. Biochem. Behav.*, 43:17–35.

Kalviainen, R., Salmenpera, T., Partanen, K., Vainio, P., Riekkinen, P., Sr. & Pitkanen, A. (1997), MRI volumetry and T2 relaxometry of the amygdala in newly diagnosed and chronic temporal lobe epilepsy. *Epilepsy Res.*, 28:39–50.

Kaufman, J., Plotsky, P. M., Nemeroff, C. B. & Charney, D. S. (2000), Effects of early adverse experiences on brain structure and function: clinical implications. *Biol. Psychiat.*, 48:778–790.

Kiser, L. J., Heston, J., Millsap, P. A. & Pruitt, D. B. (1991), Physical and sexual abuse in childhood: Relationship with posttraumatic stress disorder. *J. Amer. Acad. Child Adolesc. Psychiat.*, 30:776–783.

Kuhn, C., Pauk, J. & Schanber, S. M. (1990), Endocrine responses to mother–infant separation in developing rats. *Devel. Psychobiol.*, 23: 395–410.

Lau, C., Cameron, A. M., Antolick, L. L. & Stanton, M. E. (1992), Repeated maternal separation in the neonatal rat: Cellular mechanisms contributing to brain growth sparing. *J. Devel. Physiol.*, 17:265–276.

Lauder, J. M. (1983), Hormonal and humoral influences on brain development. *Psychoneuroendocrinology*, 8:121–155.

Lawson, A., Ahima, R. S., Krozowski, Z. & Harlan, R. E. (1992), Postnatal development of corticosteroid receptor immunoreactivity in the rat cerebellum and brain stem. *Neuroendocrinology*, 55:695–707.

Lee, G. P., Bechara, A., Adolphs, R., Arena, J., Meador, K. J., Loring, D. W. & Smith, J. R. (1998), Clinical and physiological effects of stereotaxic bilateral amygdalotomy for intractable aggression. *J. Neuropsychiat. Clin. Neurosci.*, 10:413–420.

Levine, S., Johnson, D. F. & Gonzalez, C. A. (1985), Behavioral and hormonal responses to separation in infant rhesus monkeys and mothers. *Behav. Neurosci.*, 99:399–410.

Liederman, J. (1998), The dynamics of interhemispheric collaboration and hemispheric control. *Brain Cogn.*, 36:193–208.

Liu, D., Diorio, J., Tannenbaum, B., Caldji, C., Francis, D., Freedman, A., Sharma, S., Pearson, D., Plotsky, P. M. & Meaney, M. J. (1997), Maternal care, hippocampal glucocorticoid receptors, and hypothalamic–pituitary–adrenal responses to stress. *Science*, 277:1659–1662.

Lyss, P. J., Andersen, S. L., LeBlanc, C. J. & Teicher, M. H. (1999), Degree of neuronal activation following FG-7142 changes across regions during development. *Brain Res. Devel. Brain Res.*, 116:201–203.

Magarinos, A. M., Deslandes, A. & McEwen, B. S. (1999), Effects of antidepressants and benzodiazepine treatments on the dendritic structure of CA3 pyramidal neurons after chronic stress. *Eur. J. Pharmacol.*, 371: 113–122.

Maiti, A. & Snider, R. S. (1975), Cerebellar control of basal forebrain seizures: Amygdala and hippocampus. *Epilepsia*, 16:521–533.

Matthews, K., Dalley, J. W., Matthews, C., Tsai, T. H. & Robbins, T. W. (2001), Periodic maternal separation of neonatal rats produces region- and gender-specific effects on biogenic amine content in postmortem adult brain. *Synapse*, 40:1–10.

McEwen, B. S. (2000a), Allostasis, allostatic load, and the aging nervous system: Role of excitatory amino acids and excitotoxicity. *Neurochem. Res.*, 25:1219–1231.

———— (2000b), Effects of adverse experiences for brain structure and function. *Biol. Psychiat.*, 48:721–731.

Meaney, M. J., Diorio, J., Francis, D., Widdowson, J., LaPlante, P., Caldji, C., Sharma, S., Seckl, J. R. & Plotsky, P. M. (1996), Early environmental regulation of forebrain glucocorticoid receptor gene expression: Implications for adrenocortical responses to stress. *Devel. Neurosci.*, 18:49–72.

Mesulam, M. M. (1981), Dissociative states with abnormal temporal lobe EEG: Multiple personality and the illusion of possession. *Arch. Neurol.*, 38:176–181.

Muller, R. J. (1992), Is there a neural basis for borderline splitting? *Compr. Psychiat.*, 33:92–104.

Ostrowski, N. L. (1998), Oxytocin receptor mRNA expression in rat brain: Implications for behavioral integration and reproductive success. *Psychoneuroendocrinology*, 23:989–1004.

Passero, S., Nardini, M. & Battistini, N. (1995), Regional cerebral blood flow changes following chronic administration of antidepressant drugs. *Prog. Neuropsychopharmacol. Biol. Psychiat.*, 19:627–636.

Patel, P. D., Lopez, J. F., Lyons, D. M., Burke, S., Wallace, M. & Schatzberg, A. F. (2000), Glucocorticoid and mineralocorticoid receptor mRNA expression in squirrel monkey brain. *J. Psychiat. Res.*, 34:383–392.

Pedersen, C. A. (1997), Oxytocin control of maternal behavior: Regulation by sex steroids and offspring stimuli. *Ann. N. Y. Acad. Sci.*, 807:126–145.

Perry, B. D. & Pollard, R. (1998), Homeostasis, stress, trauma, and adaptation: A neurodevelopmental view of childhood trauma. *Child Adolesc. Psychiat. Clin. North Amer.*, 7:33–51.

Pinchus, J. H. & Tucker, G. J. (1978), *Behavioral Neurology.* New York: Oxford University Press.

Plotsky, P. M. & Meaney, M. J. (1993), Early postnatal experience alters hypothalamic corticotropin-releasing factor (CRF) mRNA, median eminence CRF content and stress-induced release in rats. *Mol. Brain Res.*, 18:195–200.

Post, R. M., Rubinow, D. R. & Ballenger, J. C. (1984), Conditioning, sensitization and kindling: Implications for the course of affective illness. In: *Neurobiology of Mood Disorders*, ed. R. M. Post & J. C. Ballenger. Baltimore, MD: Williams & Wilkins, pp. 432–466.

Putnam, F. W. (1993), Dissociative disorders in children: Behavioral profiles and problems. *Child Abuse Negl.*, 17:39–45.

Pynoos, R. S., Steinberg, A. M., Ornitz, E. M. & Goenjian, A. M. (1997), Issues in the developmental neurobiology of traumatic stress. *Ann. N. Y. Acad. Sci.*, 821:176–192.

Rauch, S. L., van der Kolk, B. A., Fisler, R. E., Alpert, N. M., Orr, S. P., Savage, C. R., Fischman, A. J., Jenike, M. A. & Pitman, R. K. (1996), A symptom provocation study of posttraumatic stress disorder using positron emission tomography and script-driven imagery. *Arch. Gen. Psychiat.*, 53: 380–387.

_____ Whalen, P. J., Shin, L. M., McInerney, S. C., Macklin, M. L., Lasko, N. B., Orr, S. P. & Pitman, R. K. (2000), Exaggerated amygdala response to masked facial stimuli in posttraumatic stress disorder: A functional MRI study. *Biol. Psychiat.*, 47:769–776.

Reiman, E. M., Raichle, M. E., Robins, E., Butler, F. K., Herscovitch, P., Fox, P. & Perlmutter, J. (1986), The application of positron emission tomography to the study of panic disorder. *Amer. J. Psychiat.*, 143:469–477.

Reis, D. J., Kobylarz, K., Yamamoto, S. & Golanov, E. V. (1998), Brief electrical stimulation of cerebellar fastigial nucleus conditions long-lasting salvage from focal cerebral ischemia: Conditioned central neurogenic neuroprotection. *Brain Res.*, 780:161–165.

Riva, D. & Giorgi, C. (2000), The cerebellum contributes to higher functions during development: Evidence from a series of children surgically treated for posterior fossa tumours. *Brain*, 123:1051–1061.

Rosen, G. D., Finklestein, S., Stoll, A. L., Yutzey, D. A. & Denenberg, V. H. (1984), Neurochemical asymmetries in the albino rat's cortex, striatum, and nucleus accumbens. *Life Sci.*, 34:1143–1148.

Ross, E. D., Thompson, R. D. & Yenkosky, J. (1997), Lateralization of affective prosody in brain and the callosal integration of hemispheric language functions. *Brain Lang.*, 56:27–54.

Salmenpera, T., Kalviainen, R., Partanen, K. & Pitkanen, A. (2001), Hippocampal and amygdaloid damage in partial epilepsy: A cross-sectional MRI study of 241 patients. *Epilepsy Res.*, 46:69–82.

Sanchez, M. M., Young, L. J., Plotsky, P. M. & Insel, T. R. (2000), Distribution of corticosteroid receptors in the rhesus brain: Relative absence of glucocorticoid receptors in the hippocampal formation. *J. Neurosci.*, 20: 4657–4668.

Sapolsky, R. M., Armanini, M. P., Packan, D. R., Sutton, S. W. & Plotsky, P. M. (1990), Glucocorticoid feedback inhibition of adrenocorticotropic hormone secretagogue release: Relationship to corticosteroid receptor occupancy in various limbic sites. *Neuroendocrinology*, 51:328–336.

_____ McEwen, B. S. & Rainbow, T. C. (1983), Quantitative autoradiography of [3H]corticosterone receptors in rat brain. *Brain Res.*, 271:331–334.

_____ & Meaney, M. J. (1986), Maturation of adrenocortical stress response: Neuroendocrine control mechanisms and the stress hyporesponsive period. *Brain Res. Rev.*, 11:65–76.

_____ Uno, H., Rebert, C. S. & Finch, C. E. (1990), Hippocampal damage associated with prolonged glucocorticoid exposure in primates. *J. Neurosci.*, 10:2897–2902.

Schaaf, K. K. & McCanne, T. R. (1998), Relationship of childhood sexual, physical, and combined sexual and physical abuse to adult victimization and posttraumatic stress disorder. *Child Abuse Negl.*, 22:1119–1133.

Schenk, L. & Bear, D. (1981), Multiple personality and related dissociative phenomena in patients with temporal lobe epilepsy. *Amer. J. Psychiat.*, 138:1311–1316.

Schiffer, F., Teicher, M. H. & Papanicolaou, A. C. (1995), Evoked potential evidence for right brain activity during the recall of traumatic memories. *J. Neuropsychiat. Clin. Neurosci.*, 7:169–175.

Schmahmann, J. D. (1991), An emerging concept: The cerebellar contribution to higher function. *Arch. Neurol.*, 48:1178–1187.

_____ (2000), Cerebellum and brainstem. In: *Brain Mapping*, ed. A. W. Toga & J. C. Mazziotta. San Diego, CA: Academic Press, pp. 207–259.

Sheline, Y. I., Sanghavi, M., Mintun, M. A. & Gado, M. H. (1999), Depression duration but not age predicts hippocampal volume loss in medically healthy women with recurrent major depression. *J. Neurosci.*, 19: 5034–5043.

Shin, L. M., Kosslyn, S. M., McNally, R. J., Alpert, N. M., Thompson, W. L., Rauch, S. L., Macklin, M. L. & Pitman, R. K. (1997), Visual imagery and perception in posttraumatic stress disorder: A positron emission tomographic investigation. *Arch. Gen. Psychiat.*, 54:233–241.

Silberman, E. K. & Weingartner, H. (1986), Hemispheric lateralization of functions related to emotion. *Brain Cogn.*, 5:322–353.

Simpson, T. L., Westerberg, V. S., Little, L. M. & Trujillo, M. (1994), Screening for childhood physical and sexual abuse among outpatient substance abusers. *J. Subst. Abuse Treat.*, 11:347–358.

Snider, R. S. & Maiti, A. (1975), Cerebellar control of amygdaloid seizures. *Trans. Amer. Neurol. Assn.*, 100:17–18.

Snyder, S. & Pitts, W. M., Jr. (1984), Electroencephalography of DSM-III borderline personality disorder. *Acta Psychiat Scand.*, 69:129–134.

Stein, M. B. (1997), Hippocampal volume in women victimized by childhood sexual abuse. *Psychol. Med.*, 27:951–959.

Struve, F. A., Klein, D. F. & Saraf, K. R. (1972), Electroencephalographic correlates of suicide ideation and attempts. *Arch. Gen. Psychiat.*, 27: 363–365.

Teicher, M. H. (1988), Biology of anxiety. *Med. Clin. North Amer.*, 72:791–814.

_____ (1989), Psychological factors in neurological development. In: *Neurobiological Development, Vol. 12*, ed. P. Evrard & A. Minkowski. New York: Raven Press, pp. 243–258.

_____ (1994), Early abuse, limbic system dysfunction, and borderline personality disorder. In: *Biological and Neurobehavioral Studies of Borderline Personality Disorder*, ed. K. Silk. Washington, DC: American Psychiatric Association Press, pp. 177–207.

_____ (2000), Wounds that time won't heal: The neurobiology of child abuse. *Cerebrum*, 4(2):50–67.

_____ Andersen, S. L., Dumont, N. L., Ito, Y., Glod, C. A., Vaituzis, C. & Giedd, J. N. (2000), Childhood neglect attenuates development of the corpus callosum. *Soc. Neurosci. Abstr.*, 26:549.

_____ _____ & Hostetter, J. C., Jr. (1995), Evidence for dopamine receptor pruning between adolescence and adulthood in striatum but not nucleus accumbens. *Devel. Brain Res.*, 89:167–172.

_____ _____ Polcari, A., Anderson, C. M. & Navalta, C. P. (2002), Developmental neurobiology of childhood stress and trauma. *Psychiat. Clin. North Amer.*, 25:397–426.

_____ Feldman, R., Polcari, A., Anderson, C. M., Andersen, S. L., Webster, D. M. & Navalta, C. P. (2002), Early adverse experience and the development of borderline personality disorder. In: *Women's Health and Psychiatry*, ed. K. H. Pearson, S. B. Sonawalla & J. F. Rosenbaum. New York: Lippincott.

_____ Glod, C. A., Surrey, J. & Swett, C. (1993), Early childhood abuse and limbic system ratings in adult psychiatric outpatients. *J. Neuropsychiat. Clin. Neurosci.*, 5:301–306.

_____ Ito, Y., Glod, C. A., Andersen, S. L., Dumont, N. & Ackerman, E. (1997), Preliminary evidence for abnormal cortical development in physically and sexually abused children using EEG coherence and MRI. *Ann. N. Y. Acad. Sci., 821*, 821:160–175.

_____ _____ _____ Schiffer, F. & Ackerman, E. (1994), Possible effects of early abuse on human brain development, as assessed by EEG coherence. *Amer. J. Neuropsychopharmacol.*, 33:52.

_____ _____ _____ _____ & Gelbard, H. A. (1996), Neurophysiological mechanisms of stress response in children. In: *Severe Stress and Mental Disturbance in Children*, ed. C. Pfeffer. Washington, DC: American Psychiatric Association Press, pp. 59–84.

Tomarken, A. J., Davidson, R. J., Wheeler, R. E. & Doss, R. C. (1992), Individual differences in anterior brain asymmetry and fundamental dimensions of emotion. *J. Pers. Soc. Psychol.*, 62:676–687.

Uvnas-Moberg, K. (1998), Oxytocin may mediate the benefits of positive social interaction and emotions. *Psychoneuroendocrinology*, 23:819–835.

Villarreal, G. & King, C. Y. (2001), Brain imaging in posttraumatic stress disorder. *Semin. Clin. Neuropsychiat.*, 6:131–145.

Weinberger, D. R. (1987), Implications of normal brain development for the pathogenesis of schizophrenia. *Arch. Gen. Psychiat.*, 44:660–669.

Widom, C. S. (1999), Posttraumatic stress disorder in abused and neglected children grown up. *Amer. J. Psychiat.*, 156:1223–1229.

Williams, R. W. & Herrup, K. (1988), The control of neuron number. *Ann. Rev. Neurosci.*, 11:423–453.

Wilsnack, S. C., Vogeltanz, N. D., Klassen, A. D. & Harris, T. R. (1997), Childhood sexual abuse and women's substance abuse: National survey findings. *J. Stud. Alcohol,* 58:264–271.

Witt, D. M., Winslow, J. T. & Insel, T. R. (1992), Enhanced social interactions in rats following chronic, centrally infused oxytocin. *Pharmacol. Biochem. Behav.,* 43:855–861.

Yang, B., Wang, Y. & Cynader, M. S. (1996), Synergistic interactions between noradrenaline and glutamate in cytosolic calcium influx in cultured visual cortical neurons. *Brain Res.,* 721:181–190.

Yazgan, M. Y., Wexler, B. E., Kinsbourne, M., Peterson, B. & Leckman, J. F. (1995), Functional significance of individual variations in callosal area. *Neuropsychologia,* 33:769–779.

Yehuda, R., Teicher, M. H., Trestman, R. L., Levengood, R. A. & Siever, L. J. (1996), Cortisol regulation in posttraumatic stress disorder and major depression: A chronobiological analysis. *Biol. Psychiat.,* 40:79–88.

Chapter 12

An Agenda for Public Mental Health in a Time of Terror

Daniel B. Herman,
Barbara Pape Aaron, and
Ezra S. Susser

The shift in cultural attitudes vis-à-vis posttraumatic reactions associated with the widespread traumatization of many Americans, not just New Yorkers, could lead to a new sociopolitical reality. Epidemiologic studies from New York City documenting the consequences of 9/11 in terms of the impact on mental health of the local citizenry seem to suggest that the kind of emergency interventions and follow-up counseling made available on an ad hoc basis using mostly volunteers did have beneficial effect–though one might also weigh the beneficial impact of a national outpouring of sympathy for the city and the notably effective leadership of Mayor Giuliani and other officials in dealing with the crisis.

The authors argue that public mental health needs to be made a priority in national preparedness for future terrorist attacks. The long-term effects of the terrorist attack, as well as the effects of living in a decisively changed, and much less safe, world, remain to be scientifically assessed–these yet unknown effects will have to be figured into the planning equation.

On September 11, 2001, the United States suffered the worst terrorist attacks in its history. The destruction of the World Trade Center's twin towers was quickly followed by a series of anthrax-tainted letters that killed five people, shut down the U.S. Capitol, and caused widespread concern throughout the country. The American response was swift, with war in Afghanistan and major appropriations for military defense. The psychological impact of these events on the nation's populace was profound, leading to significant increases in mental distress and symptoms of disorder, especially among persons in close proximity to the attacks.

Faced with an imminent threat of bioterrorism, the federal government responded with a rapid and sizable increase in funding of the infrastructure for public health. Much of the money will go to a focused effort to invigorate infectious-disease epidemiology, thereby improving our capacity both to detect new pathogens and to control outbreaks of infectious diseases. This capacity is indeed a vital component of any defense against bioterrorism and will also contribute to better control of future emerging infections, such as HIV and West Nile virus.

Notably absent from the federal response, however, is another necessary component of defense against bioterrorism: public mental health. A modern terrorist campaign is designed to inflict psychological damage and thereby alter a political process (Wessely, Hyams, and Bartholomew, 2001). In the cold calculation of such a combatant, it matters not whether one or 100 or 1000 people are killed in any given attack; what matters is that the news of the attack is disseminated and engenders a state of fear and anxiety in a wide population. The real objective is to undermine the *mental* balance of a targeted community. An appropriate response, therefore, requires a determined effort to help the population withstand the mental impact of these events. Simply put, we must defend a seemingly intangible second front.

The assault on the World Trade Center illustrates the point. The smashing of a monumental structure in plain view of millions of people was clearly designed for maximum psychological impact. Many personal accounts have described the shock and dismay produced in New Yorkers who watched the towers burn from miles away (Conover et al., 2002). The towers were a soaring symbol of the city and the nation, familiar at home and abroad. Their destruction generated a profound sense of vulnerability. Surprise was a crucial element that magnified the psychological impact. The population, completely unprepared for such an event, reacted with bewilderment.

In addition to the horrific toll of death and destruction, the attack also registered unprecedented success in terms of psychological damage it inflicted. In a rapid "needs assessment" commissioned by New York state in the immediate aftermath, we estimated a minimum of half a million cases of diagnosable mental disorder consequent to September 11 (Herman, Felton, and Susser, 2001). Subsequently, published research confirmed the massive psychological impact. A telephone survey of adult residents covering most of Manhattan found that 7.5% had posttraumatic stress disorder (PTSD) related to September 11 (Galea et al., 2002). A report by Hoven and others on New York City schoolchildren in grades 4 through 12 found that 10.5% had PTSD related to September 11 (Goodnough, 2002). These studies also found substantial effects on other disorders such as depression in adults and agoraphobia (fear of public places) in children.

Thus, our original estimate of a half-million cases of mental disorder throughout the state is a minimum estimate of psychological trauma. Untold millions who witnessed the attacks through the media were surely shaken as well. Based on previous research, we believe that the psychological impact of the attacks was most profound on those who were most directly exposed to the event (by virtue of both geographical and emotional proximity) and those with histories of previous trauma exposure and other psychological vulnerabilities.

The ultimate course of these disorders remains to be seen, although preliminary data from a follow-up survey of New York City residents suggest that a significant number of PTSD cases may have resolved fairly rapidly (discussed later). Nonetheless, it is also possible that there may be delayed-onset cases that have yet to be observed. Some clinicians who have worked with those who were directly involved in the recovery and cleanup efforts after the attack are particularly concerned about this eventuality. For many of these workers, including rescue personnel, construction workers, heavy-equipment operators, and others, it is possible that their intensive involvement in the recovery effort (which lasted for almost a full year following the attack) may have actually protected them somewhat from experiencing the full psychological impact of the traumatic exposure. Now that this heroic effort has ended, it is feared that this impact may finally "hit home."

Furthermore, although symptoms of PTSD have been the most commonly studied mental health sequelae of September 11 (and other disasters as well), a broader view on the impact is needed. For example, another sign of increased stress after September 11 was an increase in the use of psychoactive substances. The previously mentioned Manhattan telephone survey also showed that cigarette, alcohol, and marijuana use increased substantially in the general population during the weeks subsequent to the attacks (Vlahov et al., 2002). This study further revealed an association between increases in cigarette and marijuana use and PTSD and between cigarette and alcohol use and depression. In contrast, there was no immediate evidence of an increase in drug use among heroin and cocaine users (Factor et al., 2002).

There is some evidence that asthma symptoms increased among New Yorkers in the period following the attacks. Although smoke and debris in the air was a likely cause, it is also suspected that psychological factors associated with stress may also have played a significant role (Fagen and Galea, 2002). Behavioral medicine experts are also interested in studying whether morbidity and mortality from myocardial infarction increased in the period immediately following the attacks. Other important health outcomes that have yet to be examined include general medical utilization and prescription drug use.

The subsequent anthrax attacks were even more precisely targeted to maximize their psychological impact. Mail laced with a highly refined form of anthrax was sent to the offices of news magazines, television stations, and prominent legislators resulting in 22 cases of illness nationwide and five deaths (Inglesby et al., 2002). This toll was many times less than the number of deaths caused each day by traffic accidents. But unlike that larger routine toll, the anthrax attacks inflicted social disruption and psychological damage across the whole country. The public health system was overwhelmed with requests for antibiotics and nasal swab testing and for examination of literally thousands of powder samples in areas far removed from any confirmed cases. Though still unmeasured, without doubt epidemic confusion and anxiety beset millions. Yet, to the best of our knowledge, the vast majority of people afflicted by anxiety had no appreciable risk of exposure to anthrax. The anthrax episode, then, was also a highly successful terrorist attack, especially in terms of the ratio of terror to physical damage.

Strengthening Psychosocial Defenses

With the scope of the problem now clear, certainly the protection of the public's mental health must be a central element in any effective defense against terrorism. And yet public health leaders have, for the most part, failed to advocate strongly for the integration of mental health considerations into the overall response to the terrorist threat. Bioterrorism preparedness as now conceived and implemented does not have a full-fledged mental health component. In some instances, mental health agencies have undertaken their own response. By and large, however, these efforts are peripheral to the mainstream public health response, neither well integrated nor well funded.

The omission of public mental health from our defense strategy is no doubt due in part to the persisting stigma attached to mental disorders. As a result, such conditions suffer general neglect in medical schools, health insurance systems, disability legislation, and many other arenas. Public health too reflects this neglect. The federal Centers for Disease Control, for instance, has paid relatively little attention to public mental health, although a World Health Organization report documents that mental disorders are leading causes of disability (Murray and Lopez, 1996).

So what can be done to limit the propagation of fear, confusion, and demoralization that leads to PTSD, depression, and other conditions, especially in the face of a public mental health system that must still be considered inadequate? Relatively little research has examined the psychological effects of terrorism; even less is documented on how to protect people from these effects. A federal funding priority, therefore, should be to fully document the mental health consequences of September 11 and to devise and test strategies to minimize those consequences. In the meantime, however, our limited database is no excuse for inaction.

We can learn much from other societies that have faced terrorist campaigns. Thus the Israelis, for many years the target of terror attacks, have actively developed strategies for withstanding them (Bleich et al., 1992). Their experience in the Gulf War of 1991 is particularly instructive. The population was repeatedly under imminent threat of an Iraqi attack with biochemical weapons. The strategic response had three elements:

- *Leadership*. Clear, consistent, and prompt public messages were broadcast by a single, familiar voice. During attacks, most radio stations converged their broadcasts; one senior official was in charge of updating the public, and his messages were translated into many languages.
- *Public education*. The army and other authorities made a systematic effort to inform the public about the nature of biochemical weapons and how to protect oneself, making use of media, schools, and community organizations. Fear was acknowledged and framed as a normal human reaction to the threat.
- *Community preparedness*. Every household was ordered to have available gas masks, a sealed room, and a battery-operated radio. Local communities undertook special efforts to properly equip vulnerable groups, such as those living alone, the elderly and frail, and new immigrants.

Political leaders can play a significant role in caring for the public's mental health, because a sense of community and social cohesion fortifies people against terror's fundamental goal of inflicting psychological trauma. In fact, the approach is consistent with a growing epidemiologic literature suggesting that social cohesion or "social capital" confers protection against morbidity and mortality (Kawachi et al., 1997). The strength of social ties may be particularly important for children. The following observation from London during World War II, by Anna Freud and Dorothy Burlingham (1943), is illuminating:

The war acquires comparatively little significance for children so long as it only threatens their lives, disturbs their material comfort, or cuts their food rations. It becomes enormously significant the moment it breaks up family life and uproots the first emotional attachments of the child within the family group. London children, therefore, were on the whole much less upset by bombing than by evacuation to the country as a protection from it.

One of history's foremost examples of the power of such social bonding dates to the 1940 Battle of Britain in World War II. Nazi bombings were designed to kill some but demoralize all. While concurrently attempting to fortify a weak air defense, Prime Minister Winston Churchill set himself the task of strengthening the resolve of his people to endure the psychological fallout of the air raids. His inspiring radio addresses, which promoted a sense of common purpose, in effect were public mental health interventions. As an example, on the very evening of September 11, 1940, Churchill spoke to the nation by radio broadcast. During the week preceding that address alone, 1200 civilians had been killed in aerial bombings. He spoke that evening of "the wickedness of the perpetrators, the repository and embodiment of soul-destroying hatred, the monstrous product of former wrongs." And he spoke of the "spirit and the tough fiber of the nation and the tough fiber of Parliamentary democracy and the value of freedom" and "of the kindling of a fire in our hearts, here and all over the world, which will glow long after all traces of this conflagration have been removed."

Likewise, in New York City in the weeks after the attacks, Mayor Rudolph Giuliani well served a stricken populace, as he took very visible command to personally keep the citizenry informed and to inspire with a sense of control and optimism. His statements also played an important role in helping citizens manage their grief by validating the feelings of overwhelming loss and pain that most New Yorkers experienced. The mayor achieved this not only by being strong and forceful but also by speaking in an emotionally authentic way. His heartfelt response to the question of how many had died—"It will be more than any of us can bear"—was especially memorable. It's clear then that statements made at the public level can have an important salutary effect on individuals' internal psychological state by helping people to manage their feelings.

Unless carefully delivered, however, statements by public officials and media representatives can arouse fear instead of alleviating it. Public spokespersons must be articulate and knowledgeable in their crucial roles, and the media should provide full and accurate information in a fashion that will not provoke distress and concern. For example, a comprehensive analysis of a new terrorist threat may be helpful; a 10-second promotional spot in which an anchor says, "New terrorist threat—more at 11" is not. And mixed messages in which government officials alarm us with detail-free "high alerts" but go on to advise us to travel normally and to "go shopping" are most likely counterproductive.

In fact, asking the population to do something sacrificial and difficult rather than to consume conspicuously is probably a better way to increase social cohesion. For such messages to be effective, however, the population must believe that the sacrifices they are being asked to make are, in fact, part of a broad national effort and are fairly distributed.

Studies of other disasters have shown that there is a substantial risk of widespread disillusionment and loss of solidarity in the community during the period following the initial "honeymoon" phase that typically follows such events. This risk is exacerbated if members of the public (including both direct victims and others) do not perceive actions by the authorities as proceeding in a fair, open, and equitable manner. This phase of disenchantment, sometimes referred to as "the disaster after the disaster," has been seen as a process of "collective secondary victimization" (Yzermans and Gerson, 2002). As the "honeymoon" phase of the September 11 attacks further wanes, we are beginning to see evidence of this process unfolding as some family members of those killed appear to feel that the terms of the proposed financial settlement are inequitable. There have also been signs of a growing backlash by other members of the public who question whether such large monetary payouts are in fact justified. These developments make it even more critical that government agencies closely monitor the public mood and take active steps to prevent these negative responses from getting out of hand.

Finally, in our view, a legitimate defense against terrorism has an important moral dimension. It must defend humane values as well as the political entities of cities, states, and nations. This implies the vigorous protection of the rights and dignity of social groups such as Muslims and others at risk of stigma and discrimination after September 11, an effort that will also contribute to maintaining social cohesion.

Treating the Trauma

In the aftermath of a major terror attack, the mental health service response typically unfolds in phases. Although described in various ways in the literature, the response includes an acute phase and a postacute phase, ultimately followed by a return to normalcy. The duration of these phases can be expected to be dictated in large part by the intensity of the disaster, the degree of ongoing threat, and the response of the community. Specific types of interventions may be required to a greater or lesser degree during each phase of the disaster response; however, we can expect to see considerable overlap of specific service needs and activities among the phases.

Services emphasized during the acute phase tend to be part of the Federal Emergency Management Administration (FEMA) model of crisis intervention, psychoeducation, and social-support–enhancing methods designed to help people cope with psychological distress caused by the disaster. Guidelines for providing psychological interventions during the first month of this phase, known as the early-intervention period, were recently considered as part of a national consensus workshop organized by the National Institute of Mental Health (2002) and other federal agencies. Its framework proposes that early mental health assessment and intervention should focus on addressing

> a hierarchy of need: starting with survival, safety, security, food, shelter, health (both physical and mental), triage (mental health triage for emergencies), orientation (helping survivors become oriented to immediate local services), communication with family, friends, and community, and other forms of psychological first aid [pp. 6–7].

Key components of early intervention include ensuring that basic needs are met; providing psychological first aid; performing ongoing assessment of individual, group, and population needs; monitoring the recovery environment; implementing outreach and disseminating information; providing technical assistance to emergency responders, caregivers, and support organizations; fostering resilience and recovery through psychoeducation, promoting social support, and looking after the bereaved; identifying, assessing, and referring to appropriate services persons in need of mental health treatment; and providing individual, family, and group mental health treatment to persons in need.

An important element of early intervention in school settings involves psychoeducation for students, parents, and school personnel, including information regarding normal reactions to disaster, tips for coping, strategies about talking with and helping children following a disaster, and identifying when to seek professional mental health services for children. Students will also likely benefit from age appropriate information about the event, age-appropriate self-help strategies, and activities they can do to help (e.g., making thank-you cards to send to firefighters or fundraising to help those directly involved in the disaster).

Psychoeducational approaches have been recommended as promising methods for working with individuals exposed to mass disaster during the acute phase, although few models have been specifically documented or evaluated. Psychoeducation was originally developed as an intervention for families who are dealing with severe mental illness but has since been adapted to address other disorders, including diabetes, cancer, Alzheimer's disease, and AIDS, as a means to both provide information and help people cope with the emotional trauma associated with these conditions (Lukens, Thorning, and Herman, 1999). The model emphasizes promoting strengths, resiliency, and increased awareness in a group setting, generally with a professional or trained peer leader. As applied to persons exposed to mass disaster, objectives of psychoeducation groups would include facilitating awareness of normal and pathological reactions to stress and trauma; increasing participants' knowledge of PTSD and related disorders; providing participants with coping, management, and other self-care skills; teaching participants to identify and recognize their own reactions and the reactions of colleagues, family members, and children as means of self- and community monitoring; helping participants process and integrate their own reactions to the traumatic experience; and strengthening self-efficacy and advocacy skills.

Many of the interventions described here are focused on individuals, families, and small groups. The need to target interventions at the broader community level, however, should not be overlooked. Citing numerous studies demonstrating the importance of positive social support and the use of it to facilitate trauma recovery, Litz, Gray, and Adler (2001) emphasize the value of implementing community-focused interventions to enhance social cohesion and mutual support. This suggests that such interventions are important during all phases following a mass disaster. These types of interventions include community-based activities that focus on bringing together members of the community to provide social and emotional support for persons who have suffered significant losses. Similar activities include organizing occasions that recognize and commemorate significant events related to 9/11.

An example of such an intervention in New York City was the Rally for Recovery that took place in November 2001 in Lower Manhattan. Organized by New York Recovers, a coalition of religious, academic, business, and community leaders, the rally was attended by several thousand New Yorkers to help their fellow citizens heal following the events of 9/11. This coalition also organized a number of community activities to commemorate the one-year anniversary of the attacks. A similar event was a community march that took place in Washington Heights in Upper Manhattan in support of the families of victims of the American Airlines plane crash that claimed the lives of more than 200 New Yorkers, primarily natives of the Dominican Republic. The response to this latter incident, which also involved coordinated outreach to the affected community by mental health treatment personnel, may serve as an excellent model of the type of response that the mental health system should be organized to deliver following mass disasters, including terrorist attacks.

To mobilize an effective and coordinated response to a sudden unanticipated disaster is a daunting challenge. The chaos that typically accompanies such a disaster makes it extremely difficult to mount the type of comprehensive response we describe. Following a disaster, there are commonly major difficulties around issues of turf, authority, and coordination, which impede the organized delivery of needed services. The response of the New York City health system after the September 11 terrorist attack is reminiscent of what has been described in previous disasters dating back to the 19th century. Among the earliest disaster responses to be well documented is the response to the cholera epidemic in Hamburg in August 1892 (Evans, 1987). Cholera struck the inhabitants of the city with terror but generated a rather fragmented and ineffectual response from the health sector. By comparison with such instances, the New York health system performed reasonably well, despite being unprepared to coordinate a concerted effort of public education, treatment, and preparedness.

In the months following major disaster or terror attack, it can be expected that the most overwhelming crisis needs will have abated somewhat as persons directly exposed to the event will likely have received concrete assistance and emotional support and as the widespread psychological distress generated by the event will have begun to diminish. As noted, the length of this period is difficult to predict and may be determined in large part by the course of future events such as actual or threatened further terror attacks. The most recent epidemiologic data collected by Galea's group seem to confirm that many New Yorkers who reported symptoms of mental disorder during the months immediately following September 11 are recovering naturally, a clear tribute to the resilience of the human psyche. For instance, the reported rate of current PTSD, related to September 11, in Manhattan residents had declined to 1.7% by January 2002 (down from 7.5% during the first month after the attacks). Rates of depression also decreased significantly (Galea et al., 2002). Despite these declining rates, the number of persons currently experiencing disorder is still enormous.

Although interventions appropriate to treating psychological distress will continue to be needed, it is likely that the subsequent focus will be on providing treatment of diagnosable mental disorders to persons whose symptoms have not resolved and to persons who have experienced delayed onsets of such disorders. Whereas early intervention and other forms of crisis assistance provided previously may help people cope with basic safety needs and feelings of psychological distress, formal mental health treatment will be required by persons experiencing severe psychological sequelae such as PTSD and depression. Although, as previously noted, relatively little empirical evidence on the effectiveness of psychological interventions used in the early-intervention phase exists, there is considerably more well-established research literature regarding effective treatments for diagnosable mental disorders most likely to result from exposure to mass violence and severe trauma. (See National Institute of Mental Health, 2002, for a current overview of the evidence on interventions in this area.)

A critical limitation in our ability to meet the urgent need for mental health interventions during all phases of a major disaster is the shortage of mental health workers who are well trained and available to be deployed when the need arises. There appears to be broad consensus in the field of disaster mental health care regarding the inadequate level of expertise among personnel in mental health and allied systems on how to best intervene when persons are exposed to violent disasters. There is, therefore, a need to provide training to a broad group of professional and nonprofessional personnel so they can respond to the diverse set of mental health issues resulting from terror events. This training ranges from teaching non–mental health personnel (including emergency responders, primary care physicians, teachers, and clergy) to provide needed support while identifying individuals requiring professional intervention (during both phases of disaster response), to intensive clinical training for mental health professionals treating persons with PTSD and other serious disorders.

An example of the latter is a major initiative organized by the New York City Consortium for Effective Trauma Treatment. A panel of nationally recognized experts in current PTSD treatment techniques is training clinical faculty members from numerous local mental health facilities. These faculty in turn will train local clinicians practicing privately or in community settings or employee-assistance programs. The preparation emphasizes the need to reach out to school clinicians, primary health care providers, and special education teachers. Just as educational needs extend beyond an exclusive focus on mental health workers, it is also important to raise the overall level of competence in dealing with trauma in many organizations, including schools, universities, hospitals, and businesses. The events of September 11 have sadly brought to wide attention the profound psychological impacts associated with trauma and disaster. Perhaps this new awareness will lead to renewed energy devoted to such training and education.

Training alone, however, is an incomplete response to shortages in competent personnel. We also need to ensure that a sufficient number of clinicians are available to intervene following a major terrorist incident. Following the September 11 attacks, many private practitioners and mental health agency staff members volunteered their services and provided crisis counseling and other therapeutic interventions. Just as the military includes a large reserve force that can be called into action during crises, we propose augmenting this workforce of clinicians by the creation of a mental health reserve corps made up of retired or part-time mental health professionals who would contribute their time and expertise on an emergency basis. Reserve corps members could lead efforts to disseminate information and to foster outreach to the public. They would also diagnose individuals with clinical cases of mental disorders and offer them appropriate treatment, whether cognitive-behavioral therapy, pharmacotherapy, family therapy, or a variety of other techniques shown to be effective. In an encouraging development, the recently passed Public Health Security and Bioterrorism Preparedness and Response Act provides a step in this direction by authorizing the creation of a registration system for health professionals who volunteer during health care emergencies (presumably to include mental health workers); the system will verify credentials, licenses, accreditations, and hospital privileges.

As this chapter was being prepared for publication, the United States was mobilizing for a broad military campaign against Iraq, triggering further domestic fears of terrorist retaliation with biological, chemical, and possibly nuclear agents. It is therefore incumbent on the federal government to recognize the need to protect the nation's mental health by focusing on psychologically informed preventive and rapid-response strategies. To reach the vast majority of the population, such efforts must go well beyond health institutions to schools, religious organizations, community groups, the military, the police, firefighters, and emergency workers. We have begun to take steps to protect our lives and property. We must guard our mental health as well.

References

Bleich, A., Dycian, A., Koslowsky, M., Solomon, Z. & Wiener, M. (1992), Psychiatric implications of missile attacks on a civilian population: Israeli lessons from the Persian Gulf War. *J. Amer. Med. Assn.*, 268:613–615.

Conover, S., Stein, Z., Susser, E. & Susser, M. (2002), New York besieged: 11 September and after. *J. Epidemiol. Community Health*, 56:2–3.

Evans, R. (1987), *Death in Hamburg: Society and Politics in the Cholera Years, 1830–1910*. New York: Oxford University Press.

Factor, S. H., Wu, Y., Monserrate, J., Edwards, V., Cueras, Y., Del Vecchio, S. & Vlahov, D. (2002), Drug use frequency among street-recruited heroin and cocaine users in Harlem and the Bronx before and after September 11, 2001. *J. Urban Health*, 79(3).

Fagen, J. & Galea, S. (2002), Self-reported increase in asthma severity after the September 11 attacks on the World Trade Center—Manhattan, New York, 2001. *MMWR Morb. Mortal. Wkly. Rep.*, 51:781–784.

Freud, A. & Burlingham, D. (1943), *War and Children*. New York: Foster Parents' Plan for War Children.

Galea, S., Ahern, J., Resnick, H., Kilpatrick, D., Bucuvalas, M., Gold, J. & Vlahov, D. (2002), Psychological sequelae of the September 11 terrorist attacks in New York City. *N. Engl. J. Med.*, 346:982–987.

_____ Boscarino, J., Resnick, H. & Vlahov, D. (2002), Mental health in New York City after the September 11 terrorist attacks: Results from two population surveys. In: *Mental Health, United States, 2001*, ed. R. W. Manderscheid. Washington, DC, U.S. Government Printing Office.

Goodnough, A. (2002), Post 9/11 pain found to linger in young minds. *The New York Times.*

Herman, D., Felton, C. & Susser, E. (2001), *New York State: Mental Health Needs Assessment Related to Terrorist Attacks in the United States.* Albany: New York State Office of Mental Health.

Inglesby, T. V., O'Toole, T., Henderson, D. A., Bartlett, J. G., Ascher, M. S., Eitzen, E., Friedlander, A. M., Gerberding, J., Hauer, J., Hughes, J., McDade, J., Osterholm, M. T., Parker, G., Perl, T. M., Russell, P. K. & Tonat, K. (2002), Anthrax as a biological weapon, 2002: Updated recommendations for management. *J. Amer. Med. Assn.,* 287:2236–2252.

Kawachi, I., Kennedy, B. P., Lochner, K. & Prothrow-Stith, D. (1997), Social capital, income inequality, and mortality. *Amer. J Public Health,* 87: 1491–1498.

Litz, B., Gray, M. & Adler, A. (2001), Early intervention for trauma: Current status and future directions. National Center for PTSD Fact Sheet.

Lukens, E., Thorning, H. & Herman, D. (1999), Family psychoeducation in schizophrenia: Emerging themes and challenges. *J. Practical Psychiat. Behav. Health,* 5:314–325.

Murray, C. L. & Lopez, A. (1996), *The Global Burden of Disease.* Cambridge, MA: Harvard University Press.

National Institute of Mental Health (2002), *Mental Health and Mass Violence: Evidence-Based Early Psychological Intervention for Victims/Survivors of Mass Violence.* Washington, DC: U.S. Government Printing Office.

Vlahov, D., Galea, S., Resnick, H., Ahern, J., Boscarino, J., Bucuvalas, M., Gold, J. & Kilpatrick, D. (2002), Increased use of cigarettes, alcohol, and marijuana among Manhattan, New York, residents after the September 11th terrorist attacks. *Amer. J. Epidemiol.,* 155:988–996.

Wessely, S., Hyams, K. C. & Bartholomew, R. (2001), Psychological implications of chemical and biological weapons. *Brit. Med. J.,* 323:878–879.

Yzermans, J. & Gerson, B. (2002), The chaotic aftermath of an airplane crash in Amsterdam. In: *Toxic Turmoil: Psychological and Societal Consequences of Ecological Disasters,* ed. J. Havenaar, J. Cwikel & E. Bromet. New York: Kluwer Academic/Plenum, pp. 85–99.

Chapter 13

Lessons for High-Risk Populations from Attachment Research and September 11

Helping Children in Foster Care

Francine Cournos

The events of 9/11 activated wide-ranging concern over the traumatization of a large population–and saw the commitment of vast resources to address its needs. The editors have elected to conclude this volume by considering a huge population of Americans in severe distress whose very existence is conveniently forgotten most of the time–children in foster-care placement. Francine Cournos is the author of City of One, *a moving testament to the suffering of these children, passages from which are reprised here. Were this book more widely disseminated, it might surpass Robertson's film,* A Child Goes to the Hospital, *in terms of social impact.*

The fact is that there are half a million children in foster care at any one time in this country. What befalls these children in the ordinary course of events as part of the daily institutional regimens of city and state agencies must not be allowed to continue. The consensus of the scientific community should now join the personal testimony of those who have survived the system in the call for fundamental change.

Our responses to the terrorist attacks of September 11 offer crucial insights into how we might create systems that can meet the mental health needs of children struggling with trauma and loss. Adults, shocked and angered by the extraordinary events of that day, immediately envisioned the distress of exposed children. Adult horror, vividly described in the chapters of this book, led to protective responses toward children, eliciting broad interest in helping them process trauma and grief. This, in turn, resulted in an unprecedented mobilization of resources, which included providing widespread education to caregivers and teachers about age-appropriate strategies for interpreting and responding to children's distress, and organizing both funded and voluntary mental health services to treat children who were symptomatic. We demonstrated that we have the capacity to respond to traumatized children in a thoughtful and generous way when we are moved to do so. And conversely, because children cannot independently advocate for resources, it is only when adults have conceptualized the suffering of children that systems can be put in place to help them.

The terrorist attacks of September 11 probably distressed adults in the United States to a greater extent than they did children. Grounded in their perspectives on history and politics, adults are in a better position to appreciate what a radical departure the events of that day were and how they would permanently alter our sense of safety. Commercial airplanes crashing into office buildings may create less shock and numbness among children, especially younger ones, whose imaginations can conjure up all sorts of frightening scenarios that carry equal potency. This may help explain Christina Hoven's (Hoven et al., 2002) finding among New York City schoolchildren that loss of a relative was a stronger determinant of psychological distress following September 11 than was proximity to Ground Zero. As Hofer (this volume) points out, children's sense of safety in the face of external threats is more strongly mediated by proximity to attachment figures than by the realistic risks posed by the threats themselves. Empirical evidence for the critical role of caregivers in mediating the emotional states of their children in situations of danger dates back to research conducted during and after World War II (Freud and Burlingham, 1944; Bowlby, 1966). September 11 made insights derived in wartime relevant to us here and now in the United States.

With those insights come a challenging question: How can we extend our attentive and caring responses to other groups of traumatized children, those who experience chronic distress but are not usually a focus of trauma initiatives? Foster children, drawn from the severe end of the spectrum of children who have been abused or neglected, number more than 500,000 at any given time and are one of the populations for whom this challenging question is most relevant. Yet foster children are rarely a topic of public discussion about or research into the effects of trauma. This is not surprising, since the foster-care system operates on a "theory of body" rather than a "theory of mind." It focuses almost exclusively on protecting children from physical abuse and neglect, while ignoring the child's, or for that matter the foster parent's, internal experience. Although physical well-being is critical, many placements are jeopardized because foster parents and foster children are treated as so many interchangeable parts, and the formation of new attachments is not conceptualized as an important part of the process.

Foster parents rarely receive the preparation and support they need to form successful new relationships with the troubled children placed in their care. Most foster children have experienced frightening and confusing changes in their interpersonal worlds. Upon placement, these children often behave in ways that suggest that caregivers are not needed (Dozier, Dozier, and Manni, 2002). As a result, placement changes and disruptions frequently occur as foster parents struggle in solitude to meet the needs of children who come to them with very damaged lives (Comfort, 2002). Placement failures in turn repeat and reinforce the cycle of trauma and loss.

There are many possible explanations for why the foster-care system operates without a theory of mind: the lack of integration of mental health services into the social service system; the large case loads and high turnover of most child-welfare workers and law guardians; the lack of interest most mental health professionals have in becoming involved with this disadvantaged and stigmatized population; the general shortage of mental health services for children; the greater weight our legal system gives to parental rights over children's needs; the placement pressures that result from a shortage of suitable foster homes; and the fact that the world of each foster child disintegrates hidden from public view. But as a former foster child, I suspect that it would also be too jarring to keep the internal experiences of foster children in mind while running the foster-care system as it currently exists (Cournos, 2002). Although September 11 evoked enormous sympathy for, and assistance to, children who witnessed the frightening events or lost loved ones on that day, how can we possibly afford to apply these same standards to abused, neglected, and abandoned children cycled through a foster-care system whose efficient operation depends on ignoring children's internal experiences?

The scientific literature on the mental health problems of foster children is limited. Most published journal articles focus on screening foster children for psychopathology and developmental delays, both of which are overrepresented in this population when compared to other socioeconomically disadvantaged children (Pilowsky, 1995). Despite the fact that as many as 84% of foster children have developmental and emotional problems (Halfon, Berkowitz, and Klee, 1992), the current foster-care system depends on placing the majority of children without regard to assessing or providing attention to these problems. Only severely troubled children who have failed numerous ordinary foster homes are transferred to more richly staffed environments, and many children gain little from foster care beyond basic survival (Rosenfeld, Wasserman, and Pilowsky, 1998). In that sense, one might say that the system for foster-care placement lacks reflective functioning (see Fonargy and Target, this volume) in that it cannot keep in mind the intentions, thoughts, and feelings of foster children or their caregivers, and therefore often fails to provide supports and services that would help them form successful and stabilizing relationships.

Because the foster-care system has difficulty responding even to severe mental health problems, it might seem a luxury to consider more generally and routinely the subjective experiences of children in placement. At the same time, one could convincingly argue that failure to represent the minds of foster children is an important factor in causing and exacerbating serious psychopathology among them. Although it would be easy to attribute the problem to a lack of funding for more adequate approaches, it could equally well be demonstrated that in the long run it is more costly not to intervene to prevent such outcomes as unemployment, incarceration, and the repetition of the cycle of childhood neglect and abuse with a new generation of children. Moreover, waiting until we are forced to respond to adverse adult outcomes poses a considerably more difficult task. Whereas psychoanalysts have long written about the indelible nature of early life experience, now a growing body of biological research supports the view that by design the human brain is meant to be formed into its final arrangement by the effects of childhood experience and that early severe stress appears to alter the structure and function of the brain (see Teicher et al., this volume). Given the potential for these irreversible effects, it is essential to intervene as early as possible. In the wake of our heightened awareness of the effects of psychological trauma following the terrorist attacks of September 11, perhaps we now have a critical opportunity to advocate for approaching distressed foster children in a more thoughtful way.

Models are already available for changing current practice. They are usually small, recently developed state-of-the-art programs that have yet to be generalized to the larger child-welfare system. Innovative programs frequently have a strong focus on the youngest children entering care, infants and toddlers under the age of three. Not only does this group constitute a significant proportion of all children in placement, but they are the ones who are most reliant on adults to represent their voices and are experiencing their most formative years in foster care with the most vulnerable developing central nervous systems and the least mature psychological defenses to cope with the frightening caregiver behaviors and disruptions they so frequently experience. Adolescent foster children are another group that needs special consideration (Wasserman, Rosenfeld, and Nickman, 2002), given the complexities of how they straddle the border between dependency and autonomy. Many of the most thoughtful approaches to foster children emphasize the same themes that emerged when providing services to children and adolescents following September 11.

Education and Collaboration

Every model foster-care program stresses the importance of mutual education and collaboration among all parties whose input will directly affect outcomes for foster children. Foster-care placement is complex, often involving the involuntary removal of children, which in turn results in extensive involvement of the law-enforcement and judicial systems (Wasserman et al., 2002). If the voices of mental health professionals are to be heard on such crucial topics as preserving the child's attachments and meeting the child's developmental needs, they must be integrated with the voices of child-welfare workers, foster-care-agency staff, biological parents and their extended families, foster parents, law-enforcement officials, law guardians, and family-court judges. Because most of these people will have received little if any formal training about the emotional and developmental needs of children, providing basic education is an essential function of mental health professionals, just as we are obliged to learn about the legal and social-welfare procedures that govern removal and placement decisions.

Responses to the events of September 11 illustrate the essential nature of such collaboration when responding to traumatic events and the dislocations that follow for those who have been directly impacted. So, for example, at the Family Assistance Center in New York City, mental health services were integrated with programs meeting other crucial needs, such as victim identification, applications for benefits, and community-level memorial services (see Coates, Schechter, and First, this volume). This resulted not only in the coordination of care but also in opportunities for mutual education. Thus, the contribution of mental health professionals involved not only direct services but also discussions with others who were involved with victims. We had to explain how children process trauma and loss, how to conceptualize the differences between childhood and adult thinking and feelings, and how to establish strategies for helping children cope successfully. In turn, we learned about the complexity of a sophisticated response to disaster, and where mental health services fit in that larger picture.

Promoting Relationship-Based Practices

Model programs for foster children attempt to shift the way the system operates so that decision making becomes more child centered and accounts for the fact that the child has a mind that is at risk, not only a body in need of protection from physical harm. Key to achieving this goal is integrating the view that children develop, function, encounter difficulties, and heal in the context of relationships (Groppenbacher, Hoard, and Miller, 2002).

Mary Dozier and colleagues have conducted extensive research on how children cope with disruptions in care (Dozier et al., 2002). One of the most important findings their work has produced is demonstrating that the foster parent's attachment state of mind, as assessed by the Adult Attachment Interview, predicted childhood attachment among babies and toddlers in foster care at nearly the same level as for birth parents and children. Based on this observation and other findings about how children can be helped to form secure attachments, Dozier's group has developed an intervention targeted to the foster parent–child dyad, which promotes nurturing behavior on the part of caregivers.

Groppenbacher and colleagues (2002) treat foster parents as co-therapists from the time of the first contact. By teaching foster parents to routinely ask themselves, "What is this child trying to tell me through his behavior?" caregivers learn that socially unacceptable or rejecting behavior may be a positive coping mechanism for the child.

Orfirer and Kronstadt (2002) emphasize the importance of presenting mental health and developmental assessments that allow the voices of children to become louder and more integrated into the child-welfare and court systems. Silver (2002) highlights the importance of advocacy by mental health professionals in achieving systems change so that foster children benefit from the early intervention services to which they are entitled yet rarely receive.

Here again, responses to the September 11 terrorist attacks taught us that without the structure of a well-organized system for responding to catastrophe, providing needed mental health services will be a chaotic hit-or-miss proposition. The challenge is to recreate the foster-care system so that it can take this obvious reality into account: children placed into foster care have experienced and will continue to experience psychological trauma that presents serious threats to becoming well-functioning and productive adults.

Prevention Strategies

Children in the foster-care system are frequently caught in the cycle of the transgenerational transmission of trauma. They are traumatized by the events that precede foster-care placement, and then their experiences within the foster-care system often lead to further trauma. Because foster children are largely drawn from very troubled families and because the child-welfare system is concerned with avoiding foster-care placement through efforts at family preservation, it is also very important to focus on biological parents at risk of losing their children.

Here again, models for intervening already exist. Brief interventions that videotape parent–child interactions and then offer the feedback of a reflective therapist have demonstrated impressive positive changes in parenting skills among traumatized caregivers who behave in frightened and frightening ways with their infants and toddlers (see Schechter, this volume). Larrieu (2002) has intervened with recently placed infants and toddlers and their foster and biological families to achieve either reunification of the child with the birth parent, or the freeing of the child for adoption when reunification is not possible. As with the interventions described in Schechter's chapter in this book, therapy involves challenging negative attributions about the parent and her child through sensitive support and interpretation. A focus on strengths is used to help modify negative behaviors that parents display with their youngsters. Larrieu notes that positive changes in mental representations often result in positive changes in behaviors, and vice versa.

Wunika's Story

Although losing a parent in the terrorist attacks of September 11 was a devastating experience that will have lifelong consequences for affected children, it did not involve the kind of frightening parental betrayal that is often present for foster children. Consider the following excerpts from an essay written by 16-year-old Wunika Hicks (1996a) about the circumstances of her life around the time of her permanent removal from her mother's care, just as she was turning nine (Wunika's father had died when she was two).

> When I look back on my past, I wish I never remembered some of the things that happened to me. My mother was abused as a child, so in return she abused me.
>
> I tried to be the best daughter for her. It just seemed as if she expected so much. I was only eight years old when I had to stay home from school to take care of my brother. When my brother was born, it seemed like that was when all my problems began.

One day my mother came home after a hard day of work. (Ha! Honestly, I don't know where she was.) She yelled at me as I was feeding my brother David, "Wunika, who the f-ck told you to give David that bottle?"

I didn't say anything, I just sat in the chair feeding my brother. I wished I could have disappeared. My mother yelled once again, "You're so damn stupid! Put David in the crib!"

I rushed to put my brother in the crib. I never envied my brother so much as I did that moment. I wished I could have been in his place. My mother loved him so much. She once told me, "I wish I never gave birth to your stupid ass." Those words stick with me today.

As I walked back into the kitchen, my mother took the boiling pot of water off the stove (filled with bottles, tops, and nipples I was sterilizing) and threw it in my face. I never yelled so much.

My mother just stood there. She didn't care. All she said was, "Shut the hell up." The skin of my face fell off. I yelled to the top of my lungs. My mother couldn't stand the noise, so she asked me, "Do you want me to give you something to cry for?"

I eventually stopped crying. My mother cleaned my face and boy, did I yell! She changed her attitude once she saw the damage she did. She apologized to me.

I never felt so much hate for her. I wanted her to hurt as I did. . . .

That night, my mother wouldn't let me sleep with her. I had to sleep on the dining-room chairs. We had mice, so I refused to sleep on the floor.

I woke up to David's yells. My mother was gone once again, and who knew when she'd return. I picked up my brother from the crib and opened the refrigerator. I took out his bottle and heated it up on the stove. He was still crying, and I felt like killing him. . . .

He loved me. He had to—I took care of him, and he depended on me. I had to feed him, change his Pampers, and answer to all his needs. Even though I hated staying home, it was worth watching him. . . .

My mother didn't come back home that night or the next. I cried so hard. I prayed nothing had happened to her. I didn't have any food, so I ate some of David's baby food (which wasn't that bad, by the way).

When my mother did return, she came with enough food to last the whole year. She acted as if she was gone for an hour. I wanted to question her, but I had to stay in my place. . . .

My mother fixed my favorite dish, lamb in tomato sauce with rice. I wondered if she was okay. All I cared about was that she was home with me.

As I slept beside her that night, I felt so much safer. I just hoped it would stay that way, that I would always feel safe with her and not be scared. But something deep inside told me that the way we were living couldn't go on forever.

That hurt me. I didn't want my mother to go, just her attitude. I knew if she went away, I'd have nothing. She was a part of me and vice versa, regardless of all the bad things. She will always be my mother, I said to myself, just before I fell asleep [pp. 34–38].

Hofer (this volume) points out that children can suffer considerable maltreatment while remaining strongly attached to an abusive care-taker. Wunika's essay powerfully illustrates this point. Despite her fear of her mother's unpredictably violent behavior, Wunika was more frightened and bereft when her mother disappeared. Although the child-welfare system can be credited with rescuing many children like Wunika and her brother from grave physical danger, without a theory of mind or a focus on attachment what are the chances that the system will help such children recover from their early traumas?

It is not surprising then that Wunika suffered another major trauma, as a result of foster-care placement. Five years after removal from her mother's home, Wunika lost all contact with her brother when he was adopted, over her strong objections. His name was changed, and she was permitted no further contact with him nor given any information concerning his whereabouts. Left to struggle with a poignant mixture of anger, guilt, and love, Wunika (1996b) declared:

I think of David every day—so much that it hurts. It hurts the most when his birthday passes. He's getting older without me.

I hope he hasn't forgotten me but remembers the times I took care of him as a mother. I don't want him to remember the times I rejected him.

I may have pushed him away when he wanted me, but that doesn't mean I don't love him. The system didn't understand my history, my pain. They took away the only family I had. Now I don't have anyone to love [pp. 32–33].

Foster care is as relevant today as it has ever been, as the global effects of terrorism, war, and infectious disease leave increasing numbers of children traumatized, orphaned, and in need of substitute care. For example, as of the end of 2001, AIDS alone had orphaned 13 million children worldwide, a number that far exceeds the capacity of extended families to raise them. Foster homes were created as alternatives to orphanages, based on findings that children's psychological health was harmed by institutional care and on subsequent evidence that children fare better in foster care. These findings have recently been replicated in developing countries (Ahmed and Mohamad, 1996). Yet foster care remains a source of further trauma for many of the children it serves.

The Author's Story

This chapter is written not only from my vantage point as a mental health professional but also from my firsthand experience as a traumatized foster child unable to accept a new caregiver. Although I was not abused, I did undergo a series of profound losses as a child, beginning with the abrupt death of my father from a cerebral hemorrhage when I was three years old. My older brother was five, and my mother was pregnant with my younger sister. My maternal grandparents moved in to help my mother support and care for us. Two years later, my grandfather died suddenly when he hemorrhaged from a peptic ulcer, and a few months after that my mother was diagnosed with breast cancer. She struggled for six years with her illness, undergoing multiple disfiguring treatments until she succumbed to lung metastases when I was 11 years old. Of the four adults who had raised me, only my grandmother was then left.

My mother's death was the saddest event of my childhood. She had been the center of my world, and I missed her terribly. By day I recreated her as an invisible presence watching over me, and I cried for her every night for almost a year. I was grieving, but I coped, and I was not traumatized in the clinical sense.

For the next two years, I lived with my grandmother. She did not speak English, had never learned to read, and was becoming increasingly forgetful, which further restricted her already limited ability to negotiate the world. But I had learned to conduct my own affairs like a miniature adult, including caring for and protecting my little sister. I thought we were getting along fine. And we were not entirely alone: I'd grown up with three sets of aunts, uncles, and cousins who lived nearby, and sometimes they came over to visit or help. But then one day the uncle who had been designated my legal guardian took me to a mysterious place where the following events transpired:

> We drove to an unfamiliar destination in Manhattan. Aunt Milly, Uncle Milton, [my little sister] Alexis, and I entered an office to meet with a woman I had never seen before. I had no idea why we had come to this place, but the adults seemed to know what was going to happen, and I had the feeling that now I was about to be let in on the secret. The woman spoke. Alexis and I would be moving to a foster home, she informed us, to live with a family that had not yet been selected. As the words sank in, rage took over. "I'll jump off the Empire State Building," I shouted, striving for the most dramatic possible statement, something that would really have effect. If I threatened something outrageous enough, they surely wouldn't go through with this. But they just humored me. The unfamiliar woman described the virtues of a new home, but I had stopped listening. I could barely distinguish between the fury I felt at my relatives and the rage I turned on myself for being so helpless. "You can't do this to me, you can't give me away if I don't want to leave." I wished I really could jump off the Empire State Building, but if I was to be loyal to my mother, I would stay in control no matter what anyone did to me or how tempted I was by my own anger [Cournos, 1999, pp. 95–96].

Thus began a process of psychological unraveling that I would later understand as a traumatized state of mind. Although I had fantasies to the contrary, I could also appreciate the fact that my parents had no control over dying. But when the aunts and uncles I was counting on made an intentional decision to abandon me, I felt betrayed and enraged.

Because the systems set up to help foster children, though well intentioned, usually focus exclusively on their physical well-being while ignoring their internal experience, increasingly the inner world of the child diverges from the ministrations of the surrounding adults. Here is an example of how this happened for me:

> The morning of my placement into foster care, I first went to [the headquarters of the foster-care agency] to have a physical examination and, I imagined, do whatever else must be done to transform me into a foster child. I had trouble believing it was happening. I was a horse and they were checking my hooves and teeth. I saw myself being sold into slavery. Before I could go to the foster home, they had to examine me for defects and diseases. I wondered what they would do if they found any.
>
> I was depleted now, exhausted, unable to make sense of this final separation from my family, beyond understanding how all the adults I was counting on could band together to exclude me. It was too painful to think about how their lives would go on without Alexis and me, go on as if we never existed. My outrage was muted by my growing detachment, my feeling that I was not fully alive. I took refuge in my firm control over my own behavior, my ability to carry out life's daily routines, however empty and meaningless they seemed. Without conscious effort or acknowledgment, I gradually obliterated any love I still had for the remaining members of my family. Eventually, even when I visited them, I felt as if I barely knew them, distant relatives I may have met once long ago, as irrelevant to my emotional life as I was to theirs [Cournos, 1999, pp. 100–101].

The act of being involuntarily taken to a foster home was the most traumatic experience of my childhood. But placement is not designed to help children process and contain their emotions, find words for the placement experience, or normalize feelings (see Coates, this volume). On the contrary, for me, being asked to strip naked in front of a stranger as a prelude to stepping into a car with strangers for the purpose of being transported to a completely unfamiliar place, intended by well-meaning foster-agency staff as assurance that I was in good physical health, felt horrible and humiliating. These adults could not hold my experience in mind, and I was losing the ability to feel centered within my own mind.

So I arrived in my foster home too disorganized, too rejecting of my own needs, too angry and detached, and too much in mourning for my biological family to easily start any new relationships. Then here is what happened with my foster mother Erma two weeks into my placement (Cournos, 1999):

"You can call me Mom now," Erma said, commanding, almost threatening after I got into bed one night. She had dropped her cheerful demeanor, staring at me with contained rage for not having come to this conclusion on my own. I suddenly had a sinking feeling, trapped here with a terrifying witch, nowhere to turn. I averted my gaze, and then, desperate, I converted my sense of helplessness into rage, answering Erma only with an internal monologue: "To me, you're nobody. I've been here only two weeks, and I haven't felt comfortable for a minute. I still have a mother, anyway, even if she's dead. My mother needs to live through me now, and I'm prepared to devote myself to this task, to stay loyal and always remember, lest she cease to exist. I don't need another mother, and it wasn't my idea to come here in the first place." I looked up. Erma was still standing over me, waiting, and I was still scared. I did as Erma said, spitting the word out, feeling thoroughly insincere, then silently apologizing to Mom for using her name. My heart began to harden against Erma.

Like other children following the death of a parent, I had reconstructed my world using the remaining relationships I still had with my family. But now, except for my sister, everyone and everything familiar was gone: my aunts and uncles, my grand-mother, [my mother's boyfriend] Sam, the library and the park, my apartment and nearly all my possessions, my school, my classmates. Faced with such a sudden and complete loss, I clung even more resolutely to my dead mother. . . . The more aggressively Erma came after me, the more I retreated into my protective shell [pp. 103–104].

Numbing of general responsiveness is one of the hallmarks of trauma. For me, it defined the crucial difference between my reaction to the death of my mother on one hand and my placement into foster care on the other. This dissociative state and many other symptoms of trauma and anxiety persisted untreated into my adult life, when I finally began to address them by seeking out psychotherapy and psychoanalysis.

However, much as Rees (this volume) describes for Guntrip and Diana, it was not during treatment but in the context of real-life experience that I first gained full emotional access to the disturbing events of my childhood. This happened when my almost two-year-old daughter suffered severe separation anxiety while she was away from many familiar people and places during a three-week summer vacation with my husband and me. As I resonated with her feelings, I felt a reactivation in full force of my own overwhelming separation terrors. I was stunned by how feelings I had tried without success to explore in therapy and analysis could hit me so powerfully at a time when I was not currently in treatment and not seeking to uncover them. Yet later, this same reaction would strike me as inevitable. Becoming a parent myself was the most potent precipitant I'd ever encountered for reevoking my childhood anxieties. My response was, in the end, a common example of how the transgenerational transmission of trauma takes place.

Fortunately, my prior treatment had set the stage for me to recognize what was occurring, and I returned to therapy. This allowed me to turn an unsettling response into a successful journey of self-exploration. My new accessibility to the past marked the beginning of more fruitful efforts to rework and reintegrate my most troubling feelings. It also increased my awareness of the degree to which I was frightening my daughter with my own separation anxiety. Disrupting the transgenerational transmission of trauma depends on this type of recognition by caregivers and on the modifications in parenting behavior that can follow (see Schechter, this volume).

Conclusion

For children, foster-care placement is experienced as the end of one world and the beginning of a strange new one. For many adults, the events of September 11 were experienced in a similar manner, and we have responded with deep concern for one another and for our children. The world would be a much safer place for foster children if this same compassion resulted in modifying the child-welfare system to meet the psychological needs of the traumatized children who cycle through it. Cost-effective models are already available for doing so. Their implementation awaits the ability of adults to represent and reflect on the inner lives of our most socially disadvantaged children.

References

Ahmed, A. & Mohamad, K. (1996), The socioemotional development of orphans in orphanages and traditional foster care in Iraqi Kurdistan. *Child Abuse Negl.*, 20:1161–1173.

Bowlby, J. (1966), *Maternal Care and Mental Health*. New York: Schocken.

Comfort, R. L. (2002), Play and learn at our place. *Bull. Zero to Three*, 22:52–56.

Cournos, F. (1999), *City of One*. New York: Norton.

————— (2002), The trauma of profound childhood loss: A personal and professional perspective. *Psychiat. Quart.*, 73:145–156.

Dozier, M., Dozier, D. & Manni, M. (2002), Attachment and biobehavioral catch-up: The ABCs of helping foster infants cope with early adversity. *Bull. Zero to Three*, 22:7–13.

Freud, A. & Burlingham, D. T. (1944), *Infants Without Families*. New York: International Universities Press.

Groppenbacher, E., Hoard, C. & Miller, S. (2002), Providing mental health services to young children in foster care: A family-by-family, moment-by-moment approach to change. *Bull. Zero to Three*, 22:33–37.

Halfon, N. G., Berkowitz, G. & Klee, L. (1992), Mental health services utilization by children in foster care in California. *Pediatrics*, 89:1238–1244.

Hicks, W. (1996a), She'll always be my mother. In: *The Heart Knows Something Different*, ed. A. Desetta. New York: Persea Books, pp. 34–38.

————— (1996b), I lost my brother to adoption. In: *The Heart Knows Something Different*, ed. A. Desetta. New York: Persea Books, pp. 30–33.

Hoven, C. W., Duarte, C. S., Lucas, C. P., Mandell, D. J., Cohen, M., Rosen, C., Wu, P., Musa, G. J. & Gregorian, N. (2002), *Effects of the World Trade Center Attack on NYC Public School Students–Initial Report to the New York City Board of Education*. New York: Columbia University Mailman School of Public Health, New York State Psychiatric Institute, and Applied Research and Consulting, LLC.

Larrieu, J. A. (2002), Treating infant–parent relationships in the context of maltreatment: Repairing ruptures of trust. *Bull. Zero to Three*, 22:16–22.

Orfirer, K. & Kronstadt, D. (2002), Working toward relationship-based child welfare practice: The SEED model after 5 years. *Bull. Zero to Three*, 22: 38–44.

Pilowsky, D. (1995), Psychopathology among children placed in family foster care. *Psychiat. Serv.*, 46:906–910.

Rosenfeld, A., Wasserman, S. & Pilowsky, D. J. (1998), Psychiatry and children in the child welfare system. *Child Adolesc. Psychiat. Clin. North Amer.*, 7:515–536.

Silver, J. A. (2002), The accidental advocate: Moving from individual case advocacy to system change. *Bull. Zero to Three*, 22:45–51.

Wasserman, S., Rosenfeld, A. & Nickman, S. (2002), Foster care and adoption. In: *Principles and Practice of Child and Adolescent Forensic Psychiatry*, ed. D. H. Schetky & E. P. Benedek. Washington, DC: American Psychiatric Publishing, pp. 97–107.

Index

DENMARK

by the same author

THE BOG PEOPLE

P. V. Glob

DENMARK

An Archaelogical History
from the Stone Age
to the Vikings

Translated from the Danish by
JOAN BULMAN

CORNELL UNIVERSITY PRESS
Ithaca, New York

International Standard Book Number 0–8014–0641–2
Library of Congress Catalog Card Number 74–148716
PRINTED IN GREAT BRITAIN

Og endnu vidner de Gamles Grave
om Slægters Følge i Danmarks Have.

Johannes V. Jensen,
5th June 1940

And still the graves of the ancients stand,
Witness to the generations that pass through
Denmark's land.

Contents

9

Illustrations

ACKNOWLEDGMENTS

photographs
Harald Andersen and P. V. Glob *plates 83–92*: Christian Blinkenberg *plates 55, 56*: Danish National Museum *plates 12, 18, 38, 39, 41, 42, 51, 52, 61, 62, 75, 76, 80, 81*: P. V. Glob *plates 2–11, 13–15, 19–24, 28–35, 37, 43–50, 53, 54, 57–60, 63–72, 79, 82, 95–101, 103, 104, 107, 112, 113, 116, 118–122, 124, 125, 126*: Victor Hermansen *plate 78*: Hans Kjær *plate 40*: Poul Kjærum *plates 105, 106*: Georg Kunwald *plates 110, 111*: Lennart Larsen *plate 36*: Carl Neergaard *plates 73, 74*: Viggo Nielsen *plate 108*: Thorkild Ramskou *plate 77*: Hans Stiesdal *plates 93, 94, 102, 115*

drawings
E. Schiödte *plate 16*: J. Kornerup *plate 17*: After C. A. Nordman *plates 25–27*: After G. Hatt *plate 109*: After J. Brøndsted *plates 114, 117*: A.P. Madsen *plate 123*

Year	Climate	Vegetation Animal Life	Cultural Period	
16,000 B.C.				
		treeless tundra dwarf birch, Arctic willow	finds in Holstein	
15,000	arctic	heather		
	Earliest Dryassic	reindeer		
14,000		birch in Jutland		
	sub-arctic	park tundra		
	Bølling	reindeer		
13,000				
	Earlier Dryassic	park tundra		hunters
12,000	sub-arctic			
	arctic	treeless tundra Polar fauna		
11,000	sub-arctic			
		scrubland with birch, willow, pine, aspen, juniper		
10,000	temperate		Bromme	
	Allerød	bear, elk, deer, wolverine, beaver		
9000				Early Stone Age hunters
	sub-arctic	park tundra	Lyngby culture	
	Later Dryassic	reindeer, wild horse, bison, mountain hare		
8000	cool, moist			
	Pre-Boreal	forest period birch, pine aurochs	Klosterlund	
7000				
		pine, birch, hazel elk, red deer, fox	Bøllund Mullerup	
	Boreal	roe deer, bear, wild pig		fishers and trappers
6000	warmer, dryer	beaver, otter, marten, hare, squirrel, wild cat, badger		
5000		capercaillie, turtle	Øgårde Holmegård	
	Atlantic	alder and oak		
	moist	mixed oak forest oak, elm, lime,		
4000		ivy, mistletoe red deer, roe deer, wild pig, lynx	kitchen middens Ertebølle	
3000		beech appears		farmers
	warm	whooper swan, great auk	Muldbjerg Havnelev	

CHRONOLOGICAL TABLE

Year	Cultivated Plants Domestic Animals	Monuments	Cultural Period		
3000 B.C.	barley, wheat ox, sheep, pig, goat	dolmens	earliest peasant culture villages		Neolithic period / Late Stone Age
2000	horse wild apple millet	passage graves low burial mounds megalithic cists stone cists cup-mark stones	the great goddess battle-axe people bell-beakers dagger period		
1000	oats, willow herb flax, pea, bean	large mounds rock engravings small mounds ship burials	chieftains trading people cremation	Early / Late Bronze Age	
Birth of Christ	rye cat, hen	mounded graves burial grounds with clay-vessel graves and stone graves flat-topped mounds monoliths	Celtic period Roman period	Early	Iron Age
	peacock	ship burials runic stones ring forts	Germanic period Viking Age	Late	
A.D. 1000		stave churches	Middle Ages		Historical time
1960		satellites	Atomic period		

2   Stabelhøj at Agri on the Island of Mols

I The Terrain

Nature and Cultivation

All over Denmark one comes upon memorials of the past, relics of cultures thousands of years old, standing like milestones along the paths our forefathers trod. By the roadside or hidden in woodland, on open heath and in cultivated fields, one sees these traces of antiquity. Where burial mounds crown the hilltops, they fill out and accentuate the rolling lines of the countryside. Nature and the hand of man have combined to present a characteristic type of scenery which has stamped itself on the national consciousness as something specifically Danish. The idea goes back very largely to the early Danish landscape painters of the middle of the last century, for whom grass-covered burial mounds and moss-grown dolmens were favoured themes. To the poets of the same period, burial monuments served as reminders of bygone generations and vanished days of national greatness.

Where the skyline rises to its highest point, a three-thousand-year-old Bronze Age burial mound almost always provides the topmost profile. This is true of the highest point in Denmark, Yding Skovhøj, which lies 173 metres above sea level, though it cannot be seen because, as its name shows (*skovhøj* means wooded mound), it is hidden by a dense thicket of maples. Yding Skovhøj lies on the plateau of Central Jutland, northwest of Ejer Bavnehøj, which with its 171 metres is in fact generally spoken of as the highest point in Denmark. It too was originally a prehistoric mound. However, it was levelled

3   Yding Skovhøj, the highest range of hills in Denmark

to the ground when someone had the idea of putting a watch-tower on the same spot, destroying its pre-eminence. To the north lies Himmelbjerg (mountain of heaven) which ruthless afforestation has cut off from the heavenly powers, rendering meaningless the name which was so appropriate only a hundred years ago.

Where these prehistoric burial mounds still rise under the open sky, they dominate the surrounding country. They provide incomparable views, and from just a few of them scattered over the country one can survey practically the whole Kingdom of Denmark. From Kigud on the plateau of eastern Vendsyssel one can see far over land and sea, right away to the white sandy desert of Råbjerg Miles and the most northerly part of Jutland. From Lundehøj in Thy one sees the waters of Limfjord with the open slopes of Morsland and other islands to south and east, and to the west the horizon fringed with sand dunes and the sea. From Hohøj on the slopes above Mariager Fjord the eye surveys a wide panorama of the woods and river valleys of Himmerland, leading deep into the county of Viborg.

Equally extensive on every side is the view from Stabelhøje, which forms the western silhouette of Mols Bjerge. From this high point one can see the whole of Djursland, vast areas of East Jutland, and the islands of Tunø, Samsø and Hjelm. In the clear, cold light of winter Vejrhøj, too, stands out on the south-easterly horizon, bringing a glimpse of Zealand into this Jutland scene.

Vejrhøj is the landmark for North-West Zealand, whether one approaches it by land or sea. Its foundation is a vast terminal moraine, which originally carried a second burial mound. There were twin mounds here, like Stabelhøje at Agri and many other mounds all over the country of both the Bronze and the Iron Ages. In many places, where they lie close together, these twin mounds are known as maiden mounds. With the surrounding hills they can be seen by the eye of the imagination as the breasts of a young woman lying asleep.

Another typical pair of mounds are those at Slots Bjergby, which command the whole of South-West Jutland, with the coasts of Funen and Langeland forming a blue horizon. The two largest prehistoric mounds in Denmark are those at the old royal seat of Jelling, and two others at Virksund in West Himmerland look far to the north and south on either side of a thousand-year-old crossing channel.

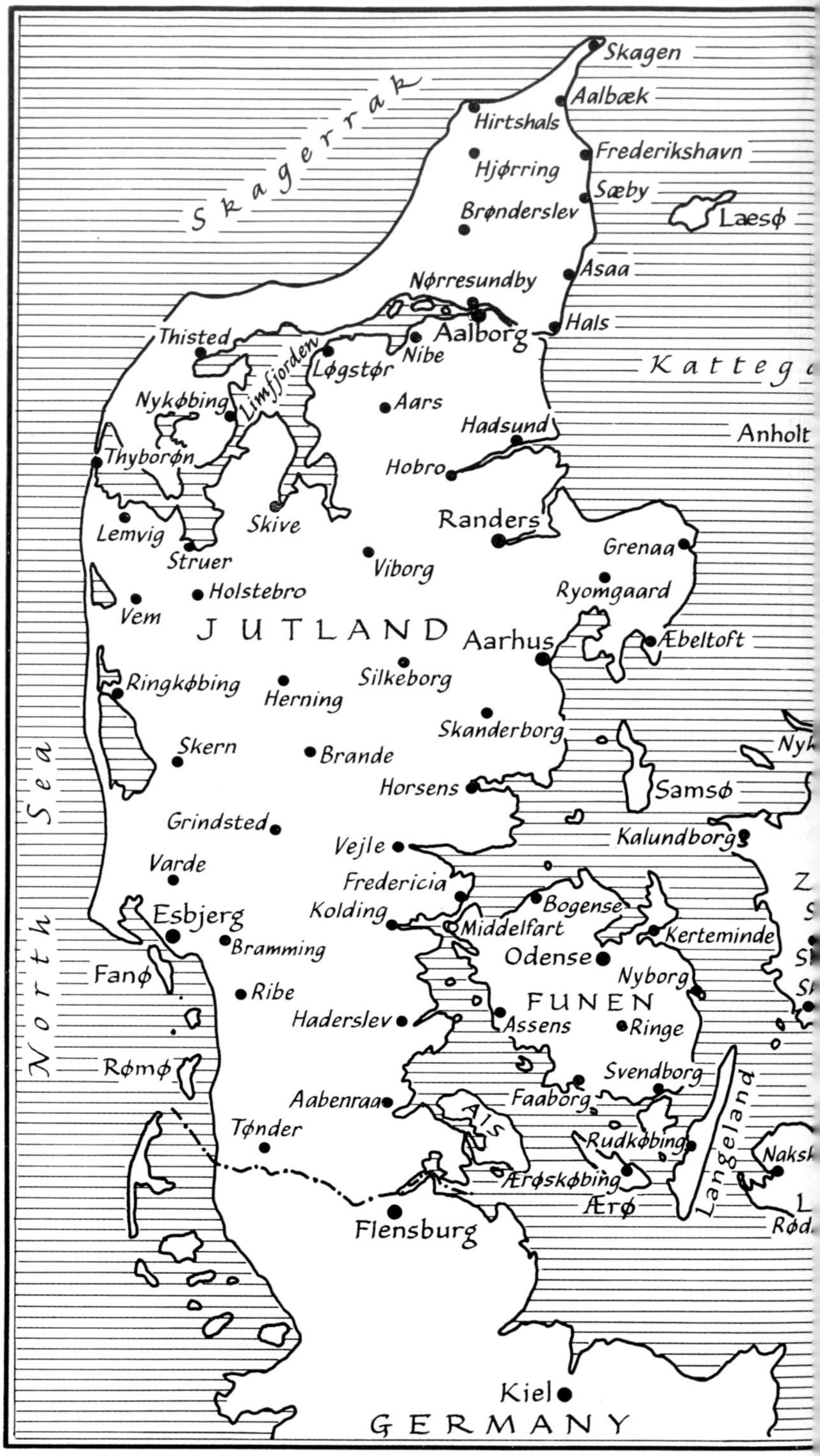

Fig 1.
Denmark

SWEDEN

Baltic Sea

Helsingør
Hillerød
Frederikssund
Copenhagen
Malmö
Roskilde
LAND
Køge
Ringsted
Store Heddinge
Næstved
Præstø
Sandvig
Neksø
Rønne
Bornholm
Stege
Møn
Stubbekøbing
Nykøbing
Falster
Nysted
Gedser

0   50   100 km

The highest point on the island of Lolland is Bavnehøj. It is one of a group of mounds near Birket and, as its name reveals (*baun* means beacon), was used in ancient times as a beacon hill, as were so many others of the burial mounds already mentioned. Even to this day bonfires are lit on them on midsummer night or Walpurgis night, before May Day, in accordance with local custom.

Since the first farming and stock-breeding peoples took over the land of Denmark about five thousand years ago, it has changed its character continuously. It became a cultivated landscape in a state of constant growth, created by man on the foundations of nature. Each immigration has brought something fresh. Climatic changes have also transformed the shape of the land. All the same, it is still possible to find places where, on account of special conditions, some particular feature of the landscape has remained as it was during one of the early periods, although they may only be very small in area.

The spacious woodland of today with its separate, slender tree-trunks is markedly different from the forest of antiquity, which was tangled, dense and impenetrable. Paths of wild animals threaded a winding network through it, and the ground was marked with the tracks of men and beasts. The openings in the forest were the work of the large ruminants, of aurochs, elk, red deer and roe deer. Clearance began in earnest when the first peasants, armed with sharp flint axes and fire, cleared spaces for fields to grow corn in, and for pastureland for their domestic animals, round their small villages.

For the first five thousand years after the Ice Age, alterations in the landscape were brought about by changes in nature. In the next five thousand years down to the present day, the changes have been mainly the work of man. The earliest of these are in the form of the burial monuments of the first peasants—the dolmens that characterize certain areas of the countryside—even if it is no longer true, as it was when Steen Steensen Blicher wrote at the beginning of the last

4 Tvillingehøje (the Twin Mounds), by Virksund
in West Himmerland

century, that in East Jutland there are dolmens and passage
graves in almost every village field. Other areas are characterized by the large mounds of the Bronze Age, especially
Himmerland and Thy, as well as certain districts in West
Jutland, though there the rounded profiles of these monuments on the skyline will soon be a part of history. This has
come about within living memory as the result of the extensive
planting of windbreaks and copses, in particular those made
with the fir-tree, so disastrous to the landscape, which is only
a few hundred years old in Denmark. The completely open
view across the plains of Jutland to a bare horizon is now
practically a thing of the past. The bent trees, shaped by the
fierce west winds of Jutland, which were as good as a compass
and by which many a traveller has guided his footsteps, are
now all sheltered behind windbreaks.

Fifteen hundred years were to pass after the building of the
large Bronze Age mounds before other monuments of equal
stature were raised—the stone-built village churches that, as
time has gone by, have grown more impressive with the addition of towers, chapels and charnel-houses. They often lie by
themselves on the hills so that they stand out like the ancient
mounds, while contemporary building has sought shelter and
protection at the foot, of necessity because, until the last
century, the materials used in village buildings were almost
exclusively wood, straw and clay. It is no accident that village
churches and burial mounds are often to be found side by side,
for the mounds like the churches were built at road junctions
and other meeting-places.

Now the landscape is changing in many places from year to
year. The changes began in earnest only a century ago, when
main roads and sweeping railway embankments were laid out,
and large dairy farms and high school buildings went up.
They have gathered speed since the Second World War. The
brightly coloured roofs of weekend cottages cover longer and
longer stretches of the coast, while ever more extensive building estates spread out from every town and village. Tall grey
or white giant silos, some round, some square, now dominate

28

5 View from Stabelhøj over Kalø Creek

the skyline more than anything else, and village churches are being constantly displaced as landscape features by swelling plantations of trees. The latest newcomers to the skyline are the Cyclops legs of radar and television masts and the human silos of tall blocks of flats.

The homely, domestic things in the changing landscape are going fast, too. Many streams are being blotted out and lakes drained away. A grazing horse on an open pasture is a rarity and cows, no doubt, will soon follow suit. When autumn falls there are few places where one can see long rows of stooks of corn emphasizing the lovely rise and fall of the land, or domed haystacks. Modern agricultural machinery—the combine-harvester, the reaping machine—has played its part in bringing the noise of engines in from the main roads over the quiet, open spaces.

Since archaeologists towards the end of the last century began exploring the country systematically, parish by parish, about a hundred thousand prehistoric monuments have been described and mapped. Only a third of them are still in existence because up to 1 July 1938 their preservation was not legally enforceable, so that shortage of stone or the need for hardcore to fill a marl-pit erased many an ancient monument. Before the preservation law, these monuments had partly been preserved by superstition. The mounds were inhabited by trolls and elves whom no one wanted to upset by desecrating their dwelling-places. It might even, in many cases, be positively dangerous: farms and houses might catch fire and sickness and death strike man and beast, should anyone be foolhardy enough to try. With education and the coming of schools, superstition vanished and with it many a prehistoric monument. Only those that were situated in heath and woodland and in uncultivated areas were left more or less untouched, until they came under the protection of the preservation law.

*   *   *   *   *

This book is intended as a guide to and an account of the relics of antiquity that may be met with on one's travels through the country. It should enable anyone to recognize the period and cultural context of most of the prehistoric monuments. There will be brief surveys of the various periods of prehistory, and the changing cultures and conditions that brought them about, as well as of the influences and immigrations from other countries that have left their mark on the monuments.

We shall discuss not only the various types of burial mound but also other traces of our ancestors that are visible in the terrain such as, for example, settlements, cultivated fields and roads. Within this limited space it is of course only possible to mention a small proportion of the hundred thousand prehistoric monuments recorded, but we shall attempt to describe and illustrate all the different types that exist.

As the burial mounds alter in appearance according to their age and culture, so too have physical conditions altered in Denmark during the ten thousand years of her prehistory, as we have seen. During the glacial periods the country lay deep-frozen under the slow-moving mass of ice, but between the glacial periods there were warm interglacial times when forests grew and both man and beast roamed abroad. After the ice ages, periods of cold and warmth, dryness and humidity succeeded one another. And at each alternation, the appearance of the countryside was changed, both as regards vegetation and animal life. Examples of these different kinds of prehistoric landscape will be mentioned and particular localities pointed out.

All over Denmark these prehistoric monuments lie as powerful testimonies to the prowess of the ancient peoples. Let us go and look at them and listen to their silent speech.

6 The land lies new-born when the tide is out, as here at Kaløl Creek

II The First Traces

Hunters, Trappers and Fishers

It is a consequence of the special climatic conditions in northern Europe that Denmark has only been inhabited without interruption for a small space of time in comparison with the long period—half a million years or more—that man has existed in other parts of the earth. About twelve thousand years ago the first small hunting tribes from the south reached the land mass by which modern Denmark lay surrounded: vast tracts covering most of the Baltic, the Kattegat and the North Sea, the three seas which in the course of succeeding millennia gradually threw up the Jutland peninsula and the numerous islands in the patterns we can now see from the air. Even Bornholm, which today lies far out in the Baltic, and from which the white chalk cliffs of Høje Møn can only be seen on particularly clear days, once formed part of the connected land mass that also included Britain, Germany and South Sweden.

From the glaciers, the inland ice that covered the Scandinavian plateau with an ice-cap two to three thousand metres thick, crawling sheets of ice repeatedly spread southwards, rendering the land uninhabitable. In the course of six hundred thousand years we have had four glacial periods, three of them affecting Denmark, and each lasting from fifty to a hundred thousand years. They were separated by interglacial periods equally long—and one still longer when the Scandinavian countries were habitable and at times warmer than at present.

7   Tundra landscape on Knudshoved Point, west of Vordingborg

When the ice-cap was at its greatest extent, the steep edge of the glacier formed a continuous wall from southern Britain through Holland into Germany, just south of Dresden, then east through Poland and into southern Russia, where from Kiev it turned northwards in a great arc following the line of the river Volga. In the lee of the cliff of ice, in France and Spain, man made his stand against the cold and the wild animals.

It was, however, the glaciers that created the fertile soil of Denmark with the material they brought down from the Scandinavian plateau and then deposited, as they thawed and melted away in the warmer periods. These glacial deposits rest on layers of chalk and limestone millions of years old, originally formed on the sea bed, but thrown up to the surface by upheavals, so that they lay there ready to receive what the ice brought down. The white chalk can be seen beneath the mantle of soil on Møns Klint, after which it runs in under the southernmost tip of Zealand and Lolland-Falster; while the later, greyish Danish sandstone is the material forming Stevns Klint in East Zealand and Sangstrup Klint in North Djursland. From there the Danish sandstone, often covered only by a thin layer of earth, runs through North Jutland to Thy. Between the chalk and sandstone and the Iron Age deposits there are layers left from the period when the ancestors of man appeared in the animal world. On Bornholm, the foundation is the old bedrock whose northern limit is the rounded granite promontory of Hammerknuden, still bearing the furrows of the glacial period on its back and covered with an open and treeless vegetation, a reminder of the way things looked before the emergence of forests in Denmark.

It has for some time been considered probable that man lived in these parts during the long interglacial periods. Finds dating from these times have been made in countries to the south and in Britain, so that hunting tribes, following the paths of the game animals to north and east, must necessarily have reached these latitudes on hunting expeditions of a few years' duration. It is only recently that decisive proof has come to hand. This is hardly surprising when one considers that, except for one area in South-West Jutland that remained free of ice during the last glacial period, the giant plough of the glaciers pushed the surface of the land into fresh shapes during each succeeding glacial period, wiping out the flimsy traces of the hunting people's settlements.

Two of the finds that have been made may date from the last or the penultimate interglacial period. They consist, first, of bones from some hunters' meal, and, second, of worked flints. The strata at Esbjerg and the bogs between Herning and Varde date back to the last interglacial period but one, an enormously long period of time—almost two hundred thousand years—which began and ended with a cold period but in between reached temperatures similar to those of today. What was land and what was sea at the time is not yet fully established. We know that the land that now lies between the west coast of South Jutland and North-West Funen was covered by sea. During the last interglacial period, which lasted at least twenty-five thousand years, the sea was as warm as the Mediterranean, as is shown by snails and mussels in the strata. There are peat bogs from this period in various parts of Jutland. The find of bones, actually two finds, comes from the peat layer from one of the two last interglacial periods. The finds were made at Hollerup near Langå in East Jutland and consist in the main of two deer skeletons, discovered in 1897 and 1912. What makes these bones so valuable is that one can see they have been split by hunters' hands—so that they could extract the tasty marrow. The way the bones had been gathered together, each animal separately, also reveals the hand of the hunter because they must have been collected together after the meal was finished. The hunters would have done this to ensure a plentiful supply of game.

The flint implements, some of which were found among mussel shells in the gravel layer of a cliff ten metres high facing Isefjord at Ejby Bro, and some on the beach at the foot of the cliff, seem to belong to the beginning of the last interglacial period but one. They are very primitive in workmanship and recall British finds of four hundred thousand years

8   Hverrestrup Hills in Himmerland, overgrown
with aspen and juniper

ago. Flint flakes and chippings, probably from the last interglacial period, have been found in the sand layer of a gravel pit at Seest near Kolding in which bones of the large mammals of the same period have from time to time been found.

There is always the possibility of discovering further traces of our earliest forefathers wherever the layers under the earth have been exposed in gravel pits and similar places. The same is true where the sea has eaten its way in and left exposed cliffs, or watercourses have cut their way down through the earth's strata. But luck comes into it, too. Only in West Jutland are the formations of the penultimate glacial period and the last interglacial period to be seen, because the glaciers of the last glacial period, which first came from the north—from the borderland between Norway and Sweden—did not move further south than the line from Viborg to Holstebro and to the north of Nissum Fjord. A later ice-stream from the east became stationary and formed the Jutland ridge which now marks the westerly limit of the ice, the land further west not being covered. The hunters may have had their summer settlements on the hill-islands and in the river valleys between them during the last glacial period. Finding traces of them on the surface would be difficult because the layer of frost in the ground in winter-time has levelled it, while the gravel and sand in the rivers of melted ice have left substantial deposits wherever they swept by. There were also habitable areas during the last glacial period in the extreme north and north-west of Norway, as is shown from various plant communities. But that primitive stone implements found in these same areas belonged to Ice Age hunters is only put forward as a possibility; as yet there is no positive proof for it.

During the hunting period, which lasted upwards of ten thousand years and ended with the coming of the farmers in *c.* 3000 B.C., the rolling surface of the land was as the ice had left it. Gradually it became covered with vegetation that followed the changing climatic periods. Only its extent changed with the rising and sinking of both sea and subsoil.

9 Park tundra with juniper and pine in the
Åsted valley, Vendsyssel

The material the ice had dragged with it was stone and
gravel, sand and clay, which deposited itself in various ways.
As the water from the melted glaciers carried it along, it sank
to the bottom in thicker or thinner layers, one on top of
another according to its weight and the speed of the current.
Where the layers are not always level but tilted or folded, it is
due to the pressure of later glaciers. In Central and West
Jutland there are wide, heath-covered plains formed by water

from the glaciers of the last glacial period, and surrounding hill-islands, which were deposited during the last glacial period but one, nearly two hundred thousand years ago, and since then have been continuously worn and levelled out by wind and weather.

A hilly, rounded landscape is a moraine formation where the material of which it is formed has not been stratified and sorted. Steep, hilly ground with flat land beyond it is terminal moraine. It marks the line along which the ice stood stationary for a long period while melting. The bottom of the moraine is slightly rolling and sometimes flat, like the heath land between Roskilde and Køge. Where the ground is full of holes, it is where lumps of ice were buried deep in the moraine and later melted. Special formations are created by rivers flowing under the mass of ice, causing long excavations and tunnel valleys (e.g. the fjords of East Jutland, which continue up through the land as valleys), or long high hills or ridges, where the rivers have gradually raised the level of the ice-masses by depositing material on the river bed. Characteristic formations are Mogenstrup Ås in South Zealand, and Strø Ås in North Zealand.

The hunting peoples did not leave monuments behind them that are visible on the landscape, as did later populations. They were at the mercy of violently changing natural conditions over which they had no control. The only traces they left are stone implements and fragments from worked flints on the surface of the ground. Where the worked flint is covered with layers of earth, it may lie in a cultural deposit in which there are remains of fires and dwellings, as well as vestiges of more perishable materials such as bone and wood.

The unbroken habitation of Denmark began when the land ice melted away leaving behind it an open, naked land without vegetation, covered by great drifts of larger or smaller blocks of stone such as may still be seen here and there in old wooded areas or in shallow water in fjords and inlets. At low tide at such places, one may still get an impression of the way the land must have looked in the distant past.

When it became habitable in the first tundra period, there was still ice in South Sweden, but bands of hunters soon made their way as far as Denmark tracking down game. Reindeer hunters were already living on the threshold of present-day Denmark, around Hamburg and in Holstein, where their settlements have been found at Meiendorf. The land was covered with tundra vegetation, including arctic willow, dwarf birch and juniper, a knee-high growth such as we meet in North Greenland. Thrift and heather were the commonest flowers, while grass and sedge provided food for the reindeer. Following a period named after finds at Bølling in Central Jutland, when the temperature rose in the hottest summer months to 5° Centigrade, and when groves of large-leaved birch and mountain ash shot up and transformed the landscape into a glorious park tundra full of herds of reindeer and wild horses, of small rodents, the pyrenean desman and the lemming, and of a number of birds such as geese, ducks and swans, a colder period then came again with tundra proper.

A warmer climate in the Allerød period, named after finds in a layer at Allerød in North Zealand, brought forests back for a time—light, open forests of birch, mountain ash and aspen, with a sprinkling of pine on Bornholm and in Holstein —and plains made bright by sun-loving plants like yellow crowfoot and cornflower, an El Dorado for reindeer, wolverine, elk, beavers and brown bear. There was plenty of game for the hunter, and one of his settlements, the oldest so far known in Denmark, has been found at Bromme, northwest of Sorø in Zealand.

For a brief period, the hunting people put up their skin tents on a sandy promontory that ran out from the east towards a little stream, the Ålerenden, and into a lake that is now a level green fen. That they were armed with bows and arrows is clear from the large number of arrowheads made from flint flakes that were found in a thin cultural layer, covered today with a layer of sand more than a metre thick. After the sunny period, with average summer temperatures of 13-14° Centigrade, the temperature fell to about 10° and transformed the landscape into park tundra again, as in the Bølling period. Only after that did the forests return and remain permanently.

During the next two thousand years the landscape changed character completely. The park tundra, with its spacious groves and clusters of trees, was replaced under constantly rising temperatures by forests in which the slender white birch predominated but where pines were also to be found. The old trees, aspen, mountain ash and willow, still persisted in the low-lying ground around large freshwater lakes and along the courses of rivers and streams. The arctic animal world disappeared northwards, while large game animals such as elk, aurochs, roe deer, brown bear and wild boar, and many smaller animals such as hares, hedgehogs, beavers and badgers, took over the forests. They were eagerly pursued by the hunters, whose settlements have been found under layers of peat at Klosterlund in Central Jutland, among other places. Denmark was at the time still joined to Britain, where a corresponding mesolithic settlement has been excavated at Star Carr, not far from the Yorkshire coast.

Rising temperatures provided living conditions for new types of trees like oak and hazel. The hazel came first, because it bears fruit that is mature for propagation within ten years, whereas with the oak this takes about half a century, and it is therefore the hazel that dominated the forest for a time, with a sprinkling of pine and birch. These flourish particularly in lighter soils. The great game animals made their paths through the wooded land to water-holes on streams and lakes encircled by great forests of reeds, the haunt of cranes, heron and bittern. In summer-time the surface of the lakes was covered over with yellow and white waterlilies. The July temperature was then 18–20° Centigrade, so that the turtle was able to live and breed in the fresh Scandinavian waters. All this is reflected in the finds at hunters' settlements on two small islands in Magle Fen at Mullerup in West Zealand, the first such finds to have been made from this period: they have given the name of Mullerup to the whole cultural group. The

10   Shore with pine trees on the south side of Asnæs

dog now followed the hunter on his expeditions, and from here on meat was supplemented by fish like pike and perch. Fishing opportunities were increased by the great rivers that forced their way up from the Baltic through the land mass where the Great and Little Belts and Øresund now lie. The beginning of the division of the country confined the population to definite areas: on Zealand and Funen to the lakes; in Jutland to the river courses. Local characteristics began to develop.

All along the river-like Gudenå (which has given its name to a hunting culture, the Gudenå culture) and other watercourses in Jutland, there are numerous dwelling sites, the characteristic tools of which are small worked pieces of flint, microliths, that may have been used both as barbs for spears and arrows, and as fish-hooks. The geometric shape of these miniature flints, triangles, half-moons and trapezia, are found all the way from Britain to the most easterly coastal areas of the Baltic in what was originally one connected cultural area, and further east to India. Similar miniature flints are known from Africa and Australia, but they are not based everywhere on a common tradition. In distant parts of the world they have been preserved through three hundred generations, and for eight thousand years.

After a time, while hazel, oak and pine formed a mixed forest with a sprinkling of elm, lime and ash, the oak gradually predominated in a Nordic primeval forest, green and sodden, and so dark and hostile that the better game animals, the elk and auroch, moved out. The hazel closed into an undergrowth of tall thin, barren stalks from lack of light. Ivy and mistletoe infested the great trees, and only in very early spring was the floor of the forest coloured with flowers like white anemone and dog's mercury. The hunters now made their way to the coasts where the broad rivers from the Baltic had grown into Belts and Sounds. The west coast of Jutland emerged, and there the marine mammals, the seals and porpoises, to some extent replaced the game animals that the primeval forest had driven away.

11   Mixed oak forest in Busene Have on Høje Møn

As we have said, the many different types of landscape that existed in the period of the hunters are still preserved here and there in remote spots where time has somehow stood still, or where nature has re-created similar conditions. The bare Ice Age landscape may, for instance, be seen at low water in fjords and inlets where the original disposition of the stones remains untouched. In winter time the picture is complete when close-packed ice forms a glacial front at the edge of the shore.

Where the ground has lain untilled for centuries one is carried back to the tundra period, as in Rejnstrup Overdrev, south of lake Tystrup, provided one can close one's eyes to the woods of Gunderslevholm and the vegetation along the lakes. Here, large and small stones lie on top of one another, as when the inland ice melted; now they are overgrown with yellow and grey lichen. Grasses and a little heather cover the whole area in the low-lying parts of which numerous small lakes reflect the blue of the sky. In the early spring, legions of small white anemones peep out everywhere, creating much the same effect as the low heathers did in the tundra period. There is similar common land in various parts of the country, but only here at Rejnstrup is it secured for posterity by protection.

Park tundra, too, is preserved here and there throughout the country. There is a reed-encircled lake in a stretch of valley among the hills of Hverrestrup, close to the main road between Ålborg and Viborg, from whose shores groves of aspen, birch, mountain ash and juniper stretch up to the grass- and heather-covered slopes that completely shut out the horizon in three directions and form a closed framework round the park tundra. The same ancient, open landscape with small lakes and dams, and scattered clumps and groves of old types of trees, is particularly to be seen on headlands and points which have lain undisturbed as grazing-ground like, for example, Knudshoved, west of Vordingborg, and the long Asnæs peninsula which bounds Kalundborg Fjord to the south. On Bornholm, a remnant of the old Almindingen common land is preserved at Ibsker Højlyng, which still lies open with its juniper, birch and pine.

46

The first real forest period of *c.* 8000 B.C. with birch and pine, has been re-created by nature in the course of the past few centuries on Lyngby Åmose near Copenhagen. The northern end of Lyngby lake has gradually turned to bog, and here, on low islands and half-submerged banks, the old forest landscape has reappeared by self-sowing: in some places with birch as the predominant tree, in others with pine. At the edges, hazel and mountain ash blend in, and at the lakeside lies the forest of reeds with its inlets that in summer time are covered with the round leaves of yellow and white waterlilies. The hunting people of the Mullerup period would feel at home here today. So would their contemporary Jutlanders at various places along river courses on the mainland. Their old fishing places on the grass-covered slopes that go down to the running water lie untouched by time. The scrub-covered slopes still rise up on either side of the valley and drifting clouds are reflected in the river water, where fish leap after spring flies.

In Jutland many of the old types of forest can be found. Oak forest with mixed vegetation is to be seen in small patches along river valleys and on low-lying ground; but mostly only low trees that have been left because there was not much timber in them, crippled as they were by the lack of nourishment in the sandy soil since it was washed out in the last glacial period. Such are the areas of Gindeskov Krat at Neder Felding and of Hørby Lunde, in Central Jutland, and of Skivum Nørrekrat in Himmerland. There is a more vigorous oak forest still covering a larger area at Hald, south of Viborg, but the best of all is Dravcd Skov just south-west of the monastery of Løgum. This retains something of the Nordic primeval forest, the humid forest that, as I have said, drove the great game animals away and forced the hunters to the coast, where they learned to make use of the salt water. Draved is still a great forest of aspen, birch and oak. To the east and west, it is bounded by bogs in which aboriginal birds and plovers abound.

Down to the end of the hunting period the shape of

12   Section through metres-thick layer of oyster shells, with stone-built fireplace, in the kitchen midden on Ertebølle Head

Denmark was constantly changing. Only then did it attain a form that is recognizable in our maps, with fjords and inlets, Belts and Sounds, and the thousand islands.

These continual changes in the relationship between land and water are a legacy from the Ice Age. The tremendous pressure exerted on the land masses by a layer of ice two or three kilometres thick was gradually released as the ice melted and evaporated in the milder climate. As a result, the land rose, but so at the same time did the sea. The rising of the land masses was long and slow in relation to the melting of the ice, and is not yet complete, but the addition of water to the world's oceans took place much more quickly. At times, certain areas of land lay deeper than they do now, and at times they lay higher.

The last hunting period falls at the end of the fourth millennium in the Atlantic period, which had a milder and moister climate than now. The average temperature in July was somewhere around 20° Centigrade. The land north-east of a line drawn between Nissum Fjord on the west coast of Jutland and the north coast of Falster lay lower. Thy and Vendsyssel were broken up into islands, while the land south-west of the line lay higher. Consequently, the coastal settlements of this period in the north-easterly parts of Denmark are now to be found a little inland and several metres above the present foreshore, and settlements in the south-western part of the country lie submerged beneath the sea at the bottom of fjords and inlets, as is the case, for example, with the great find at Kolding Fjord.

The land was covered with dense primeval forest in which lime and elm were common. Game was less plentiful. Red deer and roe deer were to be seen in small herds. Only wild pigs really flourished—on the acorns. The hunting tribes were therefore relegated to the coastline which was much more extensive than it is now. From here they could hunt marine mammals such as the grey, ringed and Greenland seals, porpoises, grampuses and dolphins. Also sought-after were the many birds, among them the extinct great auk, a diver with flipper-like wings, and the white pelican, which does not now live further north than the coast of the Black Sea.

If one follows the old line of cliffs along the shores of Roskilde fjord or Arresø, and along Mariager Fjord or Limfjord, where they rise up steeply from a flat and often very broad grass-grown or wooded foreshore, that was once the bottom of the sea, shining white oyster shells and mussel shells mark the spots where the old fishing-stations were about 3000 B.C. Kitchen middens, we call them, a name that dates from the early days of archaeology in the middle of the last century, and was for many years used internationally for similar finds in many countries. The period is now known as the Ertebølle period from the great kitchen midden finds south of Ertebølle Head on Limfjord, on the western side of Himmerland.

The site for this settlement was carefully chosen, as always happened with the fishing people. To the north, Ertebølle Head warded off the cold winds and provided shelter for the dug-out canoes that were drawn up on the foreshore. The water off the settlement was shallow so that shellfish could easily be collected on the sandbanks at low tide. That good use was made of the sea can be seen from the extremely deep layers of shells—here, as in most of the kitchen middens, consisting mostly of fine large oyster shells mixed with blue mussels, winkles and cockles. The millions of shells were left during repeated stays in the summer months. One has, however, to remember that an adult would need more than five hundred good large oysters a day to provide all his calorie requirements from this diet alone. Fortunately for both men and women, the forest animals, the fish in the fjord and the sea mammals were also within range, and they no doubt provided the bulk of the food required.

Only a few of the kitchen middens that are known mark settlements of people who were fishers pure and simple. The influence of agricultural and stock-rearing peoples is everywhere to be seen in the cultural layers in the form both of finds of the bones of sheep and domesticated cows, and of imprints of barley and wheat in clay vessels, which now began to appear as part of the ordinary domestic equipment. This development heralds a fresh period in Danish culture.

Stretches of coast as it appeared during the Ertebølle period can be seen along our shores. On the northern side of Asnæs, facing Kalundborg Fjord, rugged oaks with dense undergrowth still hold their ground. A similar glimpse of the Denmark of the kitchen-midden time can be had on the farthest point of Gylling Næs, on the north side of the inlet to Horsens Fjord. Other spots could be mentioned that reflect even older prehistoric landscapes, but everyone will be able to make rewarding discoveries in his own locality.

13   Porskjærs Stenhus, round dolmen (*runddysse*) at Knebel on Mols

III Dolmens

The Earliest Peasant Culture

The dolmen* is the most universally known of all prehistoric monuments and is constantly used as a device on public memorials and gravestones. But it is almost always reproduced in the same incorrect form—as three pointed, upright stones on which a fourth rests horizontally. Few people realize that it is in fact a magnificent monument to one of the greatest events in our history, the introduction about five thousand years ago of agriculture and stock-rearing, and was erected by the first Danish peasants as a burial chamber. Dolmens are also our earliest surviving form of monumental architecture, being built of huge boulders brought down by the glacial ice.

Through the centuries they have called attention to themselves by reason of the size of their blocks of stone, and have thus been preserved nearly down to the present day. It was not until the middle of the last century that people seriously began to demolish and destroy them, using their stones for the building of roads and railways. The superstition that had previously saved them from destruction was beginning to lose its hold.

The historian, Saxo Grammaticus, saw in the enormous

---

* The word 'dolmen' has been used in this book to translate two Danish words, *dysse* and *stendysse* (literally 'stone dolmens'), and it has a rather wider range of meaning than it usually does in English, where it generally refers to the visible stone vestiges of burial mounds. *Dysse* can mean the complete burial mound or act as an abbreviation for *stendysse*, which is close to the usual English 'dolmen'. The sense intended will be clear in context.

size of the blocks of stone forming them evidence that a race of giants had once inhabited Denmark. They were, moreover, erected on mounds, while it would have been difficult or impossible for ordinary people to move them even on level ground. This idea found expression in such names as Giants' Ovens and Giants' Tombs (passage graves), while the term Trolls' Chambers links them with the supernatural, with trolls and dwarfs, who held nature in their sway.

The megalithic tombs were thoroughly discussed by the archaeologist, Ole Worm, in his *Monumenta Danica* of 1643, which gave a comprehensive account of our prehistoric monuments for the first time. He had himself visited a number of stone graves, but his interpretations were largely based on literary sources. Thus he speaks of the dolmens as prehistoric meeting-places for the Thing where law and justice were administered, as enclosed areas for single combat, as places where the kings of old were elected, and as sacred altars where sacrifices were made to the gods. He says of the structure of these altars, i.e. the dolmens, that 'the altar is usually a mound of earth on top of which stand three enormous stones with a fourth that is both heavier and broader resting on them so as to form a sort of table. Underneath is a hollow space, sometimes empty but often filled with earth and stones, which was designed to receive the sacrificial blood. It is seldom that this does not contain flints to strike fire from; for only thus could the fire be kindled with which the sacrifice was to be burnt.' He also says that altars where there was only one circle of stones to be seen were generally built above a grave so that due sacrifice could be made once a year for the dead person. Similar ideas about stone graves were current among both scholars and laymen for another couple of hundred years until the archaeologist J. J. A. Worsaae declared in his first book, *Danmarks Oldtid* (Danish prehistory), in 1843 that dolmens and passage graves were special types of Stone Age grave. This interpretation was put forward so forcefully that it held undisputed sway for the next hundred years. It has now been established that dolmens were also sacred places in antiquity, the habitations of the dead and of their souls to which sacrifices were brought to ensure that the power of the dead was used for the good of the tribe. The dolmen and the passage grave (the stone grave of the succeeding period) are thus visible testimonies to the worship of the dead by our Stone Age ancestors. Behind them lie new religious conceptions, brought into Denmark from outside. They spread like wildfire over almost the whole country. One can trace a parallel to this movement in the Romanesque churches erected four thousand years later, for which the boulders left behind by the glaciers also provided most of the building material. The prehistoric dolmens might be said to have paid tithes to these Christian buildings in the form of their heavy stones.

All the new developments in Denmark around 3000 B.C. had begun to take place in the Middle East and Central Asia five thousand years before that. It was then that the dividing line had been set between natural conditions under which man had to maintain himself on the resources offered by nature, and man's co-operation with nature for the improvement of plant growth by the cultivation of corn and for the propagation of domestic animals. This Stone Age revolution created the conditions for larger communities than the small groups of the hunting period, for villages and towns. The day of the hunter was past when man was restricted to making do with what he could get by hunting and gathering berries in the woods, by fishing and collecting shellfish in fjords and lakes. The peasant people were now able to store the corn they harvested. Domestic animals were always available for slaughter. It was possible to forestall the constantly returning periods of hunger that winter had undoubtedly brought with it during the period of the hunters. Conditions were established for larger settlements, and indeed villages sprang up all over the country. The foundation was laid for an ordered society that could plan the tasks confronting it: building large stone graves, clearing the forests, cultivating the soil, tending domestic animals and trading in amber and flint.

14 *and* 15   Troldkirken (the Troll's Church), long dolmen
(*langdysse*) at Sønderholm, in North-West Himmerland

The foundations of the first peasant culture were sound, but they were not laid all at once. People cultivated wheat and barley, kept cows and sheep, and possibly goats and domestic pigs also. The climate was the warmest and mildest since the Ice Age, so warm that vines were able to grow right up in the Mälar region of central Sweden. The primeval forest was gradually cleared. With sharply polished, well-hafted flint axes and fire the new immigrants cut their way through the forests. The heavy timber was used for building the village houses, and branches and twigs were burnt and corn sown in the clearings, which grew more and more numerous. The forests were only opened up in earnest when pastoral peoples from Eastern Europe and Asia reached our latitudes. They had to create wide grazing areas for their cattle. The forests were therefore burnt down far and wide so that the land was opened up again—in time almost as much as it had been in the park tundra times.

But there was still sufficient game in the forests to supplement their diet: red deer, roe deer, bears and wild pigs. There was also the harvest of the sea: fish and seals, and abundant and tasty shellfish. On the coasts the old fishing peoples still survived, and they had their share of the improved standard of living, kept a few domestic animals and cultivated a little corn, as we know from the kitchen middens of the Ertebølle culture—a society of fishers, hunters and farmers, as it has remained along the west coast of Jutland down to the present day.

The new age was also apparent in the Danish landscape. The primeval forests of oak were gradually broken up into numerous smaller forests with many different kinds of trees, among them the beech, which now appeared for the first time in Denmark. Where the peasants had their villages there were extensive groves of elms, standing like bare bundles of faggots because the leaves were harvested as winter fodder for cattle. In fields that had been gradually exhausted by repeated crops of corn and then abandoned, hazel and birch were the first trees to take over since they yielded productive seed within ten years.

16   Ground plan of Porskjærs Stenhus (round dolmen) on Mols

The oldest dolmens date from the beginning of the third millennium. Before that, only very few graves are known from the end of the hunting period—one of them being found under a settlement layer at Vedbæk, where the body lay outstretched in a long pit; another under water in Korsør with a male skeleton resting on a layer of bark and a similar layer on top of him. Only the second one contained a grave gift: a knife-shaped flint flake.

Burials have been found in the large kitchen middens without a trace of coffin or grave goods, and surrounded only by thick layers of shells. That these were indeed burials is shown by the care with which the body has been placed in an outstretched position with its arms at its sides, occasionally packed round with a few stones. This was not, however, a general burial custom, otherwise a far greater number would have been found. As all these graves belong to the last part of the hunting period, and as several of the settlements show foreign influences, it may be that the burial customs of the immigrant peasant peoples have influenced the old native hunting peoples, even though burial on the actual dwelling site is known right back to the hunting cultures of the Early Stone Age. In a number of cases, human bones have been found on the hunting people's dwelling sites, among flint refuse from the manufacture of tools and the bones of wild animals; and some of the human bones have cut-marks, and others have been split open so that the marrow could be extracted—which seems to show that cannibalism took place. There are also human bones split open for the marrow in much later Stone Age finds. This shows that the beliefs giving rise to cannibalism were common in the earliest days where peasant culture prevailed, and it was probably under such an influence that cannibalism appeared in the hunting people's settlements. The idea of giving the dead man new life in future generations by cannibalism is in fact associated with the earliest agriculture, when people saw the corn buried in the earth in the spring—where it lived on until it germinated to new life and gave a fresh harvest.

Dolmens are divided into various types according to the shape of the burial chamber and the surrounding rows of stones. The oldest dolmens are small rectangular stone chambers with four side stones of equal height, completely covered by an enormous cover-stone, or cap-stone. The actual burial chamber is often no larger than would accommodate a single person lying in a crouched position and may measure 0.5×1.25 metres in ground area. The larger chambers may

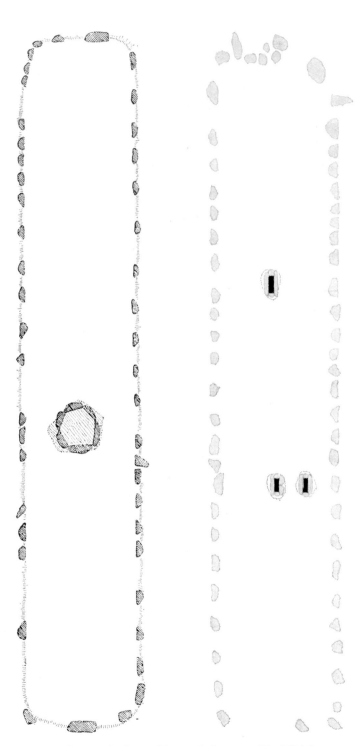

17   Ground plan of long dolmens: Troldkirken
at Sønderholm, and Ulstrup at Gunderslevholm,
Zealand

be up to 1.25 × 3.75 metres and contain several graves. A dead man will have his flint axe or stone battle-axe with him as grave goods, while the women will have their amber ornaments. Sometimes clay vessels are also found that contained food and drink for the dead, but as these are not always present the explanation may be that the vessels were sometimes made of wood (we know such vessels from contemporary bog finds), and so have not left visible traces.

Contemporary with the dolmens built of heavy blocks of stone are the graves in low mounds of earth surrounded only by smallish stones forming a support for a plank surround to the graves; but the grave goods in both are the same. There were thus two quite different burial customs in the first peasant period.

The dolmen chambers are in most cases surrounded by a mound of earth, with large blocks of stone set upright in a row round the foot. The flatter side is turned outwards, and at times they are so close together that they form a wall, the spaces between the individual blocks being filled with flat pieces of stone laid horizontally. If the surrounding mound of earth and the row of stones are circular in shape, the monument is called a round dolmen (*runddysse*). If they are rectangular, a long dolmen (*langdysse*). The round dolmen has practically always only one stone chamber placed in the middle of the stone circle. In one of Denmark's largest round dolmens, Porskjærs Stenhus on Knebel Mark on the island of Mols, there is a very fine burial chamber in the northern half of the circle. There was originally another chamber the remains of whose stones can still be seen in the southern half. The long dolmen, on the other hand, usually has a number of stone chambers, which may lie lengthwise or crosswise in relation to the kerb stones; or sometimes there are two lying lengthwise, parallel to one another. Long dolmens with three, four and five chambers are known in many parts of the country. But the stone chambers are not invariably covered with an earth mound. In many cases the space inside the kerb stones is merely covered with heavy boulders so that the burial chambers stand free. Many dolmen chambers are completely free-standing without either earth mound or kerb stones. However, in the majority of cases these chambers were originally enclosed in a long or round dolmen whose kerb stones and mound have now been completely removed.

When the chamber was large and a number of burials took place in succession, the enormously heavy cover-stone might have to be heaved aside each time before the dead could be placed inside. This difficult operation was avoided by making one of the side stones lower at the end of the chamber that faced south or east, thus giving access to the chamber as over a threshold with a door opening that could easily be closed with a smaller block of stone, or a piece of wood. The chamber itself was gradually made more spacious by the use of more side stones so that the ground area became five- or six-sided. The threshold stone then often became no more than a low doorstep beyond which a short passage was built with one or more pairs of side stones—sometimes also with cover-stones. These later and more complicated burial buildings are often free-standing with only the base being covered by a mound of earth or stones. Seen with the surrounding kerb stones, which are sometimes as high as a man, the chamber presents an architectural unit of great beauty, undisturbed since the Stone Age. The monumental effect is deliberate. The cover-stone, many thousands of pounds in weight, is placed in position with an eye to the effect of its massive weight at rest, and in such a way that it has not moved an inch. This is due not only to the colossal weight of the stones. Once the stones were brought into balance, they were fixed immovably by laying a thick layer of broken flints round the side stones and on the floor of the burial chamber. These both provided drainage and gave a firm foundation. In the long dolmens, the largest kerb stones are frequently placed at the narrow ends, and this produces an extremely impressive effect. Contemporary pottery work and finely-shaped axes and clubs made of hard types of stone show what a sure sense of form these early peasants had. It is the same practised eye as

18   Excavated dolmen chamber at Vig in Ods Hundred

19   Free-standing dolmen chamber at Herslev on Langeland

created the primitive but perfect Stone Age architecture of our round and long dolmens, which in most cases surpasses anything else of the kind known in Western Europe. It must in fairness be added that nature came to the aid of these Stone Age architects, for the boulders they had available had already been worn by glaciers into such lovely shapes that in many cases they only needed to be set upright to look as though they had been sculpted.

Good, typical examples of the different kinds of dolmen are to be found in practically all parts of the country, with the exception of Bornholm and the golden, heather-covered plains of Central Jutland. Two of the finest and largest round dolmens are at Vilsted, between Sorø and Holbæk, and at Knebel on Mols in East Jutland. Outstanding features of these two are the large, monumental burial chambers and the tall kerb stones placed very close together. Both of them measure about twenty metres across. Usually this type is only half the size, sometimes even less. There is a fine dolmen chamber with a passage and low door stone at Herrestrup in Ods Hundred, North-West Zealand, and a round dolmen of a corresponding type at Tåstrup on Djursland.

The long dolmens are generally considerably larger than the round ones, even though the latter usually have far larger burial chambers. A length of about a hundred metres is not unusual. Most are a good twenty metres long by six to eight wide. The longest example known is at Lindeskov, south-west of Nyborg. It measures 168 metres and is surrounded by 126 large kerb stones. At the northern end is a small burial chamber, now without a cover-stone; and there may be many others concealed in its long ridge. An unusual long dolmen at Ellested, not far away, has five stone chambers and is one of the finest monuments on Funen. There is also a very fine long dolmen in Gunderslevholm Forest. It has exposed stone packing between the kerb stones and a large, altar-like cover-stone over the unmounded burial chamber, which both Molbech and Grundtvig have described as an altar to the gods of Norse mythology. In Valby Hegn at Helsinge in North

Zealand there are no less than five long dolmens side by side. The long dolmen Grøn Jægers Høj on Fanefjord, West Møn, has 134 kerb stones standing close together round the mound, which is ten metres wide and 102 metres long, with three burial chambers. Two parallel long dolmens in Blommeskobbel on Als are distinctive, and the two connected long dolmens in Oleskoppel near by are unique. These two, which measure fourteen by thirty metres in area, are joined together along their sides like Siamese twins. Two other parallel long dolmens have been excavated in Steneng at Bredebro, north of Tønder, where the land has sunk since they were built, so that before excavation they were covered with peat and deposits from the river. Originally these two long dolmens were of more or less equal size, and had one burial chamber each, but later the more northerly one was doubled in length by additional building at either end and now has three burial chambers. Elsewhere in southern Denmark there are stone burial monuments where it can be seen that the land has sunk since they were built. There is, for example, one stone grave under water at Siø between Langeland and Tåsinge. The long dolmen Kongehøjen, at Voldstedlund, close to the Hobro-Mariager road is unusual and finely built with tall kerb stones at either end. It has two eight-sided chambers completely covered with an earth mound, to which a long covered passage from the south side gives access. This confirms that the passage grave, the type of stone burial chamber that became common in the succeeding period of the Stone Age, was already being built and exercising influence at the time.

Kongehøjen stands on high ground with views over lake and sea, but mostly the long dolmens are on low-lying ground beside lakes and watercourses. It may be due to the fact that it was considerably easier to drag the many heavy stones downhill than up. Another exception to this rule is the magnificent long dolmen called Troldkirken, which can be seen high up on a range of hills at Sønderholm in North-West Himmerland, with wide views over the inland waters of Limfjord. Rampen, a long dolmen 125 metres in length, stands on the other hand in a characteristic position at Hejselst down by the river Voers, in eastern Vendsyssel, where, like many other stone burial chambers all over the country, it marks a Stone Age crossing-place over a water-course. Round and long dolmens on the Røsnæs peninsula at Kalundborg mark the line of a road for a longish distance. In the middle of the last century there were some thirty stone burial chambers from Raklev out to Kongstrup, but only a third of them now survive, many merely as free-standing chambers.

Altogether nearly five thousand dolmens have been mapped and described in Denmark. Barely eighteen hundred still stand. Many can be detected in newly ploughed land by a patch of particularly sharp flint fragments, crushed after being made brittle by fire, that were originally used for packing the chambers and still remain on the surface. The long dolmens were by far the most numerous. A couple of thousand have been mapped, though of these only about twelve hundred remain. Of round dolmens there were barely half as many and of these three hundred or so have survived. The rest of the stone graves are either exposed stone chambers whose kerb stones have long ago been removed, or stone graves of an indeterminate type.

There are dolmens all over the country except on Bornholm, as we have seen. However, they are not equally numerous everywhere. There are fewest of them in Central and West Jutland where the sandy heath was not fertile enough for agricultural peoples. Here they are rare and are only to be found in districts where the rather more fertile moraine sand offered better prospects for cultivation. In Vendsyssel, between Frederikshavn and Hirtshals, and in northern Himmerland, the dolmens stand by themselves or in small groups, indicating an even habitation over large areas. Djursland was one of the most densely populated parts of the country at the beginning of the peasant period, and here stone graves are to be particularly found in the stretch along both sides of the now dried-out Kolindsund, in the areas around

Rønde and on the western side of Mols. Among them special mention must be made of Porskjærs Stenhus, already referred to above, and of one long dolmen of the many around Stenvad, because this is known to every Dane as the picture on the fifty-kroner note, whose purchasing power today is not much greater than that of the little blue five-kroner note of some twenty years ago on which the dolmen at Grønnesøgård in North Zealand appeared.

Along the southern parts of the east coast of Jutland the dolmens are evenly distributed beside, or on, the good soil with its moraine clay; but especially along the coasts of Bjerge Hundred, the wide peninsula between Horsens and Vejle fjords. The eastern coastal areas of the whole of South Jutland, too, are extremely rich in dolmens, in particular Als. On Funen there are dolmens all round the coast while the interior of the island is remarkably bare of monuments. The situation is different on Langeland and Aerø, and practically all the small islands of the Funen archipelago, where dolmens are plentiful.

It is Zealand, however, that is by far the richest part of the country. Large dolmens stand in great clusters one after another, not only along the coasts but inland too, particularly near lakes and watercourses. The Røsnæs peninsula, whose dolmens have much in common with those on Djursland, has already been mentioned. Also worthy of mention are the Sorø district and, in Horns Hundred, the stretch between Frederikssund and Roskilde; in addition, the area between Præstø and Vordingborg. Møn and Bogø have many dolmens as well. On Falster they are evenly distributed along the coasts, and on Lolland along the north coast and in the eastern part of the island. That they are almost entirely absent on Bornholm does not, however, indicate that the first settlers on the mainland were not interested in this island. There are traces there of many settlements, while their characteristic clay pots are known from the bogs.

It is a common feature of the whole of Denmark that the majority of the dolmens are now to be found in wooded areas.

20   The Stone Age village of Barkjær in Djursland during
excavation

On cultivated land many have been destroyed in the course of the past century, as I have said, and their stones used for the building of farms and houses. If we include all ruined dolmens of which we have knowledge, the total distribution all over the country should certainly give a more or less accurate picture of the population distribution at the time of the first peasant culture. It shows an enormous growth in population as compared with the days of the hunters, due largely to immigration and improved living conditions. How large these immigrations were we cannot say, but both the first peasants and the stock breeders who brought their herds of cattle to fresh pastures must have come north in groups of several families, if not indeed as whole tribes.

The long road followed by the first farmers and cattle-breeders to Denmark cannot as yet be traced in any detail. Both the Danish material and what material there may be for comparison in neighbouring countries is still too insubstantial. The finds indicate, however, that a number of different immigrations from different parts of the world went to the making of our peasant culture in the first long phase of the later Stone Age. It may have been the desire for fresh land suitable for corn cultivation and pasturage that started off the migrations. Another factor was the change in climate in Central and Eastern Europe where at the end of the fourth millennium it was growing steadily drier. It was to be expected that herdsmen would leave pastures that had been dried up by the sun, and move on to fresh areas. They were not attached to any particular spot, but were accustomed to moving about within a wide area according to the different seasons. The farmers, too, were more mobile in those days than they are now. After a certain number of years they were obliged to move because the soil became exhausted after a succession of crops. There were no artificial fertilizers.

The first peasant peoples may have come to Denmark from districts south of the Baltic round about the mouth of the Oder and from Rügen even before 3000 B.C. In addition, another peasant people gradually spread out from the fertile loess areas of Central Europe. They had their roots far away in the eastern parts of Asia Minor and the Middle East, where this culture in its earliest beginnings is some ten thousand years old. Two thousand years later we find it in south-east Europe, and after another two thousand years in Hungary, Czechoslovakia, Poland and Germany. It had thus taken many generations for the first peasants to burn their way through the primeval forests of Europe before they arrived at the Baltic. A few hundred years after this the cattle nomads came —from parts of Russia still further east and the adjacent territories of Asia. The finds indicate that they, too, were farming peoples on a small scale.

It appears that the first of the new peoples buried their dead in simple earthen graves under level ground or quite low mounds. Only after they had struck firm root in the fertile Danish soil, which proved suitable to their mode of life, did they begin to erect the large dolmens. The typical Danish dolmens reveal influences not only from the first peasant peoples, who in their homeland south of the Baltic used both earthen graves and stone coffins the length of a man, but also from Western Europe where there are dolmens of a very similar form. Without influences from this quarter the changes in the form of the dolmens would certainly not have taken place. Numerous large stone graves of many different types were being built in the coastal areas of Western Europe at just this period. They extend from the British Isles and Ireland down along the coasts of France where they are most numerous in Brittany—to Spain and Portugal, and on into the Mediterranean area. They are to be found on Mediterranean islands and in North Africa and Palestine. This immense dispersal points not to one coherent migratory movement but rather to the spread from country to country of certain religious ideas connected with the worship of the dead and ancestor worship, borne by smaller migrations and furthered by trade. Our Danish contribution to international trade was the golden amber from the open, sandy beaches of the west coast of Denmark.

The different types of grave developed their own local characteristics up in the north in the same way as the clay vessels of our earliest peasant peoples, for which it is difficult to find parallels elsewhere. For on their long wanderings they principally used leather bags, woven baskets and wooden vessels for keeping food, and only took to using clay after they became settled. There can hardly be any doubt that the long dolmen in its usual form reflects the long houses of the first peasants. Long houses are known from just those areas south of the Baltic from which the peasant culture came, and are to be found there in large villages standing parallel to one another as the long dolmens often do, and as we find them in Denmark in village communities in Djursland. In the same way, one might imagine that the round dolmens represented a round house of West European or East European origin, but there is also the possibility that their shape is based on the circular sacrificial temple, a circle of upright stones round a large central sacrificial stone, such as can be seen in the huge constructions in Brittany in the west of France.

Houses of the type that provided the model for the long dolmen have been found in a village settlement in Barkjær near Feldballe in Djursland. Newly-arrived tribes of peasant people built their village on a small islet in one of the innermost inlets of Kolindsund, which in the Stone Age was a highly ramified fjord. It was in an area where many hunting and fishing people lived. There are two rows of houses about a hundred metres long running parallel in an east-west direction with a street between for about ten metres. Originally there were twenty-one dwellings in each row but the addition of seven more at the east end of each brings the total number to fifty-six, possibly indicating the number of families in the village and the growth in population during the period it was occupied. The threshold stones in the houses were still in place when they were excavated and there were clear marks in the light sandy subsoil of roof-bearing poles and dividing walls of interlaced twigs. In front of the rows of houses ran a sort of pavement set with stones the size of a fist. The southern row

21 *and* 22   The Stone Age village of Barkjær. Above, trees line the edge of the island facing the sea. Below, variegations in the soil show where the individual houses stood in the southern row

of houses was about six metres wide and had only one row of central posts, the northern one being about one metre wider with two rows. What particularly shows the connection of the houses with the dwellings of the dead, the long dolmens, apart from their ground-plan and size, is that under the floor of the one at the east end of each row, between two roof-bearing posts, there were one and two graves respectively.

The street and houses covered practically the whole surface of the island, which is very small. When the peasant people chose such a tiny island for their village, it was undoubtedly out of considerations of defence. They were strangers in the land, they burnt the forests and drove away the wild animals, and they may consequently not have been on a particularly good footing with the hunters and fishers who had inhabited the wide territories round the fjord from time immemorial, or even indeed the islet in Barkjær itself, where hollows of habitations have been found containing their flint implements. Many broken fragments of dagger-axes from the village houses also point to warlike conditions. The dagger-axe was a dangerous weapon in hand-to-hand combat, a thick, finely-wrought daggerlike flint blade that was set in a haft at right angles like an axe.

The Stone Age village of Barkjær can only have been inhabited for quite a short space of time, perhaps ten or twenty years. By clearing the mainland of forest the settlers started the sand spreading, and little by little it destroyed the fields and settled in thick layers inside the houses—even while they were occupied—and over the village street. Both that and the sanding of the soil shortened the days of Denmark's oldest village.

Unfortunately it has not been possible to preserve the village for posterity. The threshold stones to our first terrace houses were taken up long ago and the whole island is now covered with plantations. Yet as one stands there one can still get an impression of the island and its surroundings as they were five thousand years ago, even though the lake no longer reflects the blue skies above. A sandy causeway then led from

the mainland in the east to the island, which is now surrounded to the south and west by green meadows instead of
the waters of Korup. On the mainland to the south, just
opposite the village, stands a long dolmen, and a near-by
round dolmen has been destroyed within living memory. In
the forest to the north of the island there is a fine dolmen
chamber.

23   Passage grave at Tustrup in North Djursland

IV 'Giants' Tombs'

The Great Goddess

The 'Giants' Tombs' (*jættestuer*) or passage graves, the enormous stone burial chambers built of blocks several tons in
weight that people used to think had been erected as the
dwellings of giants of superhuman strength, are the fine
monuments of the peasant communities of the succeeding
period.

Unlike dolmens, they are generally completely covered by a
burial mound, and are only in exceptional cases surrounded
by large, visible kerb stones. The heavy cover-stone, however,
the roof of the chamber, does occasionally protrude through
the grass-covered top of the mound like the back of some great
sleeping beast. From the east or south-east side of the mound
a covered passage leads into the chamber. It is low and
narrow, and nearly always so small that it is only possible
to get through in a crouching position or crawling on all fours.
But once one is through, the chamber opens out, large and
spacious, with its heavy side stones—often taller than a man—
and its even larger cover-stone damp and cool as though it still
had the chill of the glacier in it. If one has once been inside a
well-preserved passage grave and breathed the heavy, earth-
laden air of its dark burial chamber, lit only by a glimmer of
daylight from the door, one can never forget the peculiar
sense one has of history and antiquity, or deny the powerful
attraction of things prehistoric.

The passage grave succeeds the dolmen as burial chamber

of the Stone Age peasant communities. One might have supposed that a steadily growing population would simply have
fallen into the way of making dolmen chambers larger until
in the end they became passage graves. But this was not the
case. The dolmen chambers never provided a burial place
for the collective communities of the first peasant period.
Probably only the elders of the villages were buried in them—
who represented the community and provided the link with
the powers that gave prosperity to man, corn and animals.
Several of the earliest passage graves are not much larger than
a well-developed dolmen chamber, but the difference in
ground plan between the two types of grave is so great that a
development from the smaller type to the larger is hardly
conceivable. When the dolmen has a passage, it forms a
continuation to the chamber, whereas the passage in the
passage grave runs at right angles to an elongated chamber
and this presents a more complicated structural problem
which, even in the very earliest passage graves, is skilfully met.
Where the passage runs out from the chamber, the two side
stones are lower than the others, and across them is laid a
heavy connecting block of stone carrying the weight of the
heavy cover-stone at that point and distributing its enormous
pressure on to the two side stones. This structure turns the
entrance to the chamber into a portal, and gives architectural
value to the interior of the chamber. It is, however, often
cramping to the back, as it reaches its full height only in the
centre. The whole structure is of course covered by a mound,
unlike many dolmens with a free-standing chamber whose
architecture is meant to be seen from the outside.

The passage grave is new in Stone Age Denmark. It is a
megalithic grave (megalithic being a word derived from the
Greek *megas* meaning large, and *lithos* meaning a stone), which
has antecedents in Western Europe. Similar megalithic graves
are known in Spain, France, Britain and the coastal districts
of Ireland, but in Denmark they acquired their characteristic
form from the materials available. It is only natural that in
many cases the influence of the passage grave on the dolmen

24　Free-standing passage grave under oak trees at
Bjærgbygård on Langeland

should be clearly noticeable, for it was in the dolmen's final period that the passage grave was introduced into Denmark.

Passage graves are not numerous in comparison with dolmens. Altogether about six hundred are known, of which by far the greater number are on the islands, mainly within the same coastal areas as the dolmens. Many of them are, of course, still hidden under their domed, grass-covered mounds, as we have seen. In very dry summers, when the sun scorches the grass, a passage grave is sometimes revealed by a golden, T-shaped area on the top of a mound because the grass dries up first where the chamber (the cross stroke of the T) and the cover-stones of the passage (the upright stroke) lie just beneath the surface. Many of the smaller islands which have dolmens have no passage graves. On Bornholm, where there are no dolmens, there are some ten passage graves. In Jutland the passage graves are confined almost exclusively to the Limfjord area, to Himmerland and to the area along the east coast, while only few are known in Vendsyssel, Central and West Jutland.

Passage graves, too, may be divided into different types according to their shape. The smallest ones often have an oval chamber and are not more than two to three metres long and one and a half to two metres across, and less than a man's height. The larger ones have a rectangular chamber with rounded corners and may be about ten metres long by three metres wide, and more than man-high inside. Only a few have a completely rectangular ground-plan, among them some of the latest to be built—which are also very low inside. The passage may be from four to ten metres long and is generally very constricted, and low and narrow, so that an adult has difficulty in crawling through. In many cases the outer end of the passage has been removed in more recent times.

A special type of passage grave has one or even two chambers built on to the main chamber, a feature that is found in the passage graves of Ireland and other stone grave areas of Western Europe, the Mediterranean and further east.

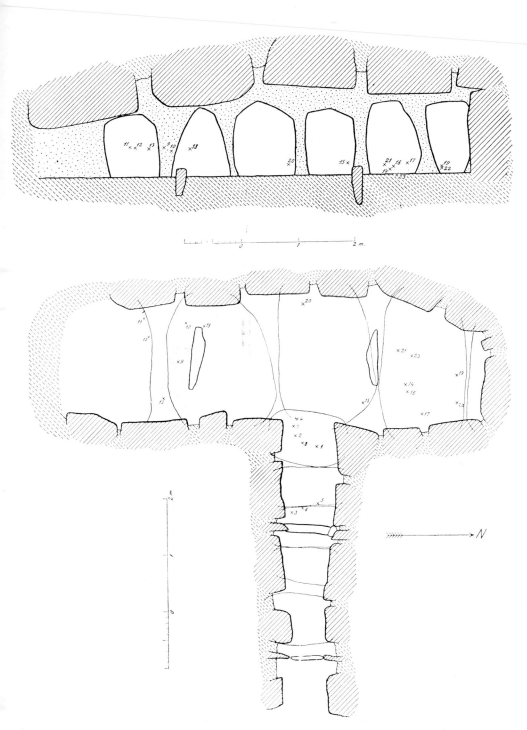

25   Ground plan and section of the passage grave in Rævehøj
at Slots Bjergby in South-West Zealand

26   Ground plan of the double passage grave called
Troldhøj at Stenstrup in Ods Hundred

This type, with the additional chamber, is by far the commonest in Jutland where there are thirteen in the area around
Limfjord, and two in East Jutland. Only two are known in
Zealand and two on Lolland. It is clear that these chambers
are not to be regarded as a general extension of the area of the
main chamber but had some special function to perform, as is

shown by the fact that they were built at the same time as the main chamber which is sometimes divided into compartments by means of upright slabs or rows of stones.

A pair of passage graves, each with its additional chamber, may be built as a double passage grave under the same mound, the two chambers being built together at the ends with a common side stone, but each with its own passage. The ordinary double passage grave is found most frequently in East Denmark, with some fifty existing on Zealand, and odd examples on Møn, Langeland, Funen and Samsø. Only ten or twelve are known in the Limfjord area, and there particularly in southern Himmerland. On rare occasions the chambers stand completely detached under the same mound. On Zealand there are long mounds with three chambers, only two of which are connected, forming a double passage grave. There is a unique case at Værslev east of Kalundborg where three chambers are built together under one mound. At Røddinge on Møn there is a double passage grave, built as one long chamber, which has later been divided by two upright stones so that the two chambers form a straight line and not, as normally, an obtuse angle. This passage grave consequently has two parallel passages.

The earth mound that encloses the passage grave is almost always round, but it can be oval or rectangular like a long dolmen. In most cases the chamber is completely covered with earth so that only an inconspicuous passage opening is visible, usually facing south-east or east, more rarely south, and only exceptionally west. The mound is often of considerable size, measuring twenty to twenty-five metres across, while a height of three or four metres is not unusual. When the mound is without external characteristics apart from the opening of the passage, this is due to the fact that during the Bronze Age it was very often increased in height and area: either burials were carried out in the actual chamber by lifting away the cover-stone, or graves were deposited above this. During the Stone Age the opening of the passage was impressive to look at, large uprights being placed close together on either side

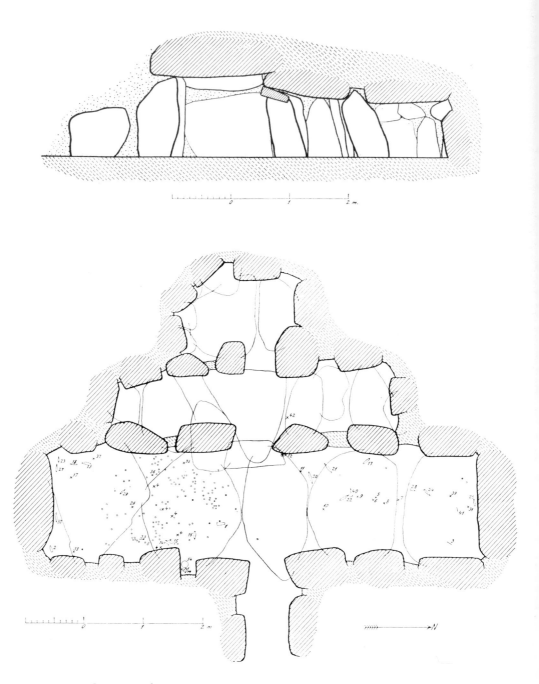

27   Ground plan and section of the passage grave called Hvisselhøj
at Alsbjerg in Øster Han Hundred. Two additional chambers have
been added behind the main chamber

of it. Sometimes they went round the whole mound. Where the mound has been investigated in more recent times these stones are exposed, as for example in the passage grave called Grønhøj close to Horsens, where the space between the metre-high kerb stones is filled in with smaller flat stones laid horizontally so as to form a compact whole; and the same may be seen in a passage grave at Tustrup on Djursland. A few passage graves on Lolland and Falster, with long, narrow chambers and a short passage, are enclosed in a rectangular mound with exposed kerb stones arranged in a rectangular frame like a long dolmen, a form that is known in north-west Germany, and may have been carried from there across the Baltic.

One occasionally sees large denuded stone chambers with quite a small mound of earth at the foot, or none at all, only a pair of threshold stones. These are passage graves from which the earth has been removed at a later period so that only the bare chamber remains. They are distinguishable from the uncovered stone chambers by their size and by the passage opening out on one of the long sides.

The passage graves are outstanding building structures. As was not the case with the dolmens, where it was the external effect that mattered, it is here the impressive interior. The outside of the stone chamber was not even intended to be seen, as is immediately obvious if one comes across one which has been completely denuded—when it looks like a pile of stones. It must have required great skill and a long tradition to construct a stone chamber of rough glacial boulders that would show such extraordinary endurance, a building that would stand unshaken for more than four thousand years. There was also a great deal of preparatory work involved. This was commented on by King Frederik VII a century ago in a paper that is still worth reading. Ideas have not in the main changed very much since then, even though the King himself exhorts his readers to think out other working methods, adding: 'He who comes closest to the truth shall always take precedence with me.'

28 Passage in passage grave seen from the chamber:
Troldhøj at Stenstrup

Some Stone Age architect directed the work, an expert in
the field with centuries of knowledge behind him to enable
him to deal with the many technical problems posed by the
erection of such a stone chamber. It is not improbable that
he would have come to Denmark from across the water to
the West and that his pupils of Jutlandish origin, after erecting
the first passage graves in the Limfjord area, would have
accompanied him further inland to build more. All the
passage graves we have were built within a single generation
or at most two. Where the examples within any particular

86

area have a characteristic style of their own, this may well
be accounted for by the building materials available on the
spot. The heavy components were probably not transported
very long distances.

The first step in building a passage grave was to drag a
considerable number of stones, large and small, to the spot
selected, so that there were plenty to choose from. Some forty
large boulders and several hundred smaller stones would be
needed for an average-sized chamber, or twice the number if
there were to be two together under the same mound. The
ground at the building site had to be dry and firm to take the
weight of the stones. The size of the chamber was to some
extent determined by the amount of building material collected, which first had to be treated, adjusted and split. There
are many indications that the builders really were able to
split the gigantic boulders, the most conclusive perhaps being
a pair of cover-stones over the two chambers of the double
passage grave called Troldhøj, in Ods Hundred, which are
the two halves of the same glacial block. The splitting, which
must have been the result of a large explosion, as the even
surfaces of cleavage show, was no doubt done with fire and
water, a technique known among primitive stonemasons
everywhere.

After exact measurement of the width and thickness of the
large boulders, the ground plan was drawn out on the selected
site. The stones forming the walls were then set upright, side
by side, supporting one another, with the flatter side—the
smooth surface—turned inwards, and an opening being
made where the passage was to be. Here was one of the more
difficult points which, as we have seen, was dealt with in the
light of experience by using somewhat lower side-stones on
either side of the passage opening, with a long, heavy stone
lintel laid across them both, the upper surface being more or
less level with the top of the other side stones. The height of
the chamber was then further increased by laying two or three
layers of horizontal slabs of stone on top of the side stones
so that the walls of the chamber were made up of several

layers. A very impressive spacious effect was thus produced, especially when these stones were pushed slightly inwards towards the centre of the chamber with the result that, when the building was completed, the interior assumed the form of a magnificent vault. This method also had the advantage that the chamber could be made slightly larger than the available cover-stone, as the vaulting at the top had the effect of narrowing the area to be covered. The spaces between the side stones were then carefully filled in with horizontal layers of split stone, laid close together, and practically always without mortar. Only in one single instance has the use of mortar been established—in one of the passage graves on Møn. The foundation of the floor was a thick layer of small pieces of flint broken by fire which acted as drainage for the chamber. On top of this was laid the floor of flat slabs of stone set in clay. The outside was also filled in with crushed flint—stones the size of a fist or a head—and over that were put thick layers of gravel and packing. Sometimes there was a layer of stamped clay on top of that, so that the back of the mound presented a smooth sloping surface from the surrounding ground to the top of the chamber. The cover-stone could then be rolled up this slope on rollers, perhaps the most difficult part of all. When one considers that these cover-stones sometimes weigh up to twenty tons and often only overlap the side-stones that have to carry them by a few inches, one realizes the delicacy of the operation. This suggestion that the cover-stone was rolled up from the back of the chamber, put forward by King Frederik VII, also explains why, as all ground-plans show, the chamber lies right over to one side of the mound. Only thus would the gradient to the top of the side-stones be low enough for it to be possible to heave the cover-stone into place.

The passage presented no great difficulties provided there were sufficient stones. These could be small enough to be rolled into place quite easily. But it, too, was carefully constructed. The threshold-stone and the projecting door-posts, one pair or more, were set in place with spaces between them

29 Chamber of Troldhøj at Stenstrup

in which doors consisting of flat slabs of stone or wood could
be supported. The remains of such stone doors, which were
also used to close the entrance from the main chamber to
subsidiary chambers, have been found in a number of passage
graves.

It was not always easy to produce stones of a sufficient size
in sufficient quantities to make a burial building in all parts
of the country where the builders of the passage graves settled.
Sometimes they had to make do with other means. In some
cases it looks as though heavy blocks of timber had been used

in combination with boulders, so that the chambers collapsed when the wood rotted away.

Even if passage graves are not equally numerous in all parts of Denmark, it is possible in most areas to visit one or more on a Sunday expedition. In the north of Jutland, in Vendsyssel, there are only a few, but these include one in Blakshøj, south of the church of Gærum, with a fine chamber eight metres long. The large triple passage grave called Hvisselhøj at Alsbjerg in Han Hundred is altogether unusual with its two chambers being built on behind the main chamber, a form for which there is no parallel closer than Malta. Lundehøj, on an open hillside at Heltborg south of Thisted, is equally impressively situated and has a fine chamber with subsidiary chambers. It was excavated in 1837 with funds from King Frederik VI's private purse, and was at the same time placed under a protection order with the proviso that an area was to be left all round the mound wide enough for the king's carriage to drive round it. This situation on high ground with wide views over sea and fjord is characteristic of many of our magnificent passage grave mounds. It is something they have in common with the Bronze Age mounds, with which they can therefore be easily confused at a distance. But there is a difference. The large Bronze Age mounds rise up in a gently rounded shape, whereas those of the Stone Age are more domed and heavier, so that one can imagine the huge mega-lithic chamber inside. Frequently there are two passage grave mounds close together, as for example at Snæbum, west of Hobro, where two very considerable mounds each cover double passage graves. One that has been excavated and repaired is Grønhøj, on Horsens, with its extremely large and fine kerb stones which continue uninterrupted on either side from the passage stones, and enclose the mound. There are two fine chambers on Hindsholm in north-east Funen, the larger one near Martofte, the other, a rather smaller one, at Brockdorff manor.

Zealand, however, is the area that is richest in passage graves, only a few of which can be mentioned. Ullershøj at

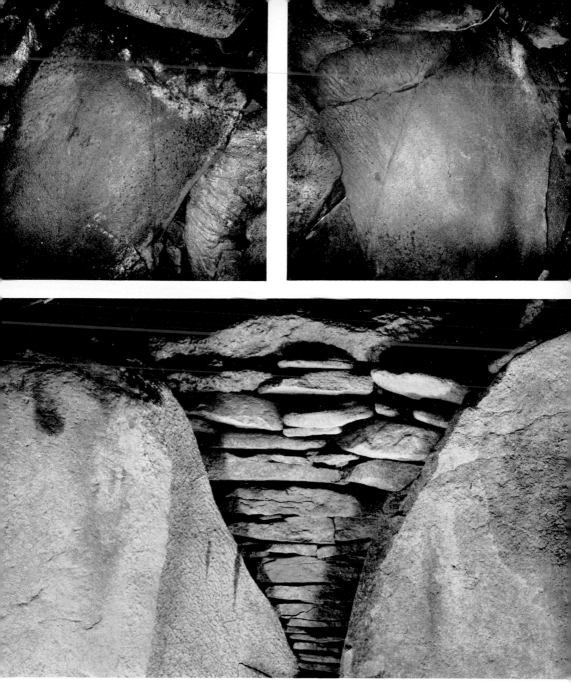

30 *and* 31   The two roof stones over the north and south
chambers of Troldhøj, deriving from the same original block

32   Dry-stone wall between the side stones of the
passage grave at Udby, near Kalundborg

Smidstrup in North Zealand, Troldstuen at Stenstrup in Ods
Hundred, and Korshøj at Ubby in the western uplands of
Kalundborg are all double passage graves that are worth a
visit. One of the best-constructed and preserved single
chambers is on Dysselodden, not far from Korshøj. Equally
fine examples are Rævehøj at Dalby with its four rows of side
stones and dome-shaped roof that rises two and a half metres
from the ground, Møllehøj at Udlejre, and Øm not far from
Roskilde. Two passage graves at Jægerspris in Horns Hundred
deserve special mention. One of them was opened up in 1744,
and a memorial tablet was placed on its mound by Crown
Prince Frederik (V) (for whom the Prince's Palace was built
where the National Museum now stands). The tablet says in
Latin: 'This grave, which was built by our pious though
heathen ancestors at least eight hundred years ago to contain
the earthly remains of four persons, and covered with enormous stones, was opened in June 1744 with reverence, and
adorned with this memorial tablet by the high-born prince
Frederik, heir to the wealth and virtues of his ancestors, the
hope, honour and glory of his people.' The inscription is by
the archaeologist bishop Erik Pontoppidan, and it refers to
the find of four urns containing burnt bones and bronze
articles in the top of the mound. Two flints were found in the
chamber 'of the kind the Peasants are accustomed to call
Thunderstones'; also some unburnt skeletons, concerning
which the royal physician pronounced that one of the skulls
was deformed though it was of normal size like the others.
The other passage grave was investigated in 1776 by
Frederik V's son, Prince Frederik, the heir presumptive, after
which it was remodelled in accordance with the style of the
time, an entrance portal being erected in honour of the
prince's mother, Juliane—after whom the mound has been
called ever since. The mound was scaled down and planted,
and memorial stones to legendary Danish and Norwegian
kings from Dan to Harald Hildetand and Harald Hårdråde
were set up in a circular space round it.

Møn is another area rich in passage graves, in particular

33 Temple building at Tustrup in Djursland

34 Skulls in the passage-grave chamber in Rævehøj
at Slots Bjergby

35 Troldebjerg at Illebølle on Langeland. The
village of the passage-grave period lay round its foot

the parish of Damsholte with Kong Asgers Høj, which has a
chamber ten metres long, and Klekkendehøj with its double
chamber and two parallel passages close together. Møn's
passage graves have the peculiar characteristic that they are
narrowest in the middle, opposite the passage. The best
known on Lolland is Kong Svends Høj under Pederstrup with
a stone chamber twelve and a half metres long, the longest
in Denmark. It lies in a rectangular mound surrounded by a

94

rectangular frame of uprights, like a long dolmen. The fact
that the passage faces west makes this monument even more
remarkable.

A group of stone monuments at Tustrup in North Djursland
must have special mention. They consist of a round dolmen,
a free-standing dolmen chamber, a passage grave and a
temple building situated in heath-covered terrain beside an
overgrown sunken road leading to the Hevring valley. This
protected site is well worth a visit, not least because its whole
appearance is very similar to that of corresponding stone
graves in deserted parts of Ireland. The temple lies at the
centre of a semicircle of a radius of fifty metres, which contains the three stone graves. Of the temple building itself all
that now remains is a horseshoe-shaped arrangement of stones
a metre high, with paving round the inside. The building was
open to the north-east, facing the rising sun at midsummer.
There is a block of stone in the centre of the opening, possibly
the base for a pillar which would have carried a turf-covered
roof on a foundation of birch bark. In the middle of the
building is a pit around which stood a number of sacrificial
vessels. Among them were ten bowl-shaped and beautifully
ornamented clay vessels with raised bases, each with a clay
spoon. This was the shrine of the temple, the dwelling-place
of the powers that ruled over the fortunes of the family. But
these were not the only powers to which prayers and sacrifices
were offered there. The dead also had their share. Sacrifices
to them were placed in clay vessels behind the tall kerb stones,
or on flat slabs laid on top of the kerb stones on either side of
the entrance to the passage grave. This was where people
assured themselves of the goodwill and help of the dead after
first cleansing the place through the power of fire. There are
cup marks on top of the cover-stones of many passage graves
which show that sacrifices were offered on megalithic graves
even during the Bronze Age. Whether this custom persisted
uninterrupted in certain places is not known, but the writer
Martin A. Hansen tells the story of a man who had been
employed as a young man after the First World War on the

farm at Roskilde on whose land the Øm passage grave stands. Every year just before Christmas, he related, two of the farm workers were sent out to clean and straighten up the chamber, after which the farmer's wife set a bowl of porridge there on Christmas Day itself 'for the giants and the spirit that dwelt there'.

The Tustrup temple building is not the only one of its kind known from the period of the passage graves, but it is the only one preserved on its original site. A similar building, only a little later, has been excavated at Ferslev in Himmerland where some forty sacrificial vessels stood round a long fire in the centre of the floor.

The passage grave was thus both grave and sanctuary for the edifice of which it formed part, and in comparison with the dolmen was a mass grave. In Zealand, in particular, a great many burials were made for which not only the chamber but the passage was well used. It must be added, however, that not all the burials belong to the same limited period of time. Some may date from the succeeding period when the flint dagger was the man's most important weapon and display object, or even from the Bronze or Iron Ages. At the excavation of Troldstuen at Stenstrup more than a hundred skeletons were found, and seventy and ninety-two respectively in the passage graves at Borreby and Slots Bjergby in South-West Zealand. In proportion to the number of skeletons, which show that men, women and children were buried there, the grave goods are not numerous. Among the men's things may be mentioned flint axes, battle-axes with haft-holes, arrowheads, chisels and knives. Amber beads and animals' teeth with holes bored through them doubtless belonged to the women, while clay vessels of food may have been placed there for either men or women. On Bornholm, however, flint axes are rare among grave goods and their place is taken by flakes from polished flint axes. This is undoubtedly due to the fact that all the flint for larger tools had to be imported into the island from places in Skåne and Zealand where flint was plentiful, so that people contented

36 The Great Goddess still gazes at us from the clay
vessels of the passage graves

themselves with giving the dead a small part in earnest of the
whole axe. Apart from these offerings at the entrances to the
graves, which were temples for ancestor worship, remains
which had previously been buried in the chamber were
sometimes moved out to the entrance. This may have been
done by newly-arrived tribes that had taken the ready-built
burial buildings into use as their own. These people came from

the other side of the Baltic where the migrations in Central Europe that later reached Denmark had forced them to leave their villages.

As to the question of who it was that brought the passage graves to Denmark, and what their society was like, we know very little. We may say, however, that these megalithic graves belong to a West European cultural group with connections right down to the Mediterranean. Our knowledge of their settlements, which might have provided information, is slight, as the only village that has so far been completely investigated dates from such an early stage in the middle Neolithic period —to which the passage graves belong—that it is doubtful whether its inhabitants could have been the builders of the passage graves. This village is in Langeland, east of Illebølle. It was built around a long hilly outcrop, Troldebjerg. A long house almost seventy metres in length, divided up for several families, lay furthest to the south along the western side facing Gammellung Fen and parallel with it—that was then the edge of the lake. North of this were the sites of a row of ten round huts, the back walls of which were dug into the hillside with the entrances facing the fen. There was a similar number of round houses along the eastern side of the hill, and there are traces of individual houses to the north and south, so that the buildings formed a closed ring round Troldebjerg. On the rounded hilltop there are only traces of a pit from which the Stone Age women took the clay for their attractively ornamented pots, fragments of which have been found in their thousands scattered along the edge of the lake in front of the houses. Troldebjerg was thus designed as a circular village containing both round and long houses, unlike Barkjær, which was a long village with long houses only. If one tries to estimate the number of inhabitants in these two ancient villages, one realizes first that there cannot have been much fewer of them than in an average Danish village in the middle of the last century, and second that their need for burial places was by no means catered for by either the dolmens or the long dolmens. This disproportion is most evident at Barkjær with its many habitations for the living and very limited space for a few dead in the surrounding dolmen graves. These can only have been intended for a few select people, among them doubtless the leader of this collective peasant community, who was also presumably the person providing the link with the powers that ruled over the village. Other people in the village must have had to be content with earth graves, which can no longer be traced as they had no grave goods. A rather larger village community such as that of Troldebjerg could not have found space enough even in a spacious passage grave. They must therefore have belonged to great families of the aristocracy rather than to village communities. This agrees with all that we otherwise know about the distribution and origin of passage graves.

The many different types of megalithic grave, of which the passage grave is one, are found in the coastal areas of Western Europe—not by any means everywhere, but arranged in groups around fjords or bays, or places further inland to which rivers give access. Often there are large megalithic graves on small islands. Such a peculiar distribution is sometimes interpreted as an indication of a colonization that spread from the Mediterranean over the whole of this enormous area. It has even been suggested that some megalithic missionary activity and trade lay behind the movement. There is much to corroborate this, among other things the fact that graves separated from one another by enormous distances in terms of the transport conditions of the time sometimes show a close connection. On the Shetland Islands, for example, there is a rock grave, the Dwarfinstone, cut out of a huge boulder that is just like the original rock graves of the Mediterranean. The ground plan of the three-chambered passage grave of Hvisselhøj, in the Limfjord area, could have originated from the temple graves of the Mediterranean islands of Malta and Gozo where the great mother-goddess, the origin of all things, was worshipped. That she was also worshipped here in Denmark is shown by the representations of her eyes on the clay vessels in the passage graves and the predominance in these graves of women's ornaments over all other objects. In some these are the only objects present, which might perhaps be regarded as an indication that it was a woman who stood at the head of the clan of passage grave builders.

The 'mission' which brought the passage graves was connected with the mother-goddess in whose honour the great megalithic graves on Malta and Gozo were first built as temples, later being used as graves. This mother-goddess, whose function it was to foster and preserve all life, is known from the Early Stone Age onwards. In the form in which we meet her on the clay vessels of the Danish finds of the mid-Neolithic period, she came to Denmark with the megalithic culture from the Mediterranean via Western Europe. Her symbols in Crete and the Aegean islands, to which she was brought from the Middle East and Anatolia, were, among other things, the axe and the snake we find carved on the stone tombs of Brittany. Her eyes gaze at us from the stones of the Irish megalithic graves with the same expression as they do from the clay vessels of the passage graves. We also find in them the double axe, both as a display weapon and as an amulet in amber. Possibly the axe was the symbol of office of the woman who stood at the head of the passage grave people.

The great families that erected the passage graves could not have carried out the work themselves alone, but would only have directed it with help from the village communities, which must have fallen quickly into a position of subservience to this upper class. It was they who sailed the great seas, organized trade in amber and flint, and brought gold, copper and bronze into the country. Ready-made articles like dagger-axes of copper, ornamented gold discs and magnificent gold collars the shape of a new moon, were brought from Ireland. It was natural for these people to choose the open hillside with wide views to distant horizons, just as the Bronze Age traders did. But their days, too, were numbered. Peoples from the East invaded the land, and the building of passage graves ceased.

V The Battle-axe People's Grave Mounds

A Conquering People

Low heather- and grass-covered mounds along river valleys and old lake shores, where water is now replaced by green meadows, mark the places in the interior of Jutland and along its western coasts where a people came to rest after long wanderings from the plains of distant Asia and through the mainland of Europe. The grave mounds were built by the Battle-axe people who invaded Jutland four thousand years ago and were caught in its net, surrounded by a sea they had never seen before.

These grave mounds are generally about ten metres across, one metre high, and stand in groups of about ten or twenty together. They date from the latest period of the passage grave people and normally cover graves only intended for one person, so that their culture has been called the single grave culture. But as the battle-axe is characteristic of the men's graves, the bearers of this culture are known in Denmark as the Battle-axe people. Men, women and children are buried in the mounds, which can easily hold several graves, but, with fresh interments, they were very often increased in height and width. The graves often cover a long period of time and show different forms of axe and clay vessels; and where the burials can be shown to have been contemporaneous, they are almost always of a man and a woman. Normally each grave contains

37   Low grave mounds of the Battle-axe culture close
to Karup River, between Fly and Skive

only one body, which in the older graves rests on a bed paved
with small stones, surrounded and covered with planks that
are held together and supported by stones the size of a fist
or a head. Occasionally two skeletons have been found in one
particularly large grave, and then they are either of a man
and a woman or of two men buried together. The oldest

graves are always about half a metre to a metre below the surface, seldom more, and are called the bottom graves. After that the earth was merely removed from the top so that the next graves lay level with the surface, and these are called ground graves accordingly. The latest graves were almost always placed on top of older mounds, which were filled out and enlarged. They consequently lay considerably above the base of the mound and were therefore called upper graves.

There is a striking difference in the orientation of the men's and women's graves during the first period, when the Battle-axe culture was pure and before it had been influenced by the surrounding peasant people. All the older graves lie in an east-west direction, but in the men's graves the dead man always lies on his right side with his legs bent as though he were still on horseback, and his head at the west end of the grave, looking towards his distant homeland and the rising sun. The women, on the other hand, lie with their heads at the east end of the coffin, and on their left sides, looking to the south and the sunset in the west. Very often a man's and a woman's grave are found side by side or opposite each other in a mound in a way that suggests burial at more or less the same time, which may perhaps show that the Battle-axe people practised monogamy. Where two men are buried in the same coffin or side by side under the same mound, it may perhaps tell of blood brotherhood that is continued into the kingdom of the dead. The fact that the burials do not normally follow one another in chronological succession in a mound or group of mounds seems to show that the Battle-axe people led a wandering existence even within the small area of Jutland, and that they were nomadic herdsmen, even if the cultivation of corn was not unknown to them. It is probable, therefore, that their society was run on patriarchal lines, possibly in contrast to matriarchal conditions among the passage grave people.

We can also tell that the Battle-axe people were herdsmen first and foremost from the fact that in north-west Europe as in Jutland they settled outside the existing areas of peasant

38 *and* 39 Man's grave with battle-axe, and woman's grave with amber beads, unearthed in mounds at Hastrup in Tyregod parish and Torupgårde in Alslev parish respectively

culture where the good soil was. This is reflected in the botanical layers of the Jutland fens, which show that in the period of the Battle-axe people the cleared patches were not allowed to return to woodland, but were regularly grazed by large herds of cattle.

The objects found under the low mounds in Jutland are completely different in form and method of manufacture from those found in the passage graves or the graves in level ground in this area. It is particularly the treatment of the good Danish flint that springs to mind, because not only did the Battle-axe people shape it into tools and weapons by chipping and polishing it, as had been the custom in Denmark from .olden days; they also used a crushing technique which is only used for other types of rock in areas where flint either does not exist or is a rarity. The Battle-axe people were strangers in Denmark and not a branch of the passage grave people, as has been suggested.

In the women's graves the chief and almost the only grave goods are amber beads, which were worn in long strings round the neck or in tassels as earrings. Sometimes the golden amber lies in a heap in front of the woman's face so that she can gaze at her splendid treasure even in death. The men's burial equipment is very uniform. In front of the face there is almost always a finely shaped stone battle-axe with a hole for the shaft, and where the belt went there is a small flint flake which was used as a knife, possibly a razor. Also at the belt, in the more important graves, there are two magnificent large discs of amber with convex faces. Were these symbols of the sun and moon, the divinities of this inland people, who regarded the sky not as a sea but as an endless greenish-blue plain, across which the sun drove his chariot along the path of the day? Or did they merely represent the wheels of the waggons that carried the children and belongings of the Battle-axe people on their long journeys? Very occasionally the man's equipment also includes a working axe of flint and a chisel, placed behind his back on the north side of the coffin. He was not only a warrior but also a woodman, compelled by the circumstances of the country to create the necessary pasturage for his cattle and horses. Clay vessels are rarely found in the graves, for containers of skin and wood were more practical for journeys in all sorts of weather. When clay vessels are found they are slender beakers, ornamented below the rim with cord twisted from two threads which was pressed into the clay while it was still wet before firing, in a number of parallel rows—a form of ornamentation so characteristic of the clay vessels of this group of peoples that their culture has been called the 'corded ware' (*snorkeramiske*) culture.

The Battle-axe culture first appears in Jutland just after 2000 B.C. Closely related tribes had already reached Denmark by easterly routes a millennium before but had long been absorbed by the country's peasant population. This new people from far away, with immense journeyings behind them, that arrived in Jutland was only a small part of enormous masses of migrating peoples.

The home of the Jutland Battle-axe peoples lay far to the east, on the other side of the Volga, in mountainous steppe-lands that continue uninterrupted into central Asia—where in the third millennium a nomadic cattle-breeding culture developed in a marginal zone outside the urban cultures of the Middle East but showing little influence from them. During the course of the fourth and third millennia the climate on these distant plains grew warmer and warmer. As rainfall decreased at the same time, the grass-covered plains on which numerous nomadic peoples had had their beasts and their tents turned to arid steppe, and with time it became unfit to produce sufficient food for cattle or men. Tribe after tribe dispersed in long caravans of waggons, led by men on horseback, to seek new pastures in other parts of the world. These were the Indo-Europeans, who broke out of their homeland and scattered in every direction. Wherever they came they caused amazement and fear, for in most places no one had ever before seen men on horseback. In the Indus valley these barbarians destroyed a fine urban culture with large, well-ordered communities, giving nothing in exchange.

In Greece, where their traces have been found in Thrace and Macedonia, the horseman was assumed to be half horse, half man, a memory that is preserved in the myth of the centaur, whose wildness and thirst for wine and love roused universal terror and admiration.

Some tribes penetrated through Poland and Germany right up to Jutland, while others settled along the paths of migration, wherever they found sufficiently good living conditions. Colonies were formed in Asia Minor, where they were called Hittites; others settled in the Moscow area, the people of the Tatyanovo culture; and others along the shores of the Baltic, in Poland, Central Europe and Holland. A few tribes even reached Sweden via south-west Finland and spread down from the Mälar districts to Skåne, Zealand and Norway. Their mark is boat-shaped axes, which is why the bearers of this culture are known in Sweden by the name of the Boat-axe people.

Wherever the Battle-axe people came they made themselves masters over the peasants and any others who were settled in the area. Prepared and well armed as they were, it was in most cases an easy matter to subdue peaceful farmers. The effects of their first onslaught in Central Europe had been felt right up to the Danish islands where farming tribes from the Elbe areas sought refuge from across the Baltic. It was these people who cleaned out many of the passage graves and were thus able to continue to bury their dead in stone graves, as they had been accustomed.

In Jutland the Battle-axe people immediately occupied all the large river valleys in West Jutland, the Gudenå valley and the smaller valleys that run into it. The first wave of their attack brought them right up to the areas around Viborg and from there westwards to the sea and further up into Thy. Finds from this area seem to show that the Battle-axe people were halted in Himmerland and northern Thy by the passage grave people, with help from whatever other elements of the population there were that buried their dead in earth graves. Later on, these areas too were subdued. Kindred tribes were by then already in process of occupying the Islands, East Jutland and Vendsyssel from bases along the south coast of the Baltic, possibly having been forced to quit their homes by equally warlike people from Western Europe known as the Bell Beaker people. This name comes from the shape of their clay vessels, which nearly always accompanied them into the grave together with a long-distance weapon resembling a bow, and also a short triangular bronze dagger for close combat.

The Battle-axe people, the single grave people of Jutland, at the time of their first invasion of Denmark were nomads who brought with them the domestic horse and possibly also the goat. In addition they kept large herds of oxen and flocks of sheep. Warlike and peaceful cohabitation with the surrounding village communities had the result that they also practised more agriculture themselves. But the independence of the old village communities was a thing of the past. The Battle-axe people became a master race, which together with the Bell Beaker people, with whom they had allied themselves, carried the country forward into a fresh cultural period. This marks the threshold of the brilliant Scandinavian Bronze Age, which gathered not only the whole of Denmark, but also southern Sweden, Norway and south-west Finland as well as large parts of northern Germany, the triangle between the rivers Oder and Elbe, into one great cultural circle. One of the bases of this greatness was the kinship and connections between the Battle-axe and the Bell Beaker peoples and tribes in parts of Europe where bronze was produced and where trade routes from the whole of our continent converged. But before bronze actually became almost the only material used for weapons and tools and the Danish Bronze Age began, there was a period of unification in the last great section of the Neolithic Age, with many different forms of grave, which tell of fresh incursions of peoples from outside.

VI Megalithic Cists and Stone Cists

On the Threshold of the Bronze Age

The influx of the Battle-axe people stopped the building of passage graves, first in Jutland, and later on the Islands, and set the course of future events. The single grave consequently became the most usual form of grave, but the latest Battle-axe people to reach the Islands and East and North Jutland also built large mass graves of stone and smaller stone cists for their dead. As both single graves and stone cists were covered with rounded mounds, which are indistinguishable in appearance and situation from the grave mounds of earlier and succeeding periods, the last period of the Neolithic Age has only set its own stamp on the landscape where the stone-built graves stand denuded.

The earliest of the Battle-axe people's stone graves are built of heavy blocks of stone that are only rarely split, like those that were used for the latest dolmens, with which they have many features in common. Their ground plan, as with many of the dolmens, is of a large four-sided or pear-shaped chamber with a short passage leading out at the end, sometimes with a threshold stone and portal stones, as found in the latest dolmens. The similarity has led to these megalithic cists, as the Battle-axe people's large stone graves are called, being regarded as a final development of the dolmen, showing influence from the passage graves in the shape of the passage,

40　Stone cists at Gravlev in Himmerland

the numerous cover-stones to the chamber and the mound of earth completely concealing it. The megalithic cist is, however, a new form which the Battle-axe people brought with them from the southern side of the Baltic.

The earliest megalithic cists are found at Orebygård on North-West Lolland, on Løjt peninsula in Åbenrå Fjord and on Vejle Fjord, and in addition in Himmerland and in neighbouring districts to the north and south, where they are particularly numerous, also in the later forms. If very few megalithic cists were built on the Islands, this is probably due to the fact that the Battle-axe people to a large extent made use of existing dolmens and passage graves for the burial of their dead.

The large megalithic cists in North Jutland are built of thinner and more split-up stones than either the dolmens or the passage graves. They are mass tombs with spacious chambers that measure two or three metres in length and one and a half to two in width, in which up to ten people were buried. The chamber is covered normally by three or four cover-stones, while the passage, which is quite short and measures about one metre square, is covered by a single stone and always faces south. The corresponding megalithic cists on the Islands, of which only a few are known, have no separate passage and are orientated west-east. The grave goods in the earlier cists are battle-axes, amber ornaments and decorated clay beakers, while the axe is replaced in the later cists by flint daggers and arrowheads and clay beakers without ornamentation, equipment which reveals fresh influences from Western Europe, especially northern France.

Megalithic cists with a special entrance, with lintel and threshold stones and a large, spacious chamber, the ceiling of which in the cists of North Jutland is supported by stone pillars, remind one very much of a house. The idea has, in fact, been put forward that this type of tomb was modelled on the dwellings of the living, the type known by the Greek name of *megaron*, house, which had the same ground plan as earlier Greek temples. The fact that graves of this time were built entirely of wood and in the same form, makes the relationship with dwelling-houses probable.

The latest megalithic cists to be built, and also a closely related form known as stone cists (*hellekister*), because both cover-stones and side stones consist of flat slabs of stone, known as *heller*, which had not been split for the purpose, date

41 *and* 42   Megalithic cists: Myrpold on Løjt at
Åbenrå, and cist at Vive north of Mariager Fjord

from the last phase of the Late Stone Age, the Late Neolithic period. These stone cists, which are the length of a man or somewhat longer, are covered by mounds and in North Jutland are normally orientated to the south, while those on the Islands are orientated east-west. The largest are intended for several burials. A few quite small stone cists, only one metre long and barely half as wide, have been found at burial places under level ground.

The single graves, now appearing as a layer containing flint daggers, arrowheads, amber beads, and more rarely un-decorated clay vessels, were originally cists made of planks of wood or hollowed-out tree trunks which had now come into use. They are very often deposited in the top of the Battle-axe people's earlier grave-mounds, which when the new burials were made were enlarged by the addition of more earth. A few single graves, however, are placed deep underground and covered generally with large mounds, lying on the open hill-side. These certainly show the immigration of fresh tribes from the south to those parts of North and Central Jutland where they are mostly found.

Only a few megalithic cists and stone cists still stand on their original sites. The fragile material of which they are frequently built necessitated their transfer to open-air museums where they were re-erected. Two of the earliest type, however, are still on the original spot, one a megalithic cist with a passage to the south in a mound on Orebygårds Mark near Saks-købing; the other on Løjt peninsula, a megalithic cist with a passage to the east. This latter is called Myrpold and offers a wide view over Åbenrå Fjord. It is now completely denuded, but was originally covered with a mound and surrounded by a stone circle. There is a spacious megalithic cist without a passage on Svalhøjgårds Mark at Vive high above Mariager Fjord, while stone cists may be seen denuded in the church-yard of Horne Church in Vendsyssel, and covered by a mound at Skodsborg railway station in North Zealand.

The many different types of grave in the closing phase of the Stone Age, the middle of the second millennium B.C., and

43 *and* 44   Sangstrup Klint in North Djursland, and
the layer of black flint in the chalk cliffs

articles of bronze and gold as grave goods, reflect an uneasy period with movements of peoples and extensive trade connections. Artisans were no doubt even then—as in recent centuries—travelling journeymen who moved about from place to place. A leading position among them was occupied by the smiths, who worked in bronze. Even towards the end of the Stone Age, so much copper and bronze had been imported into Denmark, poor in metal as it was, that these were the most important materials for weapons and tools. This presupposes an extensive and well-developed trade that may have been to some extent in native hands and controlled by a ruling class. Only some of the goods that were traded southwards and to the west were of native origin: first and foremost the magical amber from the white west coast of Jutland, which flowed like a golden stream through Central Europe, over the Brenner Pass, and opened up direct communications between Scandinavia, the metal-producing countries, and the Mediterranean. Metal flowed northwards as a counter-stream. What goods may have passed through Denmark from Norway and northern Sweden, we have no idea. One might imagine that beautiful furs and equally beautiful women were among them. From Denmark a stream of flint moved northwards, at a time when this was a material that had long been replaced by metal for weapons and many tools. Flint was obtained partly from open strata, partly by regular mining operations in chalk strata underground.

The open flint strata lie in grass-covered banks along our coasts, where they were left five thousand years ago by the sea. Such strata are to be found at Køge Bay and in Sangstrup Cliff in North-East Djursland, and were searched through systematically by the flint smiths, who sorted out all the usable material and gave it a first rough shaping. One can see, from the pieces that have been abandoned, that the articles they were most anxious to make were working axes, blades for corn sickles and pieces for striking fire.

There is evidence of the mining of flint in northern Himmerland and in Thy, where the chalk strata rise to the surface. Mining is known elsewhere in Europe in the first metal period, as for example in the Hybla Geleatis mountains of Sicily, whence it spread all over the island. In the south of England, too, shafts and passages were hewn out at this time down to flint-bearing strata in the hard chalk formations.

The first flint mines proper in Denmark were excavated in the chalk strata of Skovbakken south of Ålborg. There in the last phase of the Stone Age shafts were dug approximately one metre across at the top and to depths of almost five metres. At the bottom, the shafts widened out on all sides, following the flint seams, and several passages were so long that they joined up with other shafts, forming extensive mine systems. They have all been covered over again now, so that nothing is to be seen on the surface. Still older flint mines have been found in Sennels Ås at Hov Kalkværk north of Thisted. Here there is shaft after shaft covering a wide area of the top of the ridge, several score in all, so that the whole area is exploited to the greatest degree possible. The shafts are four or five metres across at the top, but they narrow as they go down and at a depth of about three to five metres, where the black flint strata lie, they widen out again forming galleries that run for three, four or five metres into the white chalk. In some cases different seams of flint have been worked at different levels, in others the bottom seams have had to be abandoned. When it was found that no more usable flint could be obtained from one particular shaft, this was filled in again with the lumps of chalk previously removed. Then another shaft was started alongside. Finds of spoilt flint axes show that the Thy flint mines belong to the third millennium B.C.

If one comes down from the north along the main road to Thisted, one sees Sennels Ås to the east as a long, green-clad hill against the blue horizon of Limfjord. On the western side of this hill is a deep, whitish-grey scar, Hov Kalkværk, and above it lie the flint mines, one of which is preserved, roofed over and open to visitors, a visible testimony to the mining operations conducted in this country thousands of years ago.

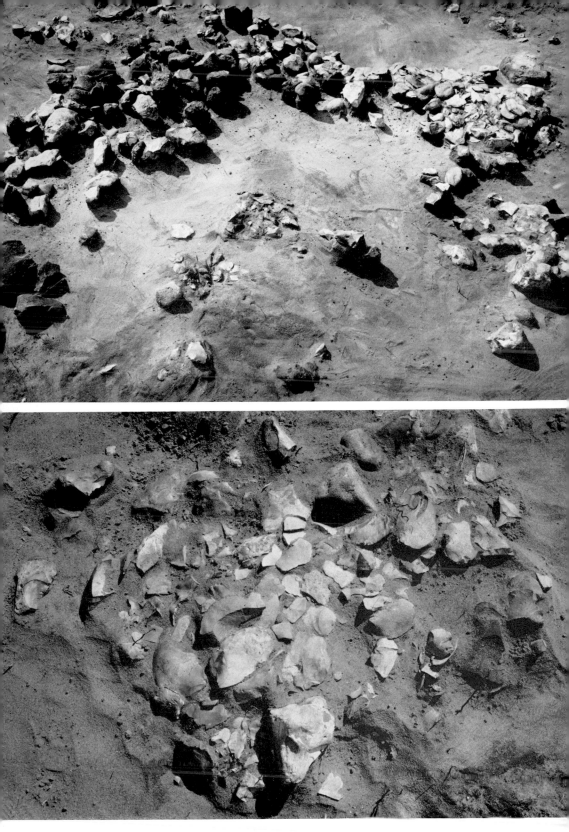

45 *and* 46   Flint-smith's workshop with material from
Sangstrup Klint, unearthed under a bank on the shore
at Fornæs

47   Flint mine in Sennels Ås, north of Thisted

VII Large Bronze Age Mounds

Chieftains and Traders

The Bronze Age mound is an even more characteristic feature of the Danish landscape than the dolmen. Everywhere the burial monuments of this period crown the largest ranges of hills, lying in rows along the ridges, breaking and strengthening the great flowing lines of the moraine landscape left by the Ice Age. It is therefore no accident that all the highest points in Denmark are large Bronze Age mounds, as we have seen, memorials of an aristocratic people with a distinctive culture who ruled Denmark with ability during the last half of the second millennium B.C., when the Islands and Skåne formed the centre of an extensive cultural area. As I have said, this included not only the whole of Denmark, southern Sweden and Finland, south Norway and Holstein, but also the broad triangular land area of northern Germany between the Elbe and the Oder, right down to Lower Saxony. These Bronze Age peoples who were laid to rest three thousand years ago in their oak coffins under the mounds had wide horizons. They were chieftains who conducted trade in bronze and other goods and who organized its routes northwards to the Scandinavian plateau and southwards through Europe to southern Germany, Czechoslovakia, Austria and Hungary, right down to the coasts of the Adriatic and the Mediterranean.

The large burial mound was not simply a last resting-place, but also a monument to a life of greatness and power, intended

48　Burial mounds at Skovsgård in Øster Han Hundred

both to see and to be seen from far around. At that time the
contours of the land lay open, as in recent centuries before
they had been smothered by plantations of conifers. The
Bronze Age landscape had a spacious, park-like character
with scattered groups of trees and wide expanses with great
grazing flocks of sheep. The moraine hills were not so large
that the mounds could not dominate them, and in the posi-
tioning and structure of the mounds the Bronze Age people
worked ingeniously and deliberately hand in hand with
nature. For the large mounds are not placed exactly on the
highest points, but a little to the side, where the hill begins to
slope, and this in itself gives the monuments a characteristic
poise. Secondly, their profile is not like that of the Ice Age
hills, but more rounded and slightly pointed at the top, a
shape they have maintained for thousands of years because
they were not just made of heaped-up earth and gravel but
were carefully built of grass turfs, further supported by stone
circles, stone walls and paving concealed under the base of the
mound. Originally the outermost of these stone kerbs or walls

49   Bronze Age landscape with grazing sheep,
by Tystrup Lake near Sorø

lay out in the open but it has in some instances been replaced
by a wattle fence.

There is in most cases a clear-cut difference of position
between Bronze Age mounds and the round Stone Age burial
mounds, which sometimes enables one to distinguish the one
from the other. The Stone Age single-grave mounds, in which
the Battle-axe people lie buried, are mainly to be found—as
already mentioned—in the interior and west of Jutland,
gathered in groups in flat terrain along river valleys; whereas
the Bronze Age mounds in the same area lie higher up, on the
hill ranges. Stone Age mounds are quite low and reach a
height of two metres only in cases where later burials have
taken place, increasing the size of the mound, while Bronze
Age mounds for either a man or a woman very often reach a
height of three or four metres in the first instance, with a
diameter of fifteen to twenty-five metres. Where later burials
have taken place in the Bronze Age, with the addition of
extra material, they reach still greater sizes. Thus the burial
mounds of Borum Eshøj, Store Kongshøj and Garderhøj,

50   Støvhøj on Rakkeborg Hede, in South-West Himmerland

known for their well-preserved oak coffins, measure from thirty-three to thirty-eight metres in diameter and seven to eight in height. A few mounds which enclose Stone Age passage graves and megalithic cists, and also the latest mounds containing dagger graves, have measurements on the same scale. They are often situated on high-lying ground. Where their size is due to later additions in the Bronze Age, they cannot, of course, be distinguished from the mounds of that period. Nor are they distinguishable in the landscape from mounds containing dagger graves, which introduce the Bronze Age burial mound customs. Mounds which completely cover the stone graves within are a different matter altogether. They are more domed, like the sun when it stands half above the horizon. The vaulted profile gives an added weightiness, corresponding with the concealed chamber weighing many tons within, as compared with the Bronze Age rounded profiles covering the lighter oak coffin.

These round, domed burial mounds are not the only kind erected in the Early Bronze Age. The Bronze Age people also used long mounds as burial monuments. They are known chiefly from the northern part of the Jutland peninsula and are much rarer in the rest of the country with the exception of South Jutland, where there are a few. They may, like the long dolmens, have been erected this way from the start. Occasionally, however, they have arisen as a result of a third Bronze Age grave being placed between two round mounds which stood close together, and earthed over so that the whole presented the appearance of one long mound. This is the way in which, among others, Muldbjerg in the county of Ring-købing arose. It is approximately forty-three metres long by twenty-four wide, but narrowing in the middle, so that the ground plan looks like the outline of a very thick figure of eight. It provided one of the best known and best preserved men's costumes of the Bronze Age: a fringed cap, a cape and a short tunic, all of wool. Unlike the Stone Age long dolmens, the Bronze Age long barrows are not surrounded by visible upright kerb stones. Like the round barrows, they have smaller stones under the base of the mound. As they are also rounded off at the ends and run up steeply, so that seen from the end they look like a round barrow, they can almost always be easily distinguished from a long dolmen.

Rarer than the long barrows are the flat Bronze Age barrows with steep sides and a completely flat top, which look as though the upper half of a large barrow has been removed with a knife. These are to be found dotted here and there in

51   Oak coffin standing unopened on its layer of stones
in the burial mound

52 The coffin opened. One can see the young girl's fair hair, tunic, belt buckle and string skirt lying on a cowhide

Jutland and are almost always of very considerable size. Thus several of them measure up to about fifty metres across at the base, three metres in height and thirty-five across the flat, circular top. The largest is a flat barrow at Nustrup in South Jutland which is sixty-seven metres in diameter, but only about two metres high. Another well-preserved example of this particular type of barrow is that at Navtrup, in north-west Salling. These flat barrows are often known to the local population as dance barrows, a name which undoubtedly provides a clue to the object of the flat surfaces, which must have served as a stage for processions and dancing in connection with the worship and cult of the dead in the Bronze Age. It has been demonstrated a number of times that the flat barrows contain ordinary Bronze Age burials, so that in that respect they are no different from the ordinary burial mounds of the time.

Originally the large Bronze Age mounds covered a single burial, either of a man or of a woman, which shows that the two sexes were equal in death. More rarely two burials were made at the same time; but it is not uncommon for later burials to be inserted into the same mound, thus directly continuing the burial customs of the Battle-axe people. In this way the one mound is converted into a family sepulchral monument. A typical example is Borum Eshøj west of Århus. In the centre of the mound was an oak coffin, in which lay the mummified remains of an old man with cap, cape and tunic of woollen material. Chips of wood showed that the oak coffin had been hollowed out on the spot. Later on, another oak coffin had been placed in the same mound containing a young man, whose clothes and equipment were also well preserved. There was a further oak coffin, just inside the kerb stones on the eastern side of the mound, in which rested an elderly woman wearing a tunic and skirt of woollen material, a hair-net made by the 'sprung' technique, a belt with two elaborate tassels and a neck ring, arm and finger rings of bronze, as well as a belt buckle, dagger and other equipment, which showed her high position. Since all three oak coffins

53 Row of mounds between Hurup and Vestervig in Thy

were at the base of the same mound, and appear to be of the same date, it is natural to regard the mound as a family burial place, even though only an anthropological relationship could be established between the two men. Occasionally several more burials have been discovered in one large barrow, but in many cases these are of such different ages that there is no need to assume any link of kinship between the individual graves, although this may be possible.

The oak coffin came into use towards the end of the Stone Age: an oak trunk split lengthwise and hollowed out, one half forming the lid, the other the actual coffin. The oak trunk coffin is known from several finds in association with the latest Battle-axe people's things, but only became general all over the country in the Bronze Age. In some cases hollowed-out oak planks are laid round the coffin, making a sort of double sarcophagus. Plank coffins, too, are still in use and even the stone coffin, which persists particularly in the western Limfjord area, in Thy and on Mors, as well as around Isefjord, Roskilde Fjord and Kalundborg.

The usual custom with the first burial was to lay the coffin on a layer of stones on the surface of the ground; less often a pit was dug for it below ground. It was then covered over, sometimes with a heap of stones or a layer of meadow turf, after which the burial mound proper was piled up over it, consisting of carefully laid heather or grass turf mixed with earth or gravel. For the most part all that now remains of the oak coffin itself is a brownish residual layer a millimetre thick on the stone bed. In certain circumstances, where a layer of iron has formed above and below the coffin, creating an airtight space enclosing a moist mass, of which the coffin itself was the core, both the coffin and its contents have been preserved by the action of the tannic acid extracted by the moisture from the oak. It is from graves such as this that the marvellous Bronze Age costumes come.

The enormous quantities of grass and heather turf that went into the making of the many large Bronze Age mounds must have laid waste huge areas of grazing land, if one considers that one single mound required the turf from two and a half to four acres of land, which must have lain bare for a long time afterwards. It was possibly not the intention of the master people, either, that the pastures round their burial monuments should be usable immediately afterwards. The cutting of the thousands of turfs must have involved a great deal of work, so that there must have been a numerous subject class available for this labour. It is possible that the work of lifting the turfs was lightened by the use of an ox-drawn ard, the Bronze Age plough, with which the turf could be squared out, for squared patterns made by ploughing in two directions at right angles to each other can sometimes be seen under the Bronze Age burial mounds. These dark furrows in the light soil may represent old fields, or be simply the tracks of the turf ard.

Apart from the stones which formed a bed and cover for the coffin, one single ring or several rings of larger stones were placed round it, to serve as protection for the dead man against evil powers; but at the same time they had a practical function, to prevent the mound from widening. These circles often consist of a single row of stones, though occasionally they extend to elaborately contrived broad walls of larger upright stones with flat stones stacked between them. A paving of smaller stones was sometimes laid like a collar round the inside of the stone circle, continuing under the mound. Small, isolated patches of paving at the base of the mound may have been places of sacrifice used in connection with the burial ceremonies.

On Bornholm and in many parts of Sweden and Norway where heather and grass turf were not easy to come by, but where there were always stones in abundance, the Bronze Age mounds were built exclusively of piled-up stones, either entirely without a covering of earth or with only quite a thin one. These piles of stones are known as cairns. The largest of all is Bredarö at Kivik in south-east Skåne. A stone-built coffin with pictures painted on the inside was discovered under this in 1748; it had been covered by an enormous flat-topped cairn about seventy-five metres across, the largest in

Scandinavia. The pictures on the inside of the coffin obviously depict the ceremonies connected with the burial: processions, horse-racing, stallion fighting and the blowing of *lurs* (long, curved Bronze Age trumpets).

There are large Bronze Age mounds all over Denmark, mostly on coasts and fjords. Standing beside them, the view over the surrounding landscape is magnificent and almost always includes water, even if it is only a narrow strip of silver on a distant horizon. There are many lovely heather-covered mounds, singly or in groups, on the plateau of Vendsyssel, and in the parishes of Tolne, Mosbjerg and Gærum near Frederikshavn. Thy is particularly rich in large groups of fine mounds, which set their stamp on the landscape more strongly here than in other parts of the country. They run in long lines from the Limfjord coast and ridge of hills westwards to the sea, where the old trading stations lay. A group of some fifty mounds on Ydby Heath, the Ancient Churchyard, as it is called in Thy, is unique.

Himmerland, too, has a wealth of Bronze Age mounds. They cover wide areas, following the high ground along the river valleys, and are sparse only in the most easterly quarter around Lille Vildmose Fen, which is old sea bed, and in the wooded districts of Rold. Special mention must be made of the fine, well-preserved range of mounds at Øster Hornum, on Hverrestrup Hills, Tuelsbjerge at Vester Tostrup and Hornshøje north of Klejtrup lake, all of which lie in more or less uncultivated terrain and follow high hill ranges in a north-west to south-east direction. Further down through fertile East Jutland the mounds are more scattered, for centuries of agriculture have long ago levelled the majority. But here again it is the high ground beside fjords and river valleys that has in particular drawn them in close rows or groups, marking out old roads and boundaries. Stabelhøje and Trehøje on Mols are famous for their beautiful situation and wide views over land and sea. In Central and West Jutland the low-lying Stone Age mounds are the most numerous, but the large, heather-covered Bronze Age mounds dominate the hill

54   Group of mounds at Vorbjerg in Nim Hundred

ranges. They follow the hills south of Struer and Lemvig in particularly dense rows, beginning at Sevel and ending at Bovbjerg, where there was a considerable trading station. They indicate an ancient transport artery that followed the boundary between the fertile clay soils from the glaciers of the last glacial period and the golden moorlands which, together with the old hill islands formed in the penultimate glacial period, contain fewest ancient monuments. A similar situation can be seen in South Jutland, where the rows of Bronze Age mounds follow the hills in a south-east to north-west direction, but also follow the old Army Road north-south along the boundary between the good soil and the poor soil. Along the coasts the groups of mounds mark the trading stations. There again the moors and sandy soil are empty.

On Funen, Bronze Age mounds are rarer. They follow the coast all round the island and are only very sparsely represented inland where large areas are completely without monuments. Langeland has a row of large mounds along the cliff at the inland end of Tryggelev Cove, which has an excellent natural harbour for a trading station and which, like so many other places, emphasizes the importance of the sea as a means of communication in the Bronze Age.

Zealand was once rich in burial mounds, but here again certain parts are less favoured in that large areas of the interior are completely without Early Bronze Age mounds. The coast is their favoured territory. There is a fine group of large mounds on Bakkebjerg south of Rågeleje in North Zealand, and many others all round the coasts where the woods have provided protection. Vejrhøj on Sejrø Bay in North-West Zealand is known for its size and its superb position. Syvhøje west of Nykøbing, which once dominated the landscape, is now, like so many other groups of mounds, concealed by plantations of trees. Mention must also be made of Dutterhøje, in the hilly country between Fårevejle and Asnæs. On the southern islands the mounds mostly lie in groups near the coast, the finest being at Birket church on North Lolland, while Bavnehøj, one of a large group of which many are still preserved, is the highest point on the island. On Bornholm also the coastal areas are the most favoured.

By and large one may say that Bronze Age burial mounds show the extent of settlements and the position of roads. Where they lie close together, there has been a main seat of one of the great Bronze Age families somewhere in the vicinity. By looking at a map of the country's burial mounds one can trace the old routes from the coasts to the inland

55 *and* 56   Small stone coffin, closed and open, in mound at Smerup on Thyholm. A bronze sword lies on top of the burnt human bones

settlements, and from there on to the other coastal areas from which ships sailed with Scandinavian goods to trading places far away, to bring back gold and bronze in return.

How many large mounds were erected in the country is not known with any certainty, but the available material seems to indicate that there were about fifty thousand. It seems a large number when one considers that many of them contain two graves of the Early Bronze Age, but as this period comprises five hundred years, it means that only a hundred large mounds were built in the whole country every year. If two hundred men and women of the trading people died every year, it would give a total population in that class of about four thousand. Apart from this there was, of course, a far larger population of subject people who provided the labour for the more menial tasks, farming and stock-rearing, hunting and fishing, handicrafts and whatever else had to be done in a trading community of this sort.

It is the finds from the large mounds that bring us really close to the people and culture of the Bronze Age, their wealth of beautiful weapons and ornaments of bronze and gold, and their handsome clothing. Where conditions have been particularly favourable, organic materials such as cloth, horn and wood are still preserved and provide us with a wonderfully complete picture of the life these people lived three thousand years ago.

The men's graves contain bronze swords and axes, and the richest ones, fine twisted gold arm rings as well. The dead were buried in their everyday clothes: a knee-length tunic which was fastened over one shoulder with a strap, and a round cape which was worn over both shoulders with the front edge turned back to form a sort of collar and *revers*. On his head the man wore a round cap, and leather sandals on his feet. The Bronze Age chieftain was clean-shaven and wore his hair short.

The woman's dress consisted of a short-sleeved tunic, sometimes adorned with embroidery, and either a short skirt elaborately fashioned of string, or a long, ankle-length lower garment. Her hair was either cut short in a page-boy style or piled up high in an attractive manner and covered with a large-meshed hair net or a woven cap. Both the ornaments found in the graves and the clothes themselves speak of taste and refinement among the Bronze Age women. For example, the short-haired Egtved girl wore a beautiful belt buckle with spiral ornamentation and two bronze arm rings. The distinguished Skrydstrup woman wore only a pair of thin gold rings in her ears and a horn comb in her belt. The similarity in grave furniture and method of burial for men and women probably reflects a corresponding equality between the sexes among the upper class in the Bronze Age.

The decisive difference between the Stone Age and the Bronze Age was that stone was supplanted as the most important material for weapons and tools by bronze, an alloy of about 90 per cent copper and 10 per cent tin, because of its superiority in many respects. How great the jump was from the one age to the other, and how great an organization and talent for trade lay behind it, is shown by the fact that, whereas the good flint had been the most important raw material for weapons and tools in Denmark for thousands of years and was easily obtainable all over the country, every single ounce of bronze had to be imported over long distances and exchanged for home-made goods. In the Stone Age, therefore, everyone could obtain material for weapons and tools. In the Bronze Age it was the rulers of the country who controlled the import of metals. It is difficult to understand how it could ever have been possible to obtain sufficient bronze to cover the colossal demand there must have been. Not only was enough metal required to replace the wastage of tools in constant use; it was also needed for new weapons and ornaments for each succeeding generation since so many personal belongings accompanied their owners to the grave. Sacrifices to the powers that watched over life and fortune also swallowed up a large proportion of metal imports.

Various new developments in Bronze Age agriculture may no doubt be attributed to extended trade connections. For example, a number of new cultivated plants appear for the first time in this period. Willow herb, the seeds of which were suitable for food for both men and beasts, was used for porridge and as a fodder plant, while white goose-foot was cultivated for its rich fat and albumen content. Among the grains, millet and oats are also new, the latter only coming into general cultivation in the Iron Age. There may also have been a change of emphasis in that stock-rearing, with its main stress on sheep and oxen, seems to have expanded considerably at the expense of agriculture as against the position among the large peasant communities of the Stone Age.

The foundations of the vast trading organization of the Bronze Age were laid, as we have seen, by the Battle-axe and Bell Beaker people of the Stone Age who, as a result of their kinship with tribes in the metal-producing countries of Europe, were able to create the conditions necessary to lead the people of Scandinavia on to the high-level and distinctive culture of the Bronze Age. It is thus the popular migrations of the Stone Age that lie behind the emergence of the Bronze Age in Northern Europe, where both the capacity and the talent existed to create an independent cultural area. The picture here is everywhere the same: a rich trading class with military and maritime power, which enabled it to secure the trade routes, and a numerous subservient class that worked at handicrafts and agriculture and served as oarsmen in the trading people's fleets.

VIII Small Bronze Age Mounds

The Cremation Period

Cremation first appears in Denmark as a burial custom towards the end of the Stone Age. Up to that time the dead had always been buried, interred unburnt, and this custom remained the prevailing one in Denmark all through the Early Bronze Age. Only one earlier case of cremation is known. A pile of burnt human bones, covered with a little heap of sand, was found in a small sandpit under a settlement layer of the period of the coastal fishing culture at the end of the Early Stone Age, at Vedbæk in North Zealand. This isolated case should not perhaps be regarded as cremation proper, more probably as a human sacrifice, and possibly in connection with cannibalism, several examples of which are known in the final phase of the Early Stone Age when influence from the peasant culture can be established. Traces of fire have been found several times in the passage graves and Battle-axe graves, but here there is no question of cremation. It is not until the final phase of the Stone Age that we know of a series of graves showing cremation—the Limfjord area ones —in which the grave goods, daggers and arrowheads of flint, were also on the funeral pyre, though accompanying clay vessels do not show any marks of fire. These graves, six in all, seem to show a new custom introduced into North Jutland by kinsfolk of the Battle-axe people from north-west Germany and Holstein. Whether it was this immigration of people who brought cremation as their burial custom—a custom which

57   Bronze Age mounds at Tryllere Dansen in the forest
of Klinteskoven on Høje Møn

persists through the Early Bronze Age and gradually becomes
general—we do not know; but it is hardly likely, as only very
few graves are known showing cremation in the first period
of the Bronze Age, and these have a distinctive character. For
example, in the coffin of a young woman buried at Egtved
there was a bundle containing the burnt bones of a child
aged eight or nine, and in a stone coffin of the same period at

Erslev on Mors a heap of burnt human bones was found at the feet of the buried woman. In both these cases the cremation of a human being may have been a special sacrifice to the person buried. In the second part of the Early Bronze Age, 1,139 inhumation graves are known and only 34 graves containing burnt bones, and in the third part, 1,315 inhumation graves and 336 cremation graves; after that, in the succeeding stage of the Bronze Age, inhumation graves are completely super- seded by cremation. So that, even though cremation can be traced through a long period, the decisive change-over took place during a relatively short space of time, and is therefore undoubtedly connected with a complete revolution in reli- gious ideas ushering in the period we call the Late Bronze Age. The dead no longer had their dwelling-place in the burial mounds, but instead the soul was freed from the body with the help of fire, and flew to a distant land of the dead, where it was reborn. We find this explanation given in the funeral hymns of the Hindus, which tell us that fire, as the servant of God, conveys the dead to the kingdom where gods and ancestors dwell. The same belief occurs amongst the Indian tribes of the Pacific coast of America, who also practise cremation:

'Unless the body is burnt the soul will never reach the land of the dead' . . . 'In the hot smoke it rises up to the shining sun to rejoice in its warmth and light; then it flies away to the happy land in the west.'

A find in a cremation grave in Himmerland suggests that the survivors, in their concern for the dead, sought to assist this celestial flight. Mixed with the burnt bones of a young person were the burnt bones of the wings of at least six jack- daws and two crows, as well as two crows' feet. We cannot doubt the intention behind the laying of so many wings on the pyre along with the dead: the twelve small wings and four large ones were to bear the soul safely to the land of the dead.

The first example of cremation shows no change in grave goods or in structure of mound. The burnt bones, always carefully cleansed of charcoal from the pyre, are strewn evenly along the bottom of the spacious oak coffin or man-sized stone coffin and covered with the dead person's clothes, weapons and ornaments, which are not marked by fire and therefore have not been on the funeral pyre. Such cremation graves are always covered by a large mound. It was soon realized, however, that both the grave itself and the mound above it could be made smaller, both because the cremated bones took up less space, and the large grave goods gradually fell out of use. In the end stone coffins became quite small, oak coffins were replaced by caskets of wood or bark, and the magnificent bronze swords by small replicas, while the ornaments were restricted to a few toilet articles: a small button, rings and such-like. At the same time a completely new type of grave came into use, the funeral urn of baked clay, which was large enough to take both the cremated bones and the grave goods. Often the large mounds of the Early Bronze Age were chosen for depositing these various forms of cremation grave, a hole being simply dug in the mound and the cremated bones in their container or small stone coffin placed inside and the hole covered over again. It was nearly always the south or east side that was chosen for this purpose. The north side was avoided altogether. This was the shadow side, where the sun's rays hardly penetrated, where darkness brooded.

New grave mounds were constantly being built, however, as was in many cases necessary, because in the Late Bronze Age people from many areas moved further inland—into parts where Bronze Age peoples had never lived before. Late Bronze Age mounds are almost always small, usually only half a metre or a metre high and five to ten metres across, but they are clustered together in larger groups than in the Early Bronze Age. Burial mounds with a diameter of ten to fifteen metres and a height of one and a half to two metres were only rarely built, but both these and the much smaller mounds sometimes contain a number of cremation graves, the largest as many as twenty. As in earlier times, the mounds contain stone circles surrounding the graves, one single one

58   Stone circle with monolith in Frejlev Forest on Lolland

or a number of concentric circles of which the outer one,
marking the foot of the mound, is sometimes visible.

Burial mounds from the second half of the Bronze Age, the
Late Bronze Age, *c.* 900 to 450 B.C., are now hardly to be
found except in woodland and uncultivated areas. Where the
plough has moved backwards and forwards through the centuries, every trace above ground has been long ago destroyed
because the mounds were so small. Every now and then stone

circles are taken up, urns and cremation graves broken up and scattered by the ploughshare. It has happened, however, that the kerb stones round a small mound have protected it from complete demolition, as on the little island of Venø in Limfjord, where the story goes that a smith used to live in a low mound known as Sorthøj and broke people's ploughshares with his hammer if they came too close to the foot of it. It was obviously the kerb stones that broke the points of intrusive ploughs.

It is not possible to assign a definite date to all the low and often quite insignificant burial mounds that are scattered all around in Danish woodlands, for similar mounds were built all the time from the Late Bronze Age right through the Iron Age, up to and into the Viking Age. Most of them, however, belong to the Late Bronze Age as excavations in various parts of the country have shown.

Late Bronze Age burial mounds are especially common in the woods of southern Denmark, where there are often so many together that they form positive cemeteries. In the forest of Guldborgland on Lolland, for example, and in the forest south-east of Maribo Søndersø there are about a hundred of these low mounds within a very limited area. Other large groups may be found in many other wooded areas of Lolland-Falster. Frejlev Forest, where many ancient monuments lie concealed, including round and long dolmens, passage graves and a great many quite low mounds surrounded by stone circles, is well worth a visit. Many of the small mounds and stone circles have a large upright stone, a monolith, standing beside them. On the island of Møn, the forest of Klinteskoven in particular contains a great many small burial mounds. There is a group standing by itself in Busene Have, a small wood at the southernmost tip of Høje Møn facing the Baltic. This wood is antiquity itself. Along the rocky shore stand dark fir-trees and crab-apples, behind are old gnarled oaks in a dense undergrowth of hazel and thorn bushes, concealed among which are ten burial mounds arranged in a semi-circle, all with low kerb stones. On

59 *and* 60   Stone circle graves unearthed at Hostrup on
Røsnæs, and Hårbølle Hestehave on Møn

61 *and* 62   Urn graves discovered in mounds at Bøgeskov
in Houlbjerg Hundred, Central Jutland, and at Grurup in Thy

Zealand there are numerous groups of Late Bronze Age mounds in the woods under Næsbyholm on Tystrup Lake, and on Stevns in Gjorslev Bøgeskov and on the Asnæs peninsula near Kalundborg. On Langeland these low mounds are preserved in the *stubhaver*, parcelled-out areas overgrown with scrub which are often left lying between the cultivated lands belonging to the various villages. That these areas have been left uncultivated since the Bronze Age is doubtless due in part to the stone-filled graves, which have made cultivation difficult. It is not easy to pick out the mounds in this *stubhaver* wilderness, of which only a twelfth part is cut annually for distribution among the owners. The most accessible is a *stub* close to the road through Lisse Fen, in which there are more than ten graves. In the rest of Denmark the low Late Bronze Age mounds are scattered and more difficult to recognize, as for example on Als and in North Jutland where many similar mounds were built in the Late Iron Age. In Central and West Jutland they are liable to be confused with the Battle-axe people's mounds and with mounds formed naturally by drifting sand. The many groups of mounds in the coastal areas show once more that this was where the trading stations were in the Late Bronze Age too, and that all the time that bronze was the most important material for weapons and tools it had to be imported from overseas.

63   Ship pictures, sun symbols and footprint figures on the
Madsebakke rock surface at Allinge on Bornholm

IX Cup Marks and Rock Engravings

Sacred Signs of the Bronze Age

When the sun stands low in the sky and shadows are long, a wealth of pits, lines and figures is revealed on certain stones as its rays strike against them. These stone pictures, which are only barely visible in ordinary daylight and in addition are almost always overgrown with lichen of various shades of grey, brown and yellow, are most often the work of nature— lines carved on boulders by glaciers, weatherings that have revealed the inner structure on the surface, or even the marks of ploughshares and other agricultural implements. Just occasionally, however, the pictures on a stone are not all nature's work but were carved by men in ancient times; these are known in Danish as *helleristninger,* because they were carved or *ristet* on *heller*: flat stones or smooth rock surfaces. Pits made by man are known on at least five hundred glacial boulders, while other pictures have only been found on a hundred loose stones and a few solid rock faces on Bornholm, where they are accompanied by a great many cup marks.

The cup mark is a circular, cup-shaped hollow cut into a block of stone and normally from four to six centimetres across and two to eight centimetres deep. Where several occur together, certain ones are usually considerably larger and deeper than the others—which are grouped round the larger ones, often in a circle so as to form a rosette. The number of cup marks on each individual block of stone varies considerably. There may be just a few together or anything up to about fifty, occasionally even more, either concentrated together like part of the Milky Way or evenly distributed like an astronomical chart on one or more surfaces of the boulder. They have therefore even been interpreted, somewhat fancifully, as ancient astronomical charts.

The cup mark, carved into loose boulders or fixed rock faces, extends over wide areas in most parts of the world. In India it is the symbol of fertility and the female sex sign, which has led to its being interpreted as the image of the actual procreative urge or as a representation of the hollow centre of a plant stalk. The cup mark has been explained ever since the beginnings of archaeological research in a variety of ways: for example, as a map of burial mounds or—where it is found in conjunction with ship designs—as a mooring post. In view of its similarity to the hole made by rotating a stick to strike fire, it has been regarded as a sacred symbol for fire; and where the marks form a circle round a larger hole, as an image of the sun; while scattered cup marks have been interpreted as a symbol of the sun inspired by the patches of sunlight in a wood on a summer's day when the foliage is at its thickest. In some parts of Sweden cup marks are known as elves' mills, and on special festivals offerings such as small coins, scraps of fat, tiny dolls, pins and so forth are laid in them right up to the present day. In Denmark when just a few of them appear on some huge monolith they are often popularly known as the fingermarks of a troll who flung the stone long ago at some particular church building. In a different school of interpretation, the hole itself is not regarded as important but its significance lies in the powdered stone that was produced when it was hollowed out, and through which was imparted some of the strength that was concentrated in the stone and gave fertility and happiness. This idea still lives on in France, where the sick and impotent bore holes in, among other things, St. Loup's stone at the church of Voanas, to be cured of fever and have their vital strength renewed.

64 *and* 65 Stones with cup marks picked out with chalk
from Stensgård in Vestermarie on Bornholm, and Nielstrup
in Djursland

The cup mark is carved all through the Bronze Age as a sacred sign, after which it falls out of use in the official faith. Owing to the simplicity of the form it is almost always impossible to determine the date of a stone with cup marks within the millennium covered by the Bronze Age, unless it is found in combination with other things by which it can be dated. The oldest stones, however, seem to have a more scattered distribution of the marks, which in the later Bronze Age are concentrated into a closer pattern with the individual hollows being frequently connected by furrows.

It is clear that the cup mark comes into use in the closing stage of the Stone Age, when it appears on stones used in building the large stone burial chambers and, in common with many other features, marks the threshold of the Bronze Age. It is equally clear that the importance of this simple sign disappears with the Bronze Age, with whose religion it is connected. With the Iron Age gods it has little power, even though its day is not altogether past. It continues as a protective sign in popular belief, a sign that liberates the power of the stone in the powder that is made when it is carved out.

The cup mark is often found on the building stones of the megalithic graves, the dolmens and passage graves, and here almost exclusively on the top of the cover-stone. It appears very rarely on the kerb stones or the side stones of the chambers or on the threshold stone. The vast majority of the marks are thus found on stones that lay exposed during the Bronze Age, with which the cup marks on these stone graves must be associated. Where they are found on the inside of the stone chamber, they must have been carved in connection with later burials in the Bronze Age which have been established in several cases. In some the cover-stone of a passage grave has been lifted and a Bronze Age tree-trunk coffin introduced into the actual chamber.

Many stones show different kinds of pittings that may easily be mistaken by the inexpert for real cup marks. With a number of stones the surface is completely covered with quite small holes not more than a quarter to half a centimetre across

66   Stone from Debel on Fuur with cup marks, human
figures and crosses

67 Wheel-crosses and cup marks on a stone in a field at
Lille Strandbygård in South Bornholm

and barely as deep, but with vertical or sometimes convex sides. They look like marks of raindrops or hailstones striking violently against the stone when it was of a softer consistency. These are nature's work. It is only by their smallness and their irregular shape that they can be distinguished from the real cup marks, which are completely circular and are incised by means of a fist-sized stone of some hard, flinty material, usually quartzite. Other 'false' cup marks, made by human hand, may be found on stones which 'Jens Vejmand' (the roadmender) used as a work-bench for breaking up stones. The resulting cup-shaped hollows are always much larger than cup marks, but not very deep, and there are usually three or four of them together, covering one end or two opposite flat ends of a block of stone that is usually triangular in shape with rounded corners, and no larger than a grown man could easily hold between his legs when sitting down. Old cleaving marks are sometimes also mistaken for cup marks. It is characteristic of these marks that they are arranged in rows, are rectangular with rounded corners, and are very deep. They belong to the time before gunpowder and dynamite came into general use for splitting stones. Wedges of dry wood, usually alder, were driven into the rectangular holes and then water was poured over the wood which immediately began to swell, splitting the stone with irresistible force in the direction marked out by the holes.

With the coming of metal and of the traders and smiths who brought it, new religious ideas entered the country— among them those that are connected with the cup marks. The paths of this simple sign may be traced westwards to Holland and Ireland, along the Atlantic coast of Europe and thence into the Mediterranean area, where it is found on megalithic graves. In the east it runs to ground in Syria, the countries around the Arabian Gulf and India, in the northern parts of which it is still regarded to this day as the female sex symbol, as I have said, often seen in conjunction with the symbol of manly strength, the linga. The women make offerings in the cup marks of the yellow corollas of flowers for fertility and happiness. No doubt the marks had the same general significance with us, even though they may also have served other religious purposes.

The cup mark is sometimes found in Denmark in combination with other signs and images in the rock engravings representing people, animals, ships, waggons, weapons, hands, foot-marks and wheels, all in a highly simplified form. They are carved into smaller blocks of stone, sometimes the cover-stones of dolmens. Only on Bornholm are large picture-surfaces, comprising a number of figures and signs, found on the ice-grooved rocks. Even richer and more varied are the pictures reflecting essential aspects of the Bronze Age religion on the huge rock surfaces of Sweden and Norway, which also carry still older representations from the days of the hunting peoples, with a quite different content.

The hunting people's pictures of the Early Stone Age show the animals they hoped to kill while hunting. The animals are therefore represented in a naturalistic style, so that there shall be no doubt as to their identity. Those most frequently depicted are the large land game animals such as the elk, reindeer, stag and bear. Sea creatures were also of importance in the hunting people's existence and whales, halibut and salmon may be seen. The depicting of these animals gave the hunters power over them, but at the same time it created a new, long life for the species on the rock surface so that its continued existence was ensured for future hunters. The earliest animal pictures are the most faithful to nature and are skilfully outlined in life size or even a little larger. Gradually as the hunting magic changed and became more abstract, the animal pictures were simplified and stylized, though never beyond the point of being recognizable. This kind of representation is not known in Denmark, where animal pictures may possibly have been drawn on the sand of the seashore or similar places prior to hunting.

Whereas the hunting people's pictures tell of hunting and fishing and the religion that was associated with these activities, the Bronze Age rock engravings reflect the life of a

68   Hand-sign on stone from Torup Mensalgård in North Funen

69 *and* 70   Ship pictures and foot-marks on rocks at Brogård
and Storløkkebakken in North Bornholm

trading community and its foundations in seafaring, agriculture and stock-rearing. Important things now were the sun and fertility, to ensure the ripening of the corn and the propagation of domestic animals; but the most important thing of all was good fortune at sea, which was to the Bronze Age people 'the path to fame and power'. It was the ship that held together the trading stations separated by the Sounds and Belts, seas and lakes, and united the Scandinavian cultural area in the Bronze Age. No other subject therefore, if we except the simple symbol of the cup mark, is more universally represented in Bronze Age rock carvings and other pictorial representations all over Scandinavia. We see the simplified outline of a very characteristic type of ship with high prow and horn-shaped elongations of the keel timber, which sometimes rises up to form high peaks at each end. There are ships carved on loose boulders from Jutland, Funen and Zealand, all of which have been taken to museums, but apart from that there are two on the cover-stones of dolmens. On Bornholm whole fleets set sail from the flat rock surfaces.

Next to the ship, the commonest Bronze Age symbol is the wheel. It may have four or eight spokes and, in common with the simple circle without a cross, symbolizes both the sun and the waggon. Foot-marks, single or in pairs, sometimes representing a naked foot, and sometimes one wearing a moccasin, are found either by themselves or in combination with cup marks or ships. Whereas the ship is characteristic of the Scandinavian Bronze Age area, the wheel and footprint are found in Western Europe. It is possible that both symbols, and the beliefs associated with them, were brought to Denmark at the same time as the cup mark. Sun-worship, however, is much older, having been brought to Denmark by the Battle-axe people and their still earlier predecessors from Eastern Europe at the beginning of the Late Stone Age. The footprint was in itself a powerful symbol of fertility and good fortune and also used for averting evil.

A group of engravings on some ten pieces of rock shows a

hand with outstretched fingers pointing in four directions, with a stump of arm which may be intersected by a cross-stroke. This representation, which is practically only known in Zealand and belongs to the beginning of the Late Bronze Age, is associated with cremation graves, cut into the cover or side stones of the small stone coffin that held the burnt bones. The numerical value of this symbol is nine and it may therefore possibly reflect a belief in re-birth, and the nine months between conception and birth, which accompanied the cremation custom north from the lands to the south-east.

Most of the Danish rock engravings are cut into smallish boulders and have therefore been taken to museums all over the country. The largest rock engravings, however, can still be seen in their original position. That applies, of course, to those on Bornholm, which are cut into the bedrock. The largest rock carving in Denmark is cut into Madsebakke, a north-west facing rock surface behind the town of Allinge. On this may be seen more than ten ships, among them one carrying a horse-drawn sun, and a wheel-cross surrounded by cup marks, footprint figures, curved lines and a great many cup marks, some of which are surrounded by a circle. The surface of the rock is somewhat weathered. As most of the pictures are not deeply cut, they can usually only be seen at all clearly in the slanting light of early morning or at sunset. There were also two flat rock surfaces, quite close to Madse-bakke, with some very fine ship pictures on them and a single figure of a man carrying a spear, but both were ruthlessly blasted away some fifty years ago. There is another rock engraving showing various ships, cup marks and a footprint, in which the individual toes are indicated by hollows of different sizes, on a slightly curved and smooth-worn rock surface known as Storløkkebakke. From it there is a magnificent view over North Bornholm and the sea, right over to the Swedish coast. It lies a few hundred metres east of Allinge railway station. An old cleavage edge runs almost right up to the tip of the prow of a large ship picture, the largest and finest of all the Danish rock-engraved ships. Just south of

71   Borrebjerg with an approach ramp at Sejrby on Sejrø

Brogård, on the heights a few kilometres south of Allinge and close to the road to Hasle, is a small curved rock surface projecting out of a thicket halfway across the road to a farm. From this five ships sail forth. Two more rocks with ship pictures are preserved in this part of North Bornholm. In the south of the island there is a flat rock with twelve wheel-crosses and a number of cup marks on it, in the middle of a field below Lille Strandbygård east of Arnager. The largest of the crosses has a double circle and two hornlike projections of the form familiar to us from the bronze helmets of the time.

On Zealand there are two ship pictures surrounded by cup marks carved into the cover-stone of a dolmen chamber at Kirke Hyllinge close to the Great Belt. Wheel-crosses and cup marks may be seen on a stone that has been incorporated as building material into the tower of Sigersted church at Ringsted; also on a stone built into the nave of Asnæs church in Ods Hundred. A sill stone in the porch of Såby church, between Roskilde and Holbæk, has a ship picture surrounded by a number of cup marks. Mention must also be made of two wheel-crosses on a building-stone in the chamber of the magnificent passage grave on the hillside above Kirke Helsinge, with its view over Reersø lake to the island of Funen, and a stone step with a wheel-cross in the porch of Taps church south of Kolding. There is a special story attached to a stone with three pairs of wheel-crosses standing on the boundary of a field at Venslev in Horns Hundred. It got in the way of the field work, so it was decided to blast it away, regardless of the signs it was known to bear. But the powers protected their sacred stone. When the charge went off, the whole stone flew up undamaged into the air and came down again with the pictures upside down. The men vowed never to touch it again. A scar running across the wheel-crosses is all that remains to be seen of this attack by humans on a three-thousand-year-old picture stone.

There must undoubtedly be many other stones with cup marks and other carvings on them all over the country that have not yet been discovered. Everyone who goes about in woods and fields and along old stone walls has the chance of making some new discovery if he keeps his eyes open—and the light is in the right direction. One of the most exciting stones, with ship pictures, sun symbols and horses on it, was discovered about twenty years ago by a young electrician out for a Sunday walk in Dyrehaven, at a place where thousands of people pass by every year. But the fact remains that when stones lie out in the open, their surfaces gradually wear away so that even carvings which were formerly quite clear have now almost completely disappeared. This applies, for example, to a fleet of ships and two wheel-crosses on the cover-stone of the lovely dolmen chamber at Herrestrup in Ods Hundred, that was discovered and drawn a good hundred years ago, but can now hardly be made out even in the most favourable lighting conditions.

A few isolated mounds of earth that lie in the open countryside like huge burial mounds, but that are natural formations, were probably used in the Bronze Age as assembly places. Several of them have a wide processional road or ramp cut into their side, leading from the surrounding country up to the top of the hill. One can imagine religious processions moving along this ramp to the flat top, which served as a stage for religious ceremonies and worship of the gods. Such mounds are still in existence at Havegård near Illebølle on Langeland, and in Nymarkshaven by Egeskov manor on Funen. Borgbjerg mound at Boeslunde north of Skælskør had a similar ramp. The rich finds made on its sides show that this mound was a sacred place in the Bronze Age. It was here that two sets of finds were made in the middle of the last century, comprising six magnificent gold vessels, two large bowls, two scoops with handles adorned with horses' heads and two beakers, obviously sacrificial gifts to the divinity of the place in the Bronze Age. The mound is now largely destroyed. The ramp is gone, except for a few vestiges to the south, and very little remains of the original flat top. Gravel pits have eaten into the hill from every side, and buildings have crept up close beside it. Now this ancient sacred place has been converted into a memorial garden for F. J. Borgbjerg, whose family took its name from the place, a late minister whose grandfather made one of the gold finds that raised the family from rags to riches. Borgbjerg is still worth a visit. The surroundings seem to be characteristic of a Bronze Age sanctuary. The huge bank lies like a broad brow exposed to the sky and the sun, two of the powerful divinities of the age. The view from the top is magnificent, taking in South-West Jutland, the Great Belt and the Småland Sea across to the distant coasts of Funen and Langeland.

Boeslunde is an example of the way churches were built in early Christian times at old places of sacrifice to which all roads led, and where people were accustomed to assemble. Boeslunde church lies to the east of the hill, over the top of which the windows of its tower look out to the sea. The miraculous well, the Spring of the Holy Cross, which was very famous in the Middle Ages when the sick used to visit it, and which may have had significance in antiquity too, lies at the foot of the hill. Nowadays, people go to the old public house on the other side of the road.

Rather later finds, dating from the beginning of the Iron Age, have been made on two equally imposing hills on the island of Sejrø: Borrebjerg and Bygbjerg, both of which have terrace-like ramps cut out of their sides. Other banks of a similar nature, dominating land and sea to the horizon, are Dyret at Onsbjerg on Samsø and Ellemandsbjerget on Helgenæs, while Dagbjerg Dås can offer only extensive views of the old moorland of Blicher. On none of these three latter banks have finds been made or excavations carried out linking them definitely with antiquity, but they are all of so distinctive a character that they must have been sacred places, not least in the Bronze Age.

X Iron Age Graves

A New Period

Iron Age burial mounds are rarely seen in the Danish land-scape. During the fifteen hundred years, up to the beginning of historical time in about the year A.D. 1000, which this period comprises, most of the graves were laid in level ground, often a great many together as in present-day cemeteries. These graves were often covered with low hillocks that have long since been levelled out by cultivation. Whatever else may have been used to mark the place of the simple grave, such as for example a small wooden grave-house, has long disappeared. Even though large burial mounds never ceased to be built right through the Iron Age, this form of burial was not general. Mounds were only erected for particularly outstanding people. While one can count Bronze Age burial mounds in thousands, the large Iron Age mounds may be numbered in tens. In appearance they are distinguishable from the rounded mounds of earlier times by having a flat top.

The Iron Age was in many respects a new period. A decisive difference between the Bronze and the Iron Ages is that iron, the most important utility material, could be produced at home, whereas every single ounce of bronze had to be im-ported from overseas. With the possibility of the domestic production of iron, a new and independent basis was created for the peasant culture, while at the same time the Bronze Age trading families received a severe blow, for their power had been so largely built up on the import of metals. All over the

163

72   Kong Ran's Mound in Randbøl churchyard,
in Central Jutland

country, wherever the necessary raw material, bog iron ore, was available for iron production, people learnt to use it very quickly. Many village communities were consequently able to make themselves independent of the old ruling class and become self-supporting. Another contributory factor in this development may have been the expansion of the Celtic tribes in Central Europe which severed the master class's trade communications with the Mediterranean for a time.

Iron production seems to have increased at a very great rate. This is not, however, to be deduced from any abundance of iron articles in the earliest finds, for these on the contrary are poor in iron—which may be due among other things to the modest scale of the grave goods. But the use of iron for weapons and tools may be assumed from the enormous quantities of bronze used for ornaments. Collars and arm rings increased out of all proportion in size and weight in the last stage of the Bronze Age and the beginning of the Iron Age. That may reflect the increasing home production of iron: more and more bronze was left over for ornaments as weapons and tools came increasingly to be made of iron.

A change of climate occurred at the beginning of the Iron Age, and over three periods of two to three hundred years it grew colder and moister. The first cooler period began about the year 500 B.C., the second about the time of the birth of Christ, and the third about A.D. 600. All through the Bronze Age the weather had been warm and dry, with only one short moister period. The beech, which had appeared in the Stone Age woods at the time of the first peasants, had led a solitary existence in forest life since then. Now it spread more and more, becoming in the end the predominant and forest-forming tree. The moist, chilly weather also caused the raised bogs to spread. These consist of millions of small mosses which absorb rain water and consequently expand steadily in humid periods. The foundations of our largest raised bogs, the wild bogs, were laid at that time. Since then they have spread unchecked and now cover villages, fields and burial mounds of the Early Iron Age. These mosses are known as sphagnum and have a reddish appearance, which has given rise to the popular name 'dog's flesh' for the moss layer of this period, easily distinguishable from the earlier brownish and denser peat layer.

The wet weather also left its mark on the country in another way. The rain washed out the nutrients from the upper layers of soil, in particular the lime, and this favoured the growth of heather. From now on, the heather spread, too quickly for the forests that had until then been the first to take over abandoned ground. Once it had got a hold, there was no contending with it and the land grew increasingly bare of trees. People had to resort to peat cutting to ensure they had sufficient fuel. Even if this change in climate undoubtedly made living conditions in some places harder for the population, it also made a significant contribution, for it furthered to a high degree the formation of bog iron ore in bogs and low-lying ground—so that all through the remainder of the Iron Age there was plenty of raw material for the production of iron. One can often see quite plainly today, in ploughed land along the Jutland river valleys, black patches full of charcoal and fragments of slag from the iron ore, marking the places where the old iron extraction was carried on. Another effect of the greater rainfall was that large areas round the edges of the hills in Central and West Jutland could now be taken in for cultivation and pastureland. Early Iron Age villages also spread into previously uninhabited areas, which had lain waste in the dry climate of the Bronze Age.

Iron Age forest landscapes may be seen in Denmark where the beech has been allowed to grow freely and form great knotted trunks and huge crowns, in striking contrast to our beautifully tended present-day beech forests which are more like colonnades. There is a characteristic Iron Age forest on Knudshoved Point that runs from Vordingborg far out into the Småland Sea west of Næstved. The Iron Age landscape begins after one has passed Knudsskov Gård and the stony reef of Draget. Tall beeches on the high rocks along the narrow northern shore mirror their broad crowns in the sea. On the headland behind, weathered oaks, domed lime trees and crab-apple, hawthorn and maple, grow among the beeches. Young animals graze free, as in the olden days, in glades between the groups of trees. Further on towards Knudshoved, the vegetation takes us back to the tundra period.

In burial customs, there is no break in the transition period from the Bronze Age to the Iron Age, only an extension and more general acceptance of cremation. Urns containing simply the burnt bones are deposited now, as previously, under low mounds, surrounded by circles of smallish stones. In South Jutland several hundred of these small mounds or hillocks may be found together forming extensive burial grounds. The smallest hillocks are not more than about a metre across and twenty to thirty centimetres high. They can reach a height of as much as half a metre and a width of four to five metres. One of the largest of these burial places, now completely destroyed, was at Årre near Varde, and contained more than a thousand hillocks. It is still possible to discover small burial grounds in these areas, where the heath maintains its hold. Further north in Jutland the urn burials are covered with circular patches of stones about ten metres across. In heath-covered ground they look like small raised patches, but on cultivated ground they are not visible once the stones have gradually been ploughed up. Untouched graves, therefore, are mostly only to be found under flat ground or inserted into the top or side of a large Bronze Age mound. The funerary patch, a pit in the ground into which the burnt bones were scraped together with remains from the funeral pyre, is particularly characteristic of Bornholm. The grave goods are few, consisting mostly of ornaments and toilet articles, and frequently are not found except in the form of burnt remains of metal, having accompanied their owner on to the funeral pyre.

The whole of the Early Iron Age from about the year 400 B.C. to the birth of Christ is known as the Celtic Iron Age, because the Scandinavian cultural area was at that time strongly under the influence of the great Celtic empires of

Central Europe. Towards the end of this period inhumation appears again and the graves are more richly furnished. The first four centuries A.D. come under the influence of the Roman Empire, which had gradually extended its frontiers to the Rhine. This period is therefore known as the Roman Iron Age, when cremation falls very much into disuse, though without completely disappearing. Burials in level ground now became usual, with the dead resting in plank coffins surrounded by their grave goods, that, apart from ornaments and toilet articles, consist mostly of a rich spread of food and drink in home-made clay vessels or costly imported Roman industrial art products of bronze, silver or glass. The dead now lie at table in their graves with their table service, food and drink set out before them, just as the Romans did in life.

In North Jutland, Vendsyssel and Himmerland there are also—in addition to the wooden coffins—large stone-built graves which were often used for more than one burial. These stone coffins are frequently very spacious, up to two metres in each direction inside and from one to one and a half metres high. They are built of heavy upright side stones, on top of which rests a layer of smaller horizontal stones, sloping inwards slightly over the burial chamber so that the heavy, flat cover-stone which forms the roof of the grave reaches from side to side more easily. This structure gives the grave a vaulted effect, a false dome, resembling that of the passage graves. A number of these impressive stone graves of the Roman Iron Age have been uncovered on their original sites. There are eight of them in Hjørring new cemetery south of the crematorium, but without their cover-stones, which had been removed before the excavation; and there is one completely preserved at Løvel Vandmølle north of Viborg, on a hill with a wide view over Skalså valley.

The large number of grave finds of the Roman Iron Age may be divided into two different kinds, of which one is mainly found on the Islands, the other on Jutland.

On the Islands the graves are always in small groups, never more than five or six together, and are frequently very richly furnished with magnificent table services of Roman imported ware. In Jutland, on the other hand, the graves are mostly gathered together in large burial grounds containing sometimes several hundred graves, arranged in rows like our present-day cemeteries. Their furniture is home-made clay pottery, usually finely shaped and well decorated, excellent quality hand-made ware. There is not much difference between the richest and the poorest in the same burial ground. Everything points to a substantial level of prosperity in domestic products.

This difference between the graves in Jutland and the Islands undoubtedly reflects a corresponding difference in social conditions, which may be due to iron. The rich east Danish graves may be those of a master people, who ruled over a numerous lower class and controlled the Iron Age trade. That is how they were able to acquire all the fine articles of bronze, silver, gold and glass. The Jutland burial grounds, by contrast, indicate a well-to-do peasant community, whose power and independence were due to the fact that bog iron ore could be found all over Jutland, so that every village community could provide itself with the necessary raw materials for tools and weapons. It should be noted in this connection that all the graves in which the dead were provided with forged equipment, the smiths' graves, are to be found within the same areas of Jutland as the large burial grounds, all of them areas in which conditions were favourable to the home production of iron.

The number of inhumation graves in the individual burial grounds of Jutland decreases considerably in the second half of the Roman Iron Age. It looks as though power had become concentrated in a smaller number of families, as on the Islands. We know that conditions were unsettled, in this and the following period, from the weapon burials and the large quantities of sacrificial weapons offered. Warlike developments may have altered social conditions and it is clear that many of the Jutland villages and burial places were abandoned just at the beginning of the Late Roman Iron Age.

Later in the Iron Age cremation again became general, and the graves so insignificant that they have only survived under particularly favourable conditions. As grave goods decreased simultaneously and almost completely disappear in the period known as the Germanic Iron Age and until the Viking Period, which begins *c*. A.D. 800, only a small number of graves of this period are known; though at the same time there is an increase in the rich finds of gold and valuable articles deposited in the ground and in bogs outside graves. This corresponds with the statement by Snorri Sturlason, the Icelandic historian, in the *Ynglingesaga*, that Odin decreed 'that all the dead should be burnt and all their possessions put on the pyre with them', and 'that everyone should come to Valhalla with as much treasure as he had had with him on the pyre, and he should also enjoy that which he had himself buried in the ground'.

There are graves of this period at Donbæk, west of Frederikshavn in Vendsyssel. They lie grouped together in a burial ground on a slope which runs down from the uplands to the beautiful valley of Bangsbo. The burial ground is overgrown with wild roses, brambles, blackthorn and old windswept trees, that give the place a strange atmosphere of antiquity. It had already been in use during the Celtic and Roman Iron Ages, with which most of the sixty-two grave mounds must be associated. The rest are low, circular or elongated hillocks, surrounded by stones, covering cremation graves the furniture of which is ornaments and toilet articles that have been burnt on the funeral pyre. There is another burial place of the same period in the northern part of Store Vildmose. Most of the mounds are now covered with sphagnum peat which has gradually grown up over them and also conceals houses and fields of the Early Iron Age. Using the finds in the graves as a basis, one can follow the constantly increasing size of the bog. The mounds nearer the centre are Early Roman Iron Age, whereas those at the edge further north are three to four hundred years later. The mounds were formerly completely hidden by layers of moss, but with

73 *and* 74 Jutland clay-vessel grave at Lisbjerg in Århus,
and stone grave at Bangsbo in Frederikshavn

cultivation the surface of the bog sank by up to a couple of metres, so that the mounds shot up everywhere like toadstools.

In the south of Denmark, on Als, the forest has preserved two burial grounds that were previously believed to be Late Bronze Age, but are actually Germanic Iron Age. Some forty low mounds lie clustered together at Havrekoppel by the open Fynshav coast, and another twenty on a slope behind Nygård, the forest rangers' station. Only two of the mounds are more than a metre high and six to seven metres across. The others are about twenty to thirty centimetres high and two metres across. They have all been surrounded by stone circles and all but two cover burnt patches caused by the funeral pyre. Five have a larger stone in the centre, and a few a pile of stones as well.

Mound graves of widely differing size and graves in level ground, both with inhumation and cremation, continue to be used into the final phase of prehistory, the Viking Age, which comprises the period from A.D. 800 to 1000. Large burial grounds of this time are known, particularly in North Jutland, for example on Ris Fattiggård at Torslev in Vendsyssel, where there were about a hundred grave mounds, large and small together, oval and round, and also twelve most unusual graves shaped like a three-pointed star. These star graves, which are now, with all the rest of the graves, completely destroyed and gone, measured from six to eight metres from the centre to one of the points and were surrounded by low kerb stones. This new Viking Age grave form is undoubtedly the result of influence from Sweden where similar graves frequently occurred both in the Viking Age and before.

The most important burial ground of the end of the prehistoric period is undoubtedly the one that has been excavated on Lindholm Høje at Nørresundby. Here vast quantities of drifting sand had covered the large burial ground, parts of a largish town and some ancient fields, thus preserving a magnificent site which is now open to visitors and under preservation order. Altogether about seven hundred graves have been investigated on this spot. Most of them are cremation graves surrounded by stones set in very varying shapes:

75 Stone circle surrounding burnt patch on burial place
at Donbæk near Frederikshavn

76 Urn graves under level ground at Errindlev on Falster

triangular, quadrilateral, circular, oval and pointed oval, sometimes with an upright stone in the centre. A few graves containing skeletons date from the sixth century, after which cremation prevails until the end of the Viking Age, when inhumation with richer grave furniture appears in about thirty graves. The cremation graves contain, apart from the cremated bones of the dead person, burnt grave goods that consist of ornaments, glass beads, knives, whetstones, playing-pieces from games, and bones of dogs and sheep, and more rarely of horses and cows. In the case of domestic animals, only the bones of the head and legs are found, so that one imagines that the fleshier parts were consumed at a great funeral feast. The sand invaded the burial ground from the very beginning. Gradually it became covered with a layer of sand four metres thick in some places. The graves therefore lie at different heights, at times completely or partially covering other graves.

There are about a hundred and fifty Viking Age cremation patches on Lindholm Høje surrounded by a framework of stones in a pointed oval shape, which are known as stone ships because, with their curved sides and tall stones at prow and stern, they resemble a real Viking ship. These stone ships are known from many parts of the country and are nearly always found in the vicinity of water, beside rivers and fjords and in many cases beside small lakes. A stone ship found on the edge of a mound at Lugnaro in Halland shows that they had already come into use in the Bronze Age, when the ship was sacred. The Lugnaro ship might well be intended to carry the dead man, whose cremated bones lay in a burial urn outside the ship to the south, to the kingdom of the dead.

There were originally some fifty stone ships on Bornholm. The same number is known in the rest of Denmark, to which must be added the hundred and fifty from Lindholm Høje. The largest Bornholm fleet was at Egely in the eastern part of the parish of Åker. This consists of eight ships. Seven of them lie side by side, but the eighth sails by itself in the wake of one of the ships of the line. They are 12.5–31.5 metres long,

77   Stone ships and stone circles on Lindholm Høje at
Nørresundby

orientated north-west to south-east, and lie close to a burial
ground containing more than a hundred cairns. There is
another collection around Enesbjerg by the slope of Højlyngen, east-north-east of Vestermarie church. A larger vessel
and a dinghy lie up on the hill itself among the cairns. These
are 29 and 8 metres long and 4.4 and 2.2 metres wide respectively. At the foot of the hill are three long ships and two

smaller boats. There is another stone ship with a tall prow close to the sea beside the road north of Listed. The other Bornholm ships are either badly damaged or completely destroyed. Some of them have been excavated, but the finds were very insubstantial, only a few fragments of clay vessels, cremated bones and pieces of charcoal, which show them to have been burial ships. These things do not allow of any definite dating, but it is probable that the Bornholm stone ships date from the end of the Late Bronze Age and should be seen in connection with the stone ships on Gotland, where there are more than fifty. Several of the Gotland stone ships contained urn graves of both the beginning and end of the Late Bronze Age.

A row of stones in a *stubhave* on Lissemose fen on Langeland had been thought to be part of a Bronze Age stone ship, but it is only the remains of a stone circle round a low Bronze Age mound, of which there are some ten thereabouts.

All the other stone ships of which we have knowledge in Denmark are probably Late Iron Age. There is a larger and a smaller one at the legendary Lejre on Zealand, on rising ground west of Kornerup river, but according to local tradition there used to be six here altogether. There was another, further north and to the west of the dried-up Lejre river, that is said to have measured a hundred and forty paces, and another east of Kornerup river. The large stone ship, which was about eighty metres long and the largest of all known examples, contained a number of inhumations of the Viking Age, to which period the stone ships must also be referred. A stone ship fourteen metres long with a tall prow stone is to be found on Ferslev Mark in Horns Hundred, but others on Zealand in Lindersvold Deer Park and on Stevns were long ago demolished.

There is a fine stone ship, whose tall prow stone has now been overturned, in the forest of Konappeskoven below Skovsgård on Langeland. One of the prow stones to the south has a circle cut in it, though this is certainly nothing to do with the stone ship and represents a later attempt to turn a prow stone into a millstone. A stone ship on the level strand at Draget on Avernakø was demolished as late as 1918.

A large stone ship at Glavendrup in the parish of Skamby on North Funen is of particular interest because it has associated with it a burial mound and a runic stone. The stone ship, which was about sixty metres long, is orientated east-west and at the east end runs up against a small Bronze Age mound, while at the west end it had as its prow stone the large runic stone which bears the longest runic inscription in Denmark, made up of a hundred and ten runic signs. It reads: 'Ragnhild set up this stone to Alle the Pale [?] the good lord of those who consecrated it, the revered thane of the housecarls [i.e. master of the housecarls]. Alle's sons made this memorial to their father and his wife to her husband, but Sote carved these runes to his master. May Thor consecrate these runes. May he be struck down who pounds [exercises violence against?] this stone or drags it away to be a memorial over another'. This fine monument of the Viking Age has been neglected through the years, but recently it has been carefully examined and put in order, and it stands now well cared for in a small grove of trees. It had of course been hoped that Alle's grave might have come to light. However, all that was found inside the rail of the stone ship was nine small cremation patches, though these may, of course, contain the burnt bones of some of Alle's oarsmen.

There is a similar monument, a stone ship forty-five metres long, between two Bronze Age mounds and with a runic stone as prow stone at the west end, on Bække Mark in South Jutland. The runic stone reads: 'Revne and Tobbe made this stone to their mother Vibrog.' Perhaps it is her deserted, empty grave that was found in an investigation in 1957 in about the middle of the ship, lying by the public highway, the old north-south Army Road of Jutland, of which sanded traces can be clearly seen at this point. The east-west orientation of the Glavendrup and Bække ships is unusual, for generally stone ships lie north-south, pointing to the sun at its noonday height and to the home of the gods in Valhalla, where the ships were to carry the dead. There is a legend that, after the battle of Bråvalla, Odin carried the dead in a golden ship to Valhalla in the south.

Other stone ships may be seen on the island of Hjarnø in Horsens Fjord where there was originally a fleet of twenty ships. Only the remains of half of that number are there now, among them King Hjarne's grave, which is about thirteen metres long. Ole Worm gives an exhaustive account of it in his *Monumenta Danica* of 1643, in which he relates among other things 'that a bull had dug out a sword from one of these mounds with his horns, and that a peasant, who had taken it, heard a voice in the night, exhorting him to put it back in its place if he did not wish a misfortune to befall him. This the man who had taken it into his keeping did not fail to do.' At a more recent investigation cremation patches were found in three of the stone ships. There are three stone ships and a large number of monoliths in among a great many small round and oval mounds in a large Viking Age burial ground at Højstrup, with a view over Tømmerby Fjord off Limfjorden. Two stone ships may be seen among small mounds on the level shore at Dynved on Als. Others, at Balle on Djursland, in Vejerslev parish beside the river Gudenåen, and on Gjenner Fjord in South Jutland have been demolished, the last-mentioned place having boasted twenty ships, large and small, that bore the name the Dannebrog Ships. The largest of all stone ships was probably the one at the old royal seat of Jelling, running up to the northern mound, Thyre's mound. Only the southern part is still distinguishable, partly covered by the south mound. It was about two hundred metres long and was truly kingly, and like the Glavendrup and Bække monuments it had a runic stone which related that it and the stone ship had been erected by King Gorm for his wife, Thyre.

No doubt the same idea lay behind the stone ship as behind the Iron Age ship burials where the dead were laid to rest or burnt in a real ship. They were vessels to sail across the waters that divided the land of the living from the kingdom of the

78 *and* 79   Stone ships at Lejre on Zealand and Glavendrup
in North Funen

dead. Real ship burials are known from numerous finds in Norway and Sweden, but in Denmark only three have been excavated, though that is enough to show that this peculiar burial custom was known all over the country at the close of the Iron Age. The first burial ship, a boat twelve metres long, was discovered in 1877 under level ground near Kongeåen at Brokær just north of Ribe, but the excavation left much to be desired and only the iron nails of the boat now remain. Another grave containing a boat five and a half metres long and one and a half wide was discovered in 1960 under a small bank at Flintingegård on Lolland, only a few metres from Guldborgsund. The boat was in a very bad state of preservation, consisting only of a few rusty ship's nails and an occasional stud. It had also been damaged by a grave that had been dug later at the northern end, and was surrounded by a stone circle. This had destroyed the upper part of the man's body and the grave goods, but the tip of an iron sword which had rested on his chest was found in the middle of the boat. A shield, of which only an iron boss remained in its original position, had been laid across the dead man's legs.

A real ship burial was found at Ladby east of Kertinge Nor early in the year 1935. It had been covered by a mound, but this had been long ago destroyed and ploughed over. One could still see, however, that there had been a long mound of considerable size there, about twenty metres in length, placed in a north-south direction. Of the ship itself, which was set on a boat-shaped, excavated bed in the subsoil, only the iron nails and the impress of its planks survived. Thanks to very careful excavation and conservation on the spot, the original shape of the ship was nevertheless successfully reproduced and preserved on the original site, where it may now be seen.

The Ladby ship was a considerable vessel about twenty-two metres in length. It is thus not much shorter than the magnificent, well-preserved Norwegian Viking ships, though it is not—as were many of them—a sea-going vessel with a high gunwale and great width. It was only about 2.85 metres wide, with low sides, but must have been capable of a tremendous speed when propelled by the thirty-two oarsmen for whom there were seats. Of oars and mast there was no trace. Even so, four iron shroud-rings on either side aft of midships show that it carried sails, though the sail must certainly have had to be lowered in a strong wind to prevent the ship capsizing. It was buried so deep that only the uppermost part of the bow and stern stood clear of the ground. Consequently the fittings they carried were still in place on the bows, which pointed south. These were a row of iron spirals that must undoubtedly have formed the neck scrolls of a terrifying dragon's head. Pointed iron spikes in the stern will have made up the dragon's tail.

The ship must have been drawn up from the south shore of Kertinge Nor on to a hill a couple of hundred metres to the south, and placed in the hollow which had already been dug, and which just about covered it. After the dead chieftain and all his equipment had been laid in place, the ship was covered over with a layer of planks laid crosswise, possibly tilted up on either side at the stern so as to form a roof-shaped burial chamber, as we know was done from the Norwegian Viking ships. Finally a great mound of earth was heaped over the vessel.

The stern of the ship, containing the burial chamber, had been plundered in earlier days for its valuables. The dead chieftain's bones had also been removed on this occasion. The robbers entered the stern over the port gunwale and hunted through everything. Only the contents of the bows failed to interest them. This rather suggests that the robbery took place at a time when the method of disposal of the valuables in a ship burial was still remembered. Almost all the Norwegian Viking ships have been plundered in a similar way, probably at a time when the family was no longer able to protect its burial monuments. Only fragments therefore remain of the magnificent equipment of the chieftain of Funen, in all more than five hundred small pieces of iron, bronze, gold, silver, tin, lead, flint, textiles, leather and down cushions. Only a few of these fragments were still recognizable, such as the

80 *and* 81   The Ladby ship in its glass case, and the burial
mound that covered it

remains of a spur, the boss of a shield and a wooden bucket with iron bands. Small pieces of gold and silver with filigree work were attached to a magnificent piece of clothing. Of the dead man himself there was no trace. On the larboard side, but outside the gunwale, lay a bundle of arrows, forty-five in all.

In the bow of the ship, which had not been touched by the robbers, was a large iron anchor with an iron chain ten metres long made of heavy oval links, which had been extended with a three-stranded bast rope. As was customary in ship burials in Sweden and Norway, the dead man's horses, eleven altogether, and the bones of a few dogs were also present. In among the animals' bones were the remains of splendid harness, an iron axe which may have been used to strike down the animals on the spot, and also a handsome knob of gilded bronze adorned with dragons' heads, which in conjunction with the other articles enables us to date the burial to the middle of the tenth century.

In the course of the excavation everything that belonged to the ship and all the major items of its contents were preserved as far as possible where they were found. The whole was then enclosed in a case of glass and steel and covered with a concrete vault, over which the mound was again thrown up. Even if the Ladby ship is far less well preserved than the Norwegian long-ships from Oseberg and Gokstad, it still has its own peculiar atmosphere of antiquity, because it stands on the spot where it was buried a thousand years ago, and has not, like the Norwegian ships, been removed to a museum. It is accessible all the year round to visitors, who are transported back to antiquity through a shaft in the side of the mound, from the light, open fjord-side in a matter of seconds.

The idea behind burial in a ship was certainly that it would carry the dead man, his gold and his possessions to Valhalla. Several hundred ship burials are known from Norway and Sweden from the end of the prehistoric period, some placed under mounds, some in natural hills or eminences close to a watercourse. A good many of the graves contain the burnt remains of the ship, which has sailed through the funeral pyre to the kingdom of the dead. Many of these ship and boat burials are several hundred years older than the Ladby ship and show how firmly rooted this burial custom was in our neighbouring countries. It was consequently at once suggested that it was a Norwegian or Swedish chieftain who was buried in the mound at Ladby. None of the articles found in the ship, however, had a foreign stamp to them, so there is reason to believe that it was a chieftain of Funen who was buried there according to foreign customs. This ship burial is associated with some ten skeleton graves containing both men's and women's equipment, and one solitary Viking Age cremation grave, which were discovered around the ship mound and are contemporary with it.

One of these graves contained a rich woman whose grave goods were two distinguished cup-shaped buckles and a splendid three-lobed ornament adorned with gripping beasts. It is probable, then, that all these graves under level ground together with the ship grave belonged to a chieftain's seat by Kerteminde Fjord.

Traces of ships have been found elsewhere. Ship's nails have been found in some of the previously mentioned cremation graves under low mounds on Als, but in such small numbers that it is more probable that old boat planks with the iron nails still in them were used in the cremation, than that whole ships accompanied the dead on the funeral pyre. Two embankments, twenty metres from the shore, have been found on the level eastern shore of Harre Vig, an inlet in Limfjord, that cuts into the fertile Salling peninsula. They are about half a metre high, twenty-five metres long and point towards the fjord. They are interpreted as being the foundations of two boat-sheds which may be of the Viking Age. There may be more embankments of the same kind on other beaches in the country.

It is worth noting that the earlier Swedish boat finds are generally from burial places in natural banks, deposited under the surface and covered only with the earth that was dug out to make space for the boat. These boat graves can therefore now be seen on the surface as long, pointed oval depressions, formed when the deck of the boat rotted away and the earth settled. One of the best known boat burial places is at Vendel church on the south-eastern end of a ridge which offers a wide view over Vendel lake and Vendel river. Here fourteen boat graves were excavated at the end of the last century, of which the seven richest belong to the period between 550 and 800, a period which in Sweden is named the Vendel period after these finds. At Valsgärde, not far from here, there is a burial ground with fifteen ship burials in a natural gravel bank above the Fyris river, from which can be seen the royal seat of the Ynglinge dynasty at Old Uppsala. The earliest graves are of about the year 700 and are very rich. In one of them the dead chieftain lay at the stern end of a boat about ten metres long surrounded by his grave goods, which consisted among other things of two swords with garnet-inlaid hilts of gilded bronze, two chopping knives, drinking horns with bronze mountings and three shields with richly ornamented mountings. A gilded helmet, decorated with bronze plates impressed with scenes of warlike pageantry and lively battle scenes, lay a little further forward in the boat. In addition the boat contained the skeletons of four horses, a saddle, remains of pigs, birds and fishes, an iron pot, a frying pan, a spit, a wooden bowl, two drinking horns, playing-pieces belonging to games, and dice.

Before excavation the boat burials at Valsgärde looked like long, pointed oval depressions in the ground where plant growth was particularly luxuriant. The question is whether it might not be possible to discover similar boat burials in Denmark on uncultivated ground in the vicinity of watercourses or by the sea. Only a few graves, poor at that, are known from the centuries immediately preceding the Viking Age; but this period was not poor, it was on the contrary Denmark's 'golden age', as is shown by the sacrificial finds of rich gold treasures from earth and bog. These include a great number of gold arm rings, finger rings and neck rings, gold ornaments adorned with filigree and polished garnets, gold fittings to scabbards and gold or silver-gilt buckles. A sword found at Bildsø north-west of Slagelse with a gilt bronze hilt, silver fittings and inset polished stones must certainly have belonged to a chieftain equal in rank and wealth to those of Valsgärde. There is therefore no reason why we should not find graves here in Denmark just as rich as the Swedish ones, or even boat burials. They have merely not been found yet. If they are under level ground, they can only be discovered by chance. We know from Valsgärde what they would look like if they lie in uncultivated areas.

We possess an eye-witness account of the way a ship burial was conducted in the Viking Age. It was given us by the Arab merchant, Ibn Fadlân, who was a member of a trade delegation sent by the caliph of Baghdad in the year 921–22 to the Bulgars of the Volga. There he met the Scandinavian Vikings, the Russ, as he calls them in his famous *Risāla*, in which he gives an account, among other things, of the burial of a chieftain. The following is an extract from it:

I saw the Russ, who had come on a trade journey and settled down beside the Volga. People with more perfectly shaped limbs I have never seen. They are tall as date-palms. Each of them carried an axe, sword and knife, from which he was never parted. The women wore neck rings of gold and silver round their necks. It was said that when a chieftain died, they had all manner of customs, of which cremation of the body was but one. I was interested therefore to find out about this, and one day I heard that a man of standing among them had died. They laid him in a grave and covered it over for ten days, until they had finished cutting and sewing his garments. When the man is rich, they gather together his possessions and divide them into three parts, of which one goes to his family, one for his clothes and one for nabi*d* [beer?], which they drink on the day his bondswoman kills herself and is burnt together with her master. When a chieftain is dead, his family says to his bondswomen and servants: 'Which of you will die with

82   Flat-topped burial mounds on Vorbjerg in Nim Hundred,
Central Jutland

him?' When one of them says 'I', she is not allowed to draw
back. A bondswoman offered herself on this occasion and they
gave two other bondswomen the task of watching over her
and following her wherever she went, washing her feet with
their hands. The bondswoman drank and sang every day
with a joyfulness which seemed to be a portent of coming
happiness.

When the day came that he and the bondswoman were

to be burnt, I went to the river where his ship lay. It had been drawn up on land and placed on timber. People began to go backwards and forwards talking, while the dead man still lay in his grave. Then they set a bench on the ship and covered it with rugs and cushions of Byzantine painted silken material. After this came an old woman called the angel of death, and spread out the rugs over the bench. She was in charge of the sewing of the death clothes, and it is also she who kills the bondswoman. She was an enormous old woman, stout and grim in appearance. When they came to the grave, they removed the earth and the woodwork and drew off the clothes the man had died in. It could be seen that he had turned black from the cold in the earth, where he lay in his grave with nabi*d*, fruit and a stringed instrument. They took everything out and apart from the colour of his skin the dead man had not changed. Then they dressed him in trousers, over-trousers, boots, tunic, and a cape of painted silk with gold buttons, and set a cap of silk and sable on his head. Then they carried him into the tent which had been set up on the ship and laid him on the carpet, supported with cushions. Bread, meat and onions were thrown before him. They cut a dog into two halves and threw it into the ship. All his weapons were laid at his side. Two horses were run into a sweat, cut into pieces with a sword and the flesh thrown into the ship. Two cows were cut up and went the same way. A cock and a hen were also killed, and thrown likewise into the ship. The bondswoman who had wished to be killed went backwards and forwards, entering into one after another of their tents, and had intercourse with the master of the tent, who said: 'Tell your master: This I have done out of love to you.'

On the Friday afternoon she was lifted up into the air three times by the men over something they had made which looked like a door frame. The first time she said: 'See there! I see my father and my mother'; the second time: 'See there! I see all my dead relatives'; the third time: 'See there! I see my master sitting in paradise, and paradise is fair and green, and with him are men and young boys; he calls to me. Let me go to him!' Then they led her to the ship, where she took off two ankle rings and gave them to the 'angel of death'. Then they took her up into the ship, but she was not allowed to enter into the tent, and they handed her a cup of nabi*d*, which she sang over and drank from and then took farewell of her women friends and was given another cup, which she sang over a long time; but then the old woman hurried up to her to get her to finish drinking and go into the tent to her master. She became confused, but the woman drew her into the tent. The men started beating on their shields, so that her cries should not be heard. Then six men went into the tent and had intercourse with her, and laid her after that by the side of her dead master. Two grasped her legs and two her hands, while the 'angel of death' laid a rope round her neck and handed the ends of it to two men, for them to pull. Then she went up with a broad-bladed dagger and stuck it in and out between the girl's ribs, while the men strangled her with the rope.

Then the one among the people who was most closely related to the dead man set light to a piece of wood. He went naked backwards towards the ship with his face to the people and he held the piece of wood in one hand while he kept the other behind his back. Thus he set fire to the wood that had been laid in position under the ship. Then all the people came up with a piece of lighted wood, which they threw onto the pyre, so that it all burnt up in a strong and terrible wind.

Not an hour had passed before the ship, the wood, the bondswoman and the chieftain had been turned to ashes and dust of ashes. At that they built on the place where the ship had stood when they dragged it up out of the river, something that resembled a round mound. In the centre of this they put a large post of birch wood and wrote on it the name of the man and his king.

This description includes a number of things that are known from investigations of Iron Age graves, among others that burial mounds were erected with a wooden support in them. That has been shown to be the case in Denmark from the period around the year A.D. 200 and up to the end of the Viking Age, when our largest burial monuments, the ten metre high twin mounds at Jelling, were built. The large Iron Age mounds thus cover a period of about eight hundred years, throughout which certain architectural features remain the same. They are most clearly distinguished from the burial mounds of earlier periods by their curved sides and flat top, which have been shown by excavations to have been intended in the actual structure of the mound. In many cases a mono-lith or large block of stone was placed on the top. Where careful excavations have been carried out, a central pole or the empty space which it occupied have been found. The mound was erected around this pole which was not, as one might suppose from the Arabian account, put up after the mound was completed. On the basis of these characteristics, mounds may be referred to the Iron Age even if they contain no graves or artefacts by which they may be dated. A very large number of mounds of the period are empty, among them some of the largest burial monuments in Scandinavia, as for example the southern Jelling mound, Galgebakke at Slots Bjergby, and Raknehaugen and Farmannshaugen in Norway. This last is fifteen metres high and the largest of all Scandinavian burial mounds, but it covered only a collection of pieces of timber. There are many explanations of why these large mounds are empty. It is related in *Skjoldungesaga* that King Ring was severely wounded and therefore had himself laid in the high poop of his ship, which was set on fire and turned out to sea. A mound was thrown up on the shore, which was given the name Ringhøj. In the *Ynglingesaga* Snorre declares that the ashes of the dead must be thrown into the sea or buried in the ground, and that a mound must be set up to outstanding men as a memorial. Other mounds were erected for chieftains who fell on expeditions in foreign

83 The Slots Bjergby mounds, Hashøj and Galgebakke

84 The foundations of a three-legged gallows

lands, in the same way as sometimes runic stones were erected for them, like for example the Swedish Valleberga stone, which concludes: 'But they lie in London.'

The flat top, which was deliberately built, may have served a special function. It is often said in the saga literature that the kings 'sat on a mound', exercised their authority from the top of a mound. The same applies to Tynwald Hill, a mound on the Isle of Man, which in a way has preserved this practice to the present day, in that changes of sovereign must be proclaimed and new laws read from its top. The same practice was also observed in Scandinavian territories, such as for example Lybers Hög north of Lund, from which the people of Skåne acclaimed Queen Margrethe's son Oluf and several subsequent kings, the last of them in 1610.

It may be a direct continuation of the old custom that a number of burial mounds, both flat-topped and others, were used well into historic time as meeting places for the Thing, later as places of execution and gallows fields. That the flat tops were also used in olden days for sacrifices of horses and other animals is shown by finds of bones, and also by the early Christian laws which forbade sacrifices on the mounds. The old custom of sacrifice was not to be uprooted altogether and has survived in some places till today. Thus the owner of a mound at Raundalen in Norway declared, when it was excavated in 1909, that when anyone died on the farm, an animal had to be slaughtered for The Tanner who lived in the mound. On the last occasion it had been a heifer, when his father died.

The post that was set up in the centre of the mound may have had a practical purpose as a centre pole when the huge monument was built, but equally it may have been intended as a dwelling-place for the soul of the dead man. This idea is known to have existed in many parts. It may also have been inscribed with the name of the dead man, as related by the Arabian merchant, Ibn Fadlân. The stones set in the form of a grave or altar at the bottom of a number of empty mounds may also have been intended as a resort for the soul.

It is an important consideration in the interpretation of the empty mounds that they did not deviate in any way, in construction or position, from the mounds in which regular burials took place.

Flat-topped Iron Age mounds may be seen in many parts of the country. They are easily distinguishable from the Bronze Age dance mounds, which are more like circular platforms than mounds.

The oldest flat-topped Iron Age mounds are those at Himlingøje in East Zealand, where four are preserved out of an original seven. A centre pole was found in two of these. One of them was completely empty, with only a small stone structure at the base. The finest examples are a group of eight large flat-topped mounds on Vorbjerg Bakke in Nim Hundred, north-west of Horsens. One of them was found to contain a Late Roman Iron Age grave, a stout central pole and a large monolith. There were overturned monoliths on three of these mounds and they have also been found on other mounds, among others Kajestenen on a mound at Kongstrup on Røsnæs. A drawing dated 1591 shows a monolith on the southern Jelling mound.

It is an interesting fact that a large proportion, roughly one-third, of the mounds that lie in our old churchyards, about seventy-five in all, are flat-topped. It shows a connection between the old sacred places of the Iron Age and the sites of the earliest Christian churches. In some cases a churchyard mound has been levelled off on top to make room for a belfry, as for example at Birket church on Lolland, which has a fine late medieval belfry now covered with boarding. There is another on a mound beside Tandslet church on Als. Hothers Høj, in Hårlev churchyard in East Zealand, is a typical flat-topped mound on which the impressive Tryggevælde runic stone may have stood. This mentions mounds and ship burials, and was probably incised by the same master as executed the Glavendrup stone. Kong Rans Høj in Randbøl churchyard in South Jutland is also flat-topped. Investigation has shown that this was built over a still older Bronze Age mound, as was very often the case. So were both the northern of the twin mounds at Slots Bjergby in West Zealand, and the north Jelling mound.

Two enormous burial mounds, Galgebakke and Hashøj, on a range of hills at Slots Bjergby a good three kilometres along the Skæls road from Slagelse, are like a landmark for the whole of South-West Jutland. From the top of these, a mere hundred metres above sea level, one can see far and wide. It was no accident that our enemies in the last World War picked on these mounds as a suitable place for a radar station, but fortunately the local parish priest and the mayor of Slagelse succeeded by courageous intervention in getting the project called off. But only for a brief moment. Now we ourselves have erected the golden phallic symbol of our age between the two Maiden mounds—a reinforced concrete television tower that has completely changed the lovely profile of this range of hills.

One of these ancient mounds was used in olden days, as its name shows (*galgebakke* means gallows hill), as an execution ground. It is only just over a hundred years since the last condemned man laid down his life on its flat top. The local paper carried the following brief account of this execution on 5th August 1847, when a mother and her twenty-three-year-old son from Halkevad were beheaded for the murder of their husband and father: 'The execution took place between seven and eight in the morning. The condemned were prepared by Pastor Boysen, Skørpinge, who spent a long time with them, singing and talking on the execution ground. Strengthened by this comfort the two of them faced death with piety and devotion. The execution was carried out particularly well by the executioner for Zealand, Mr. Dyring.' The Antvorskov district records tell of a long succession of executions in the sixteenth century for murder, child murder, incest and abortion. These were confirmed by an excavation in which some forty skeletons were discovered of both men and women, hanged or beheaded. Many of the hanged skeletons were laid out on their backs, whereas many of those beheaded lay on

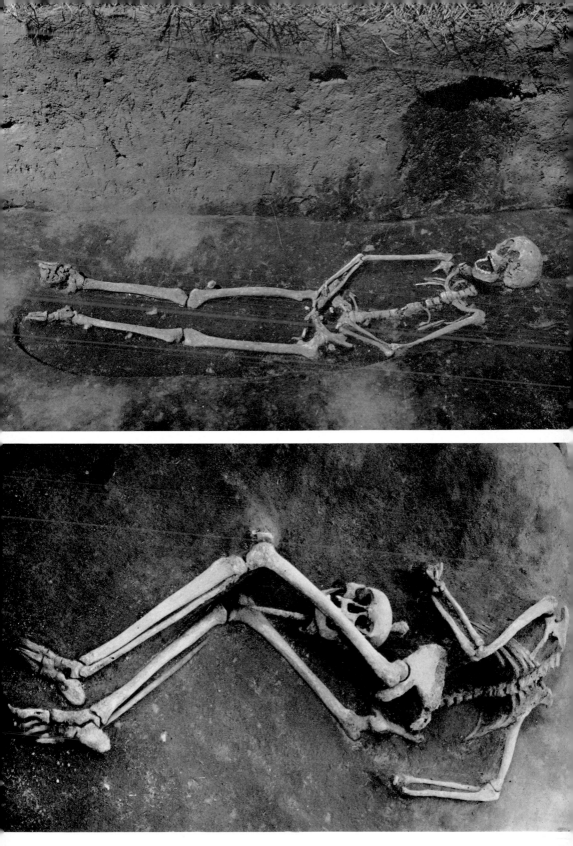

85 *and* 86   A hanged man and a beheaded man under the
turf at Galgebakke

87 *and* 88 Bronze Age graves at the bottom of Galgebakke,
and the mound that covered them

their sides with the severed head between their thighs, sometimes with a heavy hand-forged iron spike thrust through the
skull, which had been set on a stake. Little regard had been
paid, in interring the bodies, to those that were already in the
ground, and in a number of cases skeletons had been half
dug through or completely broken up, in which case they
were laid roughly together on top of the latest body to be
inserted. The piles of stone that had formed the foundation
of the three-legged gallows itself were also found. This dark
chapter in the history of the mound shows it to have been in
use nearly to the present day. It is not unusual for the larger
ancient mounds to have been used in the same way. One such
is Kanehøj, at Egeslevmagle close to the main road north of
Skælskør, within sight of Galgebakke to the south-east. The
twenty-year-old Hans Andersen was present at an execution
on this mound in 1825 and writes of it:

About this time three people were to be executed near
Skjælsgøer. A young girl of seventeen, since her father
was against her love, had persuaded her lover and the farm
hand to kill him, after she had tried herself in vain with
white arsenic. The top form was given permission to go
down and see it; we drove through the night; outside
Skjælsgøer we got out and walked to the town; I had
just precisely reached the gate when the condemned were
driven out, so I have just seen into, but not been in this
town. The girl was very pretty, but deathly pale; she was
gazing with a strange expression at the crowd and the
surrounding country; she lay in her lover's arms; he was
pink and healthy to look at; the farm hand looked pale and
yellow, with long black hair that fell down over his face.
A few other farm hands shouted out Goodbye to him: he
took off his hat and nodded. The three priests went up with
them onto the execution ground; it was such a lovely
morning; all six of them sang a hymn and I could hear the
girl's clear voice above all the others. They kissed one
another and the priests, and at the end she kissed her lover

once again. Her head did not fall until the second blow.
Now the two others followed : they laid their heads on the
same bloody block. I had come into the circle, felt that
their eyes had gazed at me; I was in a strange mood. The
executioner's assistants ate eel and drank brandy after the
execution; then the girl's old grandmother came and wept,
laid her body in a coffin, while the two men's heads were
set on stakes and their bodies broken on the wheel.

All over the country, the names tell of the same grim use of
the ancient burial mounds.

Galgebakke is fifty metres across, more than five metres
high and the story of its building covers two thousand years.
As it appears now, it is a flat-topped Iron Age burial mound,
but the first ancient mound on this spot was erected there in
the Early Bronze Age, and we will follow its construction
from that time on, though it was revealed in reverse order, for
the excavation began at the top of the mound.

A burial mound was put up on the massive Slots Bjergby
Bakke in the Early Bronze Age, about 1000 B.C., over an oak
coffin which stood right down on the subsoil, orientated east-
west, and supported by stones at the sides. This mound was
not particularly large, only thirteen to fourteen metres across
and one and a half high, but even so it stood out in the landscape, because it was placed right up on the flat top of the
slope, where the ground begins to fall away to the north-west.
Even at that time the area lay open, as commonland for
grazing and as cultivated land. It showed a layer of soil ten
centimetres thick on which the mound was erected, and in the
light-coloured, clayish subsoil a criss-cross of dark furrows
made by the ard, the Bronze Age ploughing implement. The
first grave was surrounded by a stone circle, before the mound
was piled up over it. Burials were again carried out in the
mound in the Late Bronze Age, eight times altogether, all
cremations. Two of them were urn graves, the rest small
stone coffins or burnt bones under a covering of stones. The
grave furniture they contained was small articles of bronze :

198

89 *and* 90   The small and large Iron Age mounds that
covered the Bronze Age mounds at Galgebakke

91 *and* 92 Iron-Age sacrificial pits and stones in place under Galgebakke, and a section through the body of the mound, which is built of grass turfs

razors, tweezers, awls and buttons. A side stone of one of the small coffins had a hand sign carved on the surface facing the burial chamber. These later cremation graves were inserted in the top and sides of the earlier mound from time to time all through the Late Bronze Age until the middle of the first millennium B.C., after which the mound was left undisturbed, so far as one can see, until the first two hundred years of the first millennium after the birth of Christ. The Iron Age people then erected a well-built cairn on top of the Bronze Age mound and in so doing doubled its height. It was afterwards covered with layers of subsoil sand and grass turf, thus widening the mound to about twenty-two metres. Both the cone-shaped cairn and the earth mound were encircled with a ring of large stones, but when this mound was made no grave was placed in it. It is one of the empty Iron Age mounds. It has their characteristic structural features, the flat top which is repeated in the structure of the cairn, and the vertical hole through the middle, showing that it was built round a centre pole. Beside it had stood a monolith, which was now overturned and lying on its side. A couple of urn graves had been deposited in the south side of the mound, containing small articles of bronze of the beginning of the Late Iron Age. A great deal must have happened at this time on the south side of the flat-topped mound, but at this we can only guess. Post-holes and stone paving show that a house had been built there. Deep bath-tub shaped or round pits were dug in the subsoil, in which fires had been lighted and perhaps the flesh of sacrificial animals roasted, on flat stones over red-hot charcoal, and the pit carefully covered over again. Later, metre-high monoliths were erected against the south side of the mound, standing in a layer of fragments of clay vessels and burnt bones, which can be dated to the period around A.D. 500.

How many centuries passed before another mound was raised on the spot, the greatest and last, which covered all the structures mentioned above, we do not know, but it is certainly not later than the time of Gorm the Old. An enormous pile of stones was laid over the flat-topped Iron Age mound, forming a star-shaped pattern at the top, running out from the centre in all directions. At the centre the pile was a couple of metres thick and consisted of smaller stones, but it decreased in thickness towards the foot, where the stones grew larger. This layer of stones was finally covered over with carefully laid grass turfs, which were still so easily distinguishable that each individual turf could be seen in the excavated sectors. They were all laid grass-side down to prevent the mound slipping during construction. This last large mound, which measures fifty metres across and more than five metres high, is again one of the empty Iron Age mounds. No grave has been found that is contemporary with it. But many graves came later as the unfortunates were executed, whose numbers steadily increased until the middle of the last century. In time so many of them lay under the greensward that the phosphorescent light from their bones could be seen at dusk by a sensitive eye. One evening while the excavation was in progress a man came over Bjergby Hill with a horse on his way to the knacker's in Løvegade in Slagelse. When they reached the gallows hill, the horse stopped dead and refused to go past. Nothing would induce it to go a step further and it had to be stabled at a nearby farm. Early next morning it went past the mound quite happily to Slagelse.

The finest of all ancient Danish monuments, an impressive conclusion to the burial mound custom, are the famous royal mounds at Jelling, the largest in the country, the northern one named after Queen Thyre, the southern after King Gorm. Between them are the runic stones of King Gorm and King Harald. These mounds have been investigated time after time; the runic stones were interpreted long ago, and the kings who are associated with this Jutland seat of royal power are referred to in many of the medieval literary sources. One might imagine, then, that everything of importance about them had been discovered long ago. That is far from being the case. The large runic stone was transcribed and interpreted as long ago as 1586 under King Frederik II. Ever since then, the scholarly discussion about this place where Denmark's thousand-year-old certificate of baptism is preserved in runes on the huge picture-stone has never ceased. Investigations and excavations are still going on at Jelling.

The more northerly of the two twin mounds is ascribed by centuries-old tradition to Queen Thyre. A number of excavations were carried out here in earlier days, and we have a record of one from about the middle or end of the eighteenth century: 'According to the account of an old man, Anders Jensen, so far as he could remember the Queen's Mound was excavated by men of Jelling town on king's orders in 1704, when he was present as a dragoon at the muster at Whitsuntide on Faarup field. Also he and an old woman here in the town recall that until its excavation there were always all sorts of festivities on the mound; the old woman says also that when the water ran out a pole more than thirteen *alen* [eight metres] long was thrust into a hole in the mound to see if it would reach bottom but no bottom was found.' This well in the top of the mound, which may be seen in a drawing of 1591, was believed in olden days to have healing power. It was visited for many years by cripples and sick people, but legend tells that the water lost its power after a peasant once washed his sick horse in it.

The little well on the north mound ran dry in 1819. As water was scarce in Jelling at the time, the townsfolk tried to get water again the following year by digging down to the bottom of the mound. When they reached a large timber-built chamber, the authorities halted further digging, but rumours had already spread of enormous treasures that had been brought up before the hole in the roof of the chamber was closed. Meantime experts were brought in and an investigation was undertaken, which secured the most important information about the burial chamber and salvaged what remained of its contents. If we take the results of this excavation of 1820 in conjunction with information provided by the bailiff of the parish who supervised the digging for water by the men of the town, we have a reliable account of the condition of the burial mound at the time. But the results of two other investigations of the north mound may also be added. One was undertaken in 1861 at the instigation of King Frederik VII, who after a vain search for a burial chamber in the south mound, had a gallery cut into the north mound to the burial chamber, which was repaired and then opened to the public for a number of years. Yet further information about the construction of this mound was obtained by an investigation in 1943.

The north mound is about sixty-five metres across and eight and a half metres high. It is constructed of grass and heather turf, laid upside down. Above this is a mixed layer of sand, clay and turf a metre thick and above that a layer of soil of equal thickness to ensure the growth of grass. The structure shows that the flat top twenty-five metres across is original and that the mound is thus of the ordinary flat-topped Iron Age type.

Finds made among the turfs in both this and the southern mound show us some of the tools used for this hard constructional work. The commonest are wooden spades with a long blade and a handle with a knob at the end, made in one piece. The turf was transported from the surrounding commonland on two-man hand-barrows, consisting of two long undressed spruce poles with boards between, on which the turfs were laid. A number of these hand-barrows have been left near the surface of the mound, which is very carefully laid, turf by turf, the way tiles are laid on a roof. The task of building a mound was a responsible one. This may be the mound referred to on a runic stone found in a dike in Bække churchyard, which mentions three men as mound-builders for Thyre, if this is the same as the queen at Jelling: 'Tue, kinsman of Ravn, and Funden and Gnyble, these three made Thyre's mound.' The stone is now erected on a small grass-covered hillock west of Bække church facing the main road, which here follows the same course as the old Army Road, continuing north to Jelling.

At the bottom of the north mound, inside the top of a Late Bronze Age mound, was the large timber-built chamber

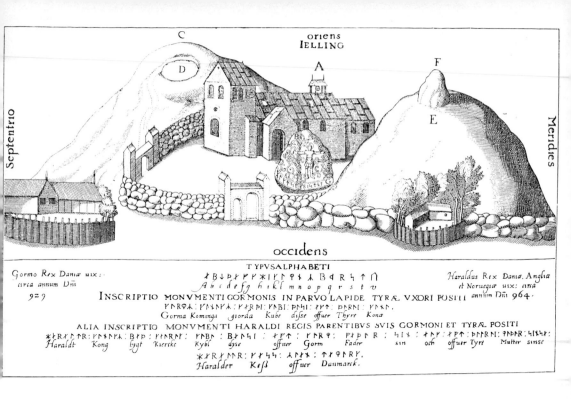

ELLING

Septentrio

oriens
IELLING

C

D

A

F

E

Meridies

occidens

TYPVSALPHABETI

ᚼᛒᛁᚦᚠᚠᚠ᛬᛬ᚼᛁᛦᚠᚠᛦᛆᚱᚼᚴᚢ
A b c d e f g h i k l m n o p q r s t v

Gormo Rex Daniæ uix:
circa annum Dñi
9=9

Haraldus Rex Daniæ, Angliæ
et Noruegiæ uix: circa
anniim Dñi 964.

INSCRIPTIO MONVMENTI GORMONIS IN PARVO LAPIDE TYRÆ VXORI POSITI

ᚠᛆᚱᚠᛆ᛬ᛦᛆᚠᚠᚠᛆ᛬ᚠᛆᚱᚦᛁ᛬ᚠᛆᛒᛁ᛬ᚦᛆᚼᛁ᛬ᛆᚠᛆ᛬ᚦᛆᚱᚿᛁ᛬ᚠᛆᚠᛆ᛬
Gorma Kominga giorda Kube dise ofuer Thyrre Kona

ALIA INSCRIPTIO MONVMENTI HARALDI REGIS PARENTIBVS SVIS GORMONI ET TYRÆ POSITI

ᚼᛦᚱᛆᚠᛆᛏᚱ᛬ᛦᛆᚿᛆᛦᛆᛖ᛬ᛒᛦᛆ᛬ᛦᛆᛆᚱᚿᛆ᛬ᛦᛆᛒᛆ᛬ᛒᛆᚿᚼᛁ᛬ᛆᛦᛆ᛬᛬ᚠᛆᚱᚠᚠ᛬ᛦᛆᛦᛆᚱᛦ᛬ᚼᛁᛏ᛬ᛆᚴᚼ᛬ᛆᛦᛆᚱ᛬ᚦᚿᛆᚱᚿᛁ᛬ᛖᛆᛏᚦᛆᚱ᛬ᚼᛁᚼᛏᛆ᛬
Haraldt Kong bygt Kiercke Kybl dise ofuer Gorm Fader sin och ofuer Tyre Mutter sinse

ᚼᛦᚱᛆᛖᛏᚱ᛬ᛦᛆᚼᚼ᛬ᛆᚿᛆᛏ᛬ᛏᛦᚴᚼᚱᛦ᛬
Haralder Kess ofuer Danmarck.

93 *and* 94   The King's Mounds at Jelling, and Rantzau's
view of 1591

which was discovered in 1820 and which had already then been opened and plundered. That could be clearly seen from the fact that four of the oak beams running across the east-west orientated burial chamber had been sawn through. These were numbers 6 and 7, and 10 and 11, counting from the east. The hole into the burial chamber was thus divided in two by the intervening beams, numbers 8 and 9, which were only sawn through and removed at the 1820 investigation in order that the earth which had fallen into the chamber from all sides during the well-digging operations, could be removed. The burial chamber measured 6.75 metres in an east-west direction, was 2.60 metres wide and 1.45 metres high. It was packed in with clay all round and also with a layer of heavy stones at the sides, and was covered over at the top with twenty-four undressed trunks of oak trees of which four, as already mentioned, had been sawn through when the grave was plundered. This must have happened long before the time of Frederik IV, for it is the actual hole made in the plundering, and the clay-packed and consequently watertight chamber, which collected the rain water and gave rise to the spring at the top of the mound, the water of which 'is said to have been so pure and sweet that people came from far and wide to take it home for tea-water'.

The burial chamber was a spacious room built of vertical planks 35 centimetres wide, lined with vertical boards on the inside and over the ceiling with boards laid lengthwise. Both ceiling and walls were covered with woollen cloth. The floor was also laid with boards on a foundation of stamped clay; the boards ran crosswise in the eastern half, and lengthwise at the western end. The chamber was divided lengthwise into two parts of equal size by a plank 4.06 metres long, which stood out 15 centimetres above the level of the floor. It was thus clear that the burial chamber had been intended for two persons, and as the south mound is one of the empty mounds, it is possible that both Queen Thyre and King Gorm rested side by side in this chamber. Possibly the queen was first buried in the stone ship that was raised for her.

Of the buried persons and the undoubtedly magnificent grave furniture only little remained. Everything lay scattered about in disorder, as it had been left by the robbers or dropped by them, among other things a small silver-gilt cup, which lay just under the hole in the ceiling. All that was left of the bodies was a small piece of a skull and a bone from a limb, which were removed at the excavation in 1861. Various fragments of animal bones were found, also a horse's tooth. When one considers that the burial chamber had been full of rainwater for several hundred years, it is not surprising that so few bones were found. The soft water must have washed out all the lime long ago, and only such few fragments as were in association with preservative materials survived.

Unique for this period among the grave goods are the little silver-gilt cup, which may have been Gorm the Old's travelling cup, and a small gold-mounted bronze cross, which Queen Thyre may have worn round her neck. Both pieces show the influence of Christianity, and also show that Gorm and Thyre may possibly not have been such benighted heathens as has been supposed. As King Harald, however, was in charge of the construction of the north mound and buried his parents there, he may as a Christian have given them two such powerful treasures as the cup and the cross to take with them, to show to St. Peter at the gates of heaven if need should arise. Of the remaining finds mention should be made of two small bird figures of gold-plated bronze, sheath mountings of iron with ornamented silver overlay, bronze mountings with gilding in pierced work, which shows among other things a cross surrounded with nail-holes, fragments of glass vessels decorated with applied glass bands of fluted work, a small piece of exquisitely woven red silken material, and a number of carved pieces of wood painted in white, red and black colours. A bearded warrior dressed in chain mail and with a snake wound round him, carved on a heavy oak panel, was a motif reminiscent of the side of the large runic stone depicting Christ. This, however, is all that the grave robbers and the passage of time have left of the magnificent kingly burial furnishings. A pair of iron rings was found on a sea chest about two metres long which stood at the western end of the ante-chamber and no doubt originally contained equipment of various sorts. The dead were not placed in individual coffins but were laid each in his own section of the west end, resting on down pillows of which there were traces, and such as are known from other contemporary graves, among others the one at Mammen between Viborg and Randers.

The Mammen grave has a great deal in common with the chamber in the northern Jelling mound. It was a large timber-built chamber under a mound and contained a uniquely well preserved chief's burial, which was completely destroyed in a frenzied hunt for treasure in 1868. The Viking chief's silk raiment worked in gold would have been a world treasure in itself, but of that mere scraps remain. There were hazel nuts among the down pillows he rested on, possibly a Christian element in a heathen grave, for the hazel was regarded as a symbol of rebirth in the medieval allegory of the Mediterranean countries. The nuts are the seed from which the dead always spring forth anew. In the green kernel is the guarantee of fresh life. The same meaning probably also lies behind the hazel sticks that were found attached to a cross in a Viking Age chamber grave underneath Hørning church on Djursland, and in early Christian graves underneath the church floor in Trans on North West Zealand and in Lund. A thick wax candle, an *alen* (just over half a metre) long, which was placed above the burial chamber at Mammen, possibly lit and burning until it was snuffed out by the filling in of the mound, must have some special story to tell. It may be a thousand-year-old altar candle, brought back by the buried Viking chief from some church in one of the Christian countries of western Europe, possibly the only one still in existence from that time in the whole of Europe. But candles were also burnt in the burial chamber in the north Jelling mound. A small wax candle was found in 1820 on one of the ceiling beams in a space between large stones. It was thought to have been left behind by the grave robbers, but the Mammen candle and another wax candle from a Viking grave at Søllested on Funen show that a candle of this sort is connected with the Viking Age burial customs, whether it was a Christian element or a protection against witchcraft and spirits.

It may have been known from olden days that the south mound, King Gorm's mound, contained no burial chamber, for there is no reliable information about excavations or finds in this mound, though of course there are legends connected with it, too. For example, it is related in the middle of the nineteenth century: 'Many years ago the entrance to Gorm's burial chamber was open; nevertheless no one dared go in, until a shepherd boy was persuaded to undertake this dangerous expedition with a rope round his waist. As it seemed too long to the peasants before he came out, they pulled on the rope, but it had been burnt in half and the shepherd boy was never seen again.' . . . 'Another time the men of Jellinge started investigating the King's Mound in the hope of finding treasure in it, but when they had dug a good way they came upon a large black dog and had to give up the work. Since then nothing has been done, for there is an old prophecy that Jellinge shall burn when Gorm's mound is opened.' It was opened, however, in 1861, when an investigation was decided upon by King Frederik VII: '. . . it is accordingly our will that King Gorm's Burial Mound, as it is called, at Jellinge shall now be investigated, in view firstly of a number of scientific questions connected therewith, secondly of any repairs to the interior that may possibly be necessary, and this with the piety and care proper to both King Gorm's memory and the cause of science.' Excavations began that same summer with the assistance of the highest experts. A gallery more than fifty *alen* (roughly thirty-one metres) long was driven into the mound in fourteen days, without result. A telegram arrived from the king: 'Fear you are working too deep in the mound, as it is only six *alen* to the middle of same . . .' Frederik VII himself inspected the

95   Queen Thyre and King Gorm's runic stone in Jelling
churchyard

investigations a number of times and in the end led the boring operations from the top. When at last everyone was satisfied that the south mound was empty, they started excavating the north mound. Since then the south mound has been thoroughly investigated—in 1941–42—when it was excavated from the top right down to the bottom, and probes were also made in the sides. It was then finally decided that this was one of the empty Iron Age mounds, but new and interesting information had been obtained about its structure.

The south mound is the largest of all the ancient Danish mounds, and possibly the last to have been built, measuring seventy-seven metres across and eleven high. It is constructed, like the north mound, of carefully laid grass and heather turf round a centre pole. Halfway up was a tent-like structure of uncertain significance, more than twenty metres long, of slender oak and birch-tree trunks, possibly a model to help in building the mound. At some time work had been discontinued long enough to allow grass to grow over the mound before it was completed to its present size.

A particularly important discovery in the last investigation was that of two rows of erect stones, standing inside the mound on the earlier surface, which if extended to the south would form an acute angle beyond the foot of the mound. These stones were erected at two-metre intervals, are about one and a half metres high and have been overgrown with lichen and moss, showing that they must have stood uncovered for twenty or thirty years, which is precisely the interval between the erection of the two runic stones, whose testimony must be taken as a basis in interpreting the Jelling monuments as a whole. It has been suggested that these erect stones formed part of a considerable-sized triangular *bautavi* or consecrated area, running from the north mound in a southerly direction —an armchair interpretation without parallel among our other ancient monuments. As already explained, it is part of a huge stone ship, which probably started from the north mound, as we know from the monuments already discussed at Bække in the south of Central Jutland and at Glavendrup on North Funen, where there are just the same three elements as at Jelling: the monolith in the point of the stone ship, the ancient mound and the runic stone.

Another exciting discovery in the 1941 excavation was the foundations of a wooden building right at the top of the south mound, ten heavy four-sided hewn oak posts set up in a rectangular ground plan of 6 × 4.5 metres with four posts on the long sides, three at the ends. Horizontal planks had been laid underneath, to prevent the posts sinking into the mound, which make it probable that they were laid at the time of the last and final reconstruction of the mound. These posts have been interpreted as parts of a defence tower or watch tower or of a belfry, but also as the remains of a burial house at the top of the mound, quite simply as the burial chamber in which King Gorm or some other royal person rested. If this last was the case, then the south Jelling mound, and with it other mounds with traces of burial structures at the top, are not in fact empty mounds. A house for the dead at the top of an otherwise empty mound is not unknown in the Viking Age, and in such cases one may assume that it was the dead man himself who had the mound erected. In *Harald Hårfager's Saga* Snorre relates that King Herlaug and King Rollaug had been three summers building a great mound that was 'walled up of stone and built with mortar and timber-work'. When the rumour spread that Harald Hårfager was approaching with an army, Herlaug had food and drink taken into the mound and had himself locked in with eleven men. Snorre also relates in the *Ynglingesaga* of Frøy that when he fell sick and his death was approaching, his men held counsel and decided to keep everyone from him. Meantime they built a mound with a door and three peep-holes. For three years after he was dead and had been laid in the mound, all taxes collected were poured through the peep-holes, gold, silver and copper each through its own hole. These stories possibly reflect some misunderstanding about burial houses, which we know existed as timber buildings of a Christianized form in various parts of Scandinavia, in Sweden right up to the eighteenth century. They may be seen in Ireland as stone houses over graves and are known and used by primitive peoples to this day. If this interpretation of the posts on the south Jelling mound as King Gorm's burial house above-ground is correct, it provides a neat confirmation of the traditional naming of the mounds.

The small runic stone lay in the porch 'as a resting stone for the weary', as the archaeologist Ole Worm said in 1621. Later on, it was erected beside the large runic stone, where it now stands. Its inscription runs: 'Gorm the king raised these stones for Thyre his wife—Denmark's ornament.' It was thus Gorm who erected this stone for his wife and the plural form 'these stones', probably refers to the whole row of standing stones of the same height as itself, which were erected south of the north mound to form the stone ship. It is therefore im-probable that King Gorm would have destroyed his own memorial to Thyre by erecting the south mound for himself.

The large picture- and runic stone, about two and a half metres high, is King Harald's memorial to his parents, Gorm and Thyre, to which his descendants added a eulogy of his own exploits. It was formerly buried in the churchyard. This was referred to in a gilded inscription on a tablet which was destroyed when Jelling church burnt down in 1679: 'Anno 1586 in the reign of King Friderik II, Caspar Markedaner of Søgaard, who at that time was Sheriff at Koldinghus, had dug up from the churchyard the stone which stands outside the church door here, and on which is an inscription which King Harald had made for his father Gorm and for his mother Queen Thyre about Anno 960.' The runic inscription, which covers the whole of one of the three sides of the stone and continues as a single line under the pictures on the two other sides, was accordingly not all cut at once. On broad, raised bands, representing the twisted body of a snake whose pointed head and cold eyes may be imagined at the top of the stone, stand the words: 'Harald the king caused this memorial to be made to his father Gorm and his mother Thyre.' After King Harald's death in 987 it was wished to record his exploits, too, and a text was drawn up for carving on the great Jelling stone: 'that Harald, who won all Denmark and Norway and made the Danes Christians'. As all the space inside the snake's body on the inscription side was practically filled up, the carver started to cut new relief bands for the long addition, but before these were finished, he realized that there would hardly be room for all the additional words there, and also that by carrying them over on to the two other sides he would achieve a pleasing synthesis of pictures and text. There was only room inside the original framework for the word 'that', and underneath he added 'Harald who won Denmark'. Below the fierce dragon picture on the side to the right he carved 'all and Norway', while the last line of runes, 'and made the Danes Christians', was fitted in on the third side underneath the picture of Christ. The pictures and the runic inscription had been merged into a whole, but rather at the expense of the original work of art, the bottom part of which was broken.

The inscription on the large runic stone, too, refers to the setting up of more than one stone, and here one may assume that, in addition to the large runic stone itself, the reference is to the standing stone that is shown in the drawing of 1591 on the top of the south mound, a picture that also shows the well on top of the mound, but not Gorm's runic stone. As Thyre died about 935 and her memorials, the runic stone and the stone ship, were erected after that and Gorm died somewhere before 950, it is perfectly possible, in view of the interval of twenty to thirty years indicated by the moss and lichen on the stones of the stone ship, that Harald whose baptism took place around 960 may have begun the south mound as a memorial to himself immediately after Gorm's death and burial in the north mound together with Thyre—who only now found her final resting place. The interruption in the construction of the south mound may support this interpretation. King Harald had no need to hurry over its construction. It may have been finally completed immediately after his death and the grave building on the top may be his mausoleum. The suggestion has been put forward with regard to the innermost south mound that it may have been put up for Harald's brother Knud, who fell as a Viking on an expedition to the West. Knud appears to have had very rare qualities and was so beloved by the people that they gave him the title Daneast, the darling of the Danes. It has also been suggested that it was built by Sven Tveskæg for his father, Harald Blåtand, who may lie buried at Roskilde in the church he himself built. But he was also given a mound at the old royal seat of the Jelling dynasty.

When King Harald turned Christian, church building spread rapidly all over Denmark, often at the old sacred places where roads converged and people were accustomed to assemble. At Jelling, traces have been found of the foundations of a stave church, which was larger than the nave of the existing church. These foundations consist of heavy boulders, the standing stones from Thyre's stone ship, which was then destroyed. There are traces which show that the first large stave church at Jelling was destroyed by fire, other royal buildings doubtless meeting the same fate, so that the old royal seat was abandoned for a time. Possibly the two runic stones were damaged at the same time, the large one by splitting, as can be seen on the dragon side from marks left by a warrior's hardened sword, while the small one shows traces of fire and is chipped at the side.

The Jelling monuments are unsurpassed in impressiveness and hypnotic power by any other ancient monument in the whole of Scandinavia. For Denmark they are an incomparable memorial of both prehistoric and early historic times. This has been felt from early days, when they were always protected by royal order. So long as there was a royal manor at Jelling, the place was more or less safe. We are told by Svend Aagesen that Prince Harald Kesja was staying at the royal manor at Jelling in 1135 when he was slain by his brother, King Erik Emune. Where this royal manor stood, and when it was destroyed, we do not know, but a two-storeyed house known as Høfdingsborgen (the chief's castle) with stables attached 'was kept ready for travellers of the royal house until 1675, when it was completely burnt down'. Since then, we are told in 1820, the priest had been required to keep rooms and stabling available at the parsonage for the same purpose. In 1636, on royal orders, both mounds were walled round with a stone wall for protection. In the present century everything possible has been done, by way of new building and extension of the churchyard, to mar this unique place. It is only in the last few years that, with the strong support of the Danish Prime Minister and Parliament, the mounds have been gradually set free again from disfiguring building. Now plastic culture threatens the sanctity of the churchyard. One can only hope that a new bill which has been put forward to preserve the churchyard in its present state and at its present size, may be carried through. It proposes quite simply that no burial places should be allowed to be established or sold around the church or mounds. Gradually, as the individual graves fall into disuse, they will either be maintained in their present state or grassed over. In this way the lovely old churchyard, which we are now doing everything in our power to wreck, would be preserved for the future as a memorial to our fine old churchyard culture, which at the moment seems to be heading for destruction. At the same time it will provide a unique setting for those magnificent monuments: the runic stones, the royal mounds, and the church.

XI Monoliths and Runic Stones

Monoliths and runic stones have already been mentioned in connection with Iron Age mounds and burial places. These upright stones bear the same testimony: they are memorial stones, the one type without inscription, though not dumb because a block of stone raised on end always speaks its own secret language, the other telling in runes by whom and for whom they were erected. The monoliths are the oldest, going back to the Early Bronze Age when, as in the Iron Age, they were erected on burial mounds. The great majority, however, are probably of the Late Iron Age and are contemporary with the runic stones, which it first became customary to erect in this country in the Viking Age. Runes, though, are much older than that, for they came into use a century or two after the birth of Christ, when they were engraved on weapons or tools, and one may suppose that the smooth sides of many monoliths were painted with runes before it became customary to incise these Scandinavian characters into the actual stone.

Many monoliths were erected on burial grounds in Jutland in the Late Iron Age, but most of them have long ago disappeared. The greatest number are at Højstrup close to Tømmerby Fjord, where about seventy-five out of an original hundred and twenty-five monoliths may still be seen among stone ships and small mounds, though some of those about a metre high may well have originally formed part of stone ships which are now destroyed. A stone known as Bjørnstenen (the Bear Stone) stands out on the edge of the cliff at Als Nordskov beside some small Late Iron Age mounds. Its name is undoubtedly of more recent date, as is that of the small mounds. They are known as Svenskegravene (the Swedish graves).

The only other part of the country where such large collections of monoliths are to be found as in North Jutland is Bornholm : there more than a thousand have been counted in various places. Only about a third of these now remain. The finest are some fifty stones at Gryet, a grove west of Neksø. These cleft boulders, up to two and a half metres high, stand singly or two or three together, in no apparent order, in a dense undergrowth of bracken, raspberry canes and blackthorn, a wilderness to which the monoliths lend an atmosphere of antiquity and consecration. There is another large collection in Louisenlund, close to the main road between Østermarie and Svaneke. This grove was acquired by King Frederik VII on a visit to Bornholm in 1851, and he named it after his beloved countess. Another impressive group of stones, some in a circle, some free-standing, may be seen on Hjortebakkerne at Skovgården close to the main road halfway between Neksø and Åkirkeby. Other Bornholm monoliths worthy of mention are Hellig Kvinde close to the Svaneke—Gudhjem main road, three stones on Frennemark south of Svaneke, and Hellig Hågen in Højlyngen at Bodilsker.

In the rest of Denmark monoliths practically only occur in West Zealand and on the small offshore islands, by themselves or a few of them together. There is one fine stone close to the shore at Tadebæk on the south-west coast of Sejrø. Another stands on the high cliffs of Tynnebjerg, north-west of Sejrby, both of them solitary Vikings, gazing out across the sea from their homeland to distant shores, where they lost their lives on warlike expeditions. Two more, *Stat fast og hans Lillebror* (Stat Fast and his Little Brother), at Ellede on Røsnæs near Kalundborg, are the last monuments left there, marking the position of a collection of low mounds which were

96　Monoliths at Frennemark in East Bornholm

long ago demolished. A little to the south and further inland
are five monoliths, *Skraedderens falske Vidner* (the Tailor's False
Witnesses), on Bøgebjerg in the parish of Reerslev. There is a
single one on the south point of the island off Skælskør in the
lake of Agersø. Others of the small islands, too, have or have
had upright stones. Finally we may mention Kajestenen at
Nostrup near Røsnæs and Saltstenen on Næsby Strand near
Skudeløbet, through which lay the entrance to the Viking

camp at Trelleborg. Both of these last two stones are on small grave mounds.

Monoliths date for the most part from the end of the Iron Age, the Viking Age. Their occurrence preponderantly in the eastern part of Denmark, as well as on the Højstrup burial ground and other burial grounds in North Jutland, whose monuments show more affinity with the burial customs of our neighbours to the north than with our own, points possibly to their having been erected under influence from Sweden. In some cases stones have been erected at the top or by the side of Bronze Age mounds, which takes the custom of erecting monoliths right back to this period. In Western Europe stones were erected beside megalithic graves, so this custom may have reached Denmark from there as early as the Late Stone Age.

The names given to many monoliths show that right up to the present time they were regarded as persons to be respected. Many have legends connected with them. The Bornholm monolith, Hellig Kvinde (Holy Woman), which stands in a group with a number of smaller stones, used to be greeted by the peasants in the evening with: 'Good Stone, Holy Woman with your ten children', and she returned the greeting loud and clear. The echo was not particularly loud, however, others report. The story is that she was a mother with nine children, who were turned to stone to escape a threatened deed of violence by their father. It was also customary within living memory for heather-gatherers and peat-cutters, driving out to Højlyngen past the two-metre high Hellig Hågen (Holy Spirit) to take off their caps and say: 'Good morning, Holy Spirit.' It stands now in a little wood in Bodilsker Plantation where no heather-gatherer greets it any more, but where Sankt Hans still receives his wreath of leaves and flowers. *Skrædderens falske Vidner*, originally six, now only five stones on Bøgebjerg, are according to the legend petrified men who had taken a false oath at the Thing and had been awarded the verdict in a quarrel about a village boundary, but on their way home, when they came to

97 Monoliths in Louisenlund in North Bornholm

the place where the boundary ran, they were turned to stone. The tailor himself had not been able to keep up with the others and he stands as the monolith Skrædderstenen (the Tailor Stone) between Bøgebjerg and Tissø. It is related of the numerous monoliths at Højstrup on Tømmerby Fjord, first that they were 'two wedding parties that came upon one another and were thereupon turned to stone', and second that they are a host of warriors who were turned to stone by a witch.

Runic stones are monoliths with short, simple inscriptions in the Scandinavian language, written in the Germanic peoples' own characters, runes, the origins of which must be sought in the alphabets of southern Europe. This angular script, arranged in bands, enables the monoliths to speak direct to us with the tongues of the Vikings themselves. Possibly many of the stones once had the voice of painted runes on their faces but their voices were silenced long ago, washed away by the rain of centuries. The majority of the runic stones are memorials to the dead, put up by their nearest relatives, usually by men for men, though also by women, particularly for their husbands, while some are erected in self-glorification.

Runes originated in the first century or two A.D. among Germanic tribes that were in close association with the Roman people whose alphabet they imitated. Then the Germani started writing themselves, adapting the foreign letters to their own needs, arranging them in their own sequence and adding any necessary signs. It is clear from the angular shape of the runes that they were originally designed to be carved in wood or some other hard material. That is also how they first appeared on articles of the second century A.D. The earliest runic inscriptions are always very short, usually only a name or a few words with magical significance, magic formulae incised or engraved on to weapons, tools and ornaments. Single examples are found scattered over a wide area from Rumania through Poland to Norway. In some cases, where they were incised on the back of an ornament or the

98   Hellig Kvinde (Holy Woman), monolith west of Svaneke

cover of a weapon, this was because their magic power worked in secret. When one sees on the ferrule of a sword: 'May Marr not spare', Marr being the name of the sword, this is to increase the ferocity of the sword. Often these short inscriptions cannot be interpreted and are magic formulae which drew their strength from the power of the runes themselves. The runic inscriptions that have come down to us from this period can only represent a very small part of a vast early Germanic runic literature now lost.

The earliest runic alphabet, the Futhark, that is found on these articles, is common to all the Germanic peoples and consists of twenty-four signs arranged in three groups, known by the Danish name of *ætter*. Every runic sign has its own name, due perhaps to the fact that it was used not only openly but in the service of magic. This long runic alphabet was later changed so that in the last few centuries of prehistory only sixteen signs were used. It is these that appear on the Danish runic stones.

It was not until shortly before the Viking Age that runic stones were erected in Denmark, but by then the custom had already been in force for some time in Norway and Sweden where runes had been cut into stones as early as the fifth century. It is probable that the custom was transferred direct from the West Germanic areas to Norway, whence it spread to Central Sweden. Here we find both upright runic stones and smaller stones in graves of the centuries just preceding the Viking Age, as for example a coffin stone in a grave at Kylver on Gotland, which contained objects of about the year 400.

In the second century of the Viking Age rather more than a hundred stones inscribed with the runes of the short alphabet were erected in Denmark, in almost every part of the country except Bornholm. There we have about twenty runic stones, all later than the Viking Age and showing influence from Sweden where the custom of erecting runic stones continued for a very long time. Many provinces of Sweden are consequently extraordinarily rich in runic monuments, while a few runic inscriptions may also be seen on fixed rock faces. There are thus about a thousand stones in Uppland alone. The later alphabet with sixteen characters is known firstly in a special Danish form, which after the year 1000 became very general in Sweden too, and secondly in a Norwegian-Swedish form.

The inscriptions on the Danish runic stones are nearly always drawn up on a set pattern and relate that A erected this stone for B, his kinsman or relative, to which are sometimes added a few words of praise for the dead man and execrations against anyone who destroyed the monument. The shortest inscriptions consist of simply a name, such as 'Hærulv' on the Hovslund stone, or the words 'Erik's stone' on the Starup stone. Longer inscriptions are found on a number of stones associated with other of the Viking Age monuments such as Bække, Glavendrup and Jelling. Of the ancient gods, only Thor is invoked in runic inscriptions, e.g. on the stone in the Glavendrup stone ship on Funen: 'May Thor consecrate these runes', while Thor's symbol, the hammer-sign, is to be seen on the fine stone that stands beside Læborg church. Protective symbols and other signs such as the cross, the trefoil, human masks and ships are found on a number of stones. Apart from these signs and pictures, ornament is rare on runic stones whose beauty consists in the exquisite shape of the stone itself and the vertical or curved band formed by the runes—which seem to impart a hypnotic power to the stone even today. The great runic stone at Jelling is unique both as a piece of carving and in the historical value of the inscription. It is a carefully selected stone of magnificent appearance and colour, three-sided, running up to a point at the top. It is almost two and a half metres high and three metres wide. It is the world's largest runic stone and of an unusual shape, picked out from among thousands of boulders. It bears the name of Denmark and is therefore unique also as a baptismal certificate, matchless and of unknown age. It is also the first Christian monument in Scandinavia. Two of its sides were set aside for carving, the third for the inscription that was to give it tongue. One side shows a battle between a vulture and a snake, symbols of the incessant struggle between Christianity and heathendom. The other shows Christ against a background of the foliage of the tree of life, his arms outstretched in blessing. Both these sides are carved in low relief with a frame of 'rope-work' filling up the corners with great intertwined curves. The third side alone was intended for writing. It is framed round the sides and top by a snake, whose long intertwined body forms parallel horizontal lines along which the characters are cut, as in the illuminated manuscripts of the time, and not, as is usual with runic stones, in vertical bands. A great craftsman has made the most of the possibilities offered by the three-sided stone and created an impressive series of pictures round its attractive shape. There is much to suggest that the sculptor was a Dane, perhaps trained abroad in the technique of stonework, but many models of contemporary art from south, west and east are represented in this outstanding piece of carving.

Originally runic inscriptions were undoubtedly in many cases picked out in strong signal colours so that they could be seen and have effect from a distance. Painting has not been established, however, on any of the runic stones in Denmark, although Swedish finds show that red, brown, blue and black were used. A Scandinavian runic stone that was found in 1832 deep in the ground in the old churchyard of St. Paul's Cathedral in London showed traces of deep blue colour. A Swedish inscription from Södermanland tells of the colouring of runic stones: 'Esbern incised and Ulf coloured.'

Most of the runic stones are shaped by nature, polished into sculpture on their long journey in the glacial ice that dragged them down from the Scandinavian plateau. Occasionally a pleasing form has been further improved by very simple shaping. Usually, however, the shape is untouched, but it must have been picked out from among hundreds of boulders. Many had already been selected as monuments a couple of thousand years before the Viking Age, for about ten carry the sacred sign of the Bronze Age, the cup sign, on their back, or

99   Chieftain Alle's runic stone acted as the prow of a stone
ship at Glavendrup in North Funen

occasionally on the rune side. One stone found at Snoldelev has the Bronze Age wheel-cross on the rune side.

Not more than a hundred runic stones are known in Denmark, most of them still being scattered around the country, though others have been taken to museums, the majority to the National Museum or the Museum of Prehistory at Århus. Only very few still stand on their original sites and in association with other monuments, and they have already been discussed. We must, however, mention again the runic stones that form part of the stone ships at Glavendrup and Bække, the Skarde stone that lay beside a mound, on which it has now been placed—beside the Ox Road from Slesvig to Rendsborg—and the Store Rygbjerg stone on a mound on Randbøl Heath. Numbers of runic stones have been found built into churches or used as building-stones in bridges and dikes. These stood originally on or by burial mounds close to the public highway, near a bridge or ford. Some of them tell of their original position themselves. The Fjenneslev stone, for example, bears the words: 'Sasser raised the stone and made the bridge.' It was found about 1830 in the old dike round Fjenneslevlille church but had undoubtedly stood in low ground in the neighbourhood where a small bridge that leads across the river Tuelå still bears the name of Sassebro. The large runic stone that was taken from Tryggevælde to the National Museum relates that it stood beside a mound and a stone ship and the inscription threatens anyone who destroyed the memorial or removed the stone from its place. This was done about 1550, when Wobislaw Wobitzer removed the stone from Hårlev and set it up in the grounds of Tryggevælde castle, but how it avenged itself on the presumptuous sheriff is not known. It is, on the other hand, told of the Glavendrup stone, which was erected by the same Ragnhild and incised by the same engraver as made the Tryggevælde stone, that a landowner wanted to move it but he fell sick when he tried to and had to leave it alone. He is said to have died, though not immediately, and to have 'vanished away like Dew before the Sun'.

The great majority of runic stones are now set up beside churches or in church porches. Many of them were found close to the spot where they now stand, whether as building stones in the church or in the church dike. Five runic stones were found, for example, at the church of Vor Frue in Århus, which cannot be an accident. It shows, in common with much else, that churches were often built close to the sacred places of the Viking Age.

Mention must also be made of a few other outstanding runic stones scattered over the country, apart from those already discussed. There are two fine examples in Sønder Vissing church in Tyrsting Hundred, south-west of Århus. One is inscribed: 'Tove, Mistive's daughter, Harald the Good's, Gorm's son's wife, caused these stones to be made for her mother', and is thus among the oldest sources of Danish history, for Harald, here given the title the Good, is presumably King Harald Blåtand, who himself erected a runic stone in Jelling. The other Sønder Vissing stone says: 'Toke made these stones for his father Abe [Ebbe], a wise man', and it has also a number of cup marks on one side, showing that it was already a sacred stone in the Bronze Age. In the same area but further north, in the porch of Sjelle church there is a tall, slender stone of reddish granite which is so worn it is no longer completely legible, but at the top is a menacing face with a plaited beard. The same mask appears on a number of stones and among others as the central figure on a fine stone by Skern church, beside the old road between Randers and Viborg. The inscription runs in a spiral band round the mask and says: 'Sasgerd, Finulv's daughter, raised this stone for Odinkar, Osbjørn's [?] son, the "well-loved" and "loyal to his king" ', while a separate inscription at the top of the stone beside the mask protects it with the words: 'Bewitched shall he be who breaks these stones.' There are three fine stones in Himmerland: Valtoke's stone, which now stands on a small mound beside Års church; Queen Asbod's stone, which has cup marks on the back, and stands on a mound beside Ravnkilde church; and the tall stone raised by 'Mother Thyre and her sons Odinkar and Gudmun', standing now in the porch of Skivum church. A stone in Tillitse churchyard, which was previously in the churchyard wall, carries not only two separate inscriptions but also a large Christian cross. It was erected by Eskil Sulkesøn to himself, and invokes both Christ and St. Michael to help his soul, thus showing the importance of runes even to Christians. This is also shown by a number of runic inscriptions on Christian gravestones, church bells, censers and similar things in the early Middle Ages. Of the many runic stones on Bornholm, almost all of which stand beside churches or in church porches, we will mention only two: the Bodilsker- and Ny Larsker stone, on which the runic stave cuts in half the body of a snake twined round a sign of the cross; and the Brogård stone, at the side of the main road a kilometre or two south of Hasle, with its long band of runes which Svenger had cut for his father, mother, brother and sister, of whom only the two men, Toste and Alvlak, are mentioned by name.

Apart from all the runic stones there are also two picture stones, one of which stands at the old crossing place at Sjellebro in Djursland and has a runic stone mask. It was to protect the place against evil powers and may once have had a neighbouring stone with runes that told who made the bridge there in the Viking days. Another picture stone, in the porch of Hørdum church in Thy, has been used as a building stone and is badly chipped along the edges, but one can still see Thor's fishing catch represented in bold, simple strokes. He is represented at the moment when he has just caught the enormous Midgard serpent on his hook, and is pulling so hard that one of his legs has gone through the bottom of the boat. The subject is well known from contemporary Swedish and English pictures. It is, however, the only one of its kind so far in Denmark. The fine representations of mythological scenes on Gotland stones, among which Odin on his eight-legged horse Sleipnir predominates, are not found in Denmark. We have to content ourselves with the few representations on the runic stones, but among these are the fine carvings on the

100 Troldestenen (the Troll Stone), with its watching face
at Sjellebro in Djursland

great Jelling stone: the vulture and the snake in combat as a symbol of the battle of Christianity against the old heathen Asa faith, and Christ spreading his arms in blessing over the good, broad land of Jutland.

XII Iron Age Settlements

Traces of the daily life of the Iron Age people, their villages with farms and houses, and their roads and fields, are usually only visible when they lie in uncultivated ground or have been excavated. As not more than about a seventh of Denmark consists of wood, heath, sand dune or bog, and as in addition most of this terrain is covered with dense vegetation or drifting sand so that the Iron Age soil is hidden, these traces are only to be found in a few areas. On cultivated ground there may still be something to see where large earthworks such as fortifications stood in ancient times, even though they have been largely levelled out by agricultural activity through the ages. In the last few decades, however, a number of constructions in various parts of the country that had long been hidden below the surface have been excavated and are now exposed to view.

A number of new methods of discovering hidden antiquities have been adopted recently. For example, a great deal that cannot be seen in the ordinary way in cultivated land from ground level becomes visible when looked at from above, from an aircraft or helicopter. This is due to the fact that ancient settlements and earthworks in some strange way take on a different tone of colour under special lighting conditions, e.g. when the early morning or evening light falls slantwise, throwing long shadows even from quite slight differences of height on the surface. The effect may be apparent even in land that has been under the plough for centuries, and in fields of growing corn. What the human eye cannot detect from the air, may still sometimes be captured on a sensitive film by a camera lens. Aerial photography has therefore become one of the best aids to present-day archaeological research.

Villages and Houses

Where Iron Age house sites lie in heathland that has not been cultivated since they were abandoned two thousand years ago, they stand out on the surface as low, rectangular banks of earth. These banks are almost always hidden by the heather and are only revealed when the heath has recently been burnt off. The metre-thick turf walls of the houses still form slight eminences, even after the passage of two thousand years. One can thus see house sites in various parts of the country and even discover them oneself in heath and woodland. One Iron Age village of the kind may be seen on a protected piece of heathland at Østerbølle in south Himmerland. There were seven long houses here, orientated in an east-west direction, in two rows. Low mounds of earth mark where the collapsed earth walls ran in a rectangular shape, with smaller similar shapes against them indicating outhouses. Other mounds can be detected round about in the heath, enclosing the fields that surrounded this Early Iron Age village. It consisted originally of twenty houses, most of which have been ploughed up. The village well can also be detected on this same site, and a small burial ground with eight inhumation graves of the ordinary Jutland type of about the time of the birth of Christ. There is a similar village with surrounding fields on Skørbæk Heath in north-west Himmerland that has been preserved in the same way. Here there are six house plots of the same date in a system of fields from one and a quarter to a quarter of an acre in size and covering an area of about two hundred and fifty acres. Of the houses, four had grass turf walls, and two walls made of posts. There is another Iron Age village of seven houses in a plantation on

101 Iron Age village erected at the Historico-Archaeological
Experimental Centre at Lejre

Gørding Heath north-east of Vemb in West Jutland. Three of
them have been excavated, one of which was without grass
turf walls but had a large, wide roof reaching right down
to the ground all round the house, a type known as *spændhus*.
It is still used in Central and West Jutland for sheep and tool
houses.

102 Refuge fort and Iron Age village in Borre Fen, Himmerland

There must undoubtedly be many similar villages in uncultivated areas waiting for someone to discover them. In
South-West Jutland, in the marshland, there are almost
certainly Iron Age houses hidden under the thick layers of
earth on the small islands that have been built up until the
present day to enable people to live securely when the storm-
floods break over the sea dikes along the west coast. Today
one gains the best impression of an Early Iron Age Jutland
village on a small islet in Borre Fen, south of Års in the heart
of Himmerland. A village was built here in the century before
the birth of Christ, on the site of a previous stronghold.
Twenty-two house plots have been excavated, but they had
not all been inhabited at the same time, for some of them were
partially covered by others. Probably about twenty houses
were in use when the village was at its largest. All the houses
were orientated east-west and grouped round a stone-paved
street, which led out over the bog along a stone-built causeway to the firm ground to the south-east. The road across the
fen is seventy metres long, three metres wide and made of
close-packed, carefully laid stones, some the size of a fist and
some a little larger. It is laid on a strong stone foundation and
supported along the sides by a row of heavy boulders, a visible
testimony to the great experience in road building possessed in
the Early Iron Age. This road continues in a loop over the
islet, where it is about two metres wide and has heavy kerb
stones, though only a single layer of paving stones. It is
crossed about halfway along by a 'gutter' and then continues
in the form of a path a metre wide towards a pond. The
houses are of very varying sizes, but all are built alike. The
largest is twenty-three metres long and six metres wide, and
the smallest not quite so wide and only half as long. They all
had grass turf walls a metre thick and a roof of heather, or
reeds, which was supported by two rows of free-standing posts
inside the house about a metre from the side walls. The people
lived in the west end, the cattle were stalled in the east. This
combined house must have been a cosy and comfortable
home for the people and their domestic animals through the

long, dark winters, with the peat fire glowing on the hearth and the cows munching the hay from the loft above the stable end of the house.

One of the houses in the Borre Fen village was burnt down while still in occupation and has lain there ever since, covered with a layer of ash, just as it was when the fire burnt out two thousand years ago. An undisturbed burnt site like this brings us close to the daily life of the Iron Age people.

The burnt house is not large, thirteen metres long and six metres wide. All round the perimeter, except at the west end, heavy stones laid side by side marked out the foundations. Inside these was a flat stone paving, possibly a foundation for benches or plank beds. In the middle of the floor, towards the west end, lay the clay platform of the hearth, burnt red and engraved with two concentric circles, one at the edge and one six centimetres further in, possibly to indicate the danger limit of the fire in this inflammable house. There were threshold stones in the middle of the side walls on both the north and south sides of the house, exactly opposite one another, and beside them traces of wood from the doors. In other burnt sites the door itself has been found, made either of woven osier in a wooden frame or of thin planks held together by grooved lists. There is usually only one door opening on one side of an Iron Age house, but in this case the two doors placed opposite each other may help to explain why the house burnt down. If both doors had been left open at once, a spark from the hearth, from which the smoke escaped through a vent in the roof, could have got caught up by the draught and been borne into the highly inflammable roof covered with heather and reeds, so that the whole house would soon have been ablaze.

Right up at the west end of the house the contents of the kitchen, scorched by the fire, lay practically undisturbed. A large quern—a saddle-quern with a fixed, hollowed-out bed and a separate grinder, on which the women of the house ground corn and seeds for bread and porridge—lay sur-rounded by numbers of clay vessels, both large ones for winter stores and smaller drinking vessels and dishes. One with a perforated bottom had been used as a colander or strainer, possibly for making cheese. By the side of the quern, which still stands in its original position on the floor of the house, lay a cake of burnt clay, full of chaff and pieces of straw. It was about the size of a good big Shrovetide bun and had a cross marked on the top. It is perhaps one of the earliest 'scrap-cakes' known to us. Many of us in Denmark remember scrap-cakes from our childhood, when bread or cakes had been made on plates or in tins and the last remains of dough were scraped together and made into a special cake, the scrap-cake, as a special treat for the children. In the old days this was put out for the pixies. In Iron Age houses, it was doubtless intended for the powers that protected the human and animal inhabitants against evil powers. It was certainly not edible with all the clay mixed up in it. Elsewhere in the house a flat lump of clay was found, its surface covered with the imprints of little fingers: perhaps a piece of potting clay left over the last time they were making clay vessels.

After they had been standing for a number of years and everything was bone dry inside, these old farmsteads caught fire very easily. We know of instances of whole villages going up in flames. One such is a small Iron Age village at Fjande beside Nissum Fjord in West Jutland where disaster struck in the first century A.D. The whole village, eight homesteads in all, burnt down, for the houses stood so close together that the fire leapt from roof to roof. After the fire they built another village over it, and insured themselves against a repetition of the disaster by digging a hole in one of the burnt plots and laying an iron axe in it with the blade pointing upwards. Possibly the fire was caused by lightning, and that was why, to prevent a similar misfortune, they put it there with its edge pointing at the sky: preventive magic, a weapon set against the weapon of the thunder, axe against axe, cutting edge against cutting edge. And the little village was not in fact burnt down again but was abandoned for quite different reasons after a number of years.

Whereas the inhabitants of the Borre Fen village were ordinary Jutland peasants, farmers with barley and oats as the most important kinds of grain and with cows and sheep as their main livestock, the inhabitants of the Fjande Iron Age village were fishermen as well, as indeed most of the village people along the coasts of Denmark have always been. The evidence for this is the presence not only of fish bones in the occupation layers but also of net-sinkers in all the houses. In one house there was actually a pile of weights, seventeen in number, of the same type as is used on the west coast to this day, corresponding to a fishing-net about twenty metres long.

A good many villages have been investigated in West Jutland, but only in a few cases has it been possible to preserve them *in situ*, as has been done at Borre Fen, where low mounds outlining the house plots stand green and light on either side of the paved village street that goes across the heather-covered islet. A characteristic feature of the Iron Age houses in the Esbjerg area is a paved stable with a drain in the middle, which can be seen in its original position in front of the Spangsbjerg school. Another of the stables from here has been moved to the grounds of Esbjerg museum. In the western part of the parish of Hostrup, north-west of Esbjerg, a number of Iron Age houses have been uncovered—among them three house sites and the narrow paved streets of a largish village of the first century A.D. at Myrtue, situated on a low headland facing the river Varde. These are short houses, eight or nine metres long, with stamped clay floors and fireplaces and without stables. At Sjælborg there are three houses marked out by low earth banks, the largest twenty-one metres long, one with a paved stable and drain and one with an underground storage cellar.

A thorough investigation that was carried out at Grøntoft, midway between Ringkøbing and Holstebro, gives us some idea of the size of West Jutland villages in the Early Iron Age. In an early village indications were found of twelve homesteads, the five long houses with stabling for from twelve to eighteen animals, and a later settlement on the same spot with

103 *and* 104   Road and ford (*below*), continuing as village
street (*above*) between house plots, in Borre Fen

thirteen or fourteen houses, both settlements showing definite traces of having been enclosed with a stockade with gates which could be locked. That is all there is to be seen at Grøntoft, but elsewhere half another village dating from the first four centuries A.D. has been unearthed due north of the dominating Vestervig abbey in Thy, east of the north-south main road. The other half lies on the west side of the road and appears now in the form of a layer about two metres thick, created by repeated rebuildings in the course of the four hundred years the village was inhabited. As is known from the excavated part, up to five or seven houses were built one on top of another. They indicate as many different habitation periods. The thick layer arose because the thick turf walls of the older houses were levelled out before marking out fresh plots for building. Between the houses, of which only one is a typical long house, run narrow paved passages, while the doorways are paved with small stones from the beach arranged in a herringbone pattern. As far as can be judged, fifteen to twenty houses were inhabited at the same time in the village—which was abandoned after a catastrophic fire.

In Vendsyssel, stone-built cellars have been known for about fifty years in the Frederikshavn area, but only recently has a direct connection been established between these and Early Iron Age houses. It was in a house on Grønhedens Mark at Stidsholt south of Sæby. The cellar runs from one corner of the stable and is about ten metres long with stone-built sides covered with flat slabs of stone. Six metres from the house the cellar expands into a small oval chamber measuring one and a half metres by ten, which confirms the account of the Roman author Tacitus, where the Germani built secret cellars that served both as store rooms and places of refuge in time of danger. There is, however, no connection with houses above ground in the case of eight stone-built cellars that have been excavated in a small bank on Løgten Mark close to the road from Frederikshavn to Gærum. These are very varied in form, dug one to one and a half metres beneath the present surface of the ground, and having one or up to three chambers. They may possibly have been covered with grass turf. Finds of broken pieces of large, roughly-made storage jars would indicate that they were used as storage rooms. They may also have been sleeping rooms for a short period. Many things go to suggest that they were only used on certain, seasonally determined occasions, whether these had to do with fishing or trade. The cellars on Løgten Mark, of which similar examples had previously been found at Donbæk, Bækmoien, Knivholt and Dalgård, have now been covered over, but they are to be made visible again in an open-air museum that is planned on the spot.

These stone-built cellars in the Frederikshavn area of the centuries preceding the birth of Christ are remarkably isolated in time and place. They are not known in earlier periods in Denmark, nor do they continue long into the Roman Iron Age. Their origin has been sought on the other side of the North Sea, in Scotland and Ireland, where stone-built underground chambers are known, generally twelve to thirty metres long, sometimes up to sixty metres, and so deep that a man can stand upright in them. A long, curved passage leads down to them, and they occasionally have a round chamber, very similar to those on Løgten Mark. They are known in Ireland in the Late Bronze Age and on into the Roman Iron Age. So much indicating foreign influence was happening in Vendsyssel at just about the time they were being built that it would not be surprising if it were established some day that immigrants from Ireland via Scotland had crossed the sea north of Grenen, in the extreme north of Denmark, to the east coast of Vendsyssel and settled there.

So far we have only discussed the houses of Iron Age peasants and fisherfolk. What sort of dwellings the tribal chiefs and great men of the time had is not yet known. Only their rich graves have been found, full of imported vessels of silver, bronze and glass. The long farmhouse, what one might call the Iron Age long house, with dwelling-place for humans at the west end and stable for animals at the east, continues right through the centuries. Its latest descendant with brick

105 *and* 106   Stone-built cellars on Løgten Mark in Vendsyssel

walls and chimneys may still be seen all over Denmark, particularly in West Jutland where it is the typical farm worker's and fisherman's house. A good impression of the Iron Age house, its structure and equipment, can be gained from a visit to Lejre in Zealand and to Hjerl Hede in Central Jutland, where reconstructions have been carried out.

Two quite different types of dwelling are known from the last few centuries of the Iron Age, first the large long house with curved walls and roof which is particularly represented in Viking Age camps and will be discussed in connection with these; and second the small, four-sided wooden house of the kind that has been excavated at Århus, Hedeby and various other early towns. At Århus the earliest Viking Age layer was found at a depth of three metres below the present surface, not far from the cathedral and inside the area which the street names show to have been the central part of the earliest town —an area bounded to the west and north by streets that bear the names The Rampart and The Moat, and to the east and west by the Århus river and the sea. There may have been a royal manor outside the actual heart of the town by Vor Frue Kirke where many runic stones have been found. The houses that have been excavated are long houses with wooden walls for dwelling-houses, and round houses with walls of interlaced twigs for storage. They were dug out down to the subsoil and opened on to a plank path that follows round the inside of the rampart which enclosed the town on the three sides facing the land and the Århus. Only one little corner of this first Viking town beneath one of our modern commercial towns has been excavated, and a part of this will be made accessible to the public in a cellar room under the bank that is to be erected on the spot. There the citizens of the capital of Jutland and others interested will be able to see the sites of the thousand-year-old dwelling-houses of the earliest inhabitants of the town.

The largest Scandinavian town in the Viking Age was Hedeby, beside the deep cove that cuts southwards far into the land from Slie Fjord. It is mentioned in the earliest historical sources and on runic stones as a trading centre that was fought over by kings. It was its fine situation for trade both with western Europe, the whole of Scandinavia and eastern Europe, that gave it its greatness and made it into the first real town in Denmark, fortified and with a protected harbour. The collection of small buildings that lay on the west side of the cove in the eighth century soon multiplied round the course of a stream to form a sizeable town with harbour and market place, which had its heyday in the tenth century. It then covered an area of some sixty-eight acres and was fortified with a heavy semi-circular rampart which completely encircled the town on the land side and continued in the form of wooden piling out into the cove, where moles and harbour lay. There was no real town plan. Only one through road led from the north gate to the south, while a stream running in from the west divided the town into a northerly and a southerly half. In this huge area houses stood side by side with their frontages opening on to narrow passages. An exception was two areas close to the ring rampart in the south-west, where the cemetery lay. The dwelling-houses had small storehouses attached. Everything is unusually well preserved in a moist soil at a depth of about half a metre. There are one-family houses in a special quarter occupied by artisans. The houses are built in very mixed styles, some of vertical planks, stave houses, others of planks laid horizontally between vertical posts, *bul* houses, and finally houses with mud-built walls. It was here that the monk Ansgar stayed from 826–29 and erected our first wooden church. Of this no trace has been found.

We have an eye-witness account of Hedeby by the Arab merchant, Al Tartushi, who visited the town from the caliphate of Cordova in Spain in its period of glory in the middle of the tenth century: 'There are wells of fresh water within it. Its inhabitants are worshippers of Sirius, apart from a small number who are Christians and possess a small church there. They celebrate a festival when they all assemble to honour the god and to eat and drink. Whoever offers a sacrificial animal, whether it be an ox or ram, a he-goat or a pig, puts up a pole at the gate of his house and fixes the sacrificial animal on to it, so that everyone may know he has made a sacrifice to the honour of his god.' Of the inhabitants, he writes: 'I never heard more hideous singing . . . the growling that comes out of their throats is like dogs howling, but even more bestial.'

About the year 900 Hedeby was subdued by Swedish Vikings, but in 934 they were driven out by the German Emperor, Henrik Fuglefänger. The Emperor Otto II held state there till his death in 983, when Sven Tveskæg reconquered it.

We learn of these events in the history of Hedeby from runic stones which are now set up at Gottorp Castle. The Swedish occupation is confirmed by a stone that was found in a bastion of the castle: 'Asfrid, Odinkar's daughter, made these stones for King Sigtryg, hers and Gnupa's son. Gorm cut the runes.' Another stone, also erected by Asfrid for Sigtryg, stood south of Hedeby by the ford across the cove. King Sven's re-conquest of the town is confirmed by a stone which in 1796 stood between two mounds close to Vedelspang south-west of Hedeby: 'Thorulv, housecarl to Sven, erected this stone to his companion Erik, who found death when men-at-arms be-sieged Hedeby; and he was a comrade, very well-born', and also by a stone which stood close to a mound beside the Ox Road between Slesvig and Rendsborg: 'King Sven raised this stone to his housecarl Skarde, who went on exploits to the west, but now found death at Hedeby.'

The largest Scandinavian Viking town ended, as many others have done, in death and destruction. It was in 1050. While the Danish king, Sven Estridsøn, was occupied else-where, King Harald Hårdråde of Norway carried out a devastating attack on Hedeby. A Norwegian poet sang of this in the court of King Harald:

> Burnt from end to end was all Hedeby in wrath,
>   a doughty deed, methinks, that shall make Sven smart.
> High rose the flames from the houses, as I stood last night before
>   dawn on the arm of the rampart.

Today if one wishes to look out over the once so mighty Hedeby, now lying hidden under the turf and divided into numerous fields in the lee of the green semi-circular earth-work, one must take up the poet's position on the northern arm of the rampart. This offers a good view over land and sea. Investigations are to be carried out in the next few years where the harbour lay; and two longships, whose burnt remains lie on the bottom of the cove, and from which weapons and equipment have already been brought up by divers, are to be raised. On the land side, too, work is to be done with an excavator to uncover new and interesting pages in the history of Denmark that Hedeby conceals.

Ancient Fields

Ancient fields have already been mentioned in connection with the Iron Age villages at Østerbølle and Skørbæk in Himmerland, and other Iron Age settlements where these are preserved on surrounding areas of heather. They can be seen in almost every part of Denmark—in North and West Jutland particularly on the heaths, and in East Jutland and on the Islands in the woods. Several hundred localities are known and most are of the Early Iron Age, especially the beginning of the period. That the soil was cultivated even at the beginning of the Late Neolithic peasant period is clear, but no fields of this time have yet been found, only traces of the ard, the ancient ploughing tool, under Stone Age mounds. The same applies for the Bronze Age, but we know that the soil was cultivated towards the end of this period in the same way as it was in the Early Iron Age, partly from Bronze Age rock engravings in Sweden that show the same type of field, and partly from finds in a few localities belonging to the end of this period. However, dating on the basis of cultivation marks is dangerous, and some of the ancient fields that have been discovered may well be considerably older than we suppose.

Three different types of ancient cleared fields are known: terraces, dike-embankments and high-backed fields. The earliest are terraces in the woods and these are formed when

248

107   Ancient fields on Giver Hede in Himmerland

108   Iron Age field on Bornholm, with heavy stones
cleared to the edge

a field is laid out on slightly sloping terrain. With repeated annual cultivation of the soil with hoe or ard a terrace is gradually formed as a steep edge builds up on the side on which the terrain drops. These terrace edges are often so slight, however, that they can only be detected by an expert, though once one has acquired an eye for them, they are easy to observe in high-lying woodland. There are good localities in the woods south of Århus, in Jægersborg Hegn, in North Zealand and in Næsbyholm Storskov by Tystrup Lake in South Zealand.

In Næsbyholm Storskov, where there are a great number of ancient monuments both of the Stone Age and the Bronze Age, there is a connected cultivated area of about five square kilometres. On steep terrain running down to the lake and on the sides of the valleys that lead down to it, terrace formations can be seen quite clearly. On flatter stretches the fields form chequerboard patterns, because low embankments gradually form on the boundaries between the individual fields, owing to the fact that soil is not removed from them as it is from the fields, and the plant growth gradually collects a certain amount of drifting soil and refuse from the fields. These banks between the fields can be quite high, particularly on the poor soil of Jutland where drifting sand has always been a difficulty. The banks and fields together are known as dike-embankments. The individual fields vary in size from half to one and three-quarter acres, but the most usual type are fields of a quarter to three-quarters of an acre. The embankments are from two to six metres wide and fifteen to thirty centimetres high, sometimes however of much more considerable size in areas of drifting sand such as Gørding Hede, where they are almost the height of a man. When the embankments are covered with heather, they are more difficult to detect, but when the heather is cut or burnt off and the sun is low in the sky, they cast so much shadow that anyone can see the chequered patterns they make.

Among the most important areas containing dike-embankments are Vindblæs Hede at Løgstør, Fly Hede south of

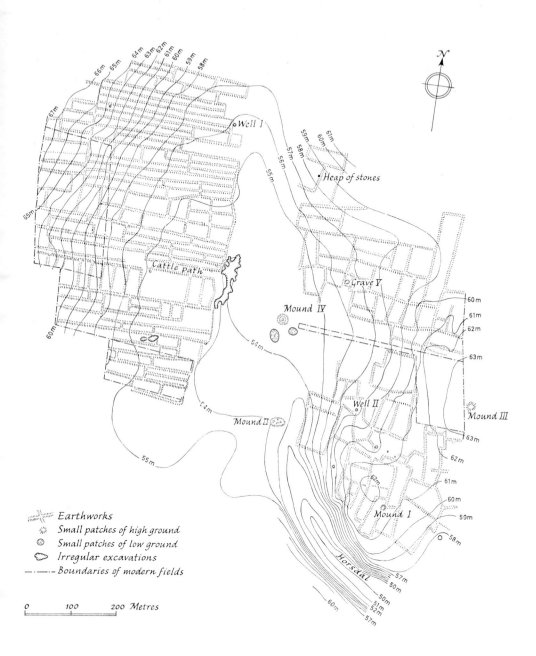

Earthworks
Small patches of high ground
Small patches of low ground
Irregular excavations
Boundaries of modern fields

0   100   200 Metres

109   Plan of ancient fields on Byrsted Heath in Himmerland

251

Skive, and Øster Lem Hede between Ringkøbing and Skern. Altogether more than a hundred abandoned fields are known in North and West Jutland, many of which have been cultivated in recent years after lying waste for something like two thousand years.

Why these fields were abandoned in the Early Iron Age, we can only guess. Possibly a cattle sickness which flared up violently in the last World War may provide the answer. It was chiefly concentrated in Vendsyssel, Central and West Himmerland, and in Central and West Jutland, more particularly in areas of cultivated heathland, though it also appeared in fenland. It was a malnutrition disease that attacked calves between the ages of two and ten months, and is attributable to lack of cobalt in the grass. The reason it broke out so violently then is that the cattle had previously obtained this substance from imported oil and linseed cake, the importation of which was completely stopped by the war. Similar conditions presumably arose for some reason in prehistoric times. The Early Iron Age saw a spread of population and of cultivation to these areas, that had been left uncultivated in the dry climate of the Bronze Age, but could be exploited with advantage in the moister climate of the Iron Age. At first all went well but after a time the lack of cobalt must have made itself felt to such an extent that cattle-breeding was affected, or possibly failed altogether, so that the fields had to be abandoned again. This may have developed into a catastrophe which, in combination with other factors, led to actual migrations of peoples. We are reminded of the migrations of the Cimbri and Teutones down through Europe, and if we are correct in placing their home in North Jutland, then this cattle sickness, which is of long standing there, and is known in Himmerland as *vosk* or *voskhed*, may be one of the reasons why they left their homeland and set out on paths of war.

Roads and Fords

Many old sunken roads and fords which are either disused or only used very little, are difficult to date but undoubtedly have their roots in antiquity. One comes upon them every-where in the woods and uncultivated areas of Denmark. Walking on the few stretches of heathland that still remain in Jutland, one cannot help stumbling now and again over deep furrows in the surface, often a number of them together in parallel rows like a freshly ploughed field. These are ancient roads that now lie hidden under the carpet of heather. After the heather has been cut or burnt one can see what a thoroughfare looked like in olden days; it will not be marked out or edged with ditches like our present-day roads. There are numerous wheel-tracks spread out over a wide area, often several hundred metres wide. On level ground people drove wherever it seemed best to drive, merely making in the main direction. If a track became too deep, they simply made a new one by the side of it. As the thoroughfare approached places where it was more difficult to get by, such as river courses, swamps or bogs, the numerous tracks converged. On the slopes of many valleys one can still see the deep wheel-ruts or furrows spread-ing out like a fan on either side of a spot where a crossing had been assured by a ford, dam or bridge.

In many places in Jutland these sunken roads are splendidly preserved, now abandoned by traffic, as for example at Tolne in Vendsyssel, at Halkjær river east of Års in Himmerland, at Løvelbro close to the Ålborg–Viborg main road, and at Mariesnåde south of Randbøl. On the Islands it is particularly in the woods that the old sunken roads are found. Here we will only mention Geelsskov between Virum and Holte, where they cut through the steep hillside, and the northern part of Nørreskoven facing the old ford at Fiskebæk between the lakes of Furesø and Farum Sø. In both these last-named places the line of the road is marked out by ancient stone graves and it is probable that here, as in many other places in the country where the dolmens lie on either side of old crossing-places, the road goes right back to the Late Stone Age, and so is more than five thousand years old.

There is no doubt that Bronze Age burial mounds, when they stand in rows along level stretches or on either side of river courses, mark the routes of roads of about 1000 B.C. This is clearly apparent in the case of one of the oldest main thoroughfares of Jutland, the old Army Road and Ox Road that runs through the peninsula from north to south and in many places follows the same route now as it did in ancient days. Bronze Age mounds follow southward routes from Viborg both east and west of Hald Lake. They meet south of Torning and the road continues down to Funder, east of the deep lake of Bøllingsø with the sources of the river Karup, and over the old Hørby ford. From Hundslund to Øster Nykirke the Army Road still retains much of its stamp of antiquity, though not the actual surface of the road, which has been metalled in the last few years. A winding road leads through Stejlebakken and Dybdal into the Heart of Jutland, the area between the sources of the rivers Skernå and Gudenå where there are magnificent ancient mounds. From there it proceeds through Tinnet Krat and past the old road-block Margrete-Dige. The heavy gold ring that, according to legend, was seen by the roadside in the days of Frode Fredegods, is supposed to have lain on a burial mound west of Jelling. A number of mounds mark where the road ran southwards to Randbøl, Bække, Skodborghus with the ferry over the Kongeå, right down past Bov to Danevirke and through Kovirke west of Hedeby—where the two large Bronze Age monuments, the Danhøje, stand close beside it.

From Jelling on to the old southern frontier of Denmark at Kovirke runic stones tell of the importance of this stretch of road in the Viking Age a thousand years ago. A superb series of these peculiarly Scandinavian memorials, beginning with the two Jelling stones, stood along this road, and most of them still stand close to their original sites. The first stone southwards is the Store Rygbjerg stone near Randbøl: 'Bryden Tue raised this stone to Bryden's wife. This stave for Thorgun will live very long.' It was found on a burial mound where it was lying with the rune side downwards, and was first discovered when it was split to make a kilometre stone. Hence its strange appearance. Part of a runic stone was found at Egtved. After

110   Ancient road through Elle Fen between Ramløse and
Tibirke, North Zealand

that come the runic stones at the Bække stone ship and at Bække church. North of Bække, just before the big cross-roads, part of the original Army Road is preserved with the old wheel-tracks. At Læborg church, only six kilometres south of Bække, stands the fine runic stone to Thyre whose two bands of inscription end with Thor's hammer-sign. On the western side of the Army Road, between Immervad and Hovslund in South Jutland, the Hærulf stone has been restored to its original position, after being on show from 1864 to 1952 in a park in Berlin. On the hills east of the stone are some twenty burial mounds, of which Strangelshøj, with a monolith more than two metres high, is visible far and wide. Where the Army Road crosses the present frontier at Bov, it passes some fifty burial mounds. A runic stone was found beside a mound on the west side of the branch of the Army Road running from Slesvig to Rendsborg that was erected by King Svend to his housecarl Skarde, who met his death at Hedeby. It has now been set up on the top of the mound, where an oak coffin, held together with iron nails and containing a man's skeleton, was excavated in 1889.

We know that the art of proper road building had been mastered in the Early Iron Age, as is shown by the village street already discussed in Borre Fen that continues as a causeway over the fen, at the same spot where a paved ford had previously led across to the island. Nor is this the only example of road building in the Early Iron Age, more than two thousand years ago. There is a good stretch of road preserved in Elle Fen in North Zealand, between Tibirke hill and the range of hills north of Ramløse. It consists, like the Borre Fen road, of a paving of smaller stones edged with larger blocks of stone and laid on a stone foundation. It is a hundred and fifty metres long and three wide and provided for traffic from Horsebjerg in the south going in the direction of Tibirke church, where the fen is narrowest. It follows an ancient crossing-place which was already in use in the Stone Age, and was laid at the beginning of the Iron Age—when rainfall increased, flooding low-lying ground and making

111   Ancient and medieval roads at Broskov in South-West
Zealand

bogs where, in the dry climate of the Bronze Age, people had been able to walk dryshod. A pathway of large stepping-stones for pedestrians runs parallel with the road.

A particularly fine road has been uncovered at Broskov between Tappernøje and Præstø in South-East Zealand. This, too, follows an ancient crossing-place over a swampy stretch of meadow with a stream. It is probably more than five hundred years later than the ones mentioned above, and is built of larger stones than those used in Borre Fen or Elle Fen. The stones are carefully fitted together so that without shaping they provide a firm surface, edged at both sides with rows of stones. The road rests on a solid foundation of stones. Towards firm land it widens out in a fan-shape, providing access for a number of sunken roads, of which three sets with double tracks are well preserved in Storkeskoven on the slopes to the north. The road is about seventy-five metres long. At the northern end it runs down in a dip, fifteen metres wide and one metre deep, which was a ford across a stream, the Hulebæk. Here the stones of the bottom and foundation are a metre across. Spear heads of about A.D. 400 indicate the approximate date of the road. In the Middle Ages another road was built at the same spot, and this covers the old one to the north. Fourteenth century horseshoes have been found on the mediaeval road. It is made of smaller stones and is broken at two points by fords, which seems to show that the Hulebæk had a double bed at the time.

Another old crossing-place must be mentioned, west of the main road between Randers and Ebeltoft where this crosses the Alling river just south of Sjellebro Kro. A stone carved with the mask of a troll, set up to protect the place in Viking days, marks the spot where four ancient roads lie hidden under the meadow. The deepest are two stone roads, one on top of another, on a bed of timber and branches. Like the Early Iron Age roads already mentioned, they are edged with heavy marking-stones. The river must have overflowed both of them for a certain distance, and it would not have been possible to get by dryshod. The two superimposed roads, of which the upper one is of the Viking Age and belongs with the troll stone, are both made of wood, with a surface of heavy timbers resting on a foundation of joists laid lengthwise on cross-beams and sunken posts. Between the ancient roads and the present main road, the sixth at this spot, are traces of the fifth road, in use from the time of Christian IV until 1860.

When the troll stone at Sjellebro was discovered only some twenty years ago, it was lying face-downwards on the meadow. People said that it was a seat for the river-man who demanded his annual human sacrifice at this spot. Once, however, it happened that for six years in succession no one was drowned. For six years the river-man's voice rang out in vain: 'The time is come, but the man is not come!' In the seventh year, a waggon on its way home from Randers market drove into Alling river and all its seven occupants perished. The account had been settled. Now the river-man on the troll stone, with his blind eyes and his plaited beard, stands gazing in vain at the main road which carries the traffic safely across Alling river on a bridge of granite and concrete.

Castle and Fortifications

Defensive constructions from ancient times are rare, though this is not to be regarded as indicating that these times were peaceful. In the earliest periods people chose places for their dwellings that were protected by nature, like the village community of Barkjær, which settled five thousand years ago on a small island that was only just large enough for a village of terrace houses. Iron Age villages were occasionally—as at Grøntoft—surrounded by a palisade, but usually there is no indication of this. Even where large earthworks were carried out, almost all traces may have been destroyed. It was the case with Denmark's oldest stronghold, built a few centuries B.C. in the southern part of Borre Fen not far from Års in Himmerland, and the two Viking strongholds of Fyrkat, west of Hobro, and of Aggersborg, north of Limfjorden. Many defensive works may therefore still be hidden under cultivated ground all over the country.

The refuge-stronghold in Borre Fen is situated on a small island that was already well protected by nature, surrounded by swamp and bog, in the lee of high hills. It covered the whole island, which is only about a hundred and fifty metres long north-south and eighty to a hundred metres wide. The fortifications consist of two moats and a rampart. One of the moats runs crosswise between the island and the mainland to the south-east where the bog is narrowest. At the bottom of the bog, which was undoubtedly originally covered with water, a ford paved with stones the size of a fist or somewhat larger runs out diagonally from the land through a break in the cross-moat. Some two hundred years later a regular causeway, which has already been discussed, was built on top of the ford, at the time the village was built.

The second moat at Borre Fen was dug the whole way round the outside of the island. It is a flat-bottomed moat, unlike those of the later ring-forts, which are sharp bottomed. This moat was dug from one and a half to two and a half metres down on the gravelly outer side of the island and the earth thrown up as a wall on the inside. As the moat is about five or six metres wide, a considerable quantity of gravel went to the making of the wall, which must have been a couple of metres high. To facilitate the task of throwing up the earth, one or two ledges were made on the inside of the moat. From them the earth could be thrown up higher. The distance from the top of the earthwork to the outside of the moat was between eight and ten metres and the height of the earthwork from the bottom of the moat about four or five metres, so that this stronghold would not have been easy to storm, if it was well manned. To make it even safer, the old layers of peat were even dug away from beyond the moat: the fortress was thus surrounded by a pitted and dangerous swamp with clear water nearest the island.

During the excavation of the Borre Fen stronghold, where the village people from round about sought refuge in time of trouble, a large number of short, pointed sticks of oak wood were found at the bottom of the moat. They were no doubt originally stuck in the sides, to spike the feet of enemies trying to storm the fort, merely protected as they were by thin leather footwear that was soaked through with the moisture of the bog. A fortunate find from an ancient peat grave nearby has shown us the footgear of the time. Two leather moccasins were found, deposited as a sacrifice in a clay vessel of the Early Iron Age, which had been protected against being eaten away by the acids in the bog by a piece of limestone which had been placed inside the clay vessel to weight it and the moccasins down in the water. The people themselves we also know. A man and two women were laid to rest, each in their ancient peat grave, to the north-west of the little Borre Fen. They are bog people who were sacrificed in the Early Iron Age.

The amount of planning and measuring that was carried out in preparation for the great earthwork in Borre Fen is brought home to us by a measuring rod of oak wood 1.35 metres long that has a button at one end and is pointed at the other. It is divided into eight equal measuring lengths of 16.5 centimetres, cut along one edge in the form of alternately convex and concave curves.

Whether the inner moat was further strengthened with palisades and whether the rampart was supported by timber-work and parapets, has not yet been established. A row of oak posts was found along the underside of the outer moat, standing about a foot apart.

During the excavation of the moat, which had filled up in the course of time with various refuse and with peat and gravel that had slipped down in alternating layers, it became apparent that in the first period after its construction the stronghold had only been used during brief periods. Fragments of clay vessels and other things were scattered fairly sparsely on the bottom, and for long distances there was nothing at all. The bottom layer had clearly been deposited during intermittent occupations. Higher up in the moat, however, was a thick cultural layer containing thousands of pieces of broken pottery dating from the building of the village on the island in the century before Christ. Even if the

112 *and* 113   Rampart and moat in Borre Fen before and
after excavation

population of the surrounding district only sought refuge on the island for brief periods, a water supply was necessary, especially if they brought their cattle with them. A deep pond had been dug for this purpose in the north-westerly corner of the island, where there was a plentiful supply of underground water.

This stronghold, more than two thousand years old, is now protected and is open to the public. A light-coloured block of stone, on which the famous sculptor of Års has reproduced the sacrificial scene from the great silver cauldron from Gundestrup Bog, stands on a dark, heather-covered hill east of the main road from Års to Hobro. From here one can look out across green, well-drained meadows that were once morass and lake, to the Borre Fen stronghold.

There is another earthwork known as Trælborg, which was also designed by nature for the purpose, but is some five hundred years later than Borre Fen, in Verst Forest about fifteen kilometres north-west of Kolding. It is situated on the south-eastern side of a large hilly area just east of the central Jutland watershed. Trælborg consists of a low oval earthwork of irregular shape, because it follows the line of the terrain. It stands only half to three-quarters of a metre above the forest floor, is about five metres wide and measures about forty metres by fifty from one outer edge to the other. Some of the earth has been taken from a moat which is fairly flat-bottomed and two or three metres wide at the top, and which runs the whole way round. The moat has always been dry because the level of the bottom varies by two metres. Trælborg was intended as a place of refuge in times of strife. Shortly before it was built there was a long house on the spot, now partly covered by the earthwork. This house contained objects dating from about the year 500, which is probably also the date of construction of the earthwork. It is eight metres long, has a fireplace in the centre and curved sides, and is thus the same type of house as was in use in the great Viking camps, the first of which was found at Trelleborg west of Slagelse.

These large, circular camps of the end of the Viking Age,

four of which are now known in various parts of the country, though none outside Denmark, were discovered by accident. In this sports-happy age it occurred to someone that the huge green arena of Trelleborg would make an ideal site for a motorcycle racecourse. Before permission was given for this, the ground was investigated. It led to the excavation of a remarkable construction which, in the same way as the Norwegian Viking ships, paints in the background to the great Viking Age.

Trelleborg is of considerably larger dimensions than the refuge stronghold of Borre Fen and covers an area greater than that of even the largest of our medieval castles: Vordingborg and Hammershus. The form was not determined by the nature of the terrain, as in the case of the refuge strongholds. Before building the ring-fort the whole area was levelled so that it could be marked off in accordance with a previously prepared plan: a definite geometrical blueprint with fixed axes and consistent symmetry, that is only broken at a few points. It is in itself unique in ancient Danish building and not until the end of the seventeenth century was any military construction of corresponding precision erected in the country.

The main construction at Trelleborg is a gigantic ring rampart that encloses an area of over four acres, on which stood sixteen completely identical Viking halls. These were built in four groups of four, each group forming an enclosed square courtyard, one in each quarter of the circular space, which was divided by roads running north-east and south-west, crossing at the centre and cutting through the rampart at all four points of the compass. The houses were so arranged that eight of the gable ends faced a central space about twenty metres square.

The camp stands right at the end of the headland formed by the confluence of the rivers Tudeå and Varbyå. It was therefore necessary to do a good deal of filling-in on the south side in order to create a sufficiently large area. At the same time, full advantage was taken of the security offered by the two rivers, by building the ramparts on the banks of the rivers, which were strengthened with a foundation of heavy stones that has now broken up. The rampart, which was seventeen metres wide at ground level, was further strengthened on either side by a high palisade. The gates, through which passed wood-paved roads, were built over, so that the top of the rampart was unbroken. They could be closed with strong doors. For them both rings and massive keys have been found. On the land side the headland is cut off by a moat seventeen metres wide, the bottom of which was ten metres below the top of the rampart. It was not so deep, however, that the water from the rivers would fill it, but deep enough to collect shallow water. There was no direct connection from the eastern gate over the moat to the land. A bridge connected the mainland with the south gate, leading over to an outer camp containing houses and a burial place that was also protected by a moat and rampart.

There were thirteen large houses in the outer camp, arranged radially in relation to the centre of the main camp, and two more standing parallel to these, in line with the east-west orientated houses inside the ring wall. More than a hundred graves were found in a specially demarcated area inside the outer moat, among them a number of mass graves, the largest containing ten skeletons.

The site of this large stronghold was chosen with care. It assures both access to the sea and protection by land. Trelleborg stands in a stretch of valley about four kilometres from the Great Belt, and is accessible to shipping from Musholm Bay by way of the river Næsbyå, which links the two rivers that surround the site and runs out into the Great Belt at a point still bearing the name of Skudeløbet (shipping run). The fine position of this headland was appreciated from early days. It was inhabited in the Stone Age, four thousand years ago, and again in the Early Iron Age, fifteen hundred years later.

When Trelleborg was built towards the end of the prehistoric era, the Vikings had already occupied the headland for some time. Well-like pits, whose contents seem to indicate that they may have been used for sacrifices, date from the period. It is evident that this place of sacrifice is older than the great symmetrical construction, because the sacrificial pits in many cases lie underneath the houses of the fort, and had been filled in before these were built. In one of the pits were two small children together with the head and limbs of a young he-goat that had been killed by a blow on the forehead. In another were two more children and parts of a young cow, a dog and bones of other animals, while a third contained a human skull. That the place was also inhabited at this time is known from various house sites, smaller, horseshoe-shaped buildings that may have been the dwellings of the gods, and a house about thirty metres long which was possibly the residence of the chief in charge of the sacrificial temple.

All that remained of the buildings in the great Trelleborg camp were the holes in the clay subsoil left by wall-planks and posts, and paved fireplaces. These, however, give such a clear picture that it is possible to reconstruct the appearance of the houses in all essentials by interpreting the holes in the subsoil in the light of what is already known of old Scandinavian wood-building techniques.

The sixteen buildings inside the ring wall are of the same size and are built in the same peculiar shape with truncated ends and curved sides, so that they look like sternless ships lying bottom upwards. They are twenty-nine and a half metres long and eight metres wide in the middle, but because of the curved sides only four and a half metres wide at the ends. They were all divided into three rooms, the main hall, about eighteen metres long and with a paved fireplace, in the middle, and two smaller gable rooms at each end, with two planks in the partition wall dividing these from the hall which constitute a bearing element in the roof construction. There were doorways leading all the way through in the end walls and partition walls, while the long hall also had direct access to the open, at one side to the courtyard, at the other to the street. The walls were more than the height of a man, built of broad oak planks: the alternate, grooved ones were sunk down into the subsoil while the rather thinner, tongued ones were fitted into them. The roof was covered with shingles and probably supported by long thin planks, the ends of which were sunk into the ground. There is a row of holes in the subsoil, parallel with the walls of the house, which were left by these supports and were first interpreted as being the marks of posts supporting an external gallery running round the house. It is this supposed gallery that may be seen on the full-scale model house that has been erected at the entrance to the outer camp, based on one of the houses there that measures 26.5 × 7.8 metres, and so is rather smaller than those of the main camp. Ten of the houses in the outer camp were built on this plan. The other five, on the other hand, had free-standing roof-posts inside the house, as in the Early Iron Age. They were probably used as storerooms or stables.

Trelleborg ring-fort with the surrounding area is now protected and is open to visitors all the year round. The ground plans of the houses have been marked out in the green grass that now covers the whole area. The ramparts have been repaired and in the east gate the old stonework that closed the cuttings through the ramparts has been replaced. The moats have been emptied of the refuse that in the course of time had almost hidden them. Only the burial place has not been marked out. From a tower in the centre of the inner court one has a wide view over this impressive Viking construction and the surrounding wide valley with the two river courses. The reconstructed house gives a vivid impression of the size and spaciousness of the houses, even though it contains errors such as, for example, the external gallery. As it stands now it is bare and without details, but probably some at least of the Trelleborg houses were adorned with the wild animal art of the Viking Age as we see it on two shrines from Bamberg and Cammin. These are made on the model of this type of house. There is also a certain kinship with the Norwegian stave churches, whose dragon heads still bellow at the mountains from the gable tops.

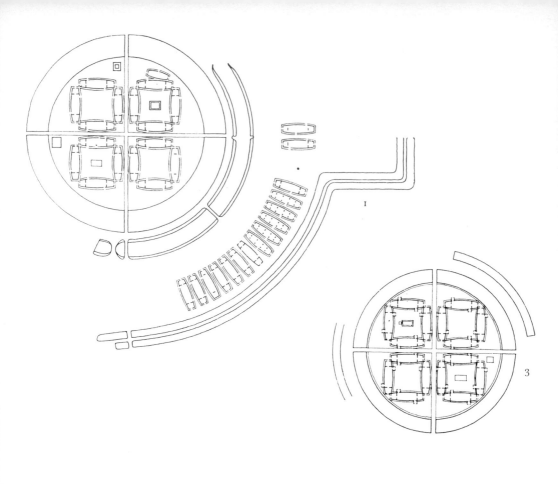

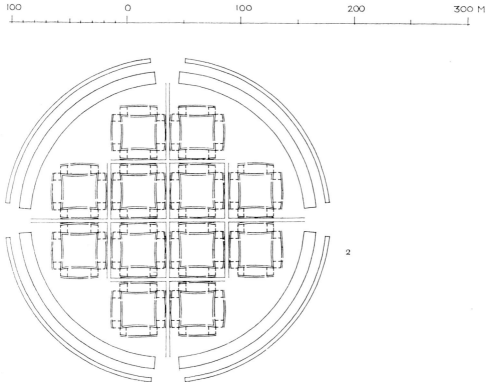

114   Plans of ring-forts: Trelleborg, Fyrkat, Aggersborg (same scale)

Fyrkat ring-fort, on a headland in Onsild River Valley about two kilometres south-west of Hobro, is built on the same plan as the central part of Trelleborg. The situation is much the same as at Trelleborg: a navigable river leading from Hobro Fjord inland to a headland covered with broad hills. Until it was excavated Fyrkat ring wall had been almost levelled, but it has now been restored to a considerable height. It has an inside diameter of a hundred and twenty metres and is about twelve metres thick, built on a basic structure of earth-filled boxes made of wooden planks, which on the outside formed palisades and parapets. It was attached to the timberwork of the inside by means of horizontal anchor-beams. A moat follows the line of the earthwork at a distance of about ten and a half metres on the high ground to west and north-east. It is a dry, sharp-bottomed moat, 7.8 metres wide and only deep enough to allow a man to stand upright, but Fyrkat gained its best protection from the river whose bank formed a steep slope running up to the rampart in the north, while to the south was a low-lying swamp that is now a mill-pond.

The sixteen houses, which form a four-sided block round a central court, one in each quarter of the circle, demarcated by the cross-roads and a ring road, are twenty-eight and a half metres long, seven and a half wide at the centre and five metres wide at the ends. They are not stave-built like the Trelleborg houses, but otherwise follow the same ground plan. The walls were of planks and half-timbering with wattle and daub. The eighteen metre long main hall had a fireplace and plank beds along the walls. The roof was supported by long planks in the partition walls, and the rafters ran into the ground about a metre from the outside of the house walls. The roof was covered with shingles or reeds, possibly with riveted boards. The doors of the main hall, both the one on to the courtyard, in the centre of which were smaller buildings, and the one on to the street were porched. Outside the west gate and inside the east gate a four-sided outline in the ground possibly marks the position of a watch tower, such as is also known from Trelleborg. Not all the houses were exclusively dwelling-houses. One of them had a smithy in it, and another appeared to have been used as a storehouse.

The burial ground was towards the north-east point of the headland. Here twenty-eight inhumation graves have been investigated, some richly furnished and some without grave goods. The latter may perhaps show Christian influence. Above the rich graves, two of which had carriage-bodies as coffins, there were fireplaces where the funeral pyre had been. The graves lay on either side of a fourteen metre plank road ending in a platform five metres wide, but neither this nor the graves have been marked on the surface. The house foundations, on the other hand, are marked out in three quarters of the fort area, the last quarter having been left untouched for investigation some time in the future when there will presumably be far better facilities for interpreting the traces of the houses underground correctly.

Finds of objects from Fyrkat show—in common with the grave goods—that the fort was only inhabited for a brief period at the end of the tenth century and that it was then completely destroyed by fire. It is now in public ownership and can be visited all the year round. One thing particularly worth seeing is a restored watermill which is driven from the mill-pond, the water of which in the old days protected the fort from the north-east. The river Onsildå no longer winds round under the crown of the fort, but makes its way direct through the wide green valley stretching out towards the steep hills in the west that formed the banks of the fjord in Neolithic times five thousand years ago.

The last Viking Age ring-fort to have been discovered, Nonnebakken in Odense, also stood beside a river leading inland from a fjord. It stood in the centre of the present town, on a ridge just south of the Odense river in the angle formed by Hunderup road and Nonnebakke road, where the Odd Fellow Lodge now stands. Information found on old maps of the town and its environs led to the discovery and was confirmed by test excavations which showed traces both of rampart and moats and of squares of houses of the Trelleborg type. This Viking fort was about the same size as Fyrkat and finds of silver treasure of the Viking period in the area set the date as about the end of the tenth century.

The largest of all the ring-forts is Aggersborg, situated on a sloping salient on the north coast of the extensive complex of Limfjord, from where so many fleets set sail on expeditions against England. The plan is the same as that of the other Viking camps but still larger, having eight more squares of houses inside the rampart, which has an inside diameter of about two hundred and forty metres. There are altogether forty-eight houses placed four by four round a courtyard, twelve in each quarter of the camp, so that the crossing streets that ran from north to south and from east to west had the side walls of four houses on either side. Because Aggersborg lies a little distance back on the headland, it was necessary here to surround it completely with a rampart. Finds show that this stronghold was contemporary with the others, but there are traces underneath it of an earlier settlement with houses of a similar type that followed a street orientated north and south. These are about two hundred years earlier than the houses of the Viking camp, and shorter. Aggersborg, too, was destroyed at one blow, and it is presumed that this was during the revolt in 1086 of the inhabitants of Vendel against King Knud den Hellige. He was killed the same year before the high altar in the church of St. Albani in Odense—on which occasion Nonnebakken may also have been stormed and burnt. By that time the great strongholds were undoubtedly already partially abandoned. The Viking raids against foreign shores had long since ceased, and with them the importance of the ring-forts.

Only test excavations have been carried out at Aggersborg, but they were enough to establish its extent and plan. It has now all been covered over again. The large ring wall can, however, still be distinguished in the slanting evening light between the church and Aggersborg farm. A dike runs along beside a section of the ring wall and appears further on as an

undulation in the cultivated ground. Some time in the future
no doubt the wish will be felt to bring this fine stronghold,
too, into the light of day.

No more than these four ring-forts with their symmetrically
laid out blocks of houses and streets are known either in
Denmark or elsewhere, but it is possible that the future may
bring others to light. The many features they have in common
—not least the fact that they are all built with the Roman foot
as the unit of measurement, and so far as one can tell within
a very short space of time—indicate that they must have been
erected on the instructions of the same overlord and by the
same master builder in accordance with a grandiose plan for
the whole country, which presumably also included the most
southerly earthwork of Danevirke. In the erection of Trelleborg the average size of the unit of measurement used (the
Roman foot) was 29.33 centimetres. It forms the basis of all
the more important measurements. Thus the houses inside the
rampart are a hundred feet long, in the outer camp ninety
feet, and the rampart itself is sixty feet wide. At Fyrkat the
houses are ninety feet long, those at Aggersborg a hundred
and ten feet. One overlord who might have been capable of
carrying out the demanding task of building these ring-forts
is the king, Sven Tveskæg, who only began his Viking raids
against England in the 990s and consequently had need of
firm strongholds at home, both to train the necessary fighting
men and to secure his kingdom during his absences. As no
direct model for these constructions is known abroad, nothing
definite can be said about their origin. The actual form of the
houses with their curved side walls is older than the ring-forts,
as we know from the earlier buildings at Trelleborg and
Aggersborg. Use of the Roman unit of measurement and the
arrangement of the individual houses in great military strongholds may, on the other hand, have been introduced from
abroad, most probably from the East with which there were
such strong connections just at that time. Roman traditions
of military construction may have lingered on in the Byzantine kingdom to the end of the Viking Age. It may be from

115   Fyrkat ring-fort in the Onsild river valley at Hobro

here that the Danish king brought the master builders who supervised the building with the aid of a staff of Danish artisans. Not very much later, Scandinavian chiefs occupied a prominent position in the bodyguard of the Byzantine Emperor as leaders of the native corps.

The best models for the distinctive ground plan of the ring-forts are to be found further east, however. The Assyrians had built fortified camps on the same pattern as early as the first millennium B.C. This pattern persisted for two millennia and is seen in a king's residence of the tenth century A.D., Firuzabad in the centre of Persia, which was completely circular, surrounded by rampart and moat and with four gates, one in each quarter of the compass. Nor is it surprising that the ground plan of our ring-forts should have been borrowed from so far away, for connections with these countries were strong in the Viking Age and many thousands of silver coins minted in the Middle East have been found in Scandinavian soil.

A number of low, overgrown earthworks which were built either as road blocks or to enclose a definite area, may be of early date but only a few of them have been excavated for their date to be definitely established. Brovold, on Als, with a village settlement which lies right up at the head of Augustenborg Fjord, through which there was access for shipping, is of the Viking Age. This village, which was inhabited from the Viking period down to the Middle Ages and covered an area of about five acres, was protected on the land side by a huge semi-circular rampart. The sites of a number of small houses about three metres by four in ground area and with a fireplace in one corner have been uncovered between the earthwork and the fjord.

One of the more important earthworks is Rammedige, south-west of Lemvig. It is about two metres high and about fifteen metres wide, running for about half a kilometre in a north-south direction, and has a moat on the east side. It forms the boundary between the parishes of Ramme and Dybe and was built to guard the old east-west main road into North Jutland. A large group of Bronze Age burial mounds beneath the earthwork gives this place a peculiar character and atmosphere. Other similar road-blocks are Dandiget at Asfærg north-west of Randers, Trældigerne at Ikast east of Herning, and Oldmersdiget at Tinglev in South Jutland. There are several road blocks close to the old Army Road that runs from Viborg down through the heart of Jutland between the sources of the rivers Gudenå and Skernå, and out through the largest of all earthworks, Danevirke, on what was the southern frontier of Denmark in the Viking Age.

Concerning the building of the Danevirke, the Frankish annals, *Annales Regni Francorum*, for the year 808 describe how the Danish king Godfred, after he had sacked and destroyed the north German Baltic town of Reric, 'carried the merchants off with him and sailed with his whole army to the harbour called Sliesthorp. Here he stayed for some days and demanded that his country's frontiers with the Saxons should be fortified by a wall, so that this earthwork stretching from the eastern bay called Østersalt to the western ocean would protect the entire northern shore of the Eider river and would have but a single gate for carriages and horses to travel to and fro. After he had distributed this task among his chieftains he returned home.' This account refers without any doubt to the construction of the largest ancient monument in Scandinavia, the Danevirke, which was constantly extended during the following three and a half centuries to become a comprehensive and complex system of earthworks. Its strategic position was chosen from the start with such skill and care that it has retained its importance right up to the present time. In 1864 the Danish army forty thousand strong stood in newly-dug trenches in the western arm to hold the Danevirke position against advancing Prussians and Austrians. This line of defence at the base of Jutland could not, in fact, be held, because among other things, an integral part of the defences had always been the water and swamp to east, south and west, and in the winter months the frost turned these natural obstacles into bridges for the advancing enemy. In the spring of 1945 the old fortifications were again included in defence

275

preparations when the German Army dug deep anti-tank trenches in the walls against an anticipated British invasion. They were never used, however, and have now been filled in; but one realizes how far-sighted King Godfred was when he chose this particular spot for the frontier defences of his kingdom.

The main wall stretches from Gottorp in the east to Hollingsted in the west and it is astonishing that at this point Jutland is almost cut through and is only fourteen kilometres wide. The gate referred to in the Frankish annals must be the Kalegat, just west of the village of Little Danevirke, through which the old Army Road gathered together its tracks from North Jutland to emerge into the great European road network. The most easterly part of the wall covers a stretch of about fifteen kilometres, still at a height of six or seven metres, and is about thirty metres wide. It was built in a number of stages, and had a palisade and a flat-bottomed moat on the south side, and a road protected by a wall along the northern side. At one stage this stretch was further protected by a wall of huge stones set in clay, three metres high and three thick. This improvement is attributed to Queen Thyre, but there is no definite proof of such an assumption. The last major piece of work on this central and most important section of the wall from Kurborg, where the wall turns and runs west, to the Thyreborg stronghold by Lake Danevirke to the north-east, was carried out by King Valdemar the Great in the 1160s. He built a red brick wall along this section five kilometres long, two metres wide and six or seven metres high with battlements and buttresses towards the moat to the south. So important was his work considered to be that it is mentioned on the lead tablet with a Latin inscription that was placed in King Valdemar's grave in Sankt Bendts church in Ringsted. In this the king is called 'the mighty conqueror of the Slavs, glorious liberator of the oppressed fatherland, restorer and preserver of peace', while it is particularly emphasized that 'he built for the defence of the whole kingdom the wall, the first to be built of baked bricks, which is known in common parlance as Danewerch'.

116   The main rampart of Danevirke

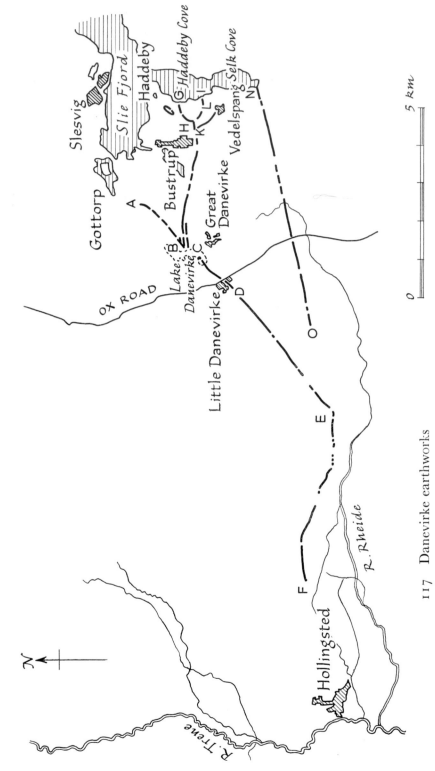

Slesvig

Slie Fjord

Gottorp

Haddeby

Haddeby Cove

G

H

Bustrup

K

L

Selk Cove

Vedelspang

N

OX ROAD

A

B

Lake
Danevirke

C

Great
Danevirke

Little Danevirke

D

O

E

R. Rheide

F

Hollingsted

R. Trene

N

5 km

0

117 Danevirke earthworks

From Kurborg the wall curves round to the west to Hollingsted. Here it is only two or three metres high, some twenty metres wide and along a stretch of about eight hundred metres takes the form of a double wall with a water-filled moat between. Along this curved section the road from the main wall continues along the northern side testifying to the extensive trade that flowed across the foot of Jutland from the great Baltic trading centres of Viking days: from Sweden's ancient capital of Birka on the island of Björkö in Lake Mälar; Grobin on the Latvian coast; Truso in the delta of the river Vistula with direct access to Byzantium; and Wollin at the mouth of the Oder in the Baltic—all to Western Europe, where trade centred largely on the flourishing town of Dorestad close to the confluence of the Rhine and Lek in Holland, possibly founded by Charlemagne. All these towns disappeared at the end of the Viking Age together with many others, such as Lindholm Høje on Limfjord and Skiringsdal at Kaupang on the western side of Oslo fjord, but have been restored to memory in recent years by the excavations of archaeologists. The great wall served as protection for Slesvig and Hedeby, which were centres of trade between east and west.

Hedeby, with its overland trade routes, may originally have been one of the main towns to be protected against enemies from the south by Godfred's wall. On the western side of Hedeby Nor there had been two or three trading stations which were linked together and surrounded by a wide semi-circular wall when the Swedes conquered it in about the year 900. Finds made in the town which grew up inside the defensive wall bear testimony to this trade. From western Europe came glass, Frankish swords and millstones of Rhenish basalt: from Norway, soap-stone for moulds and fireproof pots: from the northern coasts of the Gulf of Bothnia, whale oil and furs. The town's own artisans were also represented with products such as combs, clay vessels, ornaments and boats. When Sven Tveskæg conquered the town at the end of the tenth century, the walls had to be rebuilt. It may have been then that the semi-circular wall of Hedeby was linked up with Danevirke by a connecting wall to the east. The south front was made secure with the dead straight wall, seven kilometres long, known as Kovirke that runs from Selle Nor in the east to the swampy areas in the west around the river Rejde, and had a palisade on top and a sharp-bottomed moat on the south side. Far to the east, the broad Svansen peninsula was protected by a wall running from Slie Fjord to Vindeby Nor, the Østervold, a good three kilometres long, which has now almost completely disappeared.

When one considers how narrow the stretch of land is at Danevirke between the deepest bays on the Baltic side and the navigable stretches of river running into the North Sea on the other, one wonders that the Vikings did not cut through the land with a navigable canal. That they had mastered the art of canal building we know from the Kanhave canal that connects Stavnsfjord with the sea to the west, cutting the island of Samsø in two. It is a kilometre long and with a depth of about one and a half metres was navigable for the ships of the Viking Age. The sides were secured against earth-slips by three rows of horizontal planks placed one above the other and held in place by driven piles and pegs fixed through holes in the planks.

Possibly the double wall with a water-filled moat in between, along the curved stretch to the western end of Danevirke south of Ellingsted, was the beginning of such a waterway.

To visitors, Danevirke and the many constructions connected with it is a thing in a class by itself. From the green semi-circular rampart of Hedeby one gets a vivid impression of the largest trading town of Scandinavia in the Viking Age. One looks out across the cove to the hills of Svansen and to Slie Fjord on whose northern coast lies Hedeby's severest trade competitor in the Viking Age, the still flourishing Slesvig. One remembers the words of the Hamburg canon, Adam of Bremen: 'From that harbour ships sail out to Slav lands, Sweden and Lapland, yes even to Greece.' Long

118 Valdemar's brick wall in Danevirke

stretches of the western part of the main earthwork of Dane-virke still stand as a mighty memorial to the old southern frontier of Denmark, with grazing sheep on the crown of the wall and in the broad moat. The low heather- and grass-covered back of the curved wall loses itself in the meadows running down to the old port of Hollingsted on the river Trene, but Kovirke still lies undisturbed west of the twin mounds of Danhøje, where the old Army Road cuts through it.

XIII Hidden Traces of Antiquity

Immovable monuments and ancient objects form the visible part of our heritage from the days of antiquity. Another part, the invisible traces, is also preserved, though they only rarely reveal themselves and are often unrecognizable in their present guise. They are, among other things, the sacred places of the ancients, which were there beside every single dwelling-place and every settlement throughout the country.

There is not much possibility of detecting such traces for the millennia of the hunting and fishing peoples. Their religion was bound up with the animal world, and it was on the continued existence of this that their thoughts and actions were centred in their struggle for existence. A few animal pictures from Danish finds, and rock engravings and paintings in the caves of western Europe and on the rock faces of Norway and Sweden, tell of this. In the first peasant period the grave became a sacred place. Here sacrifices were offered to ancestors, a custom that persisted throughout all phases of the early period. In other places, too, worship was offered to the powers that ensured the prosperity and good fortune of the community. These sacred places were in the open where one stood face to face with providence. Of this Tacitus writes in his book about the Germani (the *Germania*) that they did not consider it compatible with the greatness of the heavenly powers to be shut in behind walls so that groves and copses were consecrated to them. It is consequently difficult now to identify these places, but they reveal themselves in finds, in place names and in legends associated with localities where the powers of nature manifest themselves in a strange way. People worshipped the sun and the moon, thunder and lightning, the sky, huge boulders, for the same hidden forces as they reveal today, springs from deep underground sources, some of which still run with life-giving water, and trees, which in a few cases may be of an age that takes them back to the centuries of antiquity. All these powers were strong well into Christian times and still leave vestiges. The old religions are revealed in legal provisions like, for example, the laws of Knud the Great, in which it was forbidden to worship heathen gods, the sun and the moon, sacred springs and stones. Trees are not mentioned in these laws but many a belief was associated with them, and there are many tales of Christian missionaries felling the sacred trees of heathens. The church historian, Adam of Bremen, tells of the part played by the tree and the spring in the religious ideas of late prehistoric times in an account of the temple at Uppsala in Sweden in the 1070s: nine men were sacrificed to the gods and their bodies hung in a grove close to the temple, where every tree was sanctified by the sacrifices. Between the men were hung dogs and horses, the same sacrifices as we know from Viking burials. Adam tells also of a spring in which a human being was sacrificed by drowning, and of a large sacred tree which was green both summer and winter. It seems highly probable that there were similar sacred places in Denmark in the Viking Age.

Where sacrifices to the divine powers were offered beside large blocks of stone, in springs and bogs, the sanctity of the spot is beyond question, but only exceptionally will they be found as they were then. Even so, many of these places of sacrifice still have about them a peculiar atmosphere of antiquity and sanctity, and are well worth a visit. For the places where the treasures of antiquity were offered to the gods were never chosen by chance. In the Bronze Age and the Iron Age small cauldron bogs were particularly selected as

119 Vie Fen, north-west of Odense. Denmark's largest find
of sacrificial Iron Age weapons came from here

places of sacrifice. Many gifts were deposited in them for the
gods: glorious bronze lurs, ploughs and human beings. Here
we will only mention the Ræve Bog at Gundestrup from which
the great silver vessel was brought out, Nebelgård Fen where
the Grauballe man was found, and Døstrup Fen west of
Hobro in which one of the best preserved ploughing tools of
prehistoric times had been deposited. These are all typical

285

120   Helligkorskilde (Holy Cross Well), on the shore at
Vesterlykker on Samsø

sacrificial bogs, surrounded by high banks and measuring about two hundred metres across. Many more such bogs, all over the country, could be mentioned, but here we will only linger over one, the Ræve Bog, in which, as I have said, was found the world's finest and most remarkable silver cauldron with its pictures of two-thousand-year-old gods and goddesses and sacrificial scenes. It was found packed in pieces, all the picture-adorned plates having been removed and laid in the deep bottom part of the cauldron. It was lying not at the centre of the bog but just south of the great bank on the northern side that commands and dominates the surrounding area. From this one can see south over the expanse of Borre Fen right down to the Borremose fortification, the village and the place where three of the bog people, an Iron Age man and two Iron Age women, were found. A large glacial boulder now marks the spot in the bog where the cauldron was deposited. Peat is no longer cut in the small Ræve Bog which has gradually become overgrown with thickets of alder, willow, aspen and birch. In spring the great bank to the north, covered with broom in flower, is like a flaming pyre, while an aromatic, resinous fragrance spreads from the green shoots of the bog myrtle which covers most of the surface of the bog. The whole of Ræve Bog with the surrounding hills is now protected and is gradually becoming so overgrown that it resembles the sacrificial grove Tacitus describes as the dwelling-place of the goddess of fertility, Nerthus, with her chariot: 'On an island in the ocean is a grove which has never been trodden by human beings, and in it a consecrated chariot, covered in robes.'

The spring has long been sacred on account of its life-giving properties, not least in countries where water is scarce. Here in Denmark it has been the 'water of life' ever since the Late Stone Age and many archaeological finds have been made in springs or wells sunk in springs. The divine power of springs has been sought after for five thousand years. Not until the present day has belief in the healing power they possessed died out. There are records of more than six hundred and fifty

Danish healing springs. Many of them were held in high repute as miraculous springs, and were sought by the sick and aged in their hundreds, especially on Walpurgis Night and Midsummer's Eve. Early Bronze Age sacrifices consist of weapons, as for example three swords in an old spring at Trægården in Roskilde, and a sword, spear-head and chisel at Kirkesøby. In the Late Bronze Age and Early Iron Age the objects sacrificed in the springs were women's ornaments. They were offered to the great mother-goddess who then ruled over fertility and good fortune. Mention must also be made of a hollowed-out trunk of an oak tree deposited in a spring behind Busene Have on the south-east of Møn. In this were the bones of an ox, calf, sheep, horse, pig and dog, and over them were laid magnificent women's ornaments of bronze, dedicated to the goddess: two hanging vessels, a rounded belt ornament and three spiral arm rings. Not far from this spot were found silver and gold ornaments of the Viking Age: ten neck and arm rings and a heavy plaited chain terminating in animal heads and with Thor's hammers attached, deposited fifteen hundred years later than the objects in the sacrificial spring. There is a specially strong atmosphere of antiquity about this corner of Møn at Busene Have, a small Nordic primeval forest where eight burial mounds and a monolith form a semicircle.

Many of the old springs, however, are now merely a moist spot in the earth or are completely dried up because the level of subsoil water has dropped considerably in the last few hundred years. If one wants to experience a living spring of unique beauty and power, one should visit Blåkilde which lies in the open boggy depression south of Rold Skov. The great cleft through which the spring rises is surrounded by low juniper bushes, heather and ancient bog flora. It reflects all the blues and greens of the sky in its clear depths. The bottom is covered with umber brown or olive green plants, veiled at brief intervals by clouds of grey and white which constantly well up like atomic mushrooms from underground sources in the depths of the spring. Here, however, no

121   Damestenen (the Lady Stone), at Hesselager on Funen.
The largest boulder in Denmark

pre-historic finds have as yet been made for the surface of the bog lies undisturbed round the spring, though the feeling of antiquity in this strange spot is strengthened by the series of Bronze Age burial mounds on the eastern horizon.

It is obvious that many of the huge stones of Denmark, more than a thousand of which have legends attached to them, must have been worshipped for the power that has always been attributed to stone, even if this can only be definitely established in the case of those few beside which sacrificial offerings have been found or which bear the sacred signs of the Bronze Age, cup marks and footprints. Such signs connect the stones with Bronze Age fertility rites, and it is no doubt memories of these that lie behind a number of legends about huge stones from which babies come or which turn round when they smell freshly baked bread. This is told, among other things, of the Dyvel stone at Nordby on Samsø. Some say that coarse bread should be laid out if one wants a boy, and biscuits for a girl; others that it was biscuits that brought the boy. Young childless women are supposed in earlier days to have brought dolls to the Dyvel stone to give them children. Similar legends are attached to many other large stones in Denmark.

The tree has played its own particular part in the beliefs of the ancients since the days of the Stone Age, but often only as an accessory in religious practices. Special trees were singled out for hanging up sacrifices to the gods and given names which distinguished them from all other trees. The tree was the symbol of life. To damage the specially selected tree was to bring misfortune over house and home. The greatest of all trees was the world-tree, in Scandinavian mythology the ash Yggdrasil, with its eternally green crown growing up to the clouds and overshadowing the earth. The destinies and continued existence of the world were bound up with Yggdrasil in the same way as those of every individual home with its sacred tree. The name Yggdrasil really means the terrible horse. Odin himself was called Yggra—the Terrible. Legend has it that he himself once hung swinging with the wind in the branches of the tree. At the foot of the tree flows a spring, whose water gives wisdom and powers of prophecy. There is a popular legend about a similar world-tree from Thy: a tree with three branches grows in the meadow of Ti, the god of heaven, and is so mighty that it looks as though it grew up into the clouds. It never loses its leaves, and is green both summer and winter; and it is to this tree that Ti and the other gods will tether their horses before the battle starts that will bring about the destruction and downfall of mankind.

Only very few trees now growing are so old that they go back to prehistoric times, so that one cannot expect to find a single one to which an unbroken tradition is attached. But particular activities handed down from prehistoric times may be transferred to younger trees. This applies, among other things, to the sickness trees, of which there are still some in various parts of the country. Some of them are so shaped that they form a narrow doorway through which children were pushed in order to rid them of a certain sickness. As they passed through the doorway the sickness was scraped off and they were reborn. Usually the child was naked and after the process a scrap of its clothing was attached to the tree, which thus became sacral and could not, of course, be felled. The scraps of clothing on the tree were not sacrifices, but were put there to attach the sickness to the tree, and to remove them would have involved danger of infection.

A few trees must be mentioned which have an aura of antiquity to them: the old oaks in Jægerspris Nordskov. The oldest of them all is Kongeegen (the King's Oak), which is named after the archaeologist king, Frederik VII, who according to tradition sat in person on horseback in its hollow trunk. With its circumference of almost fourteen metres at chest height it is said to be the thickest tree in Europe. By all accounts the Kongeegen is at least fourteen hundred years old, probably even older, and put out its first shoot from the acorn in the Roman Iron Age, possibly at the time of the birth of Christ. Its top went long ago, but with its primeval strength it continues to send out fresh branches from its knotted trunk. A birch grows from a hollow in its lowest branch. Storkeegen (the Stork Oak), in whose crown a stork built its nest a century ago, is not so old; neither are Snoegen (the Twisted Oak), whose main trunk is twisted, nor Bregneegen (the Fern Oak), from which grow both birch and mountain ash trees. They stand on small islands scattered about Great Elle Fen, that with its luxuriant forest of oak, birch and alder with an undergrowth of hawthorn, hazel and honeysuckle presents a splendid picture of a Scandinavian primeval forest in prehistoric times.

A great deal of information about ancient settlements and sanctuaries lies concealed in place names. As these, however, have changed considerably through the centuries, one has to work back to the oldest forms of the names, which alone make possible a correct interpretation of their origins. These have to be sought in medieval documents, deeds and titles of ownership. A very few place names are preserved in a yet older form on runic stones and in foreign chronicles. Place names are naturally very difficult to date and particularly short names have often been referred to the Stone Age or the Iron Age without adequate justification. Dating can only be done on a linguistic or historical basis, or by comparison with Scandinavian place names in those parts of western Europe where Scandinavians settled at the time of the migrations or in the Viking Age, because they took their own forms of names with them. For example, one can see from the Danelaw in England which names were current in the Viking Age and which were not. A comparison between the distribution of certain archaeological finds all over the country and in special areas has not provided a satisfactory basis for the dating of place names since the material was inadequate. No types of name can be carried back with any certainty further than the centuries following the birth of Christ, even though many short names may in their earliest forms go back to both the Bronze Age and the Stone Age.

One of the oldest known forms of compound name is the -*inge* name, which is found with the ending -*inge* on the

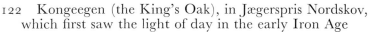

122   Kongeegen (the King's Oak), in Jægerspris Nordskov,
which first saw the light of day in the early Iron Age

Islands and -*ing* in Jutland. These were only rarely formed in
the Viking Age and are on the whole much older, which
enables us to establish the existence of Iron Age settlement
areas in particular districts. About four hundred of these
names are known from all over the country and they are all
connected with large, old settlements, half of which have

293

become parish towns. Also pre-Viking are most of the compound names ending in -*um* and -*heim*, which means settlement, -*løse*, which is found particularly on the Islands and in Skåne and possibly means pasture, -*tun*, an enclosed place or courtyard, and -*lev*, an inheritance or heritage. The majority of -*lev* names are compounded with a chief's name of the period of migrations and they occur first on Zealand, and later in Jutland, which may reflect a victorious expedition by Zealand chiefs against Jutland in the Iron Age. Names with the endings -*vang* for enclosure, -*ager* for pasture, -*by* for settlement and -*torp* for farm are mainly of the Viking Age and the Middle Ages, while -*toft* for demarcated area is of the Viking Age. Names ending in -*bod* for storage shed, -*køb* for property, -*løkke* and -*have* for enclosure, are of the Middle Ages.

All the above-mentioned compound names probably date from after the time of the birth of Christ, but many short names may be earlier than that, even if their date cannot be definitely fixed. This applies, among others, to the *ø*- and *å*-names, which are connected with old names in extinct Indo-European languages. They were in use in the oldest Indo-European name material known to us. Many of them may therefore have been brought to Denmark by the Battle-axe people nearly four thousand years ago.

A special class of place names reflects cultural conditions in prehistoric times and tells us where the sacred places were, and to whom they were dedicated. Of the sanctuaries themselves there is usually no trace. The earliest name of a divinity to be found in place names is that of the goddess of fertility, Njord, whom Tacitus calls Nerthus. It is found in the name of the North Zealand village of Nærum and in the names Nørre- and Sønder-Nærå, and may go back to the Late Bronze Age or the Celtic Iron Age when this goddess occupied a prominent position. This, however, was soon taken over by the god Frøy, who in old Danish was called Frø. His name appears in Frøs Herred, and is associated with bog, mountain and mound in Frømose at Ringsted, Frøsbjerg and Frøshøj, while the name of his goddess partner, Frøya, is to be found in the place names Frølund and Frølunde and presumably also in that of the highest point on Funen, Frøbjerg Baunehøj. Another of the older generation of gods is Ti, the god of heaven, whose name is generally associated with the names of objects in nature and particularly of woods, so that it appears in Tis-lund (grove), Tis-vilde (spring), Tis-sø (lake), Tis-bjerg (hill) and Tilst (Tis-vej = road). Whereas the name of Ti, the god of heaven, is very rare in the place names of other Scandinavian countries, that of Tor, his successor in the mythology of the Viking Age, is common all over Scandinavia, both as first and second component. It is associated particularly with nature names, as in Tors-ager (field), Tors-lund and -lunde, Tor-sø and Tors-høj (mound), but never in Denmark with words signifying sanctuary or temple. That may be due to the fact that, towards the end of the Viking Age, when it became the custom in Scandinavia to bring images of gods into the house, Tor was rather put in the shade by Odin, the god of the aristocratic chieftain class, whose name is connected with the word *vi*, in the sense of sanctuary. This is incorporated in Vi-borg, originally Vibjerg, Odense and Ondsved, while the second part of the East Jutland Onsild is presumably the Old Scandinavian *hylde* in the sense of wooden temple. But the great god Odin is also preserved to the present day in many nature-names: Onsbjerg, Vojens-høj, Vons-bæk (brook), Vons-mose (bog), and in Ons-lunde in Skåne.

The names of other gods cannot be definitely established in Danish place names, but the word God is to be found as the first component of a number of names such as Gud-bjerg, Guden-åen (river), Gud-um, Gud-me and Gud-hjem (home), and *hellig* (holy) in, among others, compounds with *å*, *bæk* and *sø*, which do not, however, always go back to early times. The Old Scandinavian name for a heathen temple, *vi*, is found in Viby and Vindinge-vi, and combined with *-heim* in the sense of a settlement in the Jutland names Vium and Vem, while *hørgh* (*hargh*), which originally meant a heap of stones, later also acquired the meaning of temple and is found in names such as Hørby and Harreby. On the other hand, the word *hov* in the sense of sacrificial temple has not been established with certainty in a single place name, though it may possibly form a component of Hovby south of Fakse in East Zealand. Where names are found containing *hov*, the word is the Old Danish *bugt* (bay). The compound Ho-høj means the high burial mound.

In view of Bronze Age sun worship, one might, without knowledge of the earlier forms of names, attribute compounds including the word *sol* (sun) to ancient sun worship, but Solgård usually means the most southerly house in the town and in Solvig and Solrød the *sol-* is the Old Scandinavian word for swamp, though the very common compound Solbjerg may in many cases be an echo of the ancient sun worship.

A number of names recall one of the ancient methods of agriculture, the burning of forests and cultivation of corn in the ashes, which is known by the Swedish name *svedjebrug*. These include the place names Stabrand and Brabrand in East Jutland, which may be compared with the Old Scandinavian word *bruni* meaning burning or fire.

Hidden traces of antiquity may also be seen in many of the holidays and festivals which now mark out the course of the year like mileposts. They are bound up with dates in the calendar, but once they exactly followed the progress of the year, the fixed courses of the sun, moon and stars. We hold Christmas and Midsummer's Day when the sun turns towards the longer and shorter days. We celebrate Easter, Whitsun and Harvest close to the time when the spring seed is sown, the leaves turn green and the corn is in the barn. All these festivals and many others were in the old days determined by nature and bound up with the processes of agricultural work. The essential meaning of such annually returning events is consequently as old as agriculture and cattle-breeding in Denmark, even though the festivals themselves have been constantly changed in the course of five thousand years by

123 *and* 124   Dolmen at Nyrup on Røsnæs a hundred years
ago and today

new social conditions and new beliefs. At the present time a thousand years of Christianity have lent their colour to the major festivals, but many minor festivities and the customs associated with them had until recently more of the past about them than the present in many parts of the country, and have only since been abandoned.

But we still celebrate Christmas at the same time of year as the ancients held their great mid-winter sacrifices for the benefit of the coming year's crops. Walpurgis night fires still flame on the hilltops when the leaves are green and are bound to the maypole, in order—as the custom formerly was—to promote the prosperity of the earth, of cattle and men, while the sun dances on Whit Sunday morning just as it did when it was a god. Midsummer Night's bonfires still blaze from the heights and along the coasts all over the country on the night when all the powers of witchcraft were let loose, but when also the healing powers of wild herbs were at their greatest and the water in the sacred springs strongest in miraculous power. Traces of antiquity still live on in secret.

XIV How to Find the Prehistoric Monuments*

Prehistoric monuments are not always visible from the public highway. Often they are hidden away in woods and bogs, in stretches of waste land and in remote corners. Most of them have little by little been mapped, so that it should not be a difficult matter to find the monuments one wishes to see in a particular district or when travelling round the country.

Since 1878, National Museum staff and many helpers have been visiting every parish there is to locate and record pre-historic monuments. The vast amount of material that has gradually been collected is now available in the form of about 150,000 dots on the parish maps of the National Museum, with notes and information about every single dot. These parish accounts are available to students in the National Museum archives. All this material is, however, available in condensed form. Johannes Brøndsted's *Danmarks Oldtid* (Prehistoric Denmark) contains maps of the whole country to scale 1 : 320,000 showing all the burial mounds, including both those which have been levelled and those which are still in existence. The stone graves are indicated by a red sign and the raised, grass-covered burial mounds by a green sign, but it is impossible to tell whether a red dot indicates a dolmen, passage grave or megalithic cist, or whether a

* See 'Appendix; The More Important Archaeological Sites in Denmark', p. 307.

burial mound is of the Stone, Bronze or Iron Age, or whether it is still there. The map was prepared to give an overall picture of the prehistoric monuments in different parts of the country and at the same time of the concentration of settlements in the Stone and Bronze Ages. It enables one to study the position of the mounds in relation to soil and terrain and to follow the routes of the old roads, which are so clearly indicated in many areas where the monuments are set in rows.

Extracts from the parish records of the National Museum are to be found in the topographical work by J. P. Trap, *Kongeriget Danmark* (The kingdom of Denmark) (1959–66), in which the most important memorials and finds in each parish are discussed, while the county records provide a wider survey. The parish records also largely form the basis of Politikens Håndbøger no. 251: *Med Arkæologen Danmark rundt* (With the Archaeologist round Denmark) (1966), in which the country is divided into seventeen provinces, each with its own survey and account of prehistoric monuments and finds. These are marked on survey maps.

All prehistoric monuments still extant are marked on the archaeological maps, *Vore Fortidsminder* (Our Ancient Monuments), published in multicolour by the Geodetic Institute in co-operation with the National Museum, to scale: 1:100,000. On these, stone graves are marked with a circle, burial mounds with a red dot, and historical monuments with a blue sign. These maps cover the whole country and each sheet has an accompanying brief account of all the more important monuments with a numbered reference to the map, thus providing the best guide there is to the prehistoric monuments of Denmark.

The maps in *Vore Fortidsminder* also indicate practically all the monuments in Denmark that are protected. If the list is not complete, this is because, first, some of the monuments may have been concealed by undergrowth when the survey was carried out and so escaped detection, and, second, the mapping is not yet complete, particularly in the case of earthworks. If some monument is missing on them, that does not mean that it is not protected, for all prehistoric monuments of Denmark are protected, under the Nature Preservation Law of 7th May 1937, which was revised in 1961, and section 2 of which runs:

2. All fixed prehistoric monuments, such as burial mounds, burial places, dolmens and monoliths, earthworks and similar fortifications, as well as ruins, are to be preserved. The question of what comes under this regulation and of the closer delimitation of the area preserved is to be determined by the National Museum on its own initiative or at the request of the owner or of the preservation tribunal or town or parish council concerned. Within an area of a hundred metres of any fixed prehistoric monument no buildings, sheds, masts, etc., may be erected nor plantations laid out, changes made in the terrain nor other measures undertaken which might to any appreciable extent disfigure or damage the prehistoric monument in question without the permission of the preservation tribunal, which shall act in consultation with the National Museum. In woods and plantations which were in existence before 1st March 1961, re-planting may, however, be carried out, but vegetation must be kept at a distance of not less than five metres from the foot of the monument. The preservation tribunal may, in consultation with the National Museum, alter the boundaries of the hundred metre zone in view of considerations of form of terrain, view, etc., provided the total area is not increased. No withdrawals of the preservation order may be made without the consent of the National Museum and the preservation tribunal. If the National Museum decides that the value of a monument has so much decreased that it has lost its significance either archaeologically or as a feature of the landscape, it will, with the agreement of the preservation tribunal, inform the owner of this fact, after which full rights of disposal revert to the owner. If the owner of a prehistoric monument thus restored to his control wishes to

demolish it completely, he must give notice not less than three months in advance to the National Museum in order that this may, if it wishes, first carry out an investigation. Any decision taken by the National Museum in relation to this regulation may, regardless of who raised the matter, whether the owner, the preservation tribunal or the town or parish council, be made the subject of appeal to the Minister of Education.

A further revision of the whole complex of laws connected with nature preservation is now in course of preparation and may be expected to be put into force in the near future.

Before the coming into force of the preservation law all preservation of prehistoric monuments was voluntary. These first preservations were marked with a granite pillar bearing the letters F.M. (*Fredet Mindesmærke*—Preserved Monument) carved on them under a king's crown. Later on the granite pillars were replaced by cement pillars bearing the same inscription, but as permission was not always granted only a small number of monuments have been marked in this way. Many ancient monuments are thus likely to remain unmarked for some years to come.

A few figures will show the importance of the passing of the preservation law for the conservation of prehistoric monuments in Denmark. In 1807 a Royal Commission for the Preservation of Antiquities was appointed, for the purpose of conserving the most important monuments all over the country. Of these a total of 185, from prehistoric times and the Middle Ages, were placed under preservation order in the years 1809–10. When it was discovered in 1847 that many of these monuments had already been demolished or wrecked, the office of Inspector for the Preservation of Antiquarian Monuments was established. The particular concern of the Inspector was to be the mapping and preservation of prehistoric monuments on a voluntary basis. This form of preservation was continued under different governments until the coming into force of the preservation law in 1937. It

125 Stone-circle grave at Hvolris north of Viborg

126 Burial mounds ploughed over at Enslev in Djursland

achieved good results but in many cases the National Museum stood helpless in the face of destruction of mounds. In 1892 the number of preserved monuments had reached a total of 1,422 and, in 1935, 7,496 were preserved under the National Museum and 217 and 69 respectively under the Geodetic Institute and the Nature Preservation Tribunals. With the new preservation law, a fresh survey of the country for preservation purposes became necessary. On the last occasion —so far as prehistoric monuments are concerned—that this was completed, in 1956, a total of 23,774 prehistoric monuments had been preserved. Of these, 2,067 were stone graves: dolmens, passage graves and megalithic cists, 19,902 were round mounds of the Stone, Bronze and Iron Ages, while the remainder were different types of monuments such as monoliths, rock engravings, stone ships, earthworks, etc. These are distributed throughout the different counties as shown in the following table:

County	Stone graves	Large mounds	Small mounds	Other monuments	Total
Frederiksborg	181	324	197	14	716
Copenhagen	131	306	150	5	592
Holbæk	317	337	217	27	898
Sorø	245	136	80	8	469
Præstø	175	265	436	28	904
Bornholm	12	127	74	874	1,087
Maribo	183	207	1,045	149	1,584
Odense	46	51	55	8	160
Svendborg	194	56	153	37	440
Hjørring	31	806	364	74	1,275
Viborg	46	1,654	965	47	2,712
Randers	184	694	525	82	1,487
Thisted	17	1,053	464	76	1,610
Ålborg	56	1,478	592	59	2,185
Århus	9	73	59	6	147
Skanderborg	11	522	389	30	952

County	Stone graves	Large mounds	Small mounds	Other monuments	Total
Ringkøbing	12	1,435	1,401	40	2,888
Vejle	29	319	374	28	750
Ribe	18	658	774	49	1,499
Haderslev	30	290	141	16	477
Åbenrå	44	86	170	18	318
Sønderborg	96	62	123	127	408
Tønder	2	115	98	1	216
Total	2,067	11,056	8,846	1,803	23,774

Nearly 24,000 legally protected and preserved prehistoric monuments in a country the size of Denmark is a good result for the recent legislation, even if it is only a third of the number that were still in existence a mere hundred years ago, and a still smaller proportion of the number there were originally. Naturally some of the monuments will continue to be destroyed in time to come to make way for houses and roads. But one must hope that so far as possible regard will be had for ancient monuments, and that they will not be needlessly sacrificed to modern requirements. Here one has specially in mind electricity pylons and television masts, which with goodwill and talent can be admirably adjusted to the Danish landscape and create new and valuable perspectives. Unfortunately these qualities are often lacking in the authorities and in their place we find that insensitive outlook which goes by the name of broad-mindedness. The ancient monuments still set their stamp on the Danish landscape and tell of our ten thousand years of prehistory, if only we will listen to their silent speech.

Fig 2. Denmark, main regions and towns

306

Appendix: The More Important Archaeological Sites in Denmark

A. JUTLAND

(i) *Vendsyssel* (xvii)*

1. Horne churchyard: stone cist with cup marks on cover stone (p. 113).
2. Tolstrup Hede: ancient fields at Gedebjerg-Huse.
3. 'Børsen': stone with cup marks erected west of St Cathrine church, Hjørring.
4. Hjørring churchyard: Iron Age stone graves at crematorium (p. 168).
5. 'Rampen': long dolmen west of Hejselt manor (p. 66).
6. Vangsgård: dolmen chamber in mound.
7. Løgten Mark: stone-built cellar (p. 242).
8. 'Blakshøj': passage grave south of Gærum church (p. 90).
9. Donbæk: burial ground with Iron Age burial mounds (p. 170).
10. Albæk Hede: ancient fields and burial mounds north of Fausholt manor.
11. Filholm: megalithic cist beside manor.
12. Hune church: runic stone in tower room.
13. Jetsmark church: runic stone in church porch.
14. Gundestrup: 2 passage graves about 600 m. south-west of Skrem railway station.
15. 'Hvisselhøj': passage grave with supplementary chamber north of Alsbjerg (pp. 84 and 90).
16. 'Grønhøj': long dolmen about 500 m. east of Bejstrup.
17. Aggersborg: Viking Age fortifications between church and manor, ploughed over (pp. 268, 271).
18. Hammer Bakker: dolmens, mounds, road tracks.
19. Lindholm Høje: burial ground with stone ships, mounds, etc. (pp. 172 5).

* The large roman numerals in brackets refer to the areas marked on maps 2–5.

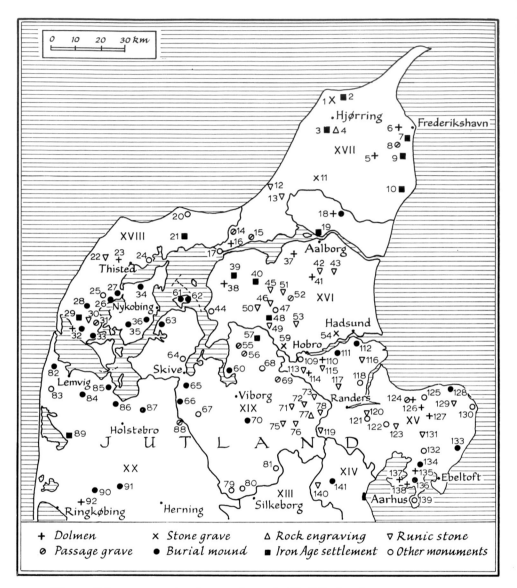

Fig 3. Monuments in the northern half of Jutland

308

(ii) *Thy and Mors* (xviii)

20. 'Troldting': dwelling-houses, burial mounds and monoliths in uninhabited land.
21. Hostrup: monolith and stone ships (p. 143).
22. Vang church: runic stone in church porch.
23. Torsted: 2 long dolmens west of town.
24. Hov Kalkværk: Stone Age flint mines (p. 116).
25. Hørdum church: Viking Age picture stone showing Thor's fishing catch (p. 230).
26. 'Høverhøj': burial mound east of Hørdum.
27. Skyum Bjerge: burial mounds.
28. Rønhede plantation: 4 burial mounds.
29. Vestervig: Iron Age house sites.
30. Hurup churchyard: runic stone.
31. 'Lundehøj': passage grave with supplementary chamber (p. 90).
32. Gettrup: stone coffin grave and mound.
33. 'Oldtidskirkegården' (ancient churchyard): mounds on Ydby Hede (p. 130).
34. 'Salgerhøj': burial mound.
35. Redsted-Vejerslev: a number of burial mounds.
36. Legindbjerge: burial mounds on protected heath area.

(iii) *Himmerland* (xvi, xix)

37. 'Troldkirken': long dolmen at Sønderholm (p. 66).
38. Årupgård: long dolmen between Vilsted and Rønhøj plantation.
39. Vindblæs: ancient fields on heath area.
40. Skørbæk Hede: Iron Age house sites and fields (pp. 234 and 248).
41. Ellidshøj: dolmen chamber in centre of town.
42. Ferslev church: runic stone in church porch.
43. Gunderup church: runic stone in church porch.
44. Ertebølle: kitchen midden south of Ertebølle Head (p. 48).
45. Skivum church: runic stone in church porch.
46. Giver church: runic stone in church porch.
47. Gundestrup: sacrificial bog (pp. 285–6).
48. Borre Fen: Iron Age refuge fort and village at Lille Binderup (p. 260).
49. Kongens Tisted: runic stone in stone wall round parsonage garden.
50. Års churchyard: runic stone on burial mound (p. 229).

51. Suldrup church: runic stone in church porch.
52. 'Stenshøj': passage grave with supplementary chamber at Suldrup.
53. Ravnkilde churchyard: runic stone on burial mound (p. 229).
54. Svalhøjgård: megalithic cist at Vive (p. 113).
55. Fjelsø: passage grave with supplementary chamber.
56. Ettrup: double passage grave.
57. Østerbølle: house sites and fields on stretch of heath (pp. 234 and 248).
58. 'Spanskhøj': passage grave at Snæbum (p. 90).
59. 'Disterhøj': megalithic cist in mound.
60. Virksund: twin mounds (p. 23).

(iv) *Fuur, Salling and Viborg Areas* (XIX)

61. 'Stendalhøje': 5 burial mounds around the highest point in Fuur.
62. 'Smediehøje': 4 burial mounds in heather.
63. Navtrup: dance mound, flat-topped Bronze Age mound (p. 126).
64. 'Ridebanen': ring-fort, burial mounds and sunken roads south of Øster Lyby.
65. Dommerby: group of 23 Stone Age and Bronze Age mounds.
66. 'Fly Høje': 7 Bronze Age mounds in rows south of Fly.
67. 'Dagbjerg Dås': sacred hill (p. 162).
68. Hvolris: stone circle graves and house sites at Vester Bjerregrav (p. 303).
69. Bigum: passage grave north of Tjele Langsø.
70. Brunshåb: group of mounds.
71. Skern: 2 runic stones at church (p. 229).
72. Ålum: 4 runic stones at church.
73. Øster Bjerregrav: 2 runic stones in church porch.
74. Ulstrup: runic stone in manor park.
75. Hjermind: runic stone in parsonage garden.
76. Sønder Vinge: runic stone at church.
77. 'Mandbjerghøj': 2 stones with engravings on site of mound north of Øster Velling.
78. Grensten: runic stone in churchyard dike.
79. Klosterlund: Early Stone Age settlement area (p. 42).
80. Tollund: stretch of bog in which Iron Age man was found.
81. Grauballe: sacrificial bog at Nebelgård, in which Iron Age man was found (p. 285).

(v) *West Jutland* (xx, xxi)

82. Hygum: group of 30 mounds.
83. 'Rammedige': defence dike and ancient mounds (p. 274).
84. Fabjerg: row of Bronze Age mounds.
85. 'Trehøje': Bronze Age mounds.
86. 'Bavnehøje': 5 mounds south of Gimsinghoved.
87. 'Tinghøje': 6 mounds on Stendis Hede.
88. Hagebrogård: passage grave.
89. Gørding Hede: Iron Age house sites and fields (p. 250).
90. 'Muldbjerg': Bronze Age long barrow (p. 18).
91. 'Trehøje': group of mounds west of Timring.
92. Ølstrup: 2 long dolmens, long barrow and round barrow east of church.
93. Øster Lem: large area showing ancient fields (p. 252).
94. Dejbjerg Præstegårdsmose: Early Iron Age sacrificial waggon.
95. Henne: group of burial mounds.
96. 'Mangehøje': group of 38 burial mounds and mounded graves.
97. Horne: runic stone at church.
98. Mejls: passage grave.
99. Nørholm: burial mounds in groups on heath east of river.
100. Skonager: ancient fields and burial mounds in heath.
101. Myrtue: Iron Age house sites (p. 240).
102. Sjælborg: Iron Age house sites with stone-built cellars (p. 240).
103. Tobøl: group of mounds of Battle-axe culture.
104. Sønder Bøl: passage grave.
105. 'Jyndovnen': long dolmen south of Klelund.
106. Klelund plantation: dolmens in south-east corner.
107. Læborg: runic stone at church (pp. 225 and 256).
108. Askov: stone with cup marks at entrance to high school.

(vi) *Mariager – Djursland* (xv)

109. 'Fyrkat': Viking fort south-west of Hobro (pp. 268–70).
110. 'Kongehøjen': long dolmen at Voldstedlund (p. 66).
111. 'Hohøj': Bronze Age mound (p. 23).
112. Vindblæs: Bronze Age mounds.
113. Glenstrup church: runic stone in church porch.
114. 'Tørslevstenen': dolmen chamber, the cover stone of which has numerous cup marks and ovals.
115. Vester Tørslev church: runic stone in church porch.
116. Dalbyover church: runic stone in church porch.

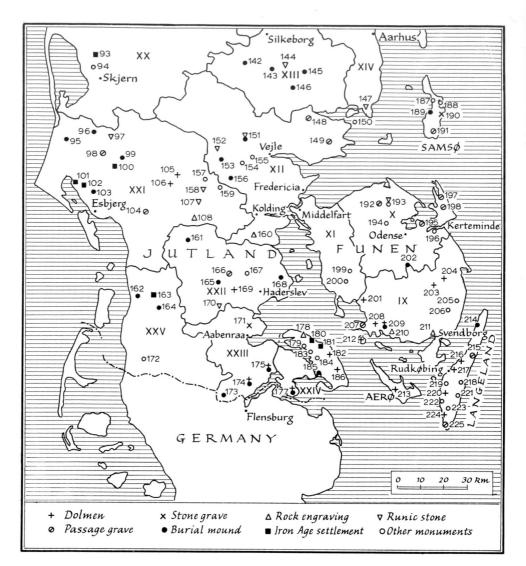

Fig 4. Monuments in West, South-East, and South Jutland, and on
Als, Funen, Samsø, Aerø and Langeland

117. Spentrup church: runic stone in church porch.
118. Hugstrup Skov: group of mounds.
119. Laurberg: runic stone in church porch.
120. Virring church: runic stone in church porch.
121. Hørning church: the Romanesque church is built over a stave church and Viking graves in mound (p. 208).
122. Sjellebro: stone with troll mask at crossing-place over Alling river (pp. 230–1 and 258–9).
123. Øster Alling: runic stone in church porch.
124. Tustrup: dolmens, passage grave and temple (pp. 85 and 95).
125. Meilgård: kitchen midden in woods.
126. Horse Fen: 2 long dolmens and 1 round dolmen.
127. Stenvad: 6 dolmens north of Dystrup lake.
128. Emmedsbo plantation: groups of mounds close to coast in east and west.
129. Rimsø: runic stone on burial mound in churchyard.
130. Fornæs: export place for flint west of Fornæs (pp. 115 and 117).
131. Kolind church: runic stone in church porch.
132. Barkjær: site of Stone Age village on south-east side of the dried-up Lake Korup (pp. 72–4).
133. 'Ormshøje': 4 Bronze Age mounds east of Balle.
134. 'Stabelhøje': Bronze Age twin mounds (pp. 20 and 29).
135. 'Porskjærs Stenhus': dolmen at Knebel (pp. 52 and 58).
136. 'Trehøje': 3 larger and several smaller burial mounds, also long-backed fields in heather.
137. Torup: stone grave.
138. 'Stenhuset': dolmen north-west of Strands.
139. 'Ellemandsbjerget': sacred hill (p. 162).

(vii) *Southern East Jutland* (XII, XIII, XIV, XXI)

140. Sjelle church: runic stone in church porch (p. 229).
141. 'Borum Eshøj': Bronze Age mound, in which clothes were found (p. 126).
142. Boest krat: row of 8 burial mounds south of Vrads.
143. 'Ottehøje': 6 out of an original 8 Bronze Age mounds near Vorbjerg (p. 193).
144. Sønder Vissing: runic stone in church and in church porch (p. 229).
145. 'Yding Skovhøj': burial mound, the highest point in Denmark (pp. 21 and 22).

146. 'Vorbjerg': Bronze Age mounds and flat-topped Iron Age burial mounds (pp. 131 and 193).
147. Gylling church: runic stone in church porch.
148. 'Grønhøj': passage grave south of Lake Bygholm (pp. 85 and 90).
149. 'Deelhøj': passage grave west of Åstrup.
150. Hjarnø: Iron Age stone ships (p. 178).
151. Jelling: burial mounds and runic stone (see Index of names).
152. Store Rybjerg: runic stone on burial mound south-east of Frederikshåb (pp. 228 and 254).
153. 'Kong Rans Høj': burial ground in Randbøl churchyard (pp. 164 and 193).
154. 'Troldeborg': Iron Age ring-fort west of Vingsted.
155. Vingsted Mølledam: Iron Age sacrificial finds made here.
156. Egtved: site of Bronze Age mound in which woman's clothing was found (pp. 138 and 254).
157. Bække Mark: burial mounds, stone ship, runic stone and road tracks (pp. 177–8).
158. Bække: runic stone west of churchyard.
159. 'Trælborg': oval Iron Age ring-fort in Verst woods north of Lunderskov (p. 263).
160. Taps church: stone with wheel-cross in church porch (p. 160).

(viii) *South Jutland and Als* (XXII, XXIII, XXIV, XXV)

161. Brøstrup: group of Bronze Age mounds west of Rødding.
162. Brøns Mølle: 2 groups of Bronze Age mounds east of the mill.
163. Birkelev: burial ground with 31 mounded graves on heath area north-east of Skærbæk.
164. Gassehøje: groups of mounds east of Skærbæk.
165. Skrydstrup: mound in which woman's Bronze Age clothing was found.
166. Over Jerstal: passage graves about 2 km. north of town.
167. Ejsbøl: sacrificial bog in which find of Iron Age weapons was made north-west of Haderslev.
168. 'Tamdruphøj': large burial mound west of Tamdrup.
169. Vedsted: 3 long dolmens at Hohnshus.
170. Hovslund: runic stone to Hærulf by the old Army Road (p. 225).
171. 'Myrpold': megalithic cist south-east of Løjt Skovby (pp. 112 and 113).
172. Gallehus: place where the 2 gold horns were found about 2 km. north of Møgeltønder.

173. Frøslev: burial mounds south-west of Frøslev.
174. Kelstrup skov: dolmens and mounds in the wood.
175. Gråsten: long dolmens and mounds in woods north of town.
176. Nydam: sacrificial bog in which Iron Age boats and weapons were found.
177. Kobbelskov: dolmens and burial mounds in wood.
178. Havnbjerg: stone with cup marks in churchyard wall.
179. Bundsø: Stone Age dwelling sites on islet in stretch of meadows by Bundsø.
180. Nygård: burial ground with Iron Age mounds (p. 172).
181. Havrekoppel: burial ground with Iron Age mounds and monolith (p. 172).
182. Oleskoppel: 2 long dolmens built together in woods near shore (p. 66).
183. Hjortspring: sacrificial bog in which Iron Age boat was found.
184. 'Brovold': semi-circular Viking Age fort (p. 274).
185. Lambjerg Indtægt: dolmens and mounds in woods.
186. Blommeskobbel: long dolmens and round dolmens in woods (p. 66).

(ix) Samsø (IVa)

187. Kanhave canal: Viking Age canal construction (p. 280).
188. Stævnsfjord: Stone Age dwelling sites under sea.
189. 'Rævebakkerne': 6 mounds near coast at Sælvig.
190. Besser: stone cist south-east of town by coast.
191. Øsby: passage grave north of town.

(x) Funen (IX, X, XI)

192. Skamby: passage grave north-east of Skamby church.
193. Glavendrup: stone ship and runic stone (see Index of names).
194. Vie Fen: sacrificial bog in which Iron Age weapons were found, north-west of Næsby (p. 285).
195. Munkebo: 2 passage graves north-west of church.
196. Ladby: Viking Age ship find in mound north of Ladby (pp. 180-4).
197. 'Mårhøj': passage grave between Martofte and Snave on Hindsholm (p. 90).
198. 'Hesthøj': passage grave north-east of Martofte railway station.
199. Bukkerup Langmose: Iron Age sacrificial bog at Søllested.
200. Kragehul: sacrificial bog in which Iron Age weapons were found, north-west of Flemløse church.

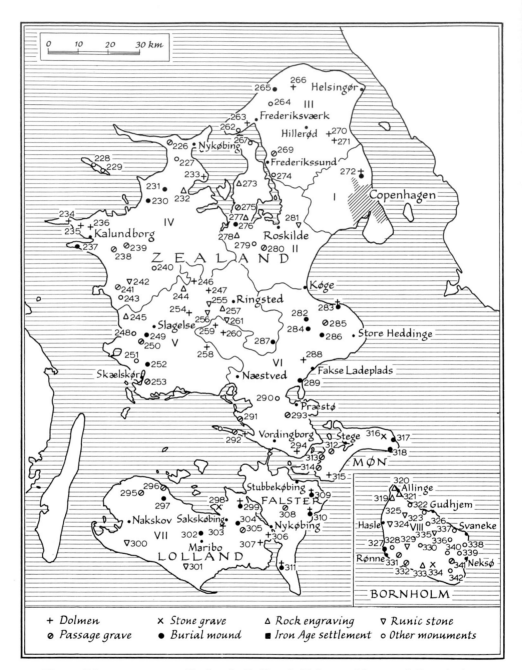

Fig 5. Monuments on Zealand, Lolland, Falster, Møn and Bornholm

316

201. Jordløse: round dolmen 2 km. south-east of Jordløse church.
202. 'Ringshøj': largest burial mound in Funen south-west of S. Nærå.
203. Ellested: 5-chambered long dolmen east-south-east of town (p. 65).
204. Lindeskov: long dolmen 2 km. west of Ørbæk.
205. 'Damestenen': Denmark's largest boulder north of Hesselager (p. 289).
206. Møllegårdsmarken: Iron Age burial ground north of Broholm.
207. Horneland: passage grave and dolmen chamber at Knoldsborg manor.
208. Alléskov (Gamle Kohave): dolmens in wood east of Fåborg.
209. Pipstorn: dolmen and mounds in wood east of Fåborg.
210. Ålstrup church: stone with cup marks built into church porch.
211. Hestehaven: stone with cup marks in woods east of Svendborg.
212. 'Klokkestenen': dolmen chamber on west side of Lyø.

(xi) *Aerø and Langeland* (ix)

213. 'Tingstedet': long dolmen west of Rise church.
214. Bremlevænge: group of mounds in southern part of woods.
215. Tved skov: double passage grave in long mound.
216. Pæregård: long dolmen.
217. Bjærgbygard: long barrow with 2 stone chambers (p. 79).
218. 'Troldebjerg': Late Stone Age village (pp. 94 and 98).
219. Lindø: Late Stone Age village.
220. 'Kong Humbles Grav': long dolmen north of Humble.
221. Konappe skov: stone ship at Ellensbjerg (p. 176).
222. 'Harnebjerg': sacred hill with Iron Age burial ground.
223. Rørlykke Fen: sacrificial bog in which lurs were found.
224. Myrebjerg: long dolmen and passage grave.
225. Hulbjerg: passage grave.

B. ZEALAND

(xii), *North-West Zealand* (iv, v)

226. 'Troldhøj': double passage grave at Stenstrup (see Index of names).
227. Trundholm: place where the 'sun chariot' was found.
228. Borrebjerg: sacred hill on Sejrø (pp. 102 and 159).
229. Tadebæk: monolith on shore (p. 288).

230. 'Vejrhøj': Bronze Age mound (p. 132).
231. 'Dutterhøje': Bronze Age mounds in row.
232. Herrestrup: rock engraving on cover stone of Dilhøj dolmen chamber (p. 161).
233. Kongsøre: round and long dolmens in woods.
234. Kongstrup: dolmen chamber.
235. Nyrup: dolmen chamber (p. 297).
236. Raklev: long dolmen and round dolmen.
237. Asnæs: Bronze Age mounds in woods.
238. Dysselodden: passage graves.
239. 'Korshøj': double passage grave at Ubby (p. 92).
240. 'Skrædderens falske Vidner': monoliths on Bøgebjerg at Rerslev (p. 222).
241. 'Rævehøj': double passage grave at Dalby, containing stone with rock engravings (p. 92).
242. Gørlev: runic stone in church porch.
243. Mullerup: Early Stone Age dwelling site in Maglemose (p. 42).
244. Munkebjergby: stone with cup marks at the church.

(xiii) *South-West Zealand* (v, vi)

245. 'Breddysse': two-chambered long dolmen at Ølandsgården with ship pictures and cup marks on cover stone.
246. Vilsted: round dolmen south of town (p. 65).
247. Store Bøgeskov: dolmens in woods west of Lake Gyrstinge.
248. 'Trelleborg': Viking Age fortification with house structures (pp. 263–72).
249. Slots Bjergby: Galgebakke and Hashøj west of town (pp. 190 *seqq.*).
250. 'Rævehøj': passage grave south-west of Slots Bjergby.
251. 'Borgbjerg': Bronze Age sacred hill west of Boeslunde church (p. 162).
252. 'Kanehøj': burial mound used as place of execution north of Skelskør (p. 197).
253. Borreby: passage grave in grounds of estate.
254. Grøfte: dolmens.
255. Fjenneslev: runic stone at church (p. 228).
256. Alsted: runic stone in church.
257. Sigersted: stone with wheel-cross and cup marks built into church tower (p. 160).
258. Gunderslevholm: long dolmen in woods (pp. 46, 60 and 65).

259. Næsbyholm Storskov: dolmens, burial mounds, stones with cup marks and ancient fields (p. 250).
260. Glumsø Østerskov: stone graves and mounds in woods.
261. Sandby: runic stone in churchyard.

(xiv) *North Zealand and Hornsherred* (I, II, III)

262. Sølager: kitchen midden in old line of sea shore.
263. 'Carlsstenen': dolmen at Grønnesøgård.
264. Tibirke: ancient road in Ellemosen (p. 256).
265. 'Maglehøje': burial mound on Bakkebjerg south of Rågeleje (p. 132).
266. Valby Hegn: long dolmens in woods (p. 65).
267. 'Kongeegen': Iron Age tree in Jægerspris Storskov (pp. 291–3).
268. 'Juliane Høj': passage grave at Jægerspris (p. 92).
269. Græse: passage grave.
270. Kirkelte Hegn: long dolmens in woods.
271. Dæmpegård: long dolmen at Tokkekøb Hegn.
272. Dyrehaven: dolmens and burial mounds.
273. Venslev: stone with wheel-cross on Venslev Mark (p. 160).
274. Skuldelev: place where Viking ship was found in Roskilde fjord.
275. 'Møllehøj': double passage grave on Kyndeløse Mark.
276. Ryegård: burial mounds in fields belonging to manor.
277. Lyndby: stone with wheel-cross and cup marks erected to mark assembly place south of town.
278. Kirke Såby: stone with ship pictures and cup marks built into church porch (p. 288).
279. Lejre: stone ships and mounds (pp. 176 and 179).
280. Øm: passage grave (pp. 92 and 95–6).
281. Hedehusene: runic stone in grounds in front of church.

(xv) *South-East Zealand and Lolland* (VI, VII)

282. Himlingøje: Iron Age burial mounds west of village (p. 193).
283. Magleby and Gjorslev: dolmens and mounds in woods by shore.
284. 'Hothers Høj': flat-topped burial mound in Hårlev churchyard (p. 193).
285. 'Maglehøj': passage grave between Hellested and Varpelev.
286. 'Elverhøj': burial mound at Hellested.
287. Bregentved: burial mounds in castle grounds and zoological gardens.

288. 'Junkershøj': long dolmen in Stubberup woods.
289. 'Troldhøje': group of mounds in Strandegård Zoological Gardens.
290. Broskov: ancient roads (pp. 257 and 258).
291. 'Månehøj': double passage grave east of Svinøvester.
292. Knudshoved Odde: dolmens, passage graves and ancient landscapes (pp. 34 and 46).
293. 'Rishøj': passage grave west of Ammendrup.
294. Stensby skov: dolmens and other stone graves.
295. 'Kong Svends Høj': passage grave in long barrow north of Pederstrup (p. 94).
296. 'Glentehøj': passage grave south of Kragenæs.
297. 'Bavnehøj': and other burial mounds at Birket (p. 132).
298. Orebygård: mound with megalithic cist (p. 110).
299. Guldborg Storskov: stone graves and mounds (p. 142).
300. Tillitse: runic stone in church porch (p. 230).
301. Tagerup: runic stone built into church porch.
302. Søholt Storskov: a number of burial mounds.
303. Radsted: long dolmen west of Radsted town.
304. Idalund: group of mounds in woods.
305. Flintinge Byskov: passage grave.
306. Nagelsti: stone dolmens.
307. Frejlev skov: stone dolmens, burial mounds and stone with cup marks and foot-marks (pp. 141 and 142).

(xvi) *Falster* (vii)

308. Listrup: passage grave north of village.
309. 'Ørnehøj': long dolmen and burial mounds in Corselitze Østerskov.
310. Halskov Vænge: long dolmens and burial mounds in woods.
311. Fiskebæk Skov: dolmens and burial mounds.

(xvii) *Møn* (vi)

312. 'Jordehøj': passage grave at Nøbølle.
313. 'Kong Asgers Høj': passage grave north-west of Sprove (p. 94).
314. 'Klekkendehøj': passage grave south of Røddinge (p. 94).
315. 'Grøn Jægers Høj': long dolmen south of Fanefjord church (p. 66).
316. Sømarke: stone grave with cup marks on cover stone west of town.

317. Klinteskoven: burial mounds (pp. 138 and 142).
318. Busene Have: burial mounds (p. 142).

(xviii) *Bornholm* (VIII)

319. Brogård: rock engraving with ships south of Allinge (p. 156).
320. Storløkkebakken: rock engraving with ships and footprints south-east of Allinge (p. 158).
321. Madsebakke: rock engravings with ships, wheel-crosses and other signs at Allinge (p. 158).
322. Stammershale: monolith and stone ships.
323. 'Hestestenene': monolith west of Gudhjem.
324. Brogård: runic stone at cross-roads south-east of Hasle (p. 230).
325. Klemensker: runic stone at church.
326. Bøgebjerg: monolith, stone coffins and mounds of Iron Age.
327. 'Tillehøje': group of mounds north of Rønne.
328. Enesbjerg and Galgebakken: cairns and stone ships (p. 175).
329. Vestermarie: 6 runic stones at church.
330. 'Gamleborg': Viking Age refuge fort.
331. 'Lundestenen': passage grave at Lundegård.
332. Arnager: passage grave.
333. Lille Strandbygård: rock engraving with wheel-cross and cup marks (pp. 152 and 160).
334. Vasegård: long barrow with stone chambers.
335. Øster Marie: 4 runic stones at church.
336. 'Louisenlund': monoliths (pp. 218 and 221).
337. 'Hellig Kvinde': monolith north-west of Svaneke (pp. 218 and 223).
338. Frennemark: monolith south of Svaneke (p. 218).
339. Gryet: monolith in grove north-west of Neksø (p. 218).
340. 'Varperne': cairns and road tracks in Pedersker woods.
341. Stensebygård: 2 passage graves south-west of Bodilsker.
342. Rispebjerg: ring-fort by river Øle.

Bibliography

This is not a complete list of works dealing with Danish prehistoric monuments. It is highly selective, giving only the most important and essential literature relating to each chapter; but from it everyone should be able to find further material on most of the subjects raised. The object has been to facilitate the task of selection among the extensive literature on our magnificent monuments. To this is added a fuller list of works concerned with the individual provinces as a basis for the study of special areas.

Abbreviations

Årbøger = *Aarbøger for nordisk Oldkyndighed og Historie.*
KUML = The annual publication of the Jysk Arkeologisk Selskab (Archaeological Society of Jutland) at Århus. (Contributions are printed in both Danish and English.)
Nat. Arb. = *Nationalmuseets Arbejdsmark.*
Nord. F. = *Nordiske Fortidsminder.*

I THE TERRAIN

General Surveys

1. Johannes Brøndsted, *Danmarks Oldtid* (Early Denmark) I–III, 1957–61.
2. A. P. Madsen, *Afbildninger af danske Oldsager og Mindesmærker: Stenalderen* (Illustrations of Danish antiquities and monuments: the Stone Age), 1868.
3. A. P. Madsen, *Gravhøje og Gravfund fra Stenalderen i Danmark: Det østlige Danmark*, 1896; *Fyen og Jylland*, 1900 (Stone Age grave mounds and grave finds in Denmark: Eastern Denmark, 1896; Funen and Jutland, 1900).

4. Sophus Müller, *Vor Oldtid* (Our prehistory), 1897.
5. Politikens Håndbøger, no. 251 : *Med arkæologen Danmark rundt* (With the archaeologist round Denmark), 1966.
6. J. P. Trap, *Kongeriget Danmark* (The kingdom of Denmark), 1959–66.
7. J. J. A. Worsaae, *Danmarks Oldtid oplyst ved Oldsager og Gravhøje* (Danish prehistory illustrated by antiquities and burial mounds), 1843.

II THE FIRST TRACES

8. Knud Dahl, *Fredede Egne på Øerne* (Protected areas on the Danish Islands), 1961.
9. Knud Dahl, *Fredede Egne i Jylland* (Protected areas in Jutland), 1962.
10. A. P. Madsen and others, *Affaldsdynger fra Stenalderen i Danmark* (Stone Age kitchen middens in Denmark), 1900.
11. Victor Madsen and others, 'Oversigt over Danmarks Geologi' (Survey of Danish geology), *Danmarks geologiske Undersøgelse*, Series V, no. 4, 1928.
12. Therkel Mathiassen, 'Gudenaa-Kulturen' (The Gudenaa culture), *Årbøger*, 1937.
13. Therkel Mathiassen, 'En senglacial Boplads ved Bromme' (A late glacial settlement at Bromme), *Årbøger*, 1946.
14. V. Nordmann, *Menneskets Indvandring til Norden* (The arrival of man in Scandinavia), 1936.
15. V. Nordmann, *Jordfundne Pattedyrslevninger i Danmark* (Remains of mammals found in the ground in Denmark), 1944.
16. J. Troels-Smith, *Nat. Arb.*, 1955, 1957 and 1960.

III DOLMENS

17. P. V. Glob, 'Barkær, Danmarks ældste landsby' (Barkær, Denmark's earliest village), *Nat. Arb.*, 1949.
18. Johs. Iversen, 'Landnam i Danmarks Stenalder' (Land seizure in the Danish Stone Age), *Danmarks Geologiske Undersøgelse*, Series II, no. 66, 1941.
19. Axel Steensberg, 'Med bragende flammer' (With roaring flames), *KUML*, 1955.

20. K. Thorvildsen, 'Dyssetidens Gravfund i Danmark' (Grave finds of the dolmen period in Denmark), *Årbøger*, 1941.
21. J. Troels-Smith, 'Ertebøllekultur—Bondekultur' (Ertebølle culture—peasant culture), *Årbøger*, 1953.
22. Ole Worm, *Danicorum Monumentorum libri sex*, 1643.

IV 'GIANT'S TOMBS' (PASSAGE GRAVES)

23. Kong Frederik den Syvende til Danmark (King Frederik VII of Denmark), *Om Byggemåden af Oldtidens Jættestuer* (On the method of building the passage graves of antiquity), 1862.
24. P. V. Glob, 'Korshøj, en Dobbeltjættestue ved Ubby i Vestsjælland' (Korshøj, a double passage grave at Ubby in West Zealand), *Fra Danmarks Ungtid*, 1940.
25. Poul Kjærum, 'Tempelhus fra Stenalderen' (Stone Age temples), *KUML*, 1955.
26. Poul Kjærum, 'Storstensgrave ved Tustrup' (Megalithic graves at Tustrup), *KUML*, 1957.
27. C. A. Nordman, 'Studier öfver ganggriftkulturen i Danmark' (Studies on the passage grave culture in Denmark), *Årbøger*, 1917.
28. C. A. Nordman, 'Jættestuer i Danmark' (Passage graves in Denmark), *Nord. F.*, Vol. II, 1918.
29. G. Rosenberg, 'To Jættestuer' (Two passage graves), *Nat. Arb.*, 1933.
30. J. Winther, *Troldebjerg* (Troldebjerg) I–II, 1935 and 1938.
31. J. Winther, *Blandebjerg* (Blandebjerg), 1943.

V THE BATTLE-AXE PEOPLE'S GRAVE MOUNDS

32. P. V. Glob, 'Den jyske Enkeltgravskultur' (The Jutland single grave culture), *Årbøger*, 1944.
33. Sophus Müller, 'De jyske Enkeltgrave fra Stenalderen' (The Stone Age single graves in Jutland), *Årbøger*, 1898.

VI MEGALITHIC CISTS AND STONE CISTS

34. H. Kjær, 'Gravkister fra Stenalderens Slutningstid' (Megalithic cists of the end of the Stone Age), *Årbøger*, 1910.
35. D. Liversage, 'En hellekiste ved Gerdrup' (A stone cist at Gerdrup), *Årbøger*, 1964.

VII LARGE BRONZE AGE MOUNDS

36. Vilhelm Boye, *Fund af Egekiste fra Bronzealderen i Danmark* (Finds of Bronze Age oak coffins in Denmark), 1896.
37. H. C. Broholm, *Danmarks Bronzealder* (Denmark's Bronze Age), I–II, 1943–44.
38. Thomas Thomsen, 'Egekistefundet fra Egtved' (The Egtved oak coffin find), *Nord. F.*, Vol. II, 1929.

VIII SMALL BRONZE AGE MOUNDS

39. H. C. Broholm, 'Studier over den yngre Bronzealder i Danmark' (Studies in the Late Bronze Age in Denmark), *Årbøger*, 1933.
40. H. C. Broholm, *Danmarks Bronzealder* (Denmark's Bronze Age) III–IV, 1946–48.
41. G. Kunwald, 'De ældste vidnesbyrd om ligbrænding i Danmarks oldtid' (The earliest evidence of cremation in Danish prehistory), *Dansk Ligbrændingsforenings Beretning for 1954.*

IX CUP MARKS AND ROCK ENGRAVINGS

42. Oscar Almgren, *Hällristningar och kultbruk* (Rock engravings and sacred practices), Stockholm, 1926–27.
43. Carl-Axel Althin, *Studien zu den bronzezeitlichen Felszeichnungen von Skåne* (Studies on the Bronze Age rock engravings in Skåne), Lund, 1945.
44. Åke Fredsjö and others, *Hällristningar i Sverige* (Rock engravings in Sweden), Stockholm, 1956.
45. P. V. Glob, 'Bornholms Helleristninger' (Rock engravings on Bornholm), *Nat. Arb.*, 1948.
46. Sverre Marstrander, *Østfolds Jordbruksristninger* (The agricultural engravings of Østfold), Oslo, 1963.
47. Henry Petersen, 'Om Helleristninger i Danmark' (On rock engravings in Denmark), *Årbøger*, 1875.

X IRON AGE GRAVES

48. Harald Andersen, 'Tomme Høje' (Empty mounds), *KUML*, 1951.
49. C. J. Becker, *Førromersk Jernalder i Syd- og Midtjylland* (The pre-Roman Iron Age in South and Central Jutland), 1961.

50. Harris Birkeland, *Nordens Historie i Middelalderen efter Arabiske Kilder* (The history of Scandinavia in the Middle Ages according to Arab sources), Oslo, 1954.

51. H. C. Broholm, 'Skibssættninger i Danmark' (Ship burials in Denmark), *Nat. Arb.*, 1937.

52. Johannes Brøndsted, 'Danish inhumation graves of the Viking Age', *Acta Archaeologica*, 1936.

53. H. Norling Christensen, 'Ældre romersk jernalders grave i Århus amt' (Early Roman Iron Age graves in the County of Århus), *Nord. F.*, Vol. IV, 2, 1954.

54. E. Dyggve, *Mindesmærkerne i Jelling* (The Jelling monuments), 1964.

55. P. V. Glob, 'Slots Bjergby Høje' (The Slots Bjergby mounds), *Nat. Arb.*, 1947.

56. K. Friis Johansen, 'Hoby-Fundet' (The Hoby find), *Nord. F.*, Vol. II, 1923.

57. J. Kornerup, *Kongehøjene i Jellinge* (The royal mounds at Jellinge), 1875.

58. A. P. Madsen and Carl Neergaard, 'Jydske Gravpladser fra den førromerske Jernalder (Pre-Roman Iron Age graves in Jutland), *Årbøger*, 1894.

59. Sophus Müller, 'Juellinge-Fundet' (The Juellinge find), *Nord. F.*, Vol. II, 1911.

60. Carl Neergaard, 'Jernalders-Gravpladserne ved Lisbjerg' (Iron Age burial grounds at Lisbjerg), *Nat. Arb.*, 1928.

61. Thorkil Ramskou, 'Viking Age cremation graves in Denmark', *Acta Archaeologica*, 1950.

62. Thorkil Ramskou, *Lindholm Høje* (The Lindholm mounds), 1960.

63. Knud Thorvildsen, 'Ladby-Skibet' (The Ladby ship), *Nord. F.*, 1957.

XI MONOLITHS AND RUNIC STONES

64. Lis Jacobsen and Erik Moltke, *Danmarks Runeindskrifter* (Runic inscriptions in Denmark), 1942.

XII IRON AGE MONUMENT⌐

Villages and Houses

65. Harald Andersen, 'Et landsbyhus på Gørding Hede' (A village house on Gørding heath), *KUML*, 1951.

66. Gudmund Hatt, *Nørre Fjand* (Northern Fjand), 1957.
67. Hans Kjær, 'Oldtidshuse ved Ginderup i Thy' (Ancient houses at Ginderup in Thy), *Nat. Arb.*, 1928.

Ancient Fields

68. P. V. Glob, 'Jyllands øde agre' (The deserted fields of Jutland), *KUML*, 1951.
69. Gudmund Hatt, *Oldtidsagre* (Ancient fields), 1949.

Roads and Fords

70. G. Kunwald, 'En Oldtidsvej ved Tibirke Bakker' (An ancient road in the Tibirke hills), *Nat. Arb.*, 1944.
71. Hugo Matthiessen, *Hærvejen. En tusindårig vej fra Viborg til Danevirke* (The Army Road. A thousand-year-old road from Viborg to Danevirke), 1930.

Fortifications

72. H. Jankuhn and others, 'Die Ausgrabungen in Haithabu' (The excavations in Haithabu), *Offa*, vols. 21–22, 1965.
73. Vilh. La Cour, *Danevirkestudier* (Danevirke studies), 1951.
74. Sophus Müller and C. Neergaard, 'Danevirke' (Danevirke), *Nord. F.*, Vol. I, 1908.
75. Poul Nørlund, 'Trelleborg' (Trelleborg), *Nord. F.*, Vol. IV, 1948.
76. Olaf Olsen, *Fyrkat* (Fyrkat), 1965.
77. C. G. Schultz, 'Aggersborg' (Aggersborg), *Nat. Arb.*, 1949.

XIII HIDDEN TRACES OF ANTIQUITY

78. Kristen Hald, *Vore Stednavne* (Danish place-names), 1965.
79. August F. Schmidt, *Danmarks Helligkilder* (The sacred springs of Denmark), 1926.
80. August F. Schmidt, *Danmarks Kæmpesten* (Denmark's great stones), 1932–33.

XIV SURVEYS OF ANCIENT MONUMENTS IN DIFFERENT DISTRICTS

VENDSYSSEL

81. P. Kjærum, 'Stensatte jernalderkældre i Vendsyssel' (Stone-build Iron Age cellars in Vendsyssel), *KUML*, 1960.

82. Sophus Müller, 'Vendsysselstudier' (Vendsyssel studies) I–III, *Årbøger*, 1911 and 1912.
83. C. A. Nordman, 'Gånggriften vid Alsbjerg' (Passage graves at Alsbjerg), *Årbøger*, 1915.
84. Th. Ramskou, 'Lindsholm Høje' (The Lindholm mounds), *KULM*, 1960.
85. Peter Riismøller, 'Om Vildmoserne Arkaeologi og Historie' (On the archaeology and history of the bogs), *Vildmose-arbejdet*, 1945.

Museums
Vendsyssel Historical Museum, Hjørring; Try Museum.

Archaeological Maps
Sheets 1–2 Hjørring-Frederikshavn, 3 Løkken, 4–5 Brøn-derslev-Sæby, 9 Løgstør, 10 Ålborg.

THY AND MORS

86. C. J. Becker, '4000-årig minedrift i Thy' (4,000-year-old mining operations in Thy), *Nat. Arb.*, 1958.
87. Johannes Brøndsted, 'Thors fiskeri' (Thor's fishing), *Nat. Arb.*, 1955.
88. Gudmund Hatt, 'Jernalderbopladsen ved Ginderup i Thy' (The Iron Age settlement at Ginderup in Thy), *Nat. Arb.*, 1935.
89. Hans Kjær, 'Oldtidshuse ved Ginderup' (Ancient houses at Ginderup), *Nat. Arb.* 1928 and 1930.
90. Hans Kjær, *Ydby Hede og dens Mindesmærker fra Oldtiden* (Ydby heath and its ancient monuments), 1916.
91. Sophus Müller, 'Bopladsfund fra Bronzealderen' (Bronze Age settlement finds), *Årbøger*, 1919.

Museums
Museum of Thy and Vester Han Hundred, Thisted; Mors-land's Historical Museum, Nykøbing, Mors.

Archaeological Maps
Sheets 7–8 Klitmøller-Thisted, 11 Vestervig, 12 Mors.

HIMMERLAND

92. Gudmund Hatt, 'Jernalders Bopladser i Himmerland' (Iron Age settlements in Himmerland), *Årbøger*, 1938.
93. Johs. V. Jensen, 'Himmerlands Arkæologi' (The archaeology of Himmerland), *Fra Danmarks Ungtid*, 1940.
94. Ole Klindt-Jensen, *Gundestrupkedlen* (The Gundestrup cauldron), 1961.
95. A. P. Madsen and others, *Ertebølle, Affaldsdynger fra Stenalderen i Danmark* (Ertebølle, Stone Age refuse heaps in Denmark), 1900.
96. Th. Ramskou, *Himmerlands Oldtidsminder* (The ancient monuments of Himmerland), 1947.

Museums

Ålborg Historical Museum; West Himmerland Museum, Års; Hobro Museum.

Archaeological Maps

Sheets 9 Løgstør, 10 Ålborg, 13 Års, 14 Mariager.

WEST JUTLAND

97. Gudmund Hatt, *Nørre Fjand* (North Fjand), 1957.
98. Therkel Mathiassen, *Studier over Vestjyllands Oldtidsbebyggelse* (Studies in the early settlement of West Jutland), 1948.
99. Sophus Müller, 'Vei og Bygd i Sten- og Bronzealderen' (Roads and buildings in the Stone and Bronze Ages), *Årbøger*, 1904.
100. Henry Petersen, *Vognfundene i Dejbjerg Præstegårdsmose* (The waggon finds in Dejbjerg Præstegård bog), 1888.
101. Th. J. Søegaard, 'Oldtidens Mindesmærker på den jyske Hede' (Ancient monuments on the Jutland heath), *Hedebogen*, 1909.
102. Axel Steensberg, 'Hardsyssels Oldtidsminder' (The ancient monuments of Hardsyssel), *Ringkøbing Amts historiske Aarbøger*, 1937.
103. Niels Thomsen, 'Myrthue, et gårdanlæg fra jernalder' (Myrthue, an Iron Age farmstead), *KUML*, 1964.
104. Niels Thomsen and others, *Historisk Vejviser over Egnen mellem Esbjerg, Varde, Ribe og Gørding* (Historical guide to the area between Esbjerg, Varde, Ribe and Gørding), 1945.

Museums

Herning Museum; Holstebro and District Museum; Lemvig Museum; Ringkøbing Museum; Skjern Museum; Struer Museum; Esbjerg Museum; Grindsted Museum; Varde Museum; Ølgod Parish Museum; Archaeological Collection at Ribe.

Archaeological Maps

Sheets 16 Lemvig, 17 Skive, 21 Ringkøbing, 22 Herning, 26 Skern, 27 Brande, 34 Varde, 35 Grindsted.

THE VIBORG AREA, SALLING AND FUR

105. N. C. Bøgelev, 'Skive-Egnens Oldtidsminder' (Ancient monuments of the Skive district), *Skivebogen*, Vol. 31, 1939.
106. P. V. Glob, *Mosefolket* (The bog people), 1965; *The Bog People*, London, 1969.
107. Hans Kjær, 'Langdyssen ved Ulvedal' (The long dolmen at Ulvedal), *Nat. Arb.*, 1932.
108. Therkel Mathiassen, 'Gudenå-kulturen' (The Gudenå culture), *Årbøger*, 1937.
109. J. J. A. Worsaae, 'Om Mammen-fundet' (On the Mammen find), *Årbøger*, 1869.

Museums

Viborg Diocesan Museum (Hvolris, the open-air section of the Museum at West Bjerregrav); Skive Museum; Klosterlund Museum; Fuur Museum; Museum on Hjerl Heath.

Archaeological Maps

Sheets 12 Mors, 13 Års, 17 Skive, 18 Viborg, 23 Silkeborg.

THE RANDERS AREA AND DJURSLAND

110. H. Hellmuth Andersen, 'Køkkenmøddingen ved Meilgaard' (The Meilgaard kitchen midden), *KUML*, 1960.
111. P. V. Glob, 'Barkær, Danmarks ældste landsby' (Barkær, Denmark's oldest village), *Nat. Arb.*, 1949.
112. Hans Kjær, 'Oldtidsmindesmærker paa Djursland og Randersegnen' (Ancient monuments in Djursland and the Randers area), *Turistforeningens Aarbog*, 1924.

113. G. Kunwald, 'Troldestenen' (The Troll Stone) (Sjellebro), *Skalk*, 1957, no. 4.

114. O. Voss, 'Kirken på Vikingens Høj' (The church on the Viking's mound) (Hørning), *Skalk*, 1960, no. 4.

Museums

Randers Museum; Djursland Museum, Grenå; Ebeltoft Museum.

Archaeological Maps

Sheets 19 Randers, 20 Grenå, 25 Æbeltoft.

EAST JUTLAND AND SAMSØ

115. P. V. Glob, 'Oldtiden i Samsø' (Samsø in ancient times), *Danmarks Midtpunkt*, 1948.

116. H. Kjær, 'Mindesmærker og Fund fra historik Tid i Jerlev Herred' (Monuments and finds of historical times in Jerlev Hundred), *Vejle Amts Årbøger*, 1912.

117. H. Kjær, 'Oldtidsminder i Sydøst-Jylland' (Ancient monuments in South-East Jutland), *Turistforeningens Årbog*, 1930.

118. Therkel Mathiassen, 'Primitive Flintredskaber fra Samsø' (Primitive flint tools from Samsø), *Årbøger*, 1934.

119. K. Thorvildsen, 'Grønhøj ved Horsens' (The green mound at Horsens), *Årbøger*, 1946.

120. O. Voss, 'Bækkemonumentet' (The Bække monument), *Fra Ribe Amt*, 1959.

Museums

Museum of Prehistory in Moesgård at Århus; Silkeborg Museum; Gudenå Museum at Rye Bro; Horsens Museum; Odder Museum; Vejle Museum; Museum at Koldinghus, Kolding; Samsø Open-air Museum, Tranebjerg.

Archaeological Maps

Sheets 24 Århus, 29 Horsens, 30 Samsø, 36 Vejle, 37 Bogense, 44 Kolding.

SOUTH JUTLAND

121. H. C. Broholm and M. Hald, 'Skrydstrupfundet' (The Skrydstrup find), *Nord. F.*, III, 1939.

122. Jens Frost, 'Om yngre Stenalder i Nordslesvig' (On the Late Stone Age in North Slesvig), *Sprogforeningens Almanak*, 1939.

123. H. Kjær, 'Fredlysning af Fortidsminder i Sønderjylland' (The protection of ancient monuments in South Jutland), *Nat. Arb.*, 1932.

124. Therkel Mathiassen, 'Bundsø' (Bundsø), *Årbøger*, 1939.

125. Sophus Müller, 'Sønderjyllands Stenalder' (The South Jutland Stone Age), *Årbøger*, 1913.

126. Sophus Müller, 'Sønderjyllands Bronzealder' (The South Jutland Bronze Age), *Årbøger*, 1914.

127. Carl Neergaard, 'Sønderjyllands Jernalder' (The South Jutland Iron Age), *Årbøger*, 1916.

128. J. Raben, *Fra Als og Sundeved* (From Als and Sundeved), 1939.

129. G. Rosenberg, 'Hjortspringfundet' (The Hjortspring find), *Nord. F.*, 1937.

Museums

Haderslev County Museum, Haderslev; Åbenrå Museum; Sønderborg Museum.

Archaeological Maps

Sheets 43 Ribe, 51 Løgumkloster, 52 Haderslev, 57 Tønder, 58 Dybbøl, 59 Sønderborg.

FUNEN AND SURROUNDING ISLANDS

130. Erling Albrectsen, 'Fyns bebyggelse i oldtiden' (Early settlements on Funen), *Årbøger*, 1946.

131. Erling Albrectsen, *Fynske Jernaldergrave* (Iron Age graves on Funen), I–II, 1954–56.

132. Erling Albrectsen, 'Stendysserne ved Holstenshus' (Dolmens at Holstenshus), *Fynske Minder*, 1955.

133. Erling Albrectsen, 'Gåsestenen (Jættestue)' ('The Gåse stone: Passage grave), *Fynske Minder*, 1955.

134. Erling Albrectsen, 'Glavendrupstenen' (The Glavendrup stone), *Fynske Minder*, 1958.
135. Hakon Berg, 'Langdolmen bei Pæregaard' (The long dolmen at Pæregaard), Langeland, *Acta Archaeologica*, Vol. XXVII, 1956.
136. H. Kjær, 'Oldtidsminder i Sydfyn' (Ancient monuments in South Funen), *Turistforeningens Årbog*, 1925.
137. H. Kjær, 'Fortidsminder i Vandæslet (Vestfyn)' (Ancient monuments in Vandæslet) (West Funen), *Turistforeningens Årbog*, 1929.
138. F. Sehested, *Fortidsminder og Oldsager fra Egnen om Broholm* (Ancient monuments and antiquities from the Broholm area), 1878.
139. F. Sehested, *Archæologiske Undersøgelser* (Archaeological investigations), 1884.
140. Jens Winter, *Langeland* (Langeland), 1929.

Museums
Funen Diocesan Museum, Odense; Svendborg Museum; Langeland Museum, Rudkøbing; Marstal Museum; Ærøskøbing Museum.

Archaeological Maps
Sheets 37 Bogense, 38 Fyns Hoved, 45 Tommerup, 46 Nyborg, 53 Fåborg, 54 Svendborg, 60 Rudkøbing.

ZEALAND AND MØN

141. Harald Andersen, 'Hovedstaden i riget' (Lejre) (The capital of the kingdom: Lejre), *Nat. Arb.*, 1960.
142. A. Avnholt, 'Oldtidsminder og Oldtidsfund i Søllerød Kommune' (Ancient monuments and ancient finds in the municipality of Søllerød), *Søllerødbogen*, 1945.
143. F. Bojsen, *Af Møns Historie* (On the history of Møn), 1905.
144. P. V. Glob, 'Nordsjællands Oldtidsminder' (Ancient monuments of North Zealand), *Turistforeningens Årbog*, 1942.
145. P. V. Glob, *Oldtidsminder i Kongens Lyngby og Dyrehaven* (Ancient monuments in Kongens Lyngby and Dyrehaven), 1948.
146. H. Kjær, 'Oldtidsminder i Vest-Sjælland' (Ancient monuments in West Zealand), *Turistforeningens Årbog*, 1931.

147. H. Kjær, 'Oldtidsmindesmærker i Sydsjælland og paa Møn' (Ancient monuments in South Zealand and on Møn), *Turistforeningens Årbog*, 1933.

148. Vilh. La Cour, *Sjællands ældste Bygder* (Zealand's earliest buildings), 1927.

149. Knud A. Larsen and others, *Naturparken mellem Farum og Slangerup* (The nature park between Farum and Slangerup), 1965.

150. Therkel Mathiassen, *Nordvestsjællands Oldtidsbebyggelse* (Ancient settlements in North-West Zealand), 1959.

151. Therkel Mathiassen, *Nordvestsjælland gennem 10,000 år* (North-West Zealand through 10,000 years), 1963.

152. P. Simonsen, 'Dyssebygden i Tokkekøb Hegn' (Dolmen building in the Tokkekøb Enclosure), *Frederiksborg Amts historiske Samfunds Aarbog*, 1944.

Museums

National Museum, Copenhagen; Roskilde Museum; Holbæk Museum; Museum for Kalundborg and Area, Kalundborg; Ods Hundred's Folk Museum, Nykøbing South; Stenstrup Museum; Næstved and District Museum, Næstved; Stevn Museum, Højerup Klint; South Zealand Museum, Vordingborg; Møn Museum, Stege.

Archaeological Maps
N.W. Zealand, N.E. Zealand, S.W. Zealand, S.E. Zealand.

LOLLAND-FALSTER

153. C. C. Haugner, *Lollands Oldtidsminder* (Ancient monuments of Lolland), 1941.

154. Therkel Mathiassen, 'Lolland-Falsters Oldtidsmindesmæker' (Ancient monuments of Lolland-Falster), *Lolland-Falsters historiske Samfunds Årbog*, 1956.

Museums
Diocesan Museum of Lolland-Falster, Maribo; Museum in the Czar's House, Nykøbing F.

Archaeological Maps
Sheets 61 Maribo, 62 Nykøbing, F, 64 Rødby, 65 Gedser.

BORNHOLM

155. J. A. Jørgensen, *Fredlyste Mindesmæker paa Bornholm* (Protected monuments on Bornholm), 1905.
156. Ole Klindt-Jensen, 'Bornholms arkæologi' (The Archaeology of Bornholm), *Bogen om Bornholm*, 1957.
157. Ole Klindt-Jensen, *Bornholm i Folkevandringstiden* (Bornholm at the time of the migrations), 1957.
158. Peter Thorsen, *Bornholms Forhistorie* (Bornholm's prehistory), 1958.
159. E. Vedel, *Bornholms Oldtidsminder og Oldsager* (The ancient monuments and antiquities of Bornholm), 1886 and 1897.

Museums
Bornholm Museum, Rønne.

Archaeological Maps
Sheet 66, Bornholm.

Index of Places, Monuments and Sites

Abbreviations are used to indicate the principal archaeological sites, as follows:

B   Bornholm
FA   Falster
FU   Funen
H   Himmerland (Jutland)
LA   Langeland and Ærø
LO   Lolland
M   Mariager-Djursland (Jutland)
MO   Møn
NWZ   North-West Zealand
NZ   North Zealand and Hornsherred
S   Southern East Jutland
SA   South Jutland and Als
SEZ   South-East Zealand
SO   Samsø
SWZ   South-West Zealand
T   Thy and Mors (Jutland)
V   Vendsyssel (Jutland)
VI   Viborg, Fuur and Salling (Jutland)
W   West Jutland

The figures in italic type refer to the numbered entries in the appendix on pp. 307–321 giving the principal sites and to the numbers in maps 3–5; and figures in bold type are numbers of illustrations.

337

General Index